# Chinese Ethnic Business

*Chinese Ethnic Business* seeks to broaden the discussion of ethnic business from an analysis of its internal dynamics to a wider focus on the influence of global economic events. It demonstrates that ethnic businesses can no longer be studied in isolation from the global picture by providing a crucial understanding of how globalization impacts on the development of Chinese businesses. The book analyzes the unprecedented changes in Chinese ethnic business resulting from the direct or indirect consequences of globalization, looking specifically at economic globalization in the key immigrant receiving countries of the US, Australia, and Canada.

Focusing on the main themes of economic globalization and Chinese community development, transnational linkages, local urban structures, homogenization, and place attachment, the team of leading international contributors place the subject of Chinese ethnic business in the wider context of ethnic businesses and globalization. Including excellent methodology such as ethnographic studies, historical analysis, geographic studies, and statistical analysis, *Chinese Ethnic Business* makes an important contribution to the field of ethnic businesses and will appeal to those studying Chinese business, immigration, race and ethnicity, and economic sociology.

**Eric Fong** is Professor of Sociology at the University of Toronto, Canada.

**Chiu Luk** is a researcher at the Centre for Urban and Community Studies, University of Toronto, Canada.

**Chinese Worlds**
The series editors are Gregor Benton, Flemming Christiansen,
Delia Davin, Terence Gomez and Frank Pieke

Chinese Worlds publishes high-quality scholarship, research monographs, and
source collections on Chinese history and society. "Worlds" signals the diversity
of China, the cycles of unity and division through which China's modern history
has passed, and recent research trends toward regional studies and local issues. It
also signals that Chineseness is not contained within borders – ethnic migrant
communities overseas are also "Chinese worlds."

**The Literary Fields of Twentieth-Century China**
*Edited by Michel Hockx*

**Chinese Business in Malaysia**
Accumulation, ascendance, accommodation
*Edmund Terence Gomez*

**Internal and International Migration**
Chinese perspectives
*Edited by Frank N. Pieke and Hein Mallee*

**Village Inc.**
Chinese rural society in the 1990s
*Edited by Flemming Christiansen and Zhang Junzuo*

**Chen Duxiu's Last Articles and Letters, 1937–1942**
*Edited and translated by Gregor Benton*

**Encyclopedia of the Chinese Overseas**
*Edited by Lynn Pan*

**New Fourth Army**
Communist resistance along the Yangtze and the Huai, 1938–1941
*Gregor Benton*

**A Road is Made**
Communism in Shanghai 1920–1927
*Steve Smith*

**The Bolsheviks and the Chinese Revolution 1919–1927**
*Alexander Pantsov*

**Chinas Unlimited**
*Gregory Lee*

**Friend of China**
The myth of Rewi Alley
*Anne-Marie Brady*

**Birth Control in China 1949–2000**
Population policy and demographic development
*Thomas Scharping*

**Chinatown, Europe**
An exploration of overseas Chinese identity in the 1990s
*Flemming Christiansen*

**Financing China's Rural Enterprises**
*Jun Li*

**Confucian Capitalism**
*Souchou Yao*

**Chinese Business in the Making of a Malay State, 1882–1941**
Kedah and Penang
*Wu Xiao An*

**Chinese Enterprise, Transnationalism and Identity**
*Edited by Edmund Terence Gomez and Hsin-Huang Michael Hsiao*

**Diasporic Chinese Ventures**
The life and work of Wang Gungwu
*Gregor Benton and Hong Liu*

**Intellectuals in Revolutionary China, 1921–1949**
Leaders, heroes and sophisticates
*Hung-yok Ip*

**Migration, Ethnic Relations and Chinese Business**
*Kwok Bun Chan*

**Chinese Identities, Ethnicity and Cosmopolitanism**
*Kwok Bun Chan*

**Chinese Ethnic Business**
Global and local perspectives
*Edited by Eric Fong and Chiu Luk*

# Chinese Ethnic Business

Global and local perspectives

**Edited by**
**Eric Fong and Chiu Luk**

Routledge
Taylor & Francis Group

LONDON AND NEW YORK

First published 2007
by Routledge
2 Park Square, Milton Park, Abingdon, Oxon OX14 4RN

Simultaneously published in the USA and Canada
by Routledge
270 Madison Ave, New York, NY 10016

*Routledge is an imprint of the Taylor & Francis Group, an informa business*

Typeset in Times New Roman by
Keystroke, 28 High Street, Tettenhall, Wolverhampton
Printed and bound in Great Britain by
TJ International Ltd, Padstow, Cornwall

*British Library Cataloguing in Publication Data*
A catalogue record for this book is available from the British Library

*Library of Congress Cataloging in Publication Data*
Chinese ethnic business : global and local perspectives / edited by
Eric Fong and Chiu Luk.
  p. cm. – (Chinese worlds)
Includes bibliographical references and index.
ISBN 0–415–39718–9 (hardback : alk. paper) 1. Minority business
enterprises. 2. Chinese–Foreign countries–Economic conditions.
3. Transnationalism. 4. Entrepreneurship–Social aspects.
I. Fong, Eric, 1960– II. Luk, Chiu-ming. III. Series.
HD2358.C44 2006
338.6′42089951–dc22                                    2006009106

ISBN10: 0–415–39718–9 (hbk)
ISBN10: 0–203–96691–0 (ebk)
ISBN13: 978–0–415–39718–6 (hbk)
ISBN13: 978–0–203–96691–4 (ebk)

# Contents

# Illustrations

**Tables**

## Figures

## Maps

# Contributors

**Guoxuan Cai** is Senior Researcher at the Guangzhou Academy of Social Sciences in China. She was Visiting Scholar at the University of California, Los Angeles, from 2000 to 2001, carrying out research on Chinese language media in the U.S. Her current research focuses on welfare reform, elderly care, and gendered migration in China.

**Gary Dymski** (Ph.D., University of Massachusetts, Amherst) is Director of the University of California Center Sacramento, and on leave as Professor of Economics at the University of California, Riverside. Gary is the author of *The Bank Merger Wave* (M.E. Sharpe, 1999) and four co-edited volumes, including *Reimagining Growth: Toward a Renewal of the Idea of Development*, co-edited with Silvana DePaula (Zed, 2005). Gary is on the editorial boards of *Geoforum* and the *International Review of Applied Economics*. He has published many articles and chapters on banking, financial fragility, urban development, credit-market discrimination, microfinance, the Latin American and Asian financial crises, economic exploitation, and housing finance.

**Eric Fong** (Ph.D., University of Chicago) is Professor of Sociology at the University of Toronto. He has published widely in the area of racial and ethnic residential patterns and ethnic businesses. His publications have appeared in various journals, including *Demography*, *International Migration Review*, and *Social Forces*. He is editor of *Inside the Mosaic* (University of Toronto press, 2006).

**Arent Greve** (Dr. Oecon., Norwegian School of Economics and Business Administration) is Professor of Organization Theory at the Norwegian School of Economics and Business Administration, Bergen. He has held visiting scholar positions at Stanford University, the University of California, Berkeley, Hong Kong University, and several others. His main research interests are topics related to social capital. He applies the concept to a variety of theoretical and empirical settings using social network analysis. Greve's research covers both organizational and individual networks looking at knowledge networks, innovation of technology, telework, migration and settlement, labor markets for immigrant professionals, and entrepreneurship. His main theoretical point of departure is the institutional theory of organizations.

**David Ip** (Ph.D., University of British Columbia, Canada) is Associate Professor in the School of Social Science at the University of Queensland in Australia. His current research investigates transnationalism and the changing identities of diaspora Chinese as well as their impact on homeland politics. His recent publications include *Experiences of Transnational Chinese Migrants in the Asia-Pacific* (Nova Sciences, 2006), *Rethinking Cultural Affinity and Business Strategies in Chinese Transnational Enterprises* (CurzonRoutledge, 2001), *Chinese Business and the Asian Crisis* (Ashgate, 2000), and *Diaspora Chinese and the Chinese Economy: An Emerging Synergy* (Macmillan, 1996).

**Linda Lee** (Ph.D, University of Toronto) recently completed her Ph.D. in sociology at the University of Toronto, focusing her research on self-employment and the family, with a particular interest on immigrant entrepreneurship. Her other research interests include ethnic and race relations, labor market participation, family, and the life course. She is working in Ottawa for the Canadian government, developing and managing large-scale, federally funded surveys. She has expanded her research activities to include field and social experiments dealing with federal programs and policies. She is currently working on the development of an interdepartmental project on immigrant language training options for Canadians.

**Peter S. Li** (Ph.D., Northwestern University) is Professor in the Department of Sociology at the University of Saskatchewan, Canada. His publications include *The Chinese in Canada* (Oxford University Press, 1988, 1998), *The Making of Postwar Canada* (Oxford University Press, 1996) and *Destination Canada* (Oxford University Press, 2003). He is also editor of *International Migration and Integration*. Li has been Director of the Board of the International Centre for Human Rights and Democratic Development, Canada, and Chair of the Economic Research Domain at the Prairie Centre for Excellence for Research on Immigration and Integration in Canada.

**Wei Li** (Ph.D., University of Southern California) is Associate Professor in the Asian Pacific American Studies Program and School of Geographical Sciences at Arizona State University. She is the editor of *From Urban Enclave to Ethnic Suburb: New Asian Communities in Pacific Rim Countries* (University of Hawai'i Press, 2006) and co-editor of *Landscapes of the Ethnic Economy* (Rowman & Littlefield, 2006). Her publications have appeared in journals including *Annals of the Association of American Geographers*, *Environment and Planning A*, *Geographic Review*, and *Urban Studies*. She serves as the Fulbright Visiting Chair in Ethnicity and Multicultural Citizenship at Queen's University, Canada (2006–7), and is the Vice Chair of the Asian Advisory Committee in the U.S. Census Bureau's Race and Ethnic Advisory Committees.

**Ivan Light** (Ph.D., University of California at Berkeley) is Professor in the Department of Sociology at the University of California, Los Angeles. His areas of research include the informal economy, entrepreneurship, ethnic groups, immigration, illegal enterprise and organized crime, urbanization, and the economy and society. His publications include *Immigration and Entrepreneurship: Culture, Capital, and Ethnic Networks* (ed.) (Transaction Publishers, 1993), *Race, Ethnicity, and Entrepreneurship in Urban America* (with Carolyn Rosenstein, Aldine de Gruyter, 1995), and *Ethnic Enterprise in America* (University of California Press, 1972).

**Lucia Lo** (Ph.D., University of Toronto) is Associate Professor in the Department of Geography at York University in Toronto, Canada. She has served as the economic domain leader of the Toronto Joint Centre for Research on Immigration and Settlement. Her research interests span across transportation modeling, urban consumer behavior, and the economic impacts of immigration. Her publications have appeared in *Geographical Analysis, Journal of Regional Science, The Canadian Geographer, The Professional Geographer, Environment and Planning A,* and the *Journal of International Migration and Integration.*

**Chiu Luk** (Ph.D., University of Minnesota) is a researcher at the Centre for Urban and Community Studies, University of Toronto. His major research interests span across residential and commercial studies with a focus on Chinese subgroups in Toronto originating from Hong Kong, mainland China, and Taiwan. As an urban/social/cultural geographer, his most current research interest lies in the interface of cultural studies, ethnic communities of the Chinese diaspora, and economic globalization.

**Emi Ooka** (Ph.D., University of Toronto) is Adjunct Lecturer in the Department of Foreign Languages and Culture Studies at Kokugakuin University and the Department of Sociology at Meiji Gakuin University, both in Japan. Her research interests include race and ethnicity, and social networks. She has published her work both in North America and in Japan, and is currently working on a study that examines the effect of friendship networks on assimilation processes among Chinese-Canadian high school students in Toronto.

**Janet W. Salaff** (Ph.D., University of California at Berkeley) is Professor of Sociology at the University of Toronto, where she is also co-appointed at the Centre for Urban and Community Studies. Her research has focused on Chinese society on the Pacific Rim. Using in-depth interviews in Hong Kong between 1971 and 1976, she has studied the effects of labor force participation of unmarried women on family status and influence. The study was published as *Working Daughters of Hong Kong* (Cambridge University Press, 1981). Some of her other publications include *Lives: Chinese Working Women* (with Mary Sheridan, Indiana University Press, 1984), *State and Family in Singapore* (Cornell University Press, 1988), and *Cowboys and Cultivators* (with Burton Pasternak, Westview Press, 1993).

**Michael A. Szonyi** (D.Phil., University of Oxford) is Associate Professor in the Department of East Asian Languages at Harvard University. He has published *Practicing Kinship: Strategies of Descent and Lineage in Late Imperial China* (Stanford University Press, 2002) and *Fuzhou Diqu Wudi Xinyang Lishi Ziliao*

*Huibian* (Historical Materials on Beliefs in the Five Emperors in the Fuzhou Region) (South China Research Press, 2006). His papers have appeared in journals including the *Journal of Chinese Religions*, *The International Journal*, and the *Journal of Asian Studies*.

**Shuguang Wang** (Ph.D., University of Alberta, Canada) is Professor and Chair in the Department of Geography at Ryerson University. His recent publications have appeared in *The Canadian Geographer*, the *Canadian Journal of Regional Science*, the *Journal of International Migration and Integration*, and *International Migration*.

**Siu-Lun Wong** (D.Phil., University of Oxford) is Professor in the Department of Sociology and Director of the Centre of Asian Studies at the University of Hong Kong. His publications include *Hong Kong's Transition: A Decade after the Deal* (ed.) (with Wang Gungwu, Oxford University Press, 1995), *Emigrant Entrepreneurs: Shanghai Industrialists in Hong Kong* (Oxford University Press, 1988), and *Sociology and Socialism in Contemporary China* (Routledge & Kegan Paul, 1979).

**Min Zhou** (Ph.D., State University of New York at Albany) is Professor of Sociology and Founding Chair of the Department of Asian American Studies at the University of California, Los Angeles. Her main areas of research are immigration and immigrant adaptation, ethnic and racial relations, Asian Americans, ethnic entrepreneurship and enclave economies, the community, and urban sociology. She is author of *Chinatown: The Socioeconomic Potential of an Urban Enclave* (Temple University Press, 1992), co-author of *Growing Up American: How Vietnamese Children Adapt to Life in the United States* (Russell Sage Foundation Press, 1998), co-editor of *Contemporary Asian America* (New York University Press, 2000), and co-editor of *Asian American Youth: Culture, Identity, and Ethnicity* (Routledge, forthcoming).

# 1 Introduction

## Chinese ethnic business and globalization

*Eric Fong and Chiu Luk*

In the last few decades, most major cities of key receiving countries have witnessed a growing visible presence of ethnic businesses. Today, when one enters a store located in these cities, it is not surprising, in fact it is quite common, to find it is owned or operated by ethnic members. Anchoring this dramatic growth have been changes in the nature of these businesses. First of all, these businesses are no longer located in the ethnic community, but are scattered through almost every part of the major cities. At the same time, ethnic malls that have emerged in suburban areas become centrifugal forces to attract a concentration of ethnic businesses, and centripetal forces to pull ethnic businesses out from the central city ethnic neighborhoods. Second, clear evidence has shown that today ethnic businesses represent a diverse array of industries. They are not limited to the traditional image of ethnic businesses as neighborhood convenience or ethnic grocery stores. Today, large numbers of computer retail shops, high-class fashion boutiques, or even financial institutions are owned by ethnic members. These changes in ethnic businesses not only highlight developments in the social processes and structures of ethnic businesses in response to larger societal changes, but also show the limitations of the conventional approach to understanding ethnic businesses.

The study of ethnic businesses has been an important topic in the social sciences. In a widely read book published in 1972, sociologist Ivan Light explored the business operations of Chinese, Japanese, and blacks in the U.S. The 1970s and 1980s then witnessed a proliferation of publications in this area. Much stimulated by the original questions asked in Light's book, these studies focused on the factors that contribute to participation in entrepreneurship and the structural operations of these businesses. In the 1990s, the study of ethnic businesses shifted to the economic dimensions of those participating in ethnic businesses (e.g., Portes and Zhou 1996; Portes and Jensen 1989; Sanders and Nee 1987). While most of the previous focuses were on the internal dynamics of the structural and economic dimensions of ethnic businesses, the understanding of how the embedded environment, the larger societal contexts exogenous to ethnic business structures, shapes ethnic businesses has not been fully addressed. In particular, as studies have demonstrated how globalization has been linked to the development of ethnic communities in recent decades (Lin 1998), the natural extension of how globalization affects the development of ethnic businesses, and how unique developments in ethnic businesses due to globalization shape the growth of ethnic communities, is long overdue.

This volume takes as its point of departure the unprecedented changes in ethnic businesses due to globalization in several major immigrant receiving countries, i.e., Canada, the U.S., and in one chapter, Australia. The discussion focuses on Chinese businesses. Chinese were chosen for this study because they are one of the major ethnic immigrant groups in all these major receiving countries. In addition, the advantage of focusing on the businesses of one specific ethnic group in different countries is that it helps filter findings linked to cultural differences among groups. An international team of scholars from various disciplines explores changes in Chinese businesses in these countries. The main body of the book focuses on a general theme: how globalization, specifically economic globalization, affects the development of Chinese businesses in these four major immigrant receiving countries. We addressed three separate but related issues: (1) How economic globalization affects the development of Chinese businesses, which in turn affects Chinese businesses in the Chinese community; (2) how transnational linkages affect the operation of Chinese businesses; and (3) how the local urban structures affected by economic globalization shape the development of Chinese businesses. By addressing these three questions, these chapters collectively provide a better picture of the relationship between ethnic businesses and economic globalization.

To advance the goals, we will situate the discussion in the study of ethnic businesses by highlighting the history of the Chinese in relation to their business activities in the three countries (Australia, Canada, and the U.S.) and by outlining the theoretical discussion of ethnic businesses, in particular Chinese businesses, in the remaining sections of this introduction. By doing so, we will relate how the chapters of this book contribute to the full picture of ethnic businesses and globalization.

Before zooming into the discussion of Chinese businesses in these three countries, we summarize some of the major findings about Chinese businesses in other countries, East and Southeast Asian countries in particular. Given the visible Chinese presence and the prominent history of Chinese businesses in East and Southeast Asia, understanding some of the major themes in relation to globalization in the region can provide a context for studying globalization and Chinese businesses in the countries of our focus, Canada, the U.S., and Australia.

## CHINESE BUSINESSES IN EAST AND SOUTHEAST ASIA AND ECONOMIC GLOBALIZATION

For decades, the study of Chinese businesses in East Asian countries has been given considerable attention by researchers. In particular, the drastic economic growth in the 1980s of three of the four "little dragons" (Hong Kong, Taiwan, and Singapore) and other Southeast Asian countries (such as Malaysia, Thailand, and the Philippines) and the overrepresentation of Chinese businesses there have generated substantial public and academic interest (Gomez and Hsiao 2001; Gomez 1999).

Although most of these studies have provided understanding of the unique characteristics of Chinese businesses (Yeung and Olds 2000), such as the prominence of networks (Kao 1993; Weidenbaum and Hughes 1996), the cultural Confucian ethnic (Fukuyama 1995; Redding 1990), and close family ties (Hamilton 2000; Redding 1996), there has been a challenge in recent decades to focus on internal business dynamics as the operations of these businesses have been increasingly affected by the global environment.

To update the examination of Chinese businesses in the region, studies have attempted to explore how these businesses have adopted new strategies and novel forms to address the consequences of economic globalization (Yeung 2000; Liu 2000). One of the strategies identified by these studies is to move away from family ties to professional management in transnational operations (Hamilton 2000; Chan and Chiang 1994). Subsequently, the unique characteristic of family-owned conglomerations is diminishing. The second strategy reported is that more Chinese businesses, especially the large corporations, are diversifying into different industries (Yeung 1998).

Another major theme in recent decades is the process of extending Chinese businesses to another country in the region (Gomez and Hsiao 2001; Yeung 2000). Some studies emphasize the supply side perspective, that the extension of Chinese businesses to other countries reflects existing networks (Wong 1988). However, some suggest that the extension is strongly related to market demands at the destination (Zhou 1998). Once the demands are realized, networks will follow. This suggestion echoes Yeung's (2000) findings that Chinese businesses usually take a joint venture approach with local businesses.

Most of these studies focus on large businesses with substantial financial capital. In this collected volume, we focus our study on the three major receiving immigrant countries (i.e., Australia, Canada, and the U.S.), where most Chinese businesses are smaller in scale (though there is growing diversity in size in recent years). The application of these findings to the understanding of globalization and Chinese businesses in these countries should be made with caution. Nevertheless, these findings provide a global context in which to understand the Chinese businesses in the three countries of our study, as some of them may have strong ties to Chinese businesses in East and Southeast Asian countries.

## CHINESE AND THEIR BUSINESSES IN AUSTRALIA, CANADA, AND THE U.S.

The history of Chinese businesses in Australia, Canada, and the United States dates back to the end of the eighteenth century. The first major Chinese immigration to these countries can be traced to the discovery of gold. Most Chinese settled in Melbourne, Australia, as gold was found in the 1850s in Ballarat and Bendigo Creek, both about 60 miles from Melbourne. Large numbers of Chinese moved to British Columbia, Canada, during the 1850s and 1860s when gold found in the Fraser River was reported. Similarly, news of gold discovered in the Sacramento River brought a larger number of Chinese to San Francisco, California, during the same period.

By the end of the eighteenth century, Chinese businesses had come into existence to meet the needs of the growing numbers of Chinese sojourners in a few cities in these countries. These businesses were spatially concentrated in the Chinese clustered areas. Subsequently, "Chinatown" took form. The unique spatial arrangements reflected the needs for mutual protection among Chinese and the limited business locational choices due to the unfriendly social environment and the unwillingness to integrate Chinese into the wider society during that period of time.

The Chinese exclusion immigration policies implemented in all of these countries in the late eighteenth century and early nineteenth century seriously curtailed the growth of their Chinese populations, which led to the stagnation of Chinese businesses.[1] During this period, most Chinese businesses were small and family based, providing laundry services to the wider society or running grocery stores in the ethnic community for co-ethnic members. Paul Siu, trained at the University of Chicago and a student of Robert Park, provided a vivid description (1998) of business operations at that time, when most of the people involved in ethnic business had little human capital and limited language ability. He suggested that ethnic businesses were a niche for economic survival, especially for kin and village members back home.

With the change of immigration policies in the 1970s in all of the three countries, Asian immigration has grown exponentially over the last two decades. The latest Australian census reported about half a million Chinese, representing about 64 percent of the three largest Asian groups in 2001 (Australian Bureau of Statistics 2003b).[2] The Canadian Census documented about 1 million Chinese in 2001 (Statistics Canada 2003a), accounting for about 26 percent of the visible minority population.[3] The U.S. census reported a total of 2.7 million Chinese in 2000 (Barnes and Bennett 2002),[4] comprising 23 percent of the Asian population.[5]

In all three countries, most Chinese settle in the major cities, such as Toronto and Vancouver in Canada, Sydney and Melbourne in Australia, and Los Angeles and New York in the U.S. In Australia, the 1996 census recorded 102,600 people in New South Wales, 48,100 in Victoria, and 20,200 in Queensland born in China or Hong Kong (Inglis 1999). The 2001 Canadian census reported about 379,555 Chinese in the Toronto census metropolitan area (CMA), 312,185 in Vancouver CMA, 46,635 in Calgary CMA, and 26,895 in Ottawa CMA. In the U.S., there were about 218,469 Chinese in the San Francisco primary metropolitan statistical area (PMSA), 334,764 in Los Angeles-Long Beach PMSA, and 386,313 in New York PMSA in 2000 (Lewis Mumford Center 2004).

The change of immigration policies in the 1970s opened the door for Chinese immigration, and the new policies of immigration status provision were no longer based only on kinship, but also on financial capital, skills, and education. Subsequently, the socioeconomic backgrounds of the Chinese community in these countries became more diverse. While most of the earlier Chinese immigrants had limited skills and a low level of education, the social and economic backgrounds of these new immigrants are more varied (Fan 2003). Although some of the new immigrants have low levels of education, a substantial proportion of them have completed a university degree, or even graduate training.

The high level of human capital and financial resources brought with these new immigrants or acquired during their stay in the host countries not only affects many aspects of their own social and economic well-being, but also sets the stage for changes in ethnic businesses. On the supply side, immigrants with high levels of human capital may not be satisfied with participation in neighborhood convenience stores or laundry shops, while those with considerable financial resources may have the capacity to invest in larger businesses. On the demand side, the socioeconomic and demographic diversity of immigrants facilitates the need for variations in services and products. Subsequently, Chinese businesses flourish in cities that have a substantial representation of Chinese. The recent rapid expansion of Chinese businesses in these cities signifies a major fundamental structural change in Chinese businesses.

## THE STUDY OF CHINESE BUSINESSES IN THREE MAJOR IMMIGRANT RECEIVING COUNTRIES

Given the long history of Chinese in Australia, Canada, and the U.S., it is not surprising to find that the study of Chinese businesses dates back to the earlier years of their arrival in the mid-eighteenth century. Typically, most of these works are a historical account of the Chinese in the country with a short section on Chinese businesses in the community (P. Li 1998; Coolidge 1969; Chiu 1967). Although they provide a glimpse of the economic activities during this period of time, most of these work are descriptive in nature. A considerable number of Chinese owned their business, and almost all their businesses were located in Chinatown. The businesses usually required little skill or investment. For example, Lai (1988) documented a variety of Chinese businesses within the Chinatown area in the late eighteenth and early nineteenth century in Canada, which typically required minimal skills, such as grocery stores and laundries. A detailed account by Chiu (1967) of the industrial and occupational representation of Chinese in California in the 1870s shows that a considerable number of them were self-employed as vendors, in businesses with little investment.

Although most studies of Chinese businesses during the exclusion period are descriptive, they provide some preliminary explanations of the emergence of Chinese business. Studies based on interviews with elderly Chinese in the U.S. and Canada suggest that Chinese started businesses during the exclusion period because it was difficult for them to find jobs in the discriminatory social environment (P. Li 1998; Nee and Nee 1972). Low skills and a small investment provided a means of survival during this difficult time (P. Li 1998). Some studies also explored the interconnectedness of these businesses by studying the organization and functions of various associations, such as the Chinese Consolidated Benevolent Association (P. Li 1998; Nee and Nee 1972). They also studied how informal business connections were formed through partnership (P. Li 1998; Nee and Nee 1972). Siu's detailed study (1998) of laundry businesses and workers in Chicago during this period further extended the discussion to the operation of these businesses. He argued that the unique working environment in laundry businesses fostered the social problems of those who worked there. Though these studies address the importance of social networks and the social embeddedness of these businesses (topics of economic sociology that have been discussed at great length in later years), these conceptual frameworks were not available before the 1970s to guide the discussion.

It was the work of Ivan Light (1972) that finally brought the discussion of Chinese businesses from the study of the Chinese diaspora and placed it in a larger theoretical context of the discussion of ethnic businesses. Inspired by Light's work and his publications at that time, other studies began to explore the participation patterns of Chinese businesses. With the emergence of network analysis in the 1960s and economic sociology in the 1980s, subsequent studies have as a common focus the structural arrangements among and within Chinese businesses. Researchers have tended to produce detailed analyses of how social and human capital affects the likelihood of individuals becoming business owners. Some have studied the effects of ethnic networks on business operations, such as recruitment and retention, or the economic patterns of those participating in Chinese businesses (Lever-Tracy *et al.* 1999; Sanders *et al.* 2002; Kwong 1996; Zhou 1992; Li 1992). In both areas, researchers have been more interested in the internal dynamics of Chinese businesses and the effects of the immediate local context on Chinese businesses. Yet, they have belied the very important fundamental changes among Chinese businesses shaped by the broader set of constraints and opportunities of the emerged and consolidated economic contexts in which they are embedded.

Given the growing significance of economic globalization, local businesses in general are increasingly linked to the flow of international capital and labor to local markets. Chinese businesses are no exception. Compounded by the fact that a large proportion of Chinese business is owned or run by immigrants, economic globalization can have a substantial impact on ethnic business development. Without doubt, the dominant economic and social forces that stem from the accelerating globalization of the world economy have been overlooked in the study of Chinese businesses. The accelerating integrated international financial markets, growing international trade, and frequent labor migration give rise to new configurations and operations of local ethnic businesses that have not been fully addressed. Only by understanding how economic globalization affects ethnic businesses can one obtain a more complete and current picture of the recent developments in ethnic businesses.

Even studies which demonstrate an awareness of the linkages between economic globalization and Chinese businesses do not fully acknowledge and explore the linkages systematically (Light 2001; Lin 1998). An earlier formulation by Wei Li (1998), a geographer, suggested that the suburban ethnic community in the U.S., the Chinese community in her case, is the consequence of globalization. However, her discussion does not further explore the exact linkages of economic globalization and Chinese businesses. Among sociologists, Lever-Tracy *et al.* (1999) studied the transnational networks of Chinese entrepreneurs in Australia. They did not go one step further to explore how these transnational linkages shape the development of Chinese businesses. Lin (1998) studied the changes in Chinatown and acknowledged the effect of economic globalization. His work focuses on change at the community level. Recent work by Kwong (1999) explored the global linkage of illegal Chinese immigrants. Yet the discussion focuses on a subgroup of the Chinese population. Although Li's study (1998) of Chinese businesses from Hong Kong in Canada acknowledged the political situation that triggered the move of those belonging to professional and business classes to Canada, he did not go on to discuss how the unique backgrounds of these entrepreneurs have shaped Chinese business development.

In the following sections, we discuss how globalization, specifically economic globalization, is related to the recent development of Chinese businesses in major immigrant receiving countries.

## ECONOMIC GLOBALIZATION AND ETHNIC BUSINESSES

Economic linkages with other countries have long been a standing feature of most national economies. However, these linkages have accelerated and intensified since World War II, due to technological developments, the decreasing cost of transportation, and emergence of international trade organizations (Chass-Dunn *et al.* 2000; Held *et al.* 1999). In the middle of the 1980s, the term "globalization" came into popular use to represent these economic linkages (Held *et al.* 1999).

Despite its common usage, the meaning of the term is elusive. "Globalization" in general refers to a global trade network represented by interconnected national economies with national and regional division of labor (Sassen 2000; Held *et al.* 1999). With emergent, intensified transnational economies, the social, cultural, political, and economic landscapes of those countries involved have undergone important changes. Although the development of ethnic businesses definitely has also resulted from the combination of political, social, and cultural aspects of globalization, our discussion will focus on economic globalization. In particular, we will concentrate on two features related to economic globalization that are widely discussed in the literature. This focus will help us to delineate the effects of economic globalization on the development of ethnic businesses.

The simple and direct reference to economic globalization usually is to the increase in foreign investment in a local economy. It is not uncommon to find today companies that coordinate market sales and production in various countries simultaneously. According to Sassen's figures, over half a million affiliates worked outside their home countries and generated about $11 trillion in sales in 1999 (Sassen 2002). This number largely echoes the growth rate of direct foreign investment from developed to developing countries, which was about 17 percent between 1988 and 1996 (Sassen 2002). All these numbers point to local markets that are tightly knit into the larger economic context. Subsequently, job growth and decline in a city sometimes may reflect not simply the state of the local economy, but rather the larger economic context.

Still another significant feature of economic globalization is the intensity and interconnectedness of labor migration. Employment opportunities in the local economy are what, in large part, drives labor migration. Further facilitated by lower transportation costs, international trade agreements, and immigration policies that target skilled workers, international labor migration has intensified in recent decades (Stalker 2000). According to recent government statistics, the U.S. accepted an average of 95,000 employment-based immigrants, which is approximately 11 percent of the annual immigration between 1986 and 2002 (U.S. Department of Homeland Security 2003). Similarly, Canada has admitted an annual average of 260,687 individuals in the skilled worker category, which comprised 7 percent of immigrants, between 1986 and 2002.

The increase in the flow of international capital and the intensity of connectedness of the labor market has had a major direct and indirect impact on the development of ethnic businesses. In the following discussion, we highlight three possible areas of studying economic globalization and ethnic businesses. In the first part, we discuss how the flow of international financial capital and human migration affects the development of Chinese businesses, which in turn affects the Chinese community. Second, we focus on how the transnational linkages of ethnic members affect the operation of Chinese businesses. After all, economic globalization is about the economic and social linkages of individual businesses with their counterparts in other countries. Third, we address how the local urban structures affected by economic globalization shape the development of Chinese businesses. Through our focus on Chinese experience, we believe that the discussion bears important implications and highlights some possible new directions for the study of ethnic businesses in general from the vantage point of globalization.

## Chinese business, economic globalization, and community development

Economic globalization transforms the nature of ethnic businesses. The transformation can be linked to two key processes: the flow of international capital, and labor migration (Sassen 1991). The flow of international capital reflects the growth of foreign investment in local areas. These foreign financial resources not only contribute to the proliferation of large transnational companies that have dominated media reports, but also foster the growth of a large number of small companies, especially ethnic businesses, whose owners are recent immigrants and other businessmen in the sending countries. Recent immigrants bring financial capital with them when they immigrate to take advantage of the growing demand for ethnic products. Businessmen in the sending countries are interested in diversifying and opening new markets in other countries (Sklar 2001). Aided by the reduced costs of entering foreign markets due to the lower costs of transnational operation and transportation, ethnic businesses are growing in the receiving countries.

The development of ethnic businesses is also affected by the increase in labor migration. Immigration policies of the major receiving countries, such as the United States, Canada, and Australia, underwent drastic changes in the 1970s. These changes were partly in response to global market competition, and led to an increase in immigrants with high levels of skill and education. With the growth of middle-class immigrants, the demand for ethnic services and products has increased and diversified, which in turn has considerably expanded the ethnic market potential.

The recent development of ethnic businesses in response to these changes due to economic globalization is echoed in some recent work on Chinese enclaves. Lin (1998) in his book observed that New York's Chinatown is no longer a gathering place for bachelors where shops are only small and family oriented. On the contrary, he suggested that foreign investment, such as the opening of branches of foreign banks and shops with substantial foreign investment, has transformed the ethnic businesses in Chinatown. Similarly, Zhou's (1992) study of New York's Chinatown documented that many businesses, such as jewelry and professional firms, are backed by resources from Hong Kong and Taiwan. Wei Li's (1998) discussion of the ethnoburb, a term she suggested to describe ethnic concentration in suburban areas, also pointed out that the expansion of ethnic businesses in the ethnoburbs largely resulted from the increased flow of international capital and labor.

In the first part of the book, authors have addressed recent developments of Chinese businesses (i.e., ethnic media, ethnic banking, and industrial diversity and dispersion) that were largely driven by international capital and labor migration and highlighted their effects on ethnic communities. These chapters address three recent developments of Chinese businesses that affect the development of ethnic communities: ethnic media, ethnic banking, and the growing diversity and dispersion of ethnic businesses. Chapter 2, by Zhou and Cai, explores the emergence and blossoming of Chinese ethnic media in North America. Ethnic media themselves are a newly developed area of ethnic business. They are unique because they are the product of globalization and at the same time the facilitator of global linkage among local ethnic members with their home country. Zhou and Cai point out that the Chinese ethnic media have grown rapidly and reach many members of the community. They suggest that the Chinese ethnic media are a product of globalization driven by international financial investment and the growth of the community due to recent immigration. Chinese ethnic media are important in providing social support and information to newly arrived Chinese immigrants, including those with skills and high levels of education. At the same time, Chinese ethnic media are crucial to enabling diversified Chinese businesses to reach their potential customers.

The second phenomenon discussed is ethnic banking. With the intensifying economic globalization, the constant flow of international capital fosters the emergence of the Chinese banking sector. The presence of Chinese banks signifies new opportunities for Chinese businesses. Li and Dymski in Chapter 3 describe in detail the emergence of Chinese banking in southern California. They differentiate between two types of Chinese banking institutions: Chinese American banks and Chinese foreign banks. The former are more locally focused and the latter are overseas branches of Asian banks. The writers have traced the development of Chinese ethnic banking sectors and suggest that the emergence of both types of Chinese ethnic financial institutions has resulted largely from the transnational movement of Chinese people and the "availability of transnational capital and the supply of ethnic millionaires." They further argue that the existence of Chinese banking is critical to the development and expansion of ethnic businesses because many ethnic Chinese firms have secured financial support from these banks.

Lo and Wang in Chapter 4 explore the extent and diversity of Chinese businesses of considerable size. They use data collected from the Dun & Bradstreet Business Directory to document the size and diversity of the medium-sized and large Chinese businesses that have a turnover of at least $50,000 in Toronto, where a large number of Chinese reside. Using this criterion, they recorded about 600 such Chinese businesses in Toronto. This number indicates that Chinese businesses are no longer small, family-owned concerns; a great number of them are relatively large in size. In addition, the findings also vividly portray a diversity of industries in which these businesses are involved. All these results point to the fact that Chinese businesses in Toronto have been transformed beyond an enclave market wherre they cluster in just a few locations.

In short, authors of various chapters in the first part of the book explore the changes in Chinese businesses. In particular, they explore recent ethnic business developments: ethnic media, ethnic banking, industrial diversity, and location dispersion. They show that these changes largely reflect the effects of economic globalization. However, economic globalization does not only affect the development of ethnic businesses, which in turn shape the ethnic community; it also affects the operations of ethnic business, the subject that we now turn to.

## Chinese businesses and transnational linkages

One important aspect of economic globalization is that it facilitates transnational linkages. With the current international flow of finances and the constant movement of workers from one country to another in the emerging global market, today's immigrants are still actively involved in and constantly maintain networks in their home countries (Portes and Zhou 1996; Glick Schiller *et al.* 1992). Based on data collected from a number of Latin immigrant groups, a recent study by Portes *et al.* (2002) suggested that more than half of self-employed immigrants are involved in transnational activities. The results clearly show that transnational linkages are common among immigrant entrepreneurs.

Transnational immigrant entrepreneurs most likely conduct their businesses between their home and receiving countries. The locational choices for such transnational business activities are obvious because these are the places with which they are most familiar. However, conducting transnational business between the two countries requires the maintenance of stable linkages. Such linkages are important to sustain business networks, to expand clientele, and to follow the local market trends (Chang and Tam 2004).

Although research has argued the importance and benefits of maintaining transnational networks among immigrant entrepreneurs, why do not all immigrant entrepreneurs maintain transnational business networks? The question is rarely addressed. Nevertheless, asking the question helps to delimit the functions of transnational business networks. Subsequently, the understanding of the nature of transnational networks is enriched.

In recent decades, studies documenting the importance of the direct and indirect impact of transnational linkages on ethnic business operation have shown how products, clients, and employees are recruited from either the sending countries or the receiving countries (Kyle 1999; Landolt 2001). In particular, there are ample studies of the transnational linkages of Mexican entrepreneurs in the U.S. and Mexico (e.g., Portes *et al*. 2002; Kyle 1999) and the "bamboo networks" of Chinese businessmen in Asian countries (e.g. Gomez and Hsiao 2001; Weidenbaum and Hughes 1996). However, few studies have explored the effects of transnational business linkages between Chinese in major immigrant receiving countries (Australia, Canada, and the U.S.) and in their sending countries (Cheng 1999). It is important to understand the transnational linkages of Chinese businesses in various countries because the transnational linkages may reflect unique cultural patterns, structural characteristics of the receiving countries, and geographic proximity between the sending and receiving countries.

In the first chapter of the second part of the book, Light (Chapter 5) compares differences in ethnic business participation between Chinese immigrants and immigrants from Central America in the U.S. Light argues that transnational linkages are important in reducing the differences in ethnic businesses of the two groups. However, he reiterates the importance of the local context, which includes group characteristics, in the local receiving areas, and of the cultural differences between the group and the host society.

Light's chapter sets the tone for the following three chapters, which look at why not all immigrant entrepreneurs have transnational business ties, if transnational linkages bring benefits to business. Although these chapters do not make direct comparisons of the transnational linkages of Chinese businesses in different cities, the authors lay the groundwork by providing important information on how transnational businesses are related to Chinese business development in the cities where the authors studied. Chapter 6, by Salaff, Greve, and Wong, explores why some Chinese from the People's Republic of China have used their transnational ties to set up their businesses in Toronto, while others have not. Using data on 50 couples from the PRC, the authors suggest that not all transnational linkages are useful. Some of the business networks in China do not help immigrants start their businesses in Canada. They point out that the usefulness of transnational linkages depends on the nature of resources offered. The study is important because it warns against an overly optimistic view of the effect of transnational linkages on ethnic business operation.

Ip in Chapter 7, using data collected in Brisbane and Sydney, two major cities in Australia, compares Chinese immigrants from Hong Kong, Taiwan, and the People's Republic of China. He found that those from Hong Kong and Taiwan arrived in Australia with transnational financial capital and ties. With financial capital, they can easily take advantage of their transnational ties and business net-works in their business operations in Australia. Without financial capital, immigrant entrepreneurs from the PRC, even those who have transnational ties, have to draw on locally developed networks to establish their businesses. When only limited support is provided by local networks, they then have to seek help from home. Nevertheless, most of the immigrants from the PRC see their businesses as local in nature. The study has shown that the availability of transnational linkages is not sufficient a condition to facilitate overseas business. Financial capital is needed to make the linkages functional.

The final chapter in this section picks up another issue related to transnational business linkages. Szonyi (Chapter 8) explores the effect of transnational linkages on the community of the sending country. Szonyi's work is based on his historical data on how one individual businessman in the late Qing Dynasty brought new perspectives and ideas back home. He provides an important glimpse of the effect of transnational linkages beyond the economic development of the local home community. He demonstrates that transnational linkages can bring cultural changes and can even have direct impact on major political reforms.

## Chinese businesses, local urban structures, and homogenization

The publication of Sassen's book *The Global City* (1991) certainly laid out a clear description of how globalization affects local city urban economies and structures. Although early researchers focused on a few cities characterized as global in nature, studies in recent years suggest that most cities are influenced by globalization to various degrees. Today, most studies try to identify the general patterns of the urban change effected by globalization (Taylor *et al.* 2002; Smith and Timberlake 2002).

One of Sassen's original observations was the effect of globalization on local economies. She suggests that the increasing flow of international capital fosters the growth of financial and service industries and the decline of manufacturing industries. Educated and skilled laborers are in greater demand and, subsequently, are highly rewarded in the labor market, while the unskilled experience more difficulty finding jobs (Stalker 2000). As research has pointed out that those involved in ethnic businesses are more likely to have lower levels of education and skill (Light and Gold 2000), the shrinking availability of manufacturing jobs in the city can have a direct and significant impact on the propensity for individuals to become entrepreneurs, and on their economic returns.

The effect of globalization on local economies can also affect ethnic businesses. The increasingly multinational nature of corporations creates more opportunities for ethnic members who are familiar with local affairs and culture in their home countries (Stalker 2000). In these circumstances, and with the aid of legislation ensuring fair employment, ethnic members may now experience less "blocked mobility," which has been suggested to be a major structural factor that encourages ethnic members to seek self-employment (Li 1998). These changes can also have considerable effects on the propensity of individuals to participate in ethnic businesses and the differential earnings between those who work inside and outside ethnic businesses.

Partly due to globalization, the growth of racial and ethnic diversity changes the ecology of the city, which in turn affects the development of ethnic businesses. One of the consequences is that the ethnic businesses of some larger groups may face a dilemma of growth. On the one hand, the increased size of the group provides the momentum to grow. On the other hand, given that the group can only support a limited number of businesses, more competition among these businesses may occur (Lieberson 1980). Another consequence of the increase of the ethnic group's size is changes in residential patterns. A higher residential concentration of ethnic members may foster the development of ethnic businesses.

In the third part of the book, Fong and Lee (Chapter 9) fully explore the effect of local urban structure, under the impact of globalization, on ethnic businesses. Although this book focuses on ethnic businesses, the study provides a larger framework by comparing earnings of workers and business owners working inside and outside the ethnic economy. Ethnic economy, despite variations in definitions, refers to the agglomeration of ethnic businesses. Drawing from the 1990 U.S. census and focusing on Chinese in 16 cities, the writers specifically address four local urban structural effects: the size of the ethnic group, residential patterns, the relative employment situation, and the state of the local economy. They found that local urban structures have a strong impact on the earnings of those who are business owners or workers inside the ethnic economy. Therefore, they suggest that the earnings or economic returns of entrepreneurs fluctuate and are subject to various local urban structures.

Economic globalization fosters migration of skilled workers. It partly contributes to the growth of the middle class in the Chinese community. Given such a context, Peter Li in Chapter 10 explores how changes in the class locations of Chinese affect the rate of participation in ethnic businesses. In addition, he investigates whether self-employed individuals still have an earnings advantage over wage earners. Drawing from 1996 census data collected in Canada, another major immigrant receiving country, Li shows that the propensity for self-employment among Chinese is similar to that of other Canadians, with the qualification that foreign-born Chinese are more likely to be self-employed. He also found earnings disadvantages among Chinese females regardless of whether they were foreign born or native born, whereas Chinese foreign-born males experience more disadvantage in economic returns than do native born.

Finally, economic globalization does not only shape the structures and processes of Chinese businesses. It also raises the issue of how much the economic and social activities related to Chinese businesses reflect local uniqueness. The discussion reflects a larger question of economic globalization: homogenization. Although economic globalization helps to diffuse products and technologies quickly from one location to another, it also poses a challenge to local communities to resist the erosion of their local uniqueness. In other words, it asks how much there is "homogenization" between home country and local destination.

The discussion by Luk (Chapter 11) addresses the issue of homogenization. The use of landmarks and famous business names back home allows Chinese businesses to define their business niche. However, the outcome can be homogenization between home country and the local destination. Nevertheless, that does not imply that globalization helps create ethnic businesses without subethnic distinction. Using data collected from Chinese businesses in Toronto, Luk argues that this phenomenon reflects the global and local linkages of ethnic businesses in terms of not only economic but also cultural interactions.

Ethnic shopping malls are a unique development, largely the results of international capital and the recent growth in the Chinese immigrant population. Most products sold in the malls are ethnic specific and reflect the most recent popular cultural trends of the sending country, an indication of homogenization. For example, shops sell the latest CDs of popular singers, the latest popular TV soap opera series, and the latest fashions in the home country. Ooka's Chapter 12 explores the effects of mall visits on how youth perceive their own ethnic identities. Her data drawn from Toronto show that frequent visits to ethnic shopping malls are associated with higher levels of ethnic identity. The chapter highlights how this new spatial arrangement of ethnic businesses attracts a younger generation of co-ethnic members. Subsequently, it can have a considerable relationship to the ethnic identity, and significant implications for the ethnic cohesiveness of the younger generation.

All these chapters are about Chinese businesses. As the Chinese are one of the largest Asian groups in most major immigrant receiving countries and they represent a considerable number of Asian ethnic businesses, these studies provide a crucial understanding of the group's business participation in these countries. We hope that this book is a beginning that will further link the literature of ethnic businesses, globalization, and studies of the overseas Chinese.

Globalization has transformed the operation of ethnic businesses. This book attempts to identify the changes, how they affect business operations, and how they shape the development of ethnic businesses. All these contributions suggest that the study of ethnic businesses should no longer focus only on their internal dynamics, but should also explore the relationship between the internal dynamics of businesses and the wider economic context that has been shaped largely by globalization. We believe that the discussion opens new avenues that link the discussion of ethnic businesses to understanding the multifaceted aspects of the topic. In particular, it paves the way for exploring new developments in ethnic businesses in the age of globalization.

## Notes

1    The Chinese Exclusion Act in the U.S. was passed in 1882; the Immigration Restriction Act in Australia was passed in 1901; and the Canadian Parliament passed the Chinese Immigration Act in 1923.

2    Information was drawn from the webpage of the Australian Bureau of Statistics (2003a), Australian Social Trends: Population—Population characteristics: Ancestry of Australia's population (http://www.abs.gov.au/ausstats/abs@.nsf/0/B85E1EB3A2BC27 4ACA256D39001BC337?Open&Highlight=0,ancestry). The three largest Asian groups included are the Chinese, Indians, and Vietnamese.

3    This information was obtained from the Statistics Canada (2003b) webpage on Canada's Ethnocultural Portrait: The Changing Mosaic (http://www12.statcan.ca/english/census 01/products/analytic/companion/etoimm/contents.cfm).

4    The calculation is based on those who reported Chinese only.
5    All numbers are based on those who reported belonging to one single Asian group.

## References

Australian Bureau of Statistics. 2003a. Report on "Australian Social Trends 2003—Population characteristics: Ancestry of Australia's population" (http://www.abs.gov.au/).

Australian Bureau of Statistics. 2003b. Australian Social Trends: Population—Population characteristics: Ancestry of Australia's population (http://www.abs.gov.au/ausstats/abs@.nsf/0/B85E1EB3A2BC274ACA256D39001BC337?Open&Highlight=0,ancestry).

Barnes, Jessica S. and Claudette E. Bennett. 2002. *The Asian Population: 2000. Census 2000 Brief* (http://www.census.gov/prod/2002pubs/c2kbr01-16.pdf).

Bureau of the Census. 1993. *We the Americans: Asians* (http://www.census.gov/apsd/wepeople/we-3.pdf).

Chan, Kwok Bun and Claire See-Ngoh Chiang. 1994. *Stepping Out: The Making of Chinese Entrepreneurs*. Singapore: Simon & Schuster.

Chang, Ly-Yun and Tony Tam. 2004. "The Making of Chinese Business Culture: Culture versus Organizational Imperatives." Pp. 23–38 in *Chinese Enterprise, Transnationalism, and Identity*, edited by Edmund Terence Gomez. London: Routledge.

Chass-Dunn, Christopher, Yukio Kawano, and Benjamin D. Brewer. 2000. "Trade Globalization since 1795: Waves of Integration in the World System." *American Sociological Review* 65: 77–95.

Cheng, Lucie. 1999. "Chinese Americans in the Formation of the Pacific Regional Economy." Pp. 61–78 in *Across the Pacific: Asian Americans and Globalization*, edited by Evelyn Hu-DeHart. Philadelphia, PA: Temple University Press.

Chiu, Ping. 1967. *Chinese Labor in California, 1850–1880: An Economic Study*. Madison, WI: University of Wisconsin Press.

Coolidge, Mary Roberts. 1969. *Chinese Immigration*. New York: Arno.

Fan, Cindy. C. 2003. "Chinese Americans: Immigration, Settlement, and Social Geography." Pp. 261–92 in *The Chinese Diaspora: Space, Place, Mobility, and Identity*, edited by Laurence J.C. Ma and Carolyn Cartier. New York: Rowman & Littlefield Publishers.

Fukuyama, Francis. 1995. *Trust: The Social Virtues and the Creation of Prosperity*. New York: The Free Press.

Glick Schiller, Nina, Cristina Blanc-Szanton, and Linda Basch. 1992. *Towards a Transnational Perspective on Migration: Race, Class, Ethnicity, and Nationalism Reconsidered*. New York: New York Academy of Sciences.

Gomez, Edmund Terence. 1999. *Chinese Business in Malaysia: Accumulation, Ascendance, Accommodation*. London: Curzon Press/University of Hawaii Press.

Gomez, Edmund Terence and Hsin-Huang Michael Hsiao. 2001. "Introduction: Chinese Business Research in Southeast Asia." Pp. 1–37 in *Chinese Business in Southeast Asia: Contesting Cultural Explanations, Researching Entrepreneurship*, edited by Edmund Terence Gomez and Hsin-Huang Michael Hsiao. Richmond, Surrey: Curzon.

Hamilton, Gary G. 2000. "Reciprocity and Control: The Organization of Chinese Family-Owned Conglomerates." Pp. 44–74 in *Globalization of Chinese Business Firms*, edited by Henry Wai-Chung Yeung and Kris Olds. Basingstoke, UK: Macmillan.

Held, David, Anthony McGrew, David Goldblatt and Jonathan Perraton. 1999. *Global Transformation: Politics, Economics, and Culture*. Stanford, CA: Stanford University Press.

Inglis, Christine. 1999. "Australia's 'New' Asian Immigration and Its Impact in a Period of

Globalization." Pp. 69–93 in *Asian Migration: Pacific Rim Dynamics*, edited by Yen-Fen Tseng, Chilla Bulbeck, Lan-Hung Nora Chiang, and Jung-Chung Hsu. Taipei: Interdisciplinary Group for Australian Studies, National Taiwan University.

Kao, John. 1993 "The Worldwide Web of Chinese Business." *Harvard Business Review* 71: 24–36.

Kwong, Peter. 1996. *New Chinatown*. New York: Hill & Wang.

———. 1999. *Forbidden Workers: Illegal Chinese Immigrants and American Labor*. New York: New Press.

Kyle, David. 1999. "The Otavalo Trade Diaspora: Social Capital and Transnational Entrepreneurship." *Ethnic and Racial Studies* 22: 422–46.

Lai, David Chuenyab. 1988. *Chinatowns: Towns within Cities in Canada*. Vancouver, WA: University of British Columbia Press.

Landolt, Patricia. 2001. "Salvadoran Economic Transnationalism: Embedded Strategies for Household Maintenance, Immigrant Oncorporation, and Entrepreneurial Expansion." *Global Networks* 1: 217–42.

Lever-Tracy, Constance, David Ip, and Noel Tracy. 1999. "Old Ties Abroad, New Friends at Home: Networks of Australian Chinese Entrepreneurs." Pp. 97–116 in *Asian Migration: Pacific Rim Dynamics*, edited by Yen-Fen Tseng, Chilla Bulbeck, Lan-Hung Nora Chiang, and Jung-Chung Hsu. Taipei, Taiwan: Interdisciplinary Group of Australian Studies, National Taiwan University.

Lewis Mumford Center for Comparative Urban and Regional Research. 2004. Metropolitan Racial and Ethnic Change—Census 2000 (http://mumford.albany.edu/census/index.asp).

Li, Peter. 1992. "Ethnic Enterprise in Transition: Chinese Business in Richmond, B.C., 1980–1990." *Canadian Ethnic Studies* 26: 120–38.

——— 1998. *The Chinese in Canada*. Second edition. Toronto: Oxford University Press.

Li, Wei. 1998. "Anatomy of a New Ethnic Settlement: The Chinese Ethnoburb in Los Angeles." *Urban Studies* 35: 479–501.

Lieberson, Stanley. 1980. *A Piece of the Pie*. Berkeley, CA: University of California Press.

Light, Ivan. 1972. *Ethnic Enterprise in America*. Berkeley, CA: University of California Press.

———. 2001. "Globalization, Transnationalism and Trade." *Asian and Pacific Migration Journal* 10: 53–80.

Light, Ivan and Steve Gold. 2000. *Ethnic Economies*. San Diego, CA: Academic Press.

Lin, Jan. 1998. *Reconstructing Chinatown*. Minneapolis: University of Minnesota Press.

Liu, Hong. 2000. "Globalization, Institutionalization, and the Social Foundation of Chinese Business Networks." Pp. 105–25 in *Globalization of Chinese Business Firms*, edited by Henry Wai-Chung Yeung and Kris Olds. Basingstoke, UK: Macmillan.

Nee, Victor and Brett De Barry Nee. 1972. *A Longtime Californ': A Documentary Study of an American Chinatown*. New York: Pantheon.

Portes, Alejandro and Leif Jensen. 1989. "The Enclave and the Entrants: Patterns of Ethnic Enterprise in Miami before and after Mariel." *American Sociological Review* 54: 929–49.

Portes, Alejandro and Min Zhou. 1996. "Self-Employment and the Earnings of Immigrants." *American Sociological Review* 66: 219–30.

Portes, Alejandro, William J. Haller, and Luis Eduardo Guarnizo. 2002. "Transnational Entrepreneurs: An Alternative Form of Immigrant Economic Adaptation." *American Sociological Review* 67: 278–98.

Redding, Gordon. 1990. *The Spirit of Chinese Capitalism*. New York: de Gruyter.

———. 1996. "Weak Organizations and Strong Linkages: Managerial Ideology and Chinese

Family Business Networks." Pp. 27–42 in *Asian Business Networks*, edited by Gary G. Hamilton. New York: de Gruyter.

Sanders, Jimy M. and Victor Nee. 1987. "Limits of Ethnic Solidarity in the Enclave Economy." *American Sociological Review* 52: 145–67.

Sanders, Jimy M., Victor Nee, and Scott Sernau. 2002. "Asian Immigrants' Reliance on Social Ties in a Multiethnic Labor Market." *Social Forces* 81: 281–314.

Sassen, Saskia. 1991. *The Global City: New York, London, Tokyo.* Princeton, NJ: Princeton University Press.

——. 2000. *Cities in a World Economy.* Thousand Oaks, CA: Pine Forge Press.

——. 2002. "Introduction: Locating Cities on Global Circuits." Pp. 1–36 in *Global Networks, Linked Cities*, edited by Saskia Sassen, New York: Routledge.

Siu, Paul C.P. 1998. *The Chinese Laundryman: A Study of Social Isolation.* New York: New York University.

Sklar, Leslie. 2001. *The Transnational Capitalist Class.* Malden, MA: Blackwell Publishers.

Smith, David and Michael Timberlake. 2002. "Hierarchies of Dominance among World Cities: A Network Approach." Pp. 117–41 in *Global Networks, Linked Cities*, edited by Saskia Sassen. New York: Routledge.

Stalker, Peter. 2000. *Workers without Frontiers.* Boulder, CO: Lynne Rienner Publishers.

Statistics Canada. 2003a. Selected Ethnic Origins, for Canada, Provinces and Territories— 20 percent Sample Data (http://www12.statcan.ca/english/census01/products/highlight/ ETO/Table1.cfm?Lang=E&T=501&GV=1&GID=0).

Statistics Canada. 2003b. Canada's Ethnocultural Portrait: The Changing Mosaic (http://www12.statcan.ca/english/census01/products/analytic/companion/etoimm/conten ts.cfm).

Taylor, Peter J., D.R.F. Walker, and J.V. Beaverstock. 2002. "Firms and Their Global Service Networks." Pp. 93–116 in *Global Networks, Linked Cities*, edited by Saskia Sassen. New York: Routledge.

Weidenbaum, Murray L. and Samuel Hughes. 1996. *The Bamboo Network: How Expatriate Chinese Entrepreneurs are Creating a New Economic Superpower in Asia.* New York: Martin Kessler Books.

Wong, Siu-lun. 1988. *Emigrant Entrepreneurs: Shanghai Industrialists in Hong Kong.* Hong Kong: Oxford University Press.

U.S. Department of Homeland Security. 2003. *Yearbook of Immigration Statistics, 2002.* U.S. Government Printing Office: Washington, DC (Table 4: Immigrants admitted by type and selected class of admission: fiscal years 1986–2002).

Yeung, Henry Wai-Chung. 1998. "Transnational Economic Synergy and Business Networks: The Case of Two-way Investment between Malaysia and Singapore." *Regional Studies* 32: 687–706.

——. 2000. "The Dynamics of the Globalization of Chinese Business Firms." Pp. 75–104 in *Globalization of Chinese Business Firms*, edited by Henry Wai-Chung Yeung and Kris Olds. Basingstoke, UK: Macmillan.

Yeung, Henry Wai-Chung and Kris Olds. 2000. "Globalizing Chinese Business Firms: Where are They Coming From, Where are They Heading?" Pp. 1–30 in *Globalization of Chinese Business Firms*, edited by Henry Wai-Chung Yeung and Kris Olds. Basingstoke, UK: Macmillan.

Zhou, Min. 1992. *Chinatown: The Socioeconomic Potential of an Urban Enclave.* Philadelphia, PA: Temple University Press.

Zhou, Yu. 1998. "Beyond Ethnic Enclaves: Location Strategies of Chinese Producer Services Firms in Los Angeles." *Economic Geography* 74: 228–51.

# Part I

# Economic globalization, and community development and Chinese ethnic businesses

# 2 Chinese language media and the ethnic enclave economy in the United States

*Min Zhou and Guoxuan Cai*

Chinese language media have been on the American scene since the earliest Chinatown but only recently have they achieved the status of an influential ethnic institution serving both social and economic functions. In much of the pre-World War II era, the Chinese immigrant community was essentially an isolated bachelors' society consisting of a small merchant class and a disproportionately male working class who were legally excluded from participating in the mainstream American economy and social life. Chinese language media did not form a significant ethnic institution at that time, because of the extremely low levels of literacy and Chinese language proficiency among many older immigrants, the limited scale of ethnic economies, and the face-to-face patterns of interaction among coethnic members in segregated enclaves. Nevertheless, occasional and back issues of newspapers and magazines published in China, and concentrating almost entirely on China or China-related events and topics, did circulate among the small Chinatown elite. There were also publications of community newspapers and newsletters, but circulation was small and was confined to Chinatown. Not until the late 1970s did Chinese language media start to take on a dual role as both an ethnic social institution and an economic enterprise.

At present, the Chinese language media in the United States are composed of publications, television, radio, and the Internet, with publications predominating. The largest and most influential newspapers include the New York-based *Chinese Daily News* (formerly *The World Journal*), the U.S. edition of the Hong Kong-based *Sing Tao Daily*, and the New York-based *China Press*. Meanwhile, numerous nationally circulated daily newspapers and weekly magazines and locally circulated community papers have mushroomed in cities and suburbs with sizeable ethnic Chinese populations. Chinese language television, radio, and online media have also been growing rapidly, especially since the early 1990s, with a strong presence in the very cities where the ethnic press has established strongholds (Kang & Lee Advertising 1998).

In this chapter, we first describe how the development of Chinese language media is affected by the phenomenal rate of contemporary Chinese immigration and the rapid diversification and globalization of the ethnic enclave economy. We then examine how Chinese language media in turn facilitate the growth of the ethnic enclave economy to grow beyond geographic and national boundaries and help non-English-speaking immigrants navigate their English-speaking host society.[1]

## IMMIGRATION, SUBURBANIZATION, AND THE RISE OF ETHNOBURBS

Chinese Americans are one of the oldest and fastest-growing ethnic groups in the United States. With the lifting of legal barriers to Chinese immigration after World War II and the enactment of a series of liberal immigration laws since the passage of the Hart-Celler Act of 1965, the Chinese American community has increased more than ten-fold, from 237,292 in 1960 to 2,879,636 (including 447,051 mixed-race persons) in 2000. According to the U.S. Immigration and Naturalization Service (USINS 2002), nearly 1.4 million immigrants were admitted to the United States from China, Hong Kong, and Taiwan as permanent residents between 1961 and 2000, and China has been on the list of top ten immigrant-origin countries since 1980. The phenomenal rate of contemporary Chinese immigration has been accompanied by two patterns of immigrant settlement: one is the time-honored path starting from inner-city ethnic enclaves and eventually "melting" into white middle-class suburbs, and the other is a distinct trend of bypassing the inner city to settle into middle-class suburbs directly upon arrival.

Historically, Chinese immigrants clustered in Chinatowns in major gateway cities. Chinatowns in San Francisco, New York, and Los Angeles were typical of the nation's oldest immigrant enclaves. But unlike early immigrants from Europe, who were expected to assimilate into the mainstream society as quickly as possible, early Chinese immigrants were legally barred from naturalization and assimilation. They were forced to take refuge in a predominantly Chinese bachelors' society, creating jobs for themselves to avoid direct competition with native workers while enabling themselves to fulfill a sojourner's dream of returning to their homeland with gold and glory (Zhou 1992). Under Chinese exclusion policies, even those who had attained adequate economic means and cultural proficiency, including the children of immigrants, found it hard to move out of the ethnic enclave because of racial exclusion in white middle-class residential neighborhoods. The lifting of Chinese exclusion acts during World War II opened up other occupational channels for the Chinese. Many of them entered the military, the shipyards, and the civil service; some were engaged in wholesale trade and operated grocery stores and other small businesses that were left vacant by the forced removal of the Japanese to internment camps (Waldinger and Tseng 1992). The decades immediately after World War II brought some residential movement out of Chinatowns among the young and socioeconomically mobile coethnics, leaving visible signs of decline and aging in these century-old enclaves.

Since the enactment of the 1965 Hart-Celler Act, which abolished the national origins quota system to allow for family reunification and employer-sponsored migration of skilled labor, old Chinatowns have persisted and thrived as new immigrants have arrived. Despite the out-movement of the "assimilated" second generation, Chinatowns have attracted new immigrants from diverse socioeconomic backgrounds, new money from overseas, and well-connected entrepreneurs who conduct businesses inter-regionally and internationally (Lin 1998; Wong 1998; Zhou 1992). However, these traditional urban enclaves no longer serve as primary centers of initial settlement as many new immigrants, especially the affluent and the highly skilled, bypass inner cities to settle into suburbs immediately after arrival. As of 2000, half of the Chinese American population lives in suburbs. Even in immigrant gateway cities such as San Francisco, Los Angeles, and New York, the majority live in neighborhoods outside Chinatown. For example, as of 2000, only 8 percent of Chinese in San Francisco, 2 percent in Los Angeles, and 14 percent in New York live in inner-city old Chinatowns.

The suburbanization of the Chinese immigrant population does not appear to be associated with the disappearance of old Chinatowns, which have actually grown and expanded in new directions, taking over decaying adjacent neighborhoods (Zhou 1992). Instead it has caused the formation of "ethnoburbs," a term used to describe suburban middle-class immigrant enclaves (Li 1997). What is distinct about the current trend is not merely the dispersion of immigrants in suburban areas, but a re-concentration of the coethnic population into new suburban immigrant enclaves.

Geographical concentration, to some extent, follows a historical pattern: Chinese Americans continue to concentrate in the West and in urban areas. California alone accounts for 40 percent of all Chinese Americans (1.1 million). Next are the states of New York and Hawaii, with 16 percent and 6 percent, respectively. However, there has also been a significant increase in the Chinese American population in other states that historically received fewer Chinese immigrants, such as Texas, New Jersey, Massachusetts, Illinois, Washington, Florida, Maryland, and Pennsylvania. While Chinese Americans have dispersed all over the country, the tendency towards ethnic concentration, especially among the foreign born, is marked. Following the drastic transformation of California's Monterey Park into the nation's first suburban Chinatown in the 1980s (Arax 1987; Fong 1994), many Chinese immigrant communities or ethnoburbs have sprung up in suburban cities. As shown in Table 2.1, there are currently 11 U.S. cities with over 100,000 people in which Chinese Americans comprise over 20 percent of the city's population. All are in California, and all but San Francisco are suburban municipalities. Traditional gateway cities have also witnessed the formation of new ethnic enclaves outside old Chinatowns, referred to as "satellite Chinatowns." Flushing and Sunset Parks in New York City, and Richmond and Sunset districts in the City of San Francisco are just a few of the most obvious cases (Wong 1998; Zhou and Kim 2003).

Suburbanization and the formation of ethnoburbs suggest a pattern of ethnic succession quite distinct from the past. It appears that once satellite Chinatowns and ethnoburbs take form, in-migration of coethnic members accelerates. Some move in directly from abroad, while others move in from Chinatown as a step up the socioeconomic ladder. However, whether in Chinatown or the ethnoburbs, Chinese immigrants face similar language and cultural obstacles. More than half

*Table 2.1* Cities* with the highest proportions of Chinese Americans, 2000

| State | City | Number of Chinese Americans in city | Share of total population in city |
|---|---|---|---|
| California | Monterey Park | 26,810 | 44.6% |
| California | Arcadia | 19,676 | 37.1% |
| California | San Gabriel | 14,581 | 36.6% |
| California | Alhambra | 31,099 | 36.2% |
| California | Rosemead | 17,441 | 32.6% |
| California | Rowland Heights | 15,740 | 32.4% |
| California | Temple City | 10,269 | 30.8% |
| California | Hacienda Heights | 13,551 | 25.5% |
| California | Cupertino | 12,777 | 25.3% |
| California | San Francisco | 160,947 | 20.7% |
| California | Diamond Bar | 11,396 | 20.2% |

Source: U.S. Census of the Population, 2000.
* Cities with population over 100,000.

the Chinese immigrants do not speak English "very well." Even those who are proficient in English still encounter barriers because of unfamiliarity with the host society. Moreover, today's Chinese immigrants have come from diverse places of origins and cultures (including different dialects) and socioeconomic backgrounds. Earlier immigrants came predominantly from villages in just a few counties in southern Guangdong, China. They were closely connected to their respective family and district associations, and they received assistance and protection from these voluntary associations once they arrived in the United States (Wong 1977; Zhou and Kim 2001).

As they strive to settle in their new homeland, many recent Chinese immigrants, including the upwardly mobile, find themselves in a paradoxical situation: they have voluntarily left their old homeland but remained emotionally attached to it; they aspire to become a part of their new homeland but are often blocked by language and cultural barriers. They need institutional support to help ease adjustment difficulties. However, existing ethnic institutions, such as family or district associations, are insufficient to meet the demands of immigrants who have come from diverse places of origins and socioeconomic backgrounds, and have settled in places not as closely knit as old Chinatowns. Chinese language media thus develop among the numerous new ethnic institutions to serve that need, providing an important tool in helping new immigrants adapt to life in a foreign land.

## DIVERSIFICATION AND GLOBALIZATION OF THE ETHNIC ENCLAVE ECONOMY

Economic development in the Chinese immigrant community is another driving force for the burgeoning Chinese language media. During the era of Chinese

Exclusion, the immigrant community was spatially isolated in Chinatowns. The ethnic economy that developed from those Chinatowns was oriented to sojourning and was confined to either ethnically specific niches, such as restaurants, or low-skilled, labor-intensive niches unattractive to native workers (Zhou 1992). Even after the repeal of the Chinese Exclusion Act during World War II and for the following two decades, Chinatown economies remained small in scale and limited in variety, as the immigrant population aged with little replenishment, and the second generation gradually moved away.

Traditional ethnic economies could not afford to support ethnic media, nor did they have much need for them. Advertising was an uncommon practice in old Chinatowns as businesses were closely intertwined with networks of coethnic members and their social organizations. Information about goods and services and business or employment opportunities was channeled primarily through word of mouth and face-to-face interaction. For example, the owner of a popular restaurant was likely to be the head of a family association and was inclined to hire his own relatives and friends, who in turn spread the word about his restaurant. A laundry worker was likely to shop at the same place as his neighbors, who could share shopping tips and exchange information about the pricing and quality of goods and services in the neighborhood. As a result, business owners and workers could meet their respective needs without having to step outside Chinatown.

Since the 1970s, there has been unprecedented Chinese immigration, accompanied by a tremendous influx of human and financial capital, which has set off a new stage of ethnic economic development (Fong 1994; Lin 1998; Zhou 1992). The U.S. census shows that from 1977 to 1987, the number of Chinese-owned firms grew by 286 percent, compared to 238 percent for all Asian-owned firms, 93 percent for black-owned firms, and 93 percent for Hispanic-owned firms. From 1987 to 1997, the number of Chinese-owned businesses continued to grow at a rate of 180 percent (from less than 90,000 to 252,577). As of 1997, there was approximately one Chinese-owned firm for every nine Chinese Americans, compared to only one Hispanic-owned firm for every 29 Hispanics and one black-owned firm for every 42 blacks. Chinese-owned business enterprises made up 9 percent of the total minority-owned business enterprises nationwide, but held 19 percent of the total gross receipts (U.S. Bureau of the Census 1991, 1996, 2001).

Most impressive has been the increase in the scale and variety of ethnic businesses in Chinatowns and Chinese ethnoburbs, a phenomenon also referred to as "the enclave economy." The enclave economy is a sociological concept that differs from the ethnic economy, in that it connotes a spatial dimension, based on the geographic concentration of ethnic businesses and coethnic populations, and a social dimension, embedded in and with profound impact on the social structures of an ethnic community (see Portes and Bach 1985; Zhou 2002). Some ethnic businesses have become incorporated into the mainstream economy, such as Computer Associates International in Long Island, New York, and Kingston Technology and Sybase in Silicon Valley, California. These ethnic businesses rely on neither a distinctive ethnic labor market nor a coethnic consumer market, and thus have relatively little tangible impact on the immigrant community as a whole, except for being celebrated as models of success. The enclave economy, in contrast, depends almost entirely on ethnic capital, labor, and consumer markets, and serves as an anchor, or identity marker, for the immigrant community (Zhou 1992). The enclave economy contains certain features of the primary sector of the mainstream economy and provides opportunities for upward mobility, such as self-employment. Nonetheless, it does remain marginal to the mainstream economy as it operates largely within a culturally and linguistically distinct environment. Even though many new ethnic businesses have expanded beyond the geographic boundaries of ethnic enclaves to tap into the mainstream consumer market, they still tend to concentrate in metropolitan areas with a visible density of coethnic consumers and businesses and to maintain close ties to the ethnic community.

Compared to the traditional Chinatown economy, the new ethnic enclave economy is much more diverse. In the past, most ethnic enterprises were restricted to retail and service sectors. Today, high-tech and durable goods manufacturing, communications, wholesale trade, FIRE (finance, insurance, and real estate), and professional services are among the fastest-growing industries in the Chinese immigrant community. These ethnic enterprises may be further diversified into various specialties. We use the medical profession as an example. In New York City, the Chinese business directory listed only 12 doctors' offices in 1958, 30 in 1973, and 300 in 1988. Among those 300 doctors, there was a wide range of specialties, from internists, pediatricians, obstetricians, and gynecologists to dentists, optometrists, orthopedists, cosmetic surgeons, acupuncturists, and chiropractors (Zhou 1992). In 2000, the number of doctors listed in New York City's Chinese business directory more than doubled that of 1988. The *2002 Chinese Consumer Yellow Pages* in Los Angeles is 3 inches thick (2,500 pages), and the listing for various herbalists and doctors of Chinese and Western medicine with various specialties takes 409 pages. New ethnic businesses are also much larger in size and scale than traditional ones. In the restaurant business, for example, traditional family-run restaurants are supplemented by trendy corporate-managed restaurants equipped with banquet halls, private dining rooms, karaoke and other entertainment facilities, and seating capacities for 500 or more.

To a great extent, the survival and growth of the enclave economy depend heavily on ethnic resources—foreign capital, pooled family savings, ethnic labor force, ethnic consumers, and transnational markets. To compete for a greater share of the ethnic consumer market, ethnic businesses can no longer depend on word of mouth or face-to-face interaction to facilitate information flow. They must find new ways to communicate with potential consumers who are diverse in dialect, origin, socioeconomic status and settlement patterns, but who share similar tastes and needs for goods and services that the larger economy cannot adequately provide. As a result, Chinese language media have emerged in the immigrant community, not simply as a service to ethnic businesses for marketing and advertising, but also as a new type of ethnic business.

## A DESCRIPTIVE PROFILE OF CHINESE LANGUAGE MEDIA IN THE UNITED STATES

Chinese language media in the United States are composed of publications, television, radio, and mostly recently online publications and broadcasting. Publications dominate the ethnic media. According to an incomplete count (Kang & Lee Advertising 1998), there are three major dailies that have a substantial U.S./Canada circulation. *Chinese Daily News*, which is affiliated with the United Daily Group based in Taiwan, is by far the largest and most influential Chinese language daily in the United States in particular and the global Chinese community in general. Since its debut in New York in 1976, *Chinese Daily News* has become an independent daily with three headquarters—New York, Los Angeles, and San Francisco—and multiple branch offices in major cities in the United States, Canada, Europe, and Latin America, and a U.S. circulation of 298,500. The second largest newspaper is the North American edition of *Sing Tao Daily*, a subsidiary of the Hong Kong-based Sing Tao Newspaper Group. *Sing Tao Daily* established its branch offices in San Francisco in the early 1960s, Los Angeles and New York in the 1980s, and Boston, Chicago, and Philadelphia in the 1990s with a U.S. circulation of 181,000. The third largest newspaper is *China Press*, which was established in 1990 in New York as an independent paper but maintains close contact with the official media machine in mainland China. *China Press* has a U.S. circulation of 120,000.

In cities where the "big three" dailies are headquartered or have branch offices, there also coexist numerous Chinese language dailies and weeklies with regional or national circulation ranging from 15,500 to 90,000. In addition, many local community newspapers and magazines have also appeared in the same cities, especially since the 1990s. Community papers, mostly owned by immigrant entrepreneurs, are published weekly or bi-weekly and have a circulation typically between 5,000 and 10,000 copies. Most of these community papers are distributed at no cost through Chinese-owned businesses (e.g., Chinese supermarkets, travel agencies, bookstores, and restaurants) but some charge customers a nominal fee. Most of the community papers and magazines are established in suburbs rather than in inner cities. In Los Angeles, for example, there are at least two dailies and six weeklies printed and circulated locally. All are headquartered in the Chinese immigrant community in LA's eastern suburbs. In Washington D.C., there are at least six local weeklies, and all are registered in Rockville, Maryland, a suburban community with an increasingly visible Chinese immigrant population.

Chinese language television is relatively new, but has developed rapidly since the mid-1980s. According to Kang & Lee Advertising (1998) and our own survey, there are three major Chinese television networks—Asian American Television (AATV), Chinese Television Network (CTN), and North American Television (NATV). These national networks broadcast in both Cantonese and Mandarin 24 hours a day, seven days a week via satellite, or through local cable systems in major cities for two to 15 hours per day. Chinese TV programming features headline news from China, Hong Kong, and Taiwan and breaking news in the United States and in the world, along with a wide variety of special reports and entertainment programs, including variety shows, popular or classic Chinese movies, Cantonese operas, and children's shows. Locally produced programs include U.S. and American Chinese community news, commentaries, and special forums on topics ranging from current affairs, local politics, education, to real estate and finance. AATV claims to reach about 87,000 households in Los Angeles via two local cable channels, usually three to six hours a day, Monday through Saturday, and as many as 100,000 more viewers via satellite dishes. Like AATV, CTN's major market is in Los Angeles and has a viewership of about 280,000 households via local cable channels, and another 285,000 via satellite dishes for its 24-hour programming. NATV, also headquartered in Los Angeles, claims to be the largest Chinese language TV network in the U.S. and to reach an estimated viewership of about 860,000 on the West Coast and in New York. In addition, there are at least 12 Chinese local TV stations, and the number is growing in cities with sizeable Chinese immigrant populations. These local stations air programs supplied by national and regional TV networks in China, Hong Kong, and Taiwan, and feed their programming to local cable systems with broadcast time varying from 30 minutes daily to eight hours daily. Except for the San Francisco-based Chinese Television Company, which was established in 1976, most of the Chinese language television stations started broadcasting in the mid- to late 1980s and the 1990s, and most serve the West Coast, reflecting the increasing waves of recent Chinese immigration and its geographic concentration. In major cities, such as Los Angeles, New York, San Francisco, Houston, and Chicago, these local Chinese TV stations claim a viewership as large as 100,000 or more.

Chinese language radio broadcasting is also a fairly recent phenomenon. At present, there are only a few Chinese radio stations, mostly located in Los Angeles, San Francisco, and New York (Kang & Lee Advertising 1998). Compared to television, radio stations produce a substantially higher proportion of their programming locally, focusing on news updates, rush-hour traffic reports, business and finance, lifestyle, shopping, entertainment, and tabloid gossip.

At the peak of the information age, Chinese language media have expanded onto the Internet, serving the greater immigrant community in North America. Two of the big three dailies launched their online editions on the Web in the late 1990s. *Chinese Daily News* can now be viewed online at <Chineseworld.com>, and *Singtao Daily* at <Singtao.com>. The Los Angeles-based *Zhong Guo Daily News* and *Taiwan Daily News* jointly maintain the website <Chinesedaily.com>. One of the most visited websites for comprehensive online media is the Chinese version of <yahoo.com>, which is not a direct translation from the English site, but contains distinctly Chinese channels and categories providing full coverage of many topics and can be viewed in both simplified and traditional Chinese writing. Another popular media site is <Sina.com>, initially developed by Chinese immigrant entrepreneurs in Silicon Valley and later merged with a Beijing-based company. <Sina.com> has now rivaled Chinese <Yahoo.com> to become one of the most visited websites around the world. Chinese language Internet media offer online news, entertainment, community news, and e-commerce in four localized websites that are produced and updated daily by local teams in China, Hong Kong, Taiwan, and North America. As of September 2000, <Sina.com> had an average of 46 million daily pageviews and 11 million registered users. Most recently, the first comprehensive Chinese language online newspaper in the United States was established by a group of Chinese immigrant entrepreneurs in Maryland. Like the printed press, this online paper features four channels—USDragon News, Chinese Community, USDragon Columns, and Leisure and Entertainment (with various categories within each channel)—and eight metropolitan editions—Washington D.C., Los Angeles, New York, San Francisco, Boston, Chicago, Houston, and Detroit. In addition, Internet users also have access to online newspapers and magazines published in China, Hong Kong, and Taiwan, and numerous other websites based in homeland locations. What distinguishes the homeland-based websites from the U.S.-based websites is the perspectives and approaches they adopt. A Chinese-American perspective and a transnational approach are clearly articulated in the U.S.-based Chinese language websites.

News coverage is the key component of all Chinese language media outlets. Whether in print, on air, or online, all outlets contain substantial news coverage, which includes: (a) local and national news highlights directly transmitted from major media outlets in China, Hong Kong, and Taiwan; (b) U.S. national and local news, current affairs, weather, and special reports produced by mainstream English language media and Associated Press) translated into Chinese; and (c) news about the local, national, and the global Chinese community produced by ethnic outlets. In addition to news coverage, most of the publications in print and online feature thematic sections on politics, community life, business/finance, entertainment/ leisure/sports, and editorial columns and reader viewpoints/letters.

In sum, content coverage in Chinese language media in the United States is not a wholesale importation from the homeland media, nor is it simply an edited translation of the mainstream American media. It responds to the varied needs of its clientele. Newspaper readers and radio listeners tend to be diverse in educational and occupational statuses, from cooks, waiters, and seamstresses, to engineers, scientists, and teachers. Online media users are predominantly middle-class professionals who are not only well educated, but also English-proficient and assimilated. TV viewers tend to be non-English speaking, older, and newer arrivals. In their increasing proportion of local reporting or locally produced programming, the ethnic media fulfill an important function as information agent by keeping immigrants of diverse backgrounds well informed of their two social worlds— Chinese and American.


## THE DUAL ROLE OF CHINESE LANGUAGE MEDIA IN THE IMMIGRANT COMMUNITY

The development of Chinese language media in the United States is, no doubt, affected by contemporary Chinese immigration and the booming ethnic enclave economy. As we shall see, the ethnic media function as both economic enterprises and social institutions. Like all mass media, Chinese language media function as economic enterprises delivering professional services to the business community and the ethnic population and generating revenues to sustain and expand themselves. Assuming that most of the Chinese immigrants who do not speak English very well and half of those who are proficient in English prefer to use Chinese language media either entirely or selectively, the ethnic consumer market in the U.S. amounts to at least 1.2 million. Taking into account the strong purchasing power of the ethnic population and the thriving ethnic economy, this market is potentially lucrative. In the ethnic media market, rates for subscriptions or listenership or viewership tend to be low-cost or free, so the major revenue comes from advertising sales to ethnic business. Through Chinese language media, ethnic businesses are able to reach out to Chinese immigrants who are residentially dispersed and go beyond the geographic confines of Chinatown and the ethnoburbs. Moreover, as economic enterprises, Chinese language media provide employment opportunities for those who have been professional journalists in their homelands but are not proficient in English, and for other individuals who are highly educated but have difficulty finding jobs that match their educational credentials.

Chinese language media also serve as an important ethnic social institution that is complementary rather than inharmonious to the host society. First and foremost, the ethnic media effectively connect immigrants to the host society in a way that is most familiar to immigrants and that keeps them informed. Regardless of outlet type, news coverage about U.S. society and the immigrant community is substantial. Without knowing any English, a Chinese immigrant can find out what is happening in the world, from headline news about a U.S. military surveillance plane crash-landing on Hainan Island, Judy Chu's election as the third Chinese American in the California State Assembly, California's energy crisis, the high court decision on marijuana use, or the postponement of the McVeigh execution, to tabloid gossip about Hollywood stars. In one of our interviews, an acupuncturist in Los Angeles's Chinatown, who is over 60 years old and does not speak English, surprised us with an incredibly vivid description of a recent NBA playoff. When we asked how he got to that level of detail, he smiled, pointed to the *International Daily News* on his desk, and said, "I watched the game on CBS, and then read the newspaper and listened to the radio on my way to work the next day. The radio had better coverage." He asked us to test him on other current events, and seemed to know more than we could ask. In this case, the Chinese language media were not only a source of information itself but also a supplement to the mainstream media. This example also suggests that non-English-speaking immigrants are acculturated via the Chinese language media.

Second, the ethnic media connect immigrants to the host society by providing them with a detailed roadmap pointing out the best possible options for them to navigate unknown and foreign territories. Upon arrival, new immigrants, even those with some proficiency in English, want to know how to go about finding suitable housing, jobs, business and investment opportunities, schools for their children, and various services. They are not well connected to the service and employment networks in the mainstream society, and their own family or friendship networks are no longer sufficient to meet these diverse needs. As information agents, the ethnic media fill the needs of new immigrants that are not met in the larger society. With some assistance, a non-English-speaking newcomer can pick up a phone to find a rental apartment and a job in the same day; there are individuals advertising housing and jobs who also speak Chinese. Locally produced newspaper forums and TV and radio programs routinely discuss topics that are of special interest to immigrants, such as changes in immigration laws, how to invest in children's education, how to purchase and finance a dream home, how to apply for a business loan, how to bridge the generational gap with their teenage children, and so forth.

Third, Chinese language media promote and reinforce the mobility goals of the immigrant community. As discussed previously, the Chinese immigrant community today has shifted its orientation from sojourning to settling, to moving up in American society rather than making money and going home. In the Chinese immigrant community, the biggest concerns are making a living, home ownership, and the education of children. In many cases, an immigrant consider himself as successful if he runs his own business or becomes a *laoban* (boss), if he owns a home (even if he lives in the basement and rents out the rest of the house), if his child goes to an Ivy League college. As ethnic institutions, the media consistently support and reinforce these mobility goals. In the local business and community sections of newspapers, for example, there are news reports and editorials or columns, as well as numerous advertisements, to inform the reader about business opportunities, the best timing and place to purchase a home, and children's problems and educational achievement. For example, *Chinese Daily News* annually publishes a chart of the latest *US News and World Report* ranking of the top 25 colleges. In a visit to a Chinatown worker's home, we saw such a chart clipped from the paper and posted on the refrigerator. We also heard people talking about these rankings during the time for college applications. Winners of various regional and national academic decathlons who are of Chinese ancestry will get front-page coverage in the major Chinese dailies, with pictures and extensive reports about their families.

Fourth, Chinese language media work to acculturate immigrants, often subtly and gradually. This may sound counterintuitive—how can ethnic language media contribute to acculturation when the key measure is the adoption of the host language? We have found that the media can influence certain habits and behavior which are not typically Chinese. One example is watching television at dinner. In Chinese families, sitting together at the dinner table is a daily ritual and also a sign of parental respect. Children are supposed to sit with their parents at the table and listen to their conversation without interruption, and they are not allowed to leave the table until everyone has finished. Now it is common for children to have dinner in front of the TV without being scolded, because many parents would want to watch their favorite Chinese language TV programs at prime time, too.

While the ethnic language media serve as a bridge between the Chinese-speaking immigrant community and the mainstream society, they also maintain their traditional function of keeping immigrants in close contact with the homeland, thus easing the psychological and emotional problems of being a foreigner. New immigrants are concerned with what goes on in their original homeland as well as in the larger U.S. society, how homeland politics and economy affect their families and friends who are left behind, and how events or policies developed in the homeland, the U.S., or elsewhere affect U.S.–China relations and their own lives in the U.S. Mainstream media outlets usually lack detailed coverage of these issues, and the ethnic media fill the gap.

Moreover, the ethnic media create a cultural space enabling immigrants to enrich their lives. New immigrants are interested in things that they have been personally connected to or have grown up with, in arts and literature, entertainment, their favorite movie/music/sports stars, the familiar faces, voices, and writings of TV anchorpersons, sports commentators, comedians, novelists, and humorists. The cultural scene in the U.S. is unfamiliar and irrelevant, and sometimes even unsettling in the case of racial stereotyping and bias and insensitive ethnic jokes. The language barrier exacerbates the sense of cultural emptiness. An immigrant writer associated this painful feeling as "being in a cultural desert." He remarked, "You try to look ahead but see no destination; you try to turn back but can't retrace your footsteps; and you end up drifting aimlessly without direction." While Chinese language media fill the emptiness by offering the familiar and thus easing the pain, they also open up a cultural space where immigrants can express in writing their experience and share it with others. In the family section of *Chinese Daily News*, for example, we have seen short stories, poems, and essays that reflect immigrant life in America.


## CONCLUSION

We have provided a general description of how contemporary Chinese immigration and the ethnic enclave economy influence the development of Chinese language media. Our descriptive analyses show that Chinese language media, while constituting ethnic businesses, also connect immigrants to the host society by providing immigrants with a detailed roadmap of what goes on around them, promoting and reinforcing the mobility goals of the immigrant community, and creating a cultural space in which immigrants can enrich their lives. Consequently, non-English-speaking immigrants seem to be well informed about the wider society when they have easy access to the ethnic language media. Assimilated immigrants who are proficient in English and have moved out of the enclaves and into the mainstream are also returning to the ethnic community in larger numbers and with greater frequency, and are subscribing or turning to the ethnic media for information and entertainment, even when they have access to mainstream media. The findings indicate that the ethnic language media, like any other ethnic institution, cannot simply be viewed as an ethnic institution isolated from the mainstream American society. Under certain conditions, which are contingent upon the premigration socioeconomic characteristics of the immigrants, the social and economic structures of the ethnic community, and global development, ethnic language media can facilitate assimilation to life in the new land.

## Notes

1   The data on which our study is based entail a content analysis of a selection of news-papers, television and radio programs, and websites, supplemented by telephone or face-to-face interviews with a snowball sample of ethnic newspaper reporters, TV and radio program producers, readers, viewers, and listeners in New York, Los Angeles, and Washington D.C., between the fall of 2000 and spring of 2001. This chapter is drawn partly from our previously published article "The Chinese Language Media in the United States: Immigration and Assimilation in American Life" (*Qualitative Sociology* 25, pp. 419–40).

## References

Arax, Mark. 1987. "Monterey Park: The Nation's First Suburban Chinatown." *Los Angeles Times*, April 6, p. 1.

Fong, Timothy P. 1994. *The First Suburban Chinatown: The Remaking of Monterey Park, California*. Philadelphia, PA: Temple University Press.

Kang & Lee Advertising, Inc. 1998. *Asian Media Reference Guide*. Third edition, online <http://www.kanglee.com>.

Li, Wei. 1997. Spatial Transformation of an Urban Ethnic Community from Chinatown to Chinese Ethnoburb in Los Angeles. Ph.D. Dissertation. Department of Geography. University of Southern California.

Lin, Jan. 1998. *Reconstructing Chinatown: Ethnic Enclave, Global Change*. Minneapolis, MN: University of Minnesota Press.

Portes, Alejandro and Robert L. Bach. 1985. *Latin Journey: Cuban and Mexican Immigrants in the United States*. Berkeley, CA: University of California Press.

U.S. Bureau of the Census. 1991. *Survey of Minority-Owned Business Enterprises, 1987*. Washington D.C.: U.S. Department of Commerce.

——. 1996. *Survey of Minority-Owned Business Enterprises, 1992*. Washington D.C.: U.S. Department of Commerce.

——. 2001. *Survey of Minority-Owned Business Enterprises, 1997*. Washington D.C.: U.S. Department of Commerce.

U.S. Immigration and Naturalization Services (USINS). 2002. *2000 Statistical Yearbook of the Immigration and Naturalization Services*. Washington D.C.: U.S. Government Printing Office.

Waldinger, Roger and Yenfen Tseng. 1992. "Divergent Diasporas: The Chinese Communities of New York and Los Angeles Compared." *Revue Européenne des Migrations Internationales* 8 (3): 91–115.

Wong, Bernard. 1977. "Elites and Ethnic Boundary Maintenance: A Study of the Roles of Elites in Chinatown, New York City." *Urban Anthropology* 6: 1–22.

——. 1998. *Ethnicity and Entrepreneurship: The New Chinese Immigrants in the San Francisco Bay Area*. Needham Heights, MA: Allyn & Bacon.

Zhou, Min. 1992. *Chinatown: The Socioeconomic Potential of an Urban Enclave*. Philadelphia, PA: Temple University Press.

——. 2002. "The Enclave Economy and Ethnic Social Structures: Variations in Neighborhood-Based Resources for Immigrant Adolescents in Los Angeles." Paper presented at Session III "Network as Context" of the Princeton Economic Sociology Conference on The U.S. Economy in Context, Princeton University, February 22–23.

Zhou, Min and Rebecca Kim. 2001. "Formation, Consolidation, and Diversification of the Ethnic Elite: The Case of the Chinese Immigrant Community in the United States." *Journal of International Migration and Integration* 2 (2): 227–47.

——. 2003. "A Tale of Two Metropolises: Immigrant Chinese Communities in New York and Los Angeles." Pp.124–49 in David Halle, ed., *Los Angeles and New York in the New Millennium*. Chicago, IL: University of Chicago Press.

# 3 Globally connected and locally embedded financial institutions

## Analyzing the ethnic Chinese banking sector

*Wei Li and Gary Dymski*

Economic development in minority communities invariably focuses on efforts to expand employment, foster business growth, and encourage investment and asset growth. Achieving these goals at the turn of the century remains a special challenge in Los Angeles: for even while racial income and wealth inequalities persist, sustained in-migration from Asia, Mexico, Europe, and Central and South America has transformed this region into a profoundly multiethnic and multiracial metropolis. If, as throughout history, southern California is a harbinger of things to come elsewhere in the U.S., then cities throughout the nation will soon face the challenge of multiethnic urban development.[1]

The influx of so many new residents in southern California, with so many different backgrounds and levels of capital and capability, has resulted in a surge of new urban development. Of particular significance is the emergence of the San Gabriel Valley as the center of a dense, multiracial population. The concentration of Hispanic and Asian American—especially Chinese American—residents has fueled robust business development, new residential communities, and a network of ethnic banks. In the past several years, our research with several co-authors has suggested the central importance of Chinese American banks in the successful development and transformation of many San Gabriel Valley communities (Dymski and Mohanty 1999; Li *et al*. 2000, 2001, 2002).[2]

The link between Chinese banks and Chinese community development is worthy of extensive study for the following two reasons:

- First, the creation of formal banking institutions is relatively new in the Chinese community. The literature on Chinese American urban economic development has focused primarily on these communities' marginal status, as exemplified in the sociological "ethnic enclave" model. Lending circles and informal financial arrangements among ethnic minorities are well known. However, contemporary Chinese communities are no longer confined to enclaves; and their financial institutions are formal banks, not "fringe banks." This shift from informal practices to the formation and expansion of formal institutions is attributable to shifting global movements of human and financial capital, the heterogeneity of this ethnic population and its businesses, and this population's increasingly dense transnational ties.

• Second, recent Chinese experience in southern California demonstrates the potential importance of ethnic banks as a developmental institution for other minority communities that have had difficulty obtaining banking services at mainstream institutions.

In this chapter, we explore the Chinese banking sector in the context of globalization and its role in minority community development; we also contrast the behavior of Chinese American banks and Chinese foreign bank offices. Southern California is our primary analytical focus, though we also discuss other parts of the U.S. We begin with a methodological note. Academic studies of banking typically fall into one of two categories—a few focus on cultural practices in banking (that is, on qualitative aspects of banking);[3] the overwhelming majority rely on quantitative sources and statistical analyses. Our study incorporates both quantitative and cultural/qualitative dimensions of banking. In addition to a wide range of secondary sources, this chapter incorporates results of face-to-face semi-structured interviews (and numerous telephone follow-up interviews) conducted over a three-year time span with top executives of 22 Los Angeles County-based Chinese American banks (a total of 39) and Chinese foreign bank offices (23).[4]

## CHINESE BANKING AS IMMIGRANT ETHNIC ECONOMY

To survive in a host society, immigrants usually concentrate on certain occupations or establish their own independent firms and business networks. These firms and networks can be termed the "ethnic economy." In any metropolitan area, the ethnic economy consists of the ethnically owned firms that tend to employ members of the same ethnic group. Ethnic economies vary in spatial form and evolve over time; they can be roughly divided into three types: ethnic economic niches, ethnic enclave economies, and contemporary integrated ethnic economies.

### The changing ethnic economy: from niches and enclaves to integrated economies

"Ethnic economic niches" were the earliest form of ethnic economy developed in America. Niches consist of certain occupations or self-employed business types, mostly pursued by first-generation immigrants as pathways to economic survival. One immigrant group may own most of the establishments in one or more economic niches, or may be concentrated in certain job types in a given locality. Chinese laundries and restaurants are one such niche. The areas of business concentration typically do not require large sums of startup capital, and thus can be supported by informal financial practices such as lending circles (Geertz 1956; Light and Bonacich 1988; Mao 1995; Tsai 1986; Wu 1974). Note that these niches are also sometimes dictated by practices of racial exclusion and discrimination in the host society.

The "enclave economy," by contrast, is an integrated set of ethnic niche activities, which forms a more or less self-contained economic system with relatively weak ties to the mainstream economy. Enclave economies are the form of ethnic economy most widely studied by social scientists.[5] Wilson and Portes (1980) define the enclave economy as the set of firms that are established by immigrant entrepreneurs. Good examples include the traditional Chinatowns across America and Cubans in Miami. These enclaves' financial needs are likely to be more extensive than in the ethnic niche economy, due to the greater scale of some enclave businesses.

The contemporary integrated ethnic economy consists of a set of ethnic businesses integrated with the mainstream economy, but with a distinct ethnic imprint. As in the ethnic enclave economy, businesses are usually owned and operated by an ethnic minority, and required labor, goods, and services may or may not be provided by members of this ethnic group. Economic restructuring in the larger society in recent years has led many ethnic economies to become both more integrated with national and international economic systems, and at the same time more bifurcated. The emphasis on family reunification in U.S. immigration law has created a large cheap labor reserve pool; at the same time, the investor category (EB-5 visa) actively recruits capitalists seeking to invest on American soil (U.S. Congress 1965, 1991). The global trend toward increasing inequality widens this intra- and inter-ethnic divide between rich capitalists and poor laborers. While the former enter the U.S. as entrepreneurs/investors, the latter can only survive in the U.S. by taking low-wage jobs.

The increased availability of transnational capital and the supply of ethnic millionaires—some belonging to new cadres of circular migrants or "transmigrants," such as the trans-Pacific "space man" (Kotkin 1991)—both increase the size of the ethnic economy and pull it into new business areas, such as large-scale custom houses and high-tech firms. For instance, Asians and Pacific Islanders owned 114,500 firms in Los Angeles County as of 1997, 14.7 percent of the total number of county firms. Among these firms, wholesale trade, FIRE (finance, insurance, and real estate), and manufacturing account for 12 percent, 9.6 percent, and 3.6 percent, and generate total sales and receipts of $28.3, $1.7, and $4.5 billion respectively.[6] Some ethnic firms involve themselves directly in global business by engaging in international trade with their home (and other) nations. By engaging in many franchising and subcontracting arrangements and by providing an increasing share of the labor and goods in the market, the ethnic economy is becoming more integrated into the mainstream economy. Ethnic banks, because of their special links with businesses and individuals in the ethnic economy, are thus increasingly important in overall economic dynamics.

The contemporary integrated ethnic economy exemplifies trends in the larger political economy: first, the shift toward service and high-tech sectors; second, the increasing demand *both* for highly educated, highly skilled, and well-paid professionals, *and* for less-educated, low-wage workers. The latter trend is leading to bifurcation in labor processes and in wage and job structures (Beauregard 1989; Sassen and Appiah 1999; Scott 1988, 1993; Storper and Walker 1989). Many contemporary Chinatowns fit the new profile of an integrated ethnic economy (Zhou 1992). Lin (1998) analyzes Chinatown's ethnic economy in New York as having a dual character: a "lower circuit," consisting of the labor-intensive sector, and an "upper circuit," consisting of the financial and real estate sector.[7] This "duality" of the ethnic economy has become widespread in those metropolitan areas with large and diverse immigrant populations, especially in those newer ethnic communities that Li has termed the "ethnoburbs" (Li 1998a).

Another important characteristic of the contemporary ethnic economy is its transnational character. Faist (2000: 214–16) notes that ethnic entrepreneurs evolve "from the ethnic niche to transnational businesses, . . . [that is] privileged entrepreneurs with relatively high amounts of financial capital." A recent study by Portes *et al.* (2002) uses a large-scale survey of three Latino immigrant groups to examine whether immigrants are increasingly working as transnational entrepreneurs. These authors find, using aggregate data, that "the forms of transnationalism can be expected to vary significantly by immigrant nationality and context of reception in ways that are not well understood today" (p. 294). What remains to be addressed is the economic and social roles of "upper circuit" transnational enterprises. Yeung and Olds (2000: 276–7) emphasize the need to "examine the *impact* of Chinese business firms on host countries (and cities)" and "the nature of the relationships between *western financial institutions* and *ethnic Chinese entrepreneurs*" (emphases in the original). We agree; but in our view, Chinese ethnic banks must also be examined as components of the overall institutional structure of finance, with attention to their impact on both the ethnic and the overall economy of metropolitan areas.

## Transforming ethnic finance: from lending circles to commercial banking

We now develop our theme by bringing ethnic finance into the analysis of the changing ethnic economy. We compare the evolution of ethnic banks with the parallel transformation of minority economic clusters (from ethnic enclaves to ethnoburbs). We focus on the experience of the Asian American communities of Chinese entrepreneurs and banks, which have some similarities with and many differences from those of other minorities. The process begins with fragmented, small lending circles among family members and professional friends, and informal savings and transactions practices. These financial relations are externally oriented: many funds are transferred to countries of origin—either to support families, accumulate assets, engage in cultural practices, or to maintain business networks. These relations are prevalent in the ethnic economic niche and enclave economy stages. The process is then gradually transformed into more integrated financial relations, increasingly oriented toward markets internal to the ethnic economy. As savings and transactions practices are accomplished within the same banking institution, the financial holdings of the ethnic community become the basis of a loan-money creation process.[8] The emphasis shifts away from transferring savings and income abroad, and toward using savings and wealth to support businesses, families, and communities in the U.S.

Who controls these emerging financial resources? Control depends on whether the group is able to develop its own formalized institutions, and on whether the non-ethnic institutions that serve it provide equitable access and credit instruments that respond to this community's needs. This transformation parallels the transition of ethnic community members themselves from migrant workers to residents.[9] It also parallels the maturation of ethnic non-banking businesses. The extent to which this triple transformation is completed depends on local circumstances—institutional frameworks, exclusionary or inclusive business and social practices, the extent of residential integration, the size of the ethnic community in question, and so on. While the diasporic process is ongoing globally for the Chinese community, there are many unique aspects to each of the "spoke" settlements that migration from population-intensive "hubs" is continually creating and recreating.

In the case of ethnic Chinese in the U.S., ethnic finance has been transformed from a mixture of remittance-based capital outflows and informal financing of domestic ethnic businesses, to a capital circulation network with full-scale commercial banking activities. In this new stage, ethnic minority-owned banks are playing a key role due to their shared basis in language, cultural background, and business practices. Ethnic Chinese banks are increasing in number because of the increasing heterogeneity of immigrants themselves, and the changing nature of the ethnic economy, as outlined above. Small-scale lending circles can no longer satisfy ethnic households' diverse financial needs, or the requirements of economic development neighborhoods. Thus, in an increasing number of U.S. metropolitan areas, informal financial practices are accompanied and even superseded by formal structures of ethnic banking.

## CHINESE AMERICAN BANKS AND CHINESE FOREIGN BANKS: ORIGINS AND DIFFERENCES

This chapter includes both Chinese American banks and Chinese foreign bank offices as "ethnic Chinese banks." Our definition of ethnic banks is based on ownership, management, and market orientation (Dymski 1999; Li *et al.* 2001, 2002): (1) banks that offer FDIC-insured deposits and are currently owned and/or controlled by ethnic Chinese in the U.S.; (2) banks that offer FDIC-insured deposits and which are partially or wholly owned by overseas owners in nations where ethnic Chinese comprise a majority; and (3) overseas banks chartered in nations wherein ethnic Chinese comprise a majority, and which explicitly include ethnic Chinese in the U.S. in their market base.

In our definition, (1) and (2)—respectively, local banks and U.S. subsidiaries of foreign banks—are considered Chinese American banks, since they are FDIC-insured, U.S.-chartered, and U.S-regulated domestic banks. By contrast, Chinese foreign bank offices are not domestic banks in the U.S.; instead they represent banks headquartered in the "Greater China" economic sphere: mainland China, Hong Kong, Taiwan, and Singapore. The activities of these foreign bank offices in the U.S. are also subject to U.S. regulatory oversight.

The above definition delineates key differences between Chinese American banks and Chinese foreign bank offices. The former are locally embedded institutions, even if the source of their capital is overseas. The latter may play some role in the local economy, but they largely serve as globally connected outposts for their headquarters offices. The following sections demonstrate that despite some similarities, these two sub-sectors have very different roles in and impacts on Chinese American community development, as well as different relationships to processes of financial globalization.

## Chinese American banks

The first U.S.-chartered banking institution owned by ethnic Chinese was Bank of Canton of California.[10] Headquartered in San Francisco, it was established in 1937, reportedly owned and controlled by one of the four then-most powerful families in China. This family's two famous daughters both became first ladies of China— Madame Sun Yat-sen (Sun Zhongshan) and Madame Chiang Kai-shek (Jiang Jieshi). The first wave of contemporary Chinese American banks emerged as anti-discrimination vehicles, especially for older-generation residents of Chinatown. Mainstream banks largely ignored the financial needs of this generation, and repeatedly denied its members' applications for commercial loans, regardless of their creditworthiness. For example, in Los Angeles in the early 1950s a group of Chinese Americans attempted to establish a savings and loan association so as to pool local residents' financial resources and provide older-generation immigrants with decent retirement housing. Their attempts were repeatedly rejected by the authorities. The two Chinese American institutions created through these efforts— Cathay Bank and East West Federal Savings—did not open until 1962 and 1972, respectively, with some assistance from white Americans (Li *et al.* 2000; Wang 1994).

The second wave of contemporary Chinese American banks in the 1980s, however, has different roots. These financial institutions serve primarily as transnational entities for the influx of ethnic Chinese immigrants in the past two decades—an influx due mainly to post-1965 changes in U.S. immigration laws and to geopolitical developments. This new wave of immigrants differs from earlier Chinese labor migrants in the nineteenth and early twentieth centuries; its members do not immigrate to the U.S. for economic survival, but instead go there seeking a political and economic safe haven for safeguarding and expanding their existing wealth. Many of them have become wealthy by owning business or working as well-paid professionals in their countries of origin. Consequently, many members of this "second wave" start to engage in cross-national economic and trade activities as soon as they settle in the U.S. (Li 1998b; Tseng 1994a, 1994b, 1995; Zhou and Tseng 2001).

The rapid growth of East Asian economies in the past 40 years has been a key source of many immigrants' large sums of disposable wealth. For instance, recent statistics show that accumulated personal wealth in Taiwan reached US$800 billion, a figure that surpassed Korea ($600 billion) and Hong Kong ($320 billion) and trailed only Japan among Asian nations.[11] This translates into about $35,000 for every resident of Taiwan. Current government regulations in Taiwan stipulate that residents can legally transfer up to US$5 million annually from the island to overseas, and businesses can transfer up to $50 million. From 1986 to 2000, an average of 11,400 Taiwanese immigrated to the U.S. annually, many of them to LA. In 2000, the suburban San Gabriel Valley alone housed more than 193,000 ethnic Chinese.[12]

The changing socio-economic profile of immigrants, in conjunction with changes in the ethnic economy, has created the need for new structures of financing. The second wave of ethnic financial institutions has carved out special niches, especially with new immigrants who lack credit histories in their destination countries. In the past two decades, Chinese transnational entrepreneurs based in other countries have added to the scale and size of the ethnic banking sector by acquiring local Chinese American banks.[13] The result has been an explosion in the number of U.S.-chartered Chinese American banks: while there was only one such bank operating in LA County in 1970 and six in 1980, the total increased to 20 by 1990, and 27 by 2000.[14] Furthermore, all four of the largest California-based Chinese American banks—United Commercial, East West, General, and Cathay[15]—are publicly traded on the NASDAQ. Tapping into this equity market integrates them into U.S. and global financial markets, a step signifying that Chinese American banks—like Chinese Americans themselves—are becoming "mainstream."

## Chinese foreign bank offices

The first Chinese foreign bank office in the U.S. was a New York office established by the Bank of China in 1936. The Bank of China was a government-owned foreign exchange bank in China at the time, and the predecessor of both mainland China's contemporary Bank of China and Taiwan's International Commercial Bank of China (ICBC).[16]

Chinese foreign bank offices did not start operating in Los Angeles until the 1980s, when two banks each from Singapore and Hong Kong opened offices, and so did ICBC and Bank of China (Dymski and Li 2004). The 1990s witnessed a proliferation of Chinese foreign bank offices, especially from Taiwan. By June 2002, 20 Chinese foreign bank offices were open in Los Angeles, including 12 from Taiwan, four from Hong Kong, three from Singapore,[17] and one from mainland China. The establishment of Chinese foreign bank offices in the U.S. results either from the financial internationalization strategies of their home governments and headquarters, or from an effort to meet the needs of ethnically Chinese businesses in the U.S.

For example, Taiwanese banks began expanding overseas when first permitted to under the financial internationalization policy of 1987. In 1994, President Lee Teng Hui pronounced that his government would support Taiwanese banks' branches anywhere in the world to aid local Chinese businesses.[18] Table 3.1 lists the years in which banks opened overseas branches; note that most Taiwanese overseas offices were established during the 1990s. One impetus for Taiwanese banks has been the Taiwan government's continuing policy of encouraging

Table 3.1 Year and place of overseas operation among Taiwanese banks

| Bank name* | U.S. | E Asia | SE or South Asia | Australia | Canada | Latin America | Africa | Europe |
|---|---|---|---|---|---|---|---|---|
| Bank of Taiwan | NY – 1990; LA – 1993 | Hong Kong – 1994 Tokyo – 1995 | Singapore – 1995 | | | | S Africa – 1992 | London – 1991 2 Amsterdam – 1992 |
| Bank SinoPac | LA – 1999 | Beijing – 1997 Hong Kong – 1999 | Ho Chi Minh C – 1998 | | | | | |
| Chang Hwa Bank Ltd. | NY – 1989; LA – 1990 | Tokyo – 1992; HK – 1994 Shanghai – 2002 | Singapore – 1997 | | | | | London – 1993 2 Amsterdam – 1991 |
| Chiao Tung Bank Co., Ltd.** | Silicon Valley – 1989 NY – 1993 | | Singapore – 1983 | | | | | |
| Chinatrust Commercial Bank | NY – 1999 | Tokyo – 2000 | 2 Indonesia – 1992/1996 2 Philippines 1993/1996 Thailand – 1994 Vietnam – 1995 Hong Kong – 1997 New Delhi – 1996 | | Vancouver – 1999 | Asunción – 1996 Asunción – 2000 Asunción – 2001 | | London – 1992 |
| E. Sun Bank | LA – 2000 | Hong Kong – 1999 | Philippines – 1998 | | | | | |
| The Farmers Bank of China | Seattle – 1991; LA – 1995 | | | | | | | |
| First Commercial Bank*** | Guam – 1978 LA & NY – 1990 | Tokyo – 1994 Hong Kong – 1994 | Singapore – 1977 Bangkok – 1995 Ho Chi Minh C – 1996 | | | San Salvador – 2000 | | London – 1984 Frankfurt – 1991 |

| Bank | US | Japan / Hong Kong / China | Southeast Asia | Australia | Canada | Panama | Europe |
|---|---|---|---|---|---|---|---|
| Hua Nan Commercial Bank Ltd.**** | LA & NY –1990 | Tokyo – 1992; Hong Kong – 93 | Phnom Penh –1998; Palau – 1998; Singapore – 1995 | | | | London – 1998; Frankfurt – 1991 |
| The International Commercial Bank of China | NY – 1936; Chicago – 1975; Houston –1980; LA – 1984 | Tokyo & Osaka –1950; Hong Kong –2000 | Bangkok – 1950; 2 Philippines –1995/97; Singapore –1997; Jakarta –1999; Ho Chi Minh C –1996; Bahrain – 1984; Malaysia –1998 | Sydney –1997; Brisbane –1999 | Toronto –1982/85; Vancouver –1992; Richmond –1996 | Panama –1974/82 | Paris – 1982; Amsterdam – 1990 |
| Land Bank of Taiwan | LA – 1997 | Hong Kong –1999 | | | | | |
| Taipei Bank | NY – 1991; LA – 1993 | Hong Kong –1998 | | | | | London – 1994 |
| Taiwan Business Bank | LA – 1995 | Hong Kong –2000 | | Sydney – 2001 | | | |
| United World Chinese Commercial Bank | LA – 1993 | Hong Kong –2001; Shanghai – 2002 | Philippines –1997; Singapore –1997; Malaysia –1998; Bangkok –1998; Ho Chi Minh C –2000 | | | | |

Source: www.boma.gov.tw/sta/bas9103-102.doc; accessed 7/29/2002.

Note:  * Including branches, representative offices, and subsidiaries, but not subsidiaries in the U.S.; as of 3/31/02.
  ** European subsidiary closed on 12/1/01.
  *** Malaysia branch closed on 2/28/02.
  **** Jakarta representative office closed on 2/28/02.

investment in Southeast Asia, as a means of averting Taiwanese corporations' (including banks') direct investment in mainland China (Chan 1997). In effect, banks' overseas operations are jointly determined by government policies and market opportunities.

The establishment of offices in the U.S. reflects these banks' efforts to internationalize. The 20 Chinese foreign banks with Los Angeles offices operate a total of 514 overseas branches/agencies or representative offices worldwide. Asian countries remain the focus of their operations, accounting for 403, or 78 percent, of their overseas offices. One Singaporean bank alone, United Overseas Bank Group, has 264 Asian branches. Outside Asia, the U.S. has the largest number of these institutions' overseas branches (41), followed by Europe (34), Australia (17), Latin America (9), Canada (7), and Africa (3).

One continuing question is whether establishing a presence in global financial centers or serving co-ethnic population bases is more critical in determining these banks' branch locations. The latter appears more important. Los Angeles, while not a major financial center, surpasses New York, the world's largest financial center, in the number of Chinese foreign bank offices. The 20 Chinese foreign banks with LA offices collectively have 15 New York offices, and one each in Chicago, Houston, San Francisco, Silicon Valley, Seattle, and Guam. Among the 26 Taiwanese banks with overseas offices, 12 have almost exclusively Asian operations; with one exception, all the others have LA offices.[19] This evidence illustrates that Chinese foreign banks are not attracted solely to world financial centers, but instead locate in areas with concentrations of ethnic Chinese population and businesses. Human and financial resources move together in the era of globalization.

## CHINESE AMERICAN AND CHINESE FOREIGN BANKS: DIFFERENT LOCAL AND GLOBAL ROLES

Table 3.2 compares the age and size of the two Chinese ethnic banking sub-sectors as of March 31, 2002. The differences in the institutional character of the two sectors come through clearly. Chinese American banks have larger overall asset and deposit volumes; as locally embedded U.S. financial institutions with branch networks, they are conduits for Chinese residents' and businesses' financial resources and needs. Chinese foreign-bank offices, subject to U.S. restrictions on their deposit sources, with limited human resources and a responsibility to serve as their headquarters' global outposts, have little role in the economic development activities of their co-ethnics.

### Residential loan activity

In the 1980s and 1990s, large numbers of Chinese immigrants achieved their "American dream" by moving to the U.S., settling in the Los Angeles area, and becoming homeowners. While the very wealthy among these immigrants made cash purchases of homes, many seeking homes applied for home purchase loans from formal financial institutions. Home Mortgage Disclosure Act (HMDA) data for Los Angeles show that Asian Americans in general have had low overall loan-to-value ratios for their home purchase loans, reflecting their higher average down payments (averaging up to 30 percent). HMDA data demonstrate the role of Chinese American banks in the racial transformation of certain suburban neighborhoods from predominantly white spaces to multiracial and multiethnic ones with large proportions of Chinese residents. Figure 3.1 demonstrates the correlation between the spatial distributions of HMDA loans originated by Chinese American banks and the distribution of Asian households in Los Angeles County. It overlays the number of home purchase loans by census tract on the changing numbers of Asian households between 1990 and 2000.[20] Figure 3.1 shows that Chinese American banks, through their home purchasing and refinancing loan activities, have contributed heavily to the geographical concentration of Asian residents in the San Gabriel Valley.

Chinese foreign bank offices have little or no involvement in this residential lending activity. No law prevents foreign bank offices from making home mortgage loans. However, complying with home mortgage loan laws (such as HMDA and the Community Reinvestment Act (CRA)) requires human resources, which means hiring compliance officers. Chinese foreign bank offices feel discouraged from any involvement in residential lending, which of course falls outside their main lines of business. They tend to refer business clients requiring home mortgages or other types of consumer loan to local Chinese American banks.

## Commercial loans

Commercial loans are another important aspect of the banking business. This type of loan includes commercial real estate loans (non-farm and non-residential), and commercial and industrial (C&I) loans (including loans for revolving working capital, equipment, and trade financing). When spatially concentrated, these commercial loans help fuel the growth of the infrastructural, commercial, and industrial bases in the places on which they focus. Many ethnic Chinese banks are particularly interested in commercial real estate lending; lending in this category is considered a safeguard for their investments, since funded properties are used as collateral. Chinese banks have thus taken an active role in transforming the San Gabriel Valley from bedroom suburbs with limited economic activities to ethnoburbs with robust (and heavily ethnic) economies ranging from services to manufacturing and import/export activities.

Ahn and Hong (1999) point out that commercial loans are more important than home mortgages for Chinese American banks. Our own exploration of FDIC data reveals that as of June 30, 2002, commercial lending by the 24 Chinese American banks based in southern California accounts for 54 percent to 99 percent of their loan portfolios; the average is 78 percent, versus an average of only 20 percent for residential real estate loans[21] (Table 3.3). In fact, local Chinese American commercial banks indicate that their strategic focus is on commercial lending to small- and medium-size businesses. This strategic emphasis conforms both with

Table 3.2 Southern California-based Chinese American and Chinese foreign banks

| Chinese American banks (24) | Year* | Total assets ($,000) | Total deposits ($,000) | Rank** | Chinese foreign banks (20)**** | HQ City | Year* | Total assets ($,000) | Total deposits ($,000) | Rank***** |
|---|---|---|---|---|---|---|---|---|---|---|
| East West Bank | 1972 | 2,897,300 | 2,549,616 | 3 | Development Bank of Singapore | Singapore | n.a. | 885,058 | 51,412 | 6 |
| Cathay Bank | 1962 | 2,511,392 | 2,160,605 | 5 | Hua Nan Commercial Bank | Taipei | 1990 | 694,923 | 45,007 | 8 |
| General Bank | 1980 | 2,501,714 | 1,958,413 | 6 | First Commercial Bank | Taipei | 1990 | 684,726 | 65,054 | 9 |
| CHINATRUST Bank (U.S.A.) | 1994 | 1,695,087 | 1,416,896 | 10 | Bank of Taiwan | Taipei | 1993 | 487,523 | 52,053 | 11 |
| Far East National Bank | 1974 | 1,226,594 | 963,290 | 12 | Shanghai Commercial Bank | Hong Kong | 1991 | 443,362 | 440,165 | 14 |
| Standard Savings Bank | 1980 | 840,179 | 649,081 | ***8 | Chang Hwa Commercial Bank | Taichong | 1992 | 414,145 | 3,127 | 15 |
| United National Bank | 1983 | 631,889 | 570,192 | 19 | United Overseas Bank | Singapore | 1977 | 405,608 | 30,869 | 17 |
| Preferred Bank | 1991 | 625,281 | 554,652 | | International Commercial Bank of China | Taipei | 1984 | 293,526 | 101,293 | |
| Universal Bank | 1990 | 355,223 | 273,408 | ***9 | Farmers Bank of China | Taipei | 1995 | 240,069 | n.a. | 20 |
| First Continental Bank | 1991 | 276,326 | 248,130 | | Land Bank of Taiwan | Taipei | 1997 | 234,602 | 32,061 | 21 |
| First Commercial Bank (USA) | 1997 | 216,547 | 178,327 | | United World Chinese Commercial Bank | Taipei | 1993 | 210,425 | 67,044 | 22 |
| Trust Bank, f.s.b. | 1977 | 214,501 | 172,091 | ***12 | | | | | | |
| Evertrust Bank | 1995 | 195,916 | 158,065 | | | | | | | |
| Omni Bank | 1980 | 183,684 | 161,432 | | | | | | | |
| Int'l Bank of California | 1980 | 176,997 | 159,561 | | | | | | | |

| Bank | Year | | | Bank | City | Year | | | Rank |
|---|---|---|---|---|---|---|---|---|---|
| Los Angeles National Bank | 1973 | 174,192 | 154,722 | Taiwan Business Bank | Taipei | 1995 | 194,092 | 1,102 | 23 |
| Grand National Bank | 1983 | 161,416 | 122,453 | Bank of East Asia | Hong Kong | 1991 | 171,105 | 3,989 | |
| Pacific Business Bank | 1995 | 157,064 | 133,696 | E. Sun Commercial Bank | Taipei | 2000 | 165,165 | 4,025 | 25 |
| United Pacific Bank | 1982 | 138,757 | 126,496 | Taipei Bank | Taipei | 1993 | 165,022 | 38,382 | 26 |
| | | | | Bank SinoPac | Taipei | 1999 | 159,440 | 4,103 | 27 |
| Guaranty Bank of California | 1992 | 126,477 | 102,082 | CITIC Ka Hwa Bank | Hong Kong | 1982 | 134,073 | 133,681 | |
| InterBusiness Bank, N.A. | 2000 | 110,894 | 86,974 | Bank of China | Beijing | 1989 | 124,636 | 61,317 | |
| Golden Security Bank | 1982 | 106,651 | 96,784 | Overseas Chinese Banking Corporation | Singapore | n.a. | 89,655 | n.a. | |
| Eastern Int'l Bank | 1985 | 83,593 | 73,733 | Wing Lung Bank | Hong Kong | 1982 | 73,290 | 27,777 | 34 |
| Asian Pacific National Bank | 1990 | 48,170 | 41,356 | | | | | | |
| Total | | 15,655,844 | 13,112,055 | Total | | | 6,270,445 | 1,162,461 | |
| Average | | 680,689 | 570,089 | Average | | | 313,522 | 58,123 | |

Sources: Chinese American banks data – http://www3.fdic.gov/sdi/main.asp; Ranking: http://www.labusinessjournal.com/tofilelabj.htm?user/user.fas/s=614/fp=3/tp=45?T=notrans&P=register.

Note: all data are as of March 31, 2002.

* Year of opening or becoming Chinese American banks; or year opening LA operation for Chinese foreign banks.

** Ranking among all Los Angeles County-based banks, unless otherwise noted.

*** Ranking among all Los Angeles County-based Savings and Loan Associations.

**** Five banks are not in the DFI database, whose data are retrieved from the FFIEC database: http://132.200.33.161/nicSearch/nicHome.html. They are: Bank of China (mainland China); ICBC (Taiwan); The Bank of East Asia, Ltd.; CITIC Ka Hwa Bank; Wing Lung Bank Ltd. (Hong Kong).

***** Rank among all 47 foreign banks registered under CA DFI.

Chinese foreign banks – http://www.dfi.ca.gov/stats/fbstats/rank4q00.htm. All of the above accessed on 9/6/2002.

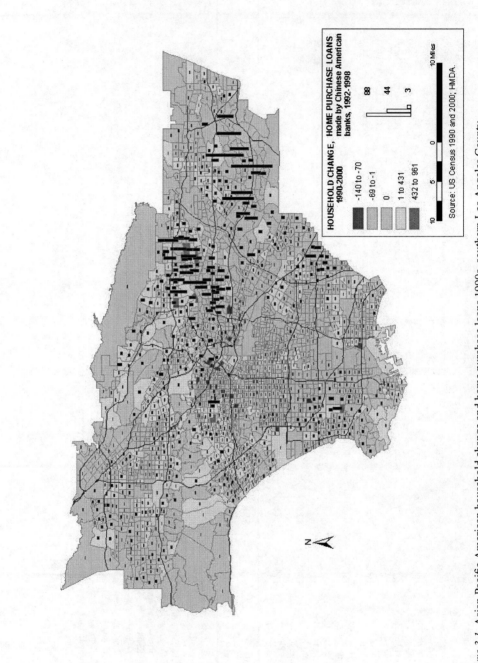

*Figure 3.1* Asian Pacific American household change and home purchase loans 1990s, southern Los Angeles County.

the CRA requirement that banks meet credit needs throughout their service areas, and also with these banks' areas of competitive advantage—as locally embedded institutions, they are very familiar with local businesses and business practices, and can more efficiently monitor business transactions and loan activities than can out-of-area or out-of-state lenders.

No publicly available data on the spatial distribution of commercial loans are available. However, CRA reports can be used as a proxy. While larger Chinese American banks often choose the entire Los Angeles County (LA MSA) as their CRA "assessment area," smaller San Gabriel Valley (SGV) based banks select the SGV (not the LA MSA) as one of their assessment areas. For instance, a March 1996 CRA report indicated that the Alhambra-based Omni Bank made 72 percent of its commercial loans and 88 percent of all its loans in its 23-city SGV assessment area.[22] Similarly, a 1998 report revealed that the San Marino-based United National Bank made 658 loans totaling $148.8 million in their SGV and Beverly Hills assessment areas, accounting for 56 percent and 65 percent, respectively, of all loans made in the 1995–1997 period.[23]

Chinese foreign banks are not subject to these regulations, so their lending behavior can be determined more by the directives of local management and/or bank headquarters. In fact, while some of these banks channel credit to local businesses, many of them are participating in syndication loans for Fortune 500 companies initiated by mainstream banks. Table 3.3 shows the loan structures of both Chinese American and foreign banks, ranked by percentage of commercial real estate loans. Compared with their Chinese American counterparts, Chinese foreign banks have higher percentages of C&I and inter-bank loans. Most of these C&I and inter-bank loans are made within the U.S., demonstrating these offices' role as global outposts for their headquarters. These banks' commercial loan portfolio includes the financing of international trade, mostly through commercial letters of credit (L/Cs). A commercial L/C is issued to facilitate trade or commerce, particularly for import and export. The FDIC releases figures for outstanding and unused portions of L/Cs; these figures reveal the scope of banks' commitment to international trade financing.[24] Table 3.4 presents data on these figures for the two sub-sectors of ethnic Chinese banks over the three years 1999–2001. It shows that with the sole exception of ICBC, trade financing is not a principal line of business for Chinese foreign bank offices. This result is consistent with our interview findings. Chinese American banks, on the other hand, have more involvement with trade financing. General Bank, for instance, ranked second among all California banks, next only to Bank of America, in terms of total consignments in California financed by banks in 2000.[25]

Figure 3.2 compares Chinese American banks with the two mainstream megabanks that operate in California, Bank of America and Wells Fargo Bank, and with all California banks over 11 years (1992–2002). During the 1997–8 Asian financial crisis, mainstream banks reduced their trade commitments, but Chinese American banks continued to increase their commitments. Their annual averages have surpassed those of all California banks, and total commitments have counted for 13 percent to 16.8 percent of all commitments made by California banks since

Table 3.3 Southern California-based Chinese American and Chinese foreign banks—loan structure

| Chinese American banks (24) | Total L&L (in $,000) | % n-f, n-r RE | % C&I | % Resid RE | % Consumer |
|---|---|---|---|---|---|
| First Continental Bank | 228,978 | 92.6 | 4.8 | 3.3 | 0.0 |
| Evertrust Bank | 131,602 | 90.3 | 3.6 | 6.2 | 0.0 |
| Asian Pacific National Bank | 30,406 | 87.7 | 2.2 | 6.6 | 3.7 |
| Int'l Bank of California | 132,947 | 83.7 | 15.7 | 0.1 | 0.7 |
| United National Bank | 467,206 | 77.7 | 12.3 | 8.8 | 0.1 |
| First Commercial Bank, U.S.A. | 127,254 | 72.9 | 24.7 | 2.5 | 0.0 |
| United Pacific Bank | 101,066 | 71.5 | 19.6 | 4.8 | 4.4 |
| CHINATRUST Bank (U.S.A.) | 1,248,749 | 69.9 | 18.7 | 5.9 | 0.4 |
| Los Angeles National Bank | 136,047 | 68.4 | 14.8 | 16.8 | 0.3 |
| Omni Bank | 136,250 | 65.5 | 3.2 | 30.1 | 1.2 |
| Golden Security Bank | 87,419 | 65.3 | 0.9 | 33.8 | 0.1 |
| Pacific Business Bank | 105,168 | 64.2 | 24.3 | 8.9 | 0.3 |
| Grand National Bank | 102,410 | 63.5 | 33.4 | 0.9 | 2.6 |
| InterBusiness Bank, N.A. | 71,887 | 59.9 | 23.0 | 14.8 | 0.1 |
| Cathay Bank | 1,722,931 | 55.2 | 23.7 | 19.7 | 0.8 |

| Chinese foreign banks (20) | Total L&L | % n-f, n-r RE | % C&I | % Loan to F.I. |
|---|---|---|---|---|
| Wing Lung Bank | 68,863 | 91.8 | 8.5 | 0.0 |
| Bank of East Asia | 151,945 | 86.4 | 13.9 | 0.0 |
| Shanghai Commercial Bank | 88,923 | 80.1 | 16.8 | 3.4 |
| Taipei Bank | 100,739 | 80.1 | 15.1 | 5.0 |
| First Commercial Bank | 181,961 | 79.1 | 21.0 | 0.0 |
| United Overseas Bank | 420,945 | 71.2 | 25.2 | 3.6 |
| CITIC Ka Hwa Bank | 46,471 | 63.7 | 33.3 | 0.0 |
| International Commercial Bank of China | 214,762 | 53.4 | 44.4 | 0.0 |
| Development Bank of Singapore | 690,260 | 52.6 | 16.4 | 30.5 |
| Farmers Bank of China | 188,418 | 46.7 | 27.0 | 26.5 |
| Bank of Taiwan | 332,563 | 40.8 | 39.3 | 20.0 |
| Chang Hwa Commercial Bank | 357,784 | 39.4 | 57.8 | 5.6 |
| Hua Nan Commercial Bank | 256,478 | 37.8 | 62.4 | 2.0 |
| Taiwan Business Bank | 179,935 | 34.8 | 44.4 | 20.6 |
| Overseas Chinese Banking Corporation | 125,362 | 29.4 | 70.6 | 0.0 |
| Bank SinoPac | 143,636 | 27.4 | 72.6 | 0.0 |

Table: Loan composition of Chinese American banks and Chinese foreign banks (as of 6/30/02)

| Bank | Total L&L | % n-f, n-r RE | % C&I | % Resid RE | % Loan to F.I. |
|---|---|---|---|---|---|
| General Bank | 1,175,007 | 54.7 | 37.0 | 5.8 | 0.1 |
| Far East National Bank | 847,634 | 54.5 | 19.1 | 23.7 | 0.1 |
| Preferred Bank | 425,738 | 54.5 | 37.9 | 6.7 | 0.1 |
| Eastern Int'l Bank | 63,053 | 54.4 | 0.0 | 45.7 | 0.3 |
| Trust Bank | 147,591 | 48.7 | 1.4 | 49.8 | 0.1 |
| East West Bank | 2,413,357 | 47.4 | 13.8 | 37.6 | 0.9 |
| Guaranty Bank of Calif. | 99,624 | 44.8 | 33.4 | 21.4 | 0.5 |
| Standard Savings Bank | 517,461 | 28.6 | 0.4 | 69.6 | 1.3 |
| Universal Bank | 305,366 | 28.3 | 6.7 | 64.4 | 0.6 |
| Average | $451,048 | 62.7 | 15.6 | 20.3 | 0.8 |
| E. Sun Commercial Bank | 84,408 | 17.8 | 82.6 | | 0.0 |
| Land Bank of Taiwan | 191,977 | 17.1 | 75.6 | | 7.8 |
| Bank of China | 88,546 | 15.7 | 78.0 | | 6.7 |
| United World Chinese Commercial Bank | 208,209 | 7.5 | 92.9 | | 0.0 |
| Average | $206,109 | 48.6 | 44.9 | | 6.6 |

Sources: Chinese American banks – www.fdic.gov; Chinese foreign banks – http://132.200.33.161/nicSearch/servlet/NICServlet?$GRP$=INSTSEARCH&REQ=DOM&MODE=SEARCH.

Note: all data are as of 6/30/02; total percentage for each individual bank may not be 100% due to rounding and/or other types of loans not included in this table.

Total L&L: total loans and leases, the one for Chinese American banks include construction and development loans + commercial RE loans.

% n-f, n-r RE: % non-farm, non-residential real estate loans; % C&I: % commercial and industrial loans; % Resid RE: % residential real estate loans; % Consumer: % consumer loans, including credit cards; % Loan to F.I.: % loans to financial institutions, including both banks and non-bank financial institutions.

Table 3.4 Southern California-based Chinese American and Chinese foreign banks—commercial letters of credit

| Chinese American banks ($,000) | 3-yr total | 06/30/2002 | 2001 | 2000 | 1999 | Chinese foreign banks ($,000) | 3-yr total | 06/30/2002 | 2001 | 2000 | 1999 |
|---|---|---|---|---|---|---|---|---|---|---|---|
| General Bank | 297,187 | 79,453 | 63,578 | 70,154 | 84,002 | International Commercial Bank of China | 2,803,160 | 400,936 | 800,490 | 800,559 | 801,175 |
| Cathay Bank | 135,762 | 32,602 | 26,923 | 44,371 | 31,866 | First Commercial Bank | 47,968 | 11,643 | 12,407 | 12,818 | 11,100 |
| CHINATRUST Bank (U.S.A.) | 86,914 | 18,993 | 18,198 | 32,709 | 17,014 | Taipei Bank | 38,948 | 11,345 | 15,486 | 6,149 | 5,968 |
| Far East National Bank | 85,889 | 28,538 | 27,061 | 19,255 | 11,035 | Development Bank of Singapore | 31,001 | 11,128 | 12,742 | 4,031 | 3,100 |
| East West Bank | 66,637 | 24,318 | 14,333 | 14,592 | 13,394 | Bank of East Asia | 24,291 | 2,768 | 4,311 | 7,598 | 9,614 |
| United National Bank | 20,850 | 4,226 | 5,323 | 5,652 | 5,649 | Bank of China | 24,179 | 2,969 | 2,379 | 6,062 | 12,769 |
| United Pacific Bank | 18,049 | 3,193 | 3,054 | 6,476 | 5,326 | Land Bank of Taiwan | 20,482 | 18 | 4,957 | 6,283 | 9,224 |
| Grand National | 15,300 | 2,092 | 1,974 | 5,807 | 5,427 | Bank SinoPac | 16,746 | 3,062 | 8,260 | 5,342 | 82 |
| Preferred Bank | 14,428 | 4,079 | 1,884 | 6,089 | 2,376 | Hua Nan Commercial Bank | 11,495 | 2,451 | 4,594 | 2,678 | 1,772 |
| Pacific Business Bank | 8,991 | 2,417 | 1,994 | 2,673 | 1,907 | Chang Hwa Commercial Bank | 7,408 | 3,472 | 2,863 | 414 | 659 |
| Los Angeles National Bank | 7,371 | 1,769 | 2,452 | 941 | 2,209 | United World Chinese Commercial Bank | 6,146 | 892 | 595 | 751 | 3,908 |
| Guaranty Bank of California | 5,609 | 2,748 | 985 | 536 | 1,340 | CITIC Ka Hwa Bank | 2,944 | 1,017 | 198 | 398 | 1,331 |
| First Commercial Bank, USA | 5,094 | 1,482 | 1,156 | 1,299 | 1,157 | Bank of Taiwan | 2,267 | 262 | 438 | 861 | 706 |
| Int'l Bank of California | 3,730 | 426 | 703 | 1,042 | 1,559 | E. Sun Commercial Bank | 2,256 | 2,256 | 0 | 0 | n.a |
| InterBusiness Bank, N.A. | 3,105 | 1,229 | 1,676 | 200 | n.a. | Wing Lung Bank | 1,695 | 1,004 | 623 | 68 | 0 |
| Universal Bank | 2,523 | 218 | 776 | 1,529 | 0 | Taiwan Business Bank | 37 | 29 | 0 | 8 | 0 |
| First Continental Bank | 2,418 | 513 | 535 | 426 | 944 | | | | | | |

| | | | | | |
|---|---|---|---|---|---|
| Evertrust Bank | 1,828 | 447 | 612 | 524 | 245 |
| Omni Bank | 906 | 520 | 175 | 130 | 81 |
| Eastern Int'l Bank | 88 | 0 | 0 | 0 | 88 |
| Asian Pacific National Bank | 0 | 0 | 0 | 0 | 0 |
| Golden Security Bank | 0 | 0 | 0 | 0 | 0 |
| Standard Savings Bank | 0 | 0 | 0 | 0 | 0 |
| Trust Bank | 0 | 0 | 0 | 0 | 0 |
| Total | 782,679 | 209,263 | 173,392 | 214,405 | 185,619 |
| Average | 32,612 | 8,719 | 7,225 | 8,934 | 8,070 |
| Farmers Bank of China | 20 | 0 | 11 | 0 | 9 |
| Overseas Chinese Banking Corporation | 0 | 0 | 0 | 0 | 0 |
| United Overseas Bank | 0 | 0 | 0 | 0 | 0 |
| Shanghai Commercial Bank | 0 | 0 | 0 | 0 | 0 |
| *Total without ICBC* | *237,883* | *54,316* | *69,864* | *53,461* | *60,242* |
| *Average without ICBC* | *12,520* | *2,859* | *3,677* | *2,814* | *3,347* |
| Total | 3,041,043 | 455,252 | 870,354 | 854,020 | 861,417 |
| Average | 152,052 | 22,763 | 43,518 | 42,701 | 45,338 |

Sources: Chinese American banks – www.fdic.gov; Chinese foreign banks – http://132.200.33.161/nicSearch/servlet/NICServlet?SGRP$=INSTSEARCH&REQ=DOM&MODE=SEARCH.

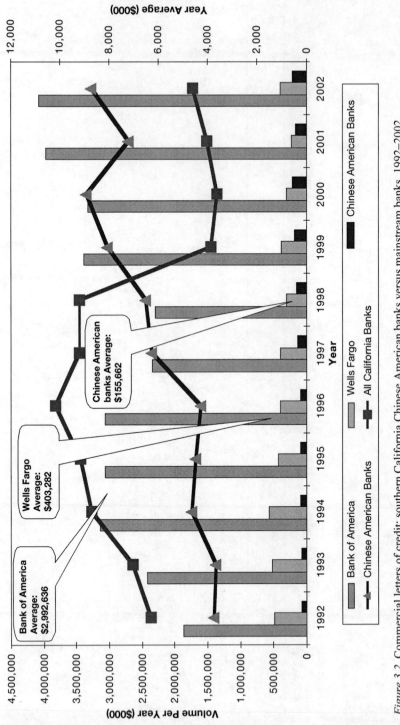

*Figure 3.2* Commercial letters of credit: southern California Chinese American banks versus mainstream banks, 1992–2002.

1999, as compared with 4 percent or less before 1998. Chinese American banks' trade commitments are large relative to their asset totals—1.34 percent, compared to Bank of America's 0.68 percent and Wells Fargo's 0.12 percent—further illustrating their orientation toward facilitating international trade.[26]

## Summary

In general, key similarities and differences exist between Chinese American and Chinese foreign banks in their local and global roles. Table 3.5 highlights several dimensions of this comparison—ownership, customer bases, deposit and loan types, and so on. The differences can be attributed to two core factors: first, differences in financial policies and regulations in the U.S. and in banks' (and immigrants') countries of origin; second, these banks' different institutional missions. Because their capital is based in their headquarters offices, Chinese foreign banks have much larger legal lending limits than Chinese American banks. Chinese foreign banks primarily target large customers from their countries of origin through referrals from headquarters. They also participate in syndication loans initiated by mainstream banks. Chinese American banks often focus on lending to small and medium-sized firms, and develop loan businesses largely on their own. They concentrate on commercial real estate and C&I loans, including trade financing. While Chinese foreign banks primarily depend on inter-bank loans or headquarters for funding, Chinese American banks absorb both local and overseas Chinese savings to fund their assets.[27] While Chinese foreign banks often depend on headquarters for loan decisions, Chinese American banks make these decisions locally, based on local knowledge.[28] In general, this permits Chinese American banks to make more expedient loan decisions.

Despite significant differences between the two ethnic financial sectors, they nonetheless complement and cooperate with each other. When Chinese foreign bank offices initiate large syndication loans, they sometimes ask Chinese American banks to participate because of their local embeddedness and familiarity with U.S. business practices. In other cases, Chinese American banks develop business ties with potential borrowers but nevertheless cooperate with Chinese foreign bank offices, especially when organizing loan commitments that exceed their legal lending limits. In recent years, some foreign banks have been developing and even implementing plans to become more locally embedded—either through purchasing local banks (as in the cases of Bank of East Asia [Hong Kong] and Bank SinoPac [Taiwan]), or through establishing their own U.S. chartered subsidiaries (such as First Commercial Bank [Taiwan]).

If more foreign banks follow this localization trend, competition between the two sectors will increase (though there will be more opportunities for cooperation between the domestic subsidiaries and agency offices of individual foreign banks that possess both). In sum, the sheer numbers and operations of the two ethnic Chinese banking sectors in Los Angeles collectively provide local Chinese households and businesses with more choices of service and broader coverage. This has promoted a more robust pace for Chinese import/export trade and business

*Table 3.5* Comparison between Chinese American banks and Chinese foreign bank offices

|  | *Chinese American banks* | *Chinese foreign bank offices* |
|---|---|---|
| Nature | U.S.-chartered domestic banks | Foreign bank U.S. operations |
| Ownership | Domestic and/or foreign | Foreign |
| Customer bases | Local Chinese and non-Chinese, some outside southern California | Local and nationwide customers (including Chinese) |
| Deposits/funding | Local and overseas | Mainly inter-bank loans |
| Loan types | Commercial RE, C & I loans largely banks' own development | Variety of loans; largely participating in syndication loans by larger banks |
| Trade financing | Mostly active | Largely not a main line of business |
| Lending limits | Small due to limited capital base | Large, depending on headquarters |
| Decision making | Local | Local and/or headquarters |

development in southern California than is found elsewhere in the U.S. Clearly, the Chinese banking sector plays a key role in local ethnic financing and economic development.

## CONCLUSION: ETHNIC CHINESE BANKS—LOCALLY EMBEDDED AND GLOBALLY CONNECTED

Our investigation has incorporated many aspects of ethnic Chinese banks' behavior, from their micro-decisions on lending to their strategic cooperation and competition, and their macro-decisions on where to lend, invest, and expand. We have emphasized the impacts of this behavior on the economic and spatial logic of ethnic community development.

This perspective permits us to shed new light on questions that are being investigated from entry points different from ours. Consider first the role of spatial factors in credit and banking market outcomes. The ethnic enclave literature has extensively studied urban ethnic communities within (given) urban environments; our research explores how the urban environment itself is transformed by the actions of ethnic bankers and their customers. Further, migration and globalization have often been examined on one of two bases: either on the movement of money while people remain stationary, or on the movement of people without considering the impact of the money that often moves with them. Our investigation takes into account the movement of both money and people across borders. This permits us to examine the dynamics of business creation and community-building by these flows of people and money—leading to a better understanding of the rise of integrated ethnic economies.

A key conclusion of our research is that these flows are structurally differentiated, not uniform. In particular, our inquiry into ethnic Chinese banking demonstrates that the growth of Chinese foreign banks is the result of Chinese diasporic countries' shifting policies regarding financial internationalization (Dymski and Li 2004), while the growth of U.S.-chartered Chinese American banks mirrors transnational flows of money and people. This sort of structural differentiation is important in understanding why some urban communities with significant numbers of people of Chinese ethnicity develop thriving economic engines and communities, whereas other communities (even with significant ethnically Chinese populations) do not.

Table 3.6 presents 12 U.S. metropolitan areas in 2000 which had large Chinese population and/or Chinese banks. We present some illustrative data on the scope of Chinese business activities, and the number of Chinese American banks and Chinese foreign bank offices in each area.[29] The Los Angeles CMSA has more Chinese businesses than the other metro areas, and ranks second to the Chicago CMSA in per capita sales and receipts; this CMSA is also the largest ethnic Chinese financial infrastructure in the nation, with 44 banks or foreign bank offices. This illustrates our analytical point that ethnic-banking infrastructure is a key factor in the robust character of local ethnic business activity. Los Angeles' Chinese population and businesses have greater and easier access to more varied financial services provided by Chinese banks than do those in other metropolitan areas.[30]

There are 25 Chinese foreign bank offices in California, representing 44 percent of all foreign banks operating in this state. This figure equals the combined total for other Asian banks and all European banks. At the same time, the year-2000 Chinese population of 980,600 in California represents 40.3 percent of all Chinese in the nation.[31] These totals suggest the co-movement of ethnic populations and their economic activities and finance.[32]

We cannot establish on the basis of our investigations (and the data in Table 3.6) whether there is a causal relationship between ethnic Chinese banking presence and Chinese economic development. However, it is reasonable to conclude that the presence or absence of ethnic Chinese banks affects the pace, scale, and stability of ethnic Chinese economic development. Large concentrations of ethnic banks can facilitate and promote ethnic business development, as in southern California; the absence of such a banking sector limits development elsewhere.[33]

This points to the need for further work on the relationship between ethnic finance and community development. The role of the Chinese American banking sector as a whole in transforming ethnic financing and promoting the contemporary Chinese ethnic economy also deserves more detailed study, especially because of the intertwining of these business and residential sectors with the changing dynamics of globalization and localization. Studies in this area may yield policy insights regarding ethnic banking and minority community development in the U.S. and in other nations.

Table 3.6 Chinese population, business, and banks in selected U.S. metropolitan areas

| CMSA or MSA Name | New York CMSA | SF CMSA | Los Angeles CMSA | Boston CMSA | DC CMSA | Chicago CMSA |
|---|---|---|---|---|---|---|
| Chinese population | 503,347 | 468,736 | 408,239 | 83,104 | 77,513 | 68,879 |
| No. of Chinese businesses | 58,767 | 42,525 | 53,623 | 4,561 | 8,211 | 5,703 |
| Sales and receipts ($000) | 18,547,507 | 23,011,026 | 27,859,208 | 1,624,086 | 2,106,568 | 5,121,006 |
| No. of businesses per 1,000 pop. | 117 | 91 | 131 | 55 | 106 | 83 |
| S&R per Chinese 1,000 population | 36,848 | 49,092 | 68,242 | 19,543 | 27,177 | 74,348 |
| No. of Chinese American banks* | 5 | 7 | 24 | 0 | 1 | 7 |
| No. of Chinese foreign banks | 19 | 5 | 20 | 0 | 0 | 1 |
| No. of Chinese per Ch Ame bank | 20,973 | 39,061 | 9,278 | n.a. | 77,513 | 8,610 |

| CMSA or MSA Name | Seattle CMSA | Houston CMSA | Philadelphia CMSA | Dallas-F.W. CMSA | San Diego MSA | Atlanta MSA |
|---|---|---|---|---|---|---|
| Chinese population | 52,914 | 48,537 | 42,959 | 33,559 | 30,750 | 22,564 |
| No. of Chinese businesses | 4,674 | 5,657 | 3,732 | 5,935 | 1,915 | 2,625 |
| Sales and receipts ($000) | 1,871,016 | 3,032,564 | 620,666 | 3,413,296 | 668,867 | 1,097,208 |
| No. of businesses per 1,000 pop. | 88 | 117 | 87 | 112 | 62 | 116 |
| S&R per Chinese 1,000 population | 35,360 | 62,479 | 14,448 | 64,506 | 21,752 | 48,626 |
| No. of Chinese American banks* | 2 | 3 | 0 | 3 | 2 | 3 |
| No. of Chinese foreign banks | 1 | 1 | 0 | 0 | 0 | 0 |
| No. of Chinese per Ch Ame bank | 17,638 | 12,134 | n.a. | 11,186 | 15,375 | 7,521 |

Sources: Chinese pop & business – (1) Census 2000 Summary File 2 (SF 2) 100-Percent Data; http://factfinder.census.gov/servlet/DTTable?_ts+4936994982.
U.S. Census Bureau       One race data ("Chinese only") are used here for Chinese population.
(2) 1997 Economic Census http://www.census.gov/epcd/mwb97.
Chinese American bank data – (1) http://www.federalreserve.gov/releases/mob/min_bnk_1st.pdf; all of the above accessed on 9/6/2002.
(2) 17th World Chinese Banking Amity Conference: Challenges and Opportunities in the New Century.

Notes: Calculations do not include those PMSAs for which Chinese businesses data are unavailable, undisclosed, or unpublishable. These PMSAs are: Kankakee in Chicago CMSA; Brazoria, and Gaveston-Texas City in Houston CMSA; Ventura in LA CMSA; Newburgh in NY CMSA; Atlantic-Cape May, and Vineland-Millville-Bridgeton in Philadelphia CMSA; and Santa Cruz-Watsonville in SF CMSA.

* Including a small number of unspecified Asian American banks.

# Acknowledgment

This project has been partially funded by a National Science Foundation grant (SES-00747754/ 0296136), and by Arizona State University's Vice Provost for Research and College of Public Programs. The authors would like to thank all interviewees for their cooperation, and acknowledge the assistance of three other members of the Ethnic Banking Project—Maria Chee, Carolyn Aldana, and Yu Zhou. Abe Chen, Daisy Hsye, and Hong Liu provided key insights into bank lines of credit. Daniel Borough, Brent Hedquist, Weidi Pang, and Jianfeng Zhang at Arizona State University provided invaluable research assistance; Anne Theriault, Karen Hoang, Li Zheroo, and Daniel Wright at the University of Connecticut transcribed and translated interviews. The authors are solely responsible for remaining errors.

# Notes

1 Census 2000 data for Los Angeles County show the following racial/ethnic population distribution: 44.6 percent Hispanic, 31.1 percent white, 12.0 percent Asian and Pacific-Islander American, 9.5 percent African American, 2.3 percent multi-race, 0.3 percent Native American, and 0.2 percent other.

2 This chapter is based on research conducted for the Ethnic Banking Project (EBP), an ongoing inter-university research project to study all minority-owned and -operated banking institutions in Los Angeles County. The multinational research team members of project, directed by Gary Dymski, are drawn from the fields of economics, geography, and anthropology. See Dymski (1999) for a detailed description of the whole project.

3 See McDowell (1997) and Schoenberger (1991).

4 Ethnic Chinese foreign bank branch/agency interviews involve those with 12 Taiwan-based banks (five interviews were conducted with managers at the international banking department in banks' Taipei headquarters and 12 with branch managers/agents in their Los Angeles offices), four Hong Kong-based banks, and two Singapore-based banks. Many of the descriptions in the following sections are based on summaries of these interviews.

5 See, for instance, Hiebert (1993); Light and Bonacich (1988); Light *et al.* (1993, 1994); Light and Karageorgis (1994); Light and Rosenstein (1995); Portes and Bach (1985); Portes and Jensen (1987); Siu (1987); Tsai (1986); Wilson and Portes (1980).

6 Calculation based on http://www.census.gov/epcd/mwb97/metro/p4480.html.

7 Lin's financial analysis shows how the banks in this ethnic economy have drawn on global capital flows and helped to restructure the local housing market; however, he does not discuss the transformation from lending circles to formal banking—the topic at the center of our previous work on ethnic banking.

8 Please refer to Li *et al.* (2002) for detailed discussion on how Cathay Bank, the first Chinese American bank in Los Angeles, contributed to the transformation of Chinatown from a cash economy to the one based on banks' commercial lending.

9 The category of "resident" is itself complex, ranging from uprooted refugees, to immigrants who settle in the destination countries without close ties to their origin countries, to "transmigrants" whose business practices and residential patterns are bi-if not multi-national.

10 This bank was acquired by another San Francisco-based Chinese American bank, United Commercial Bank, in 2003.

11 *Chinese Daily News*, August 16, 2002, A10.

12 Calculations are based respectively on the INS *Statistical Yearbook* for 1997 and 2000, and on 2000 Census SF1 data.

13  These new owners claim that these takeovers are part of a diversification strategy. See Yeung and Olds (2000, p. 20).

14  From Li *et al.* (2002, Table 1).

15  Cathay Bank and General Bank announced their merger plan in spring 2003.

16  The establishment of the People's Republic of China and the fleeing of the Nationalist government to Taiwan in 1949 caused the split of that bank; the one in Taiwan changed its name to "International Commercial Bank of China" in 1971 during a reorganization.

17  A fourth Singaporean bank which had a separate LA agency, Overseas Union Bank, was acquired by another Singaporean bank. Since the reorganization is currently in process, we still include OUB in our discussion for total number of overseas operations.

18  *Chinese Daily News*, May 9, 1994.

19  Another Taiwan bank, Chinatrust Commercial Bank, has one branch in New York, and a U.S. subsidiary bank, Chinatrust USA, headquartered in LA County. Calculation based on information collected from individual bank websites, and www.boma.gov.tw/sta/bas9103-102.doc.

20  HMDA data reveal applicants' race only for five ethnic/racial groupings. Therefore, these data capture the loan numbers and amounts made to all Asian applicants by Chinese American banks, not just to Chinese applicants.

21  These figures are the combinations of "percent non-farm and non-residential Real Estate loans" and "Commercial and Industrial loans." These figure exclude the three Chinese American banks that are chartered as saving and loans; these three institutions' commercial lending ranges from 29.1 percent to 50.1 percent—a very high percentage for thrifts.

22  http://www.occ.treas.gov/scripts/crareslt.cfm.

23  http://www.occ.treas.gov/ftp/craeval/jun98/17785.pdf.

24  The FDIC reports the amount of outstanding and unused commercial and similar letters of credit, issued or confirmed commercial letters of credit, non-monetary travelers' letters of credit, and similar non-standby letters of credit issued to facilitate trade or commerce.

25  *World Journal*, July 16, 2001.

26  Calculation based on data collected from www.fdic.gov; all data are as of 6/30/02. The figures for Bank of America and Wells Fargo include their entire operations in the U.S.

27  Available information does not permit us to identify the percentages of Chinese American bank deposits originating domestically and overseas. A recent CRA report on Far East National Bank, however, estimated that 30 percent of this bank's deposits on June 30, 2000 came from foreign countries (see http://www.occ.treas.gov/ftp/craeval/may01/16407.pdf).

28  Some Chinese foreign bank offices have discretionary authority to make smaller loans; others rely solely on their home-country headquarters regardless of loan amount, sometimes even translating loan documents from English into Chinese.

29  Since there are no nationwide economic database available for the year 2000, data from the 1997 Economic Census are used here. No authoritative list of ethnic banks exists. However, the list of U.S. minority-owned banks registered with the Federal Reserve as of March 31, 2002 provides a partial list of this banking sector (http://www.federal reserve.gov/releases/mob/min_bnk_1st.pdf). Please note this is a partial list only for those voluntarily participating in the minority banking program; and it breaks down to only four major minority groups: African American, Asian American, Native American, and Latino.

30  The lower numbers in both Atlanta MSA and Chicago CMSA are questionable: there is only one known Chinese American bank in Atlanta, and no known Chinese American banks in Chicago.

31  Calculations on California foreign bank offices and Chinese populations are based on http://132.200.33.161/nicSearch/servlet/NICServlet?as_inst=&cb_show=Submit&rb_n msrch=B&as_date=09%2F20%2F2002&rb_active=A&as_city=&as_state_cd=6&lb_s

ort=nm_lgl&REQ=AGY&MODE=RESULT&as_type=B2 and http://factfinder.census. gov/servlet/DTTable?_ts=50607003982 respectively; Chinese population figure includes only one race data.
32 An interesting point is that while Taiwanese bank offices largely locate in the Los Angeles CMSA, Hong Kong-based banks have located branch/agency offices only in the San Francisco CMSA. The LA metro area is home to large numbers of Taiwanese Chinese (and their businesses), while the SF metro area has large numbers of Hong Kong Chinese. The Bank of China, the sole mainland Chinese bank on the U.S. West Coast, is located in Los Angeles rather than San Francisco (the traditional stronghold of mainland Chinese immigrants and their business activities).
33 In addition to our work on Los Angeles in conjunction with other members of the Ethnic Banking Project, two studies have explored socio-economic differences between the Chinese in Los Angeles and New York (Waldinger and Tseng 1992; Zhou 1998). There has been no systematic study of Chinese American banks in other major metropolitan areas, nor have there been comparative studies of those places which do and do not have Chinese American banks.

# References

Ahn, Hyeon-Hyo and Jangpyo Hong. 1999. "Evolution of Korean Ethnic Banks in California." *Journal of Regional Science*, 7(2): 97–120. Korean Association of Regional Studies.

Beauregard, R.A. (ed.) 1989. *Atop the Urban Hierarchy*. Totowa, NJ: Rowman & Littlefield Publishers.

Chan, Gerald. 1997. "Taiwan's Economic Growth and Its Southward Policy in Asia." In R.F. Watters and T.G. McGee (eds.) *New Geographies of the Pacific Rim Asia Pacific*. Vancouver, WA: UBC Press. 206–22.

*China Capital Market Weekly* No. 35 September 21, 2002.

Dymski, Gary A. 1999. *Ethnic Banking in Southern California: A Multi-Disciplinary Research Project*. Mimeograph. Riverside, CA: University of California, Riverside.

Dymski, Gary A. and Wei Li. 2004. "Financial Globalization and Cross-Border Co-Movements of Money and Population: Foreign Bank Offices in Los Angeles." *Environment and Planning A*, 36(2): 213–40.

Dymski, Gary A. and Lisa Mohanty. 1999. "Credit and Banking Structure: Insights from Asian and African-American Experience in Los Angeles." *American Economic Review Papers and Proceedings*, May, 89(2): 362–6.

Faist, Thomas. 2000. *The Volume and Dynamics of International Migration and Transnational Social Spaces*. Oxford, UK: Oxford University Press.

Geertz, Clifford. 1956. *The Rotating Credit Association: An Instrument for Development*. Cambridge, MA: Center for International Studies.

Hiebert, D. 1993. "Jewish Immigrants and the Garment Industry of Toronto, 1901–1931: A Study of Ethnic and Class Relations." *Annals of the Association of American Geographers*, 83(2): 243–71.

Kotkin, J. 1991. "The Chinese Connection." *Los Angeles Times*, Dec. 22.

Li, Wei. 1998a. "Anatomy of a New Ethnic Settlement: the Chinese *Ethnoburb* in Los Angeles." *Urban Studies*, 35(3): 479–501.

——. 1998b. "Los Angeles' Chinese *Ethnoburb*: From Ethnic Service Center to Global Economy Outpost." *Urban Geography*, 19(6): 502–17.

Li, Wei, Maria Chee, Yu Zhou, and Gary Dymski, 2000. "Development Trajectory of Chinese American Banking Sector in Los Angeles." Mimeograph, Asian American Studies Institute/Geography Department, University of Connecticut.

Li, Wei, Yu Zhou, Gary Dymski, and Maria Chee. 2001. "Banking on Social Capital in the Era of Globalization—Chinese Ethnobanks in Los Angeles." *Environment and Planning A*, 33: 1923–1948.

Li, Wei, Gary Dymski, Yu Zhou, Carolyn Aldana, and Maria Chee. 2002. "Chinese American Banking and Community Development in Los Angeles County." *Annals of Association of American Geographers*, 92(4): 777–96.

Light, Ivan H. and E. Bonacich. 1988. *Immigrant Entrepreneurs: Koreans in Los Angeles, 1965–1982*. Berkeley, CA: University of California Press.

Light, I. and S. Karageorgis. 1994. "Economic Saturation and Immigrant Entrepreneurship." In Lazin Isralowitz and I. Light (eds.), *Immigration and Absorption: Issues in a Multicultural Perspective*. Beer-Sheva, Israel: Ben-Gurion University of the Negev, 89–108.

Light, Ivan H. and C. Rosenstein (eds.). 1995. *Race, Ethnicity and Entrepreneurship in Urban America*. New York: Aldine de Gruyter.

Light, Ivan, Paminder Bhachu, and Stavros Karageorgis. 1993. "Migration Networks and Immigrant Entrepreneurship." In I.H. Light and P. Bhachu (eds.), *Immigration and Entrepreneurship: Culture, Capital, and Ethnic Networks*. New Brunswick, NJ: Transaction Publishers.

Light, I., G. Sabagh, M. Bozorgmehr, and C. Der-Martirosian. 1994. "The Four Iranian Ethnic Economies in Los Angeles." In Lazin Isralowitz and I. Light (eds.), *Immigration and Absorption: Issues in a Multicultural Perspective*. Beer-Sheva, Israel: Ben-Gurion University of the Negev, 109–32.

Lin, Jan. 1998. *Reconstructing Chinatown: Ethnic Enclave, Global Change*. Minneapolis, MN: University of Minnesota Press.

McDowell, Linda. 1997. *Capital Culture: Gender at Work in the City*. Oxford, UK: Blackwell Publishers.

Mao, J. 1995. "The Rotating Credit Association and the Adaptation of Immigrants in North America." In J.H. Ong, K.B. Chan, and S.B. Chew (eds.), *Crossing Borders: Transmigration in Asia Pacific*. New York: Prentice Hall.

Portes, A. and R.L. Bach. 1985. *Latin Journey: Cuban Immigrants in the United States*. Berkeley, CA: University of California Press.

Portes, A. and L. Jensen. 1987. "What's an Ethnic Enclave? The Case for Conceptual Clarity." *American Sociological Review*, 52: 768–71.

Portes, A., W.J. Haller, and L.E. Guarnizo. 2002. "Transnational Entrepreneurs: An Alternative Form of Immigrant Economic Adaptation." *American Sociological Review*, 67(2): 278–98.

Sassen, Saskia and Kwamia Anthony Appiah. 1999. *Globalization and Its Discontents: Essays on the New Mobility of People and Money*. New York: New Press.

Schoenberger, Erica. 1991. *The Cultural Crisis of the Firm*. Oxford, UK: Blackwell Publishers.

Scott, Allen J. 1988. *Metropolis from the Division of Labor to Urban Form*. Berkeley, CA: University of California Press.

——. 1993. *Technopolis: High-Technology Industry and Regional Development in Southern California*. Berkeley, CA: University of California Press.

Siu, Paul C.P. 1987. *The Chinese Laundryman: A Study of Social Isolation*. New York: New York University Press.

Storper, M. and R. Walker. 1989. *The Capital Imperative: Territory, Technology, and Industrial Growth*. Cambridge, MA: Blackwell Publishers.

Tsai, S. H. 1986. *The Chinese Experience in America*. Bloomington, IN: Indiana University Press.

Tseng, Yen-fen. 1994a. "Suburban Ethnic Economy: Chinese Business Communities in Los Angeles." Unpublished Doctoral Dissertation. Los Angeles: University of California, Los Angeles.

———. 1994. "Chinese Ethnic Economy: San Gabriel Valley, Los Angeles County." *Journal of Urban Affairs*, 16(2): 169–89.

———. 1995. "Beyond 'Little Taipei': The Development of Taiwanese Immigrant Businesses in Los Angeles." *International Migration Review*, 24(1): 33–5.

U.S. Congress. 1965. Immigration and Nationality Act—Amendments Public Law 89–236 H.R. 2580. *U.S. Code Congressional and Administrative News, 89th Congress—First Session*. 883–987.

———. 1991. Immigration Act of 1990 Public Law 101–649. *U.S. Code Congressional and Administrative News, 101th Congress—Second Session*. St. Paul, MN: West Publishing Co.

Waldinger, R.D. and Tseng, Y. 1992. "Divergent Diasporas: The Chinese Communities of New York and Los Angeles Compared." *Revue Européenne des Migrations Internationale*, 8(3): 91–116.

Wang, Emma. 1994. "Retrospectives of Chinese American Banks." *Chinese International Daily*, Section C. Southern California Economy April 28–May 3.

Wilson, K.L. and Portes, A. 1980. "Immigrant Enclaves: An Analysis of the Labor Market Experiences of Cubans in Miami." *American Journal of Sociology*, 86: 295–319.

Wu, D.Y.H. 1974. "To Kill Three Birds with One Stone: The Rotating Credit Associations of the Papua New Guinea Chinese." *American Ethnologist*, 1: 565–84.

Yeung, H.W. and K. Olds. 2000. "Epilogue." In H.W. Yeung and K. Olds (eds.), *Globalization of Chinese Business Firms*. New York: St. Martin's Press. 275–78.

Zhou, Min. 1992. *Chinatown: The Socioeconomic Potential of an Urban Enclave*. Philadelphia, PA: Temple University Press.

Zhou, Yu. 1998. "How do places matter? A comparative studies of Chinese ethnic economies in Los Angeles and New York City." *Urban Geography*, 19(6): 531–53.

Zhou, Yu and Yen-Fen Tseng. 2001. "Regrounding the 'Ungrounded Empires': Localization as the Geographical Catalyst for Transnationalism." *Global Network*, 1(2): 131–54.

# 4 The new Chinese business sector in Toronto

## A spatial and structural anatomy of medium-sized and large firms

*Lucia Lo and Shuguang Wang*

Based on a sample of businesses extracted from the 1997 Dun & Bradstreet Business Directory, this chapter examines the sectoral composition, size distribution, and geographic distribution of medium-sized and large Chinese businesses in Toronto, and compares them to the overall business sectors in the Toronto metropolitan economy. Accompanied by locational shifts, the Chinese ethnic economy has moved away from its traditional focus on consumer goods and services to one that covers nearly the whole array of industrial activities, and has gone beyond the enclave market and middleman status. The study elucidates the functional diversity as well as the structural and economic integration of the Chinese sub-economy in the overall Toronto metropolitan economy. It also underscores the macro changes in the world's economic and international migration systems.

## INTRODUCTION

The traditional view of ethnic businesses is that they are small in scale, provide retail goods and services to co-ethnic or minority consumers, and that they cluster if their intended clients are co-ethnics (Bates 1994; Chin *et al.* 1996; Evans 1989; Jones and McEvoy 1996; Marger and Hoffman 1992; Razin 1992; Tait *et al.* 1989; Teixeira 1998). Global political and economic restructuring and international population movement in the last two decades have drastically altered the picture. Contemporary ethnic economies, such as those of the Chinese in world metropolises, include medium-sized and large firms, branch beyond retailing and the ethnic enclaves, and command transnational connections (Li 1998). It is in this context that this chapter examines the medium and larger Chinese businesses in Toronto.[1] The primary objectives are to understand the current nature and structure of ethnic businesses, to examine their industrial and spatial representation, and to compare them to the overall business sector in the Toronto metropolitan economy.

Toronto's Chinese ethnic economy has undergone much metamorphosis. Like their counterparts elsewhere, the first Chinese immigrants in Toronto faced residential, educational, and occupational segregation. Institutional discrimination produced the enclave known as Chinatown and prompted early Chinese involvement in laundry and restaurant businesses (Anderson 1991). In 1923, the year when the Chinese Exclusion Act forbidding the entry of Chinese nationals into Canada came into effect, with a population of 2,500, the Chinese in Toronto operated 203 restaurants, 47 laundries and 9 grocery stores (Thompson 1979, cited in Rhyne 1982, p. 31). By 1966, the year before the 1967 Immigration Act was introduced, the ethnic Chinese business sector had expanded to 448 firms. The proportion of restaurants declined from 78 percent in 1923 to 38.8 percent in 1966 while that of grocers increased from 3 percent to 18.1 percent and that of laundry and dry cleaning increased from 18 percent to 32.6 percent. New entries included import and export firms, gift shops, real estate, insurance and travel agents, and a few professionals (Thompson 1989, p. 108). The 1967 Immigration Act, which for the first time allowed immigrants of any race to enter Canada based on a points system, and the business immigrant program with entrepreneurial and investor components, which was much promoted in the 1980s, caused considerable change in the size and structure of the Chinese community. The emergence of an immigrant middle class has created the consumer demand and capital supply necessary for the expansion of Chinese businesses and the onset of a new ethnic economy (Chan and Cheung 1985; Li 1992), ethnic economy here defined as a set of businesses owned and operated by Chinese.

Chan and Cheung (1985), sampling from Toronto's Chinese business telephone directories, surveyed 187 businesses that existed in 1979–80: 49 percent were consumer services, including restaurant [33%], dry cleaner [4%], printing shop, movie house, driving school, travel agency, hair salon, construction company, and herbal store; 34 percent were commercial outlets such as grocery store, gift shop, photo shop, newspaper stall, retail store, wholesale store, garage, bookstore, garment manufacturing, and real estate firms; 18 percent were professional services, comprising physician, dentist, accountant, pharmacy, and interior design. Of the 187 businesses, 52.3 percent had a sales volume in the $50,000 to $100,000 range, and 47.6 percent were located outside the three Chinatowns of the larger City of Toronto (formerly Metropolitan Toronto).

Marger and Hoffman (1992), using evaluation reports on 272 immigrant entrepreneurs entering Ontario in 1986 and 1987 through the Entrepreneur Immigrant Program, looked at immigrant participation in the small business sector. Among the 142 Chinese businesses set up by business immigrants from Hong Kong and mainland China, dominance in small manufacturing (36.6%), especially the apparel industry (18.3%), was obvious. In addition, retail trade, wholesale trade, and services accounted for 31 percent, 15.5 percent, and 12.7 percent respectively.[2] These Chinese firms hired between 1 and 160 workers, with an average of 12.8. Ninety percent of the firms were located within the Toronto CMA, and of these, 47 percent were in the former City of Toronto, 36 percent elsewhere in the former Metro Toronto, and 17 percent elsewhere in the CMA.

These two studies provide a partial glimpse into the changing Chinese ethnic economy. However, they still contain traditional views on the scale and orientation of ethnic businesses. Their treatment of ethnic businesses is aspatial. Unlike those written about New York and Los Angeles (Li 1998; Lin 1998; Tseng 1994; Zhou 1992; Zhou 1996, 1998), they make little connection between ethnic businesses and the current global flows of people and capital. We therefore turn our attention to the medium-sized and large firms. In the past, medium and large businesses were often considered the efforts of native-born Canadians and established immigrants who had worked their way up. More recently, mass global movements—of ideas and technology, of people and resources—have resulted in a very different picture. Many immigrants have come with both human and financial capital, and with management experience and business acumen. Many of them are transnationals, and they establish businesses that often have transnational connections (Tseng 1994). These businesses do not necessarily target end consumers. However, they have not been studied until recently (Olds 1996; Saxenian 1999; Zhou 1998).

With Hong Kong and, more recently, mainland China being the largest immigrant-sending countries (Citizenship and Immigration Canada 2002), we dare say that the new Chinese ethnic economy is one propelled by globalization and oriented towards transnational networking (Li 1992; Li 1998; Lin 1998). It differs from its predecessor in scale and structure. "Enclave" is no longer an appropriate word to describe it; its spatial dimension differs significantly. Hence, in this chapter, we focus on the medium-sized and large Chinese businesses and contrast them with comparable businesses in the overall Toronto economy. We hope to fill a void in research on contemporary ethnic economies. While the exposition is empirical in scope and descriptive in nature, we intend to lay down some groundwork for future research.

## DATA SOURCE

An inherent question in studies on ethnic businesses has always been: What constitutes an ethnic business? Incongruous views prevail. Razin (1988) defines them as small businesses employing and serving only people of the same ethnic group, and Evans (1989) differentiates those serving the same ethnic group from those serving the general population. These definitions take a narrow and traditional view of ethnic business as small in size and co-ethnic in orientation. The reality is such that as an ethnic business becomes larger, it does not necessarily serve co-ethnics only. Hence in this chapter, we follow Portes and Jensen (1989) and confine the definition of ethnic business to business owned and operated by people of a certain ethnicity, themselves immigrants or descendants of earlier immigrants, and disregard their mix of clientele.

Our data came from the Dun & Bradstreet Business Directory (Dun & Bradstreet Canada 1997), and not from ethnic business directories. While directories such as the *Chinese Yellow Pages* (1997) or the *Chinese Consumer Directory* (1997) are traditionally tapped as sources of information about the types and variability of ethnic businesses (for example, Thompson 1989; Wang 1996), we view them as insufficient for our attempt to analyze the nature and structure of contemporary Chinese ethnic businesses. First, because of their consumer bearings, the Chinese directories may over-represent businesses that provide retail and personal services, and under-represent manufacturing, professional, and other services not necessarily targeting co-ethnic and/or other minority consumers. Second, they often include businesses that are not organized or owned by the particular ethnic group the directory targets, that is, businesses that belong to the wider general economy. Third, these directories only contain locational information about the businesses, and nothing on sales or employment, the usual size indicator of a business.

On the other hand, the Dun & Bradstreet Business Directory offers two advantages. First, it lists for each entry its standard industrial classification (SIC), number of employees, sales volume, name and title of chief executive(s), geographic and other contact details, and functional nature of the establishment. Many of these details are not available in conventional consumer directories. They allow us to identify firms owned by Chinese, and to examine their structural and spatial distribution. Second, the Directory has a section listing the total number of Toronto businesses in each industrial sector, thus allowing us to examine the industrial representation of Chinese businesses. The Dun & Bradstreet Directory, however, is not without limitations. It lists only businesses with over $50,000 in sales, thereby eliminating the smallest of businesses and making it impossible to analyze the whole spectrum of businesses. Ideally, we would like to combine the Dun & Bradstreet Business Directory and the *Chinese Yellow Pages* for a more comprehensive analysis of the Chinese business sector. However, data incompatibility is an issue. A second drawback of the Dun & Bradstreet Directory is that the inaccuracy rate of the listings has been repeatedly reported as fairly high. Given that this is also true of ethnic consumer directories and that a better database is not available, we take a leap of faith that the error distribution among Chinese businesses in the Dun & Bradstreet Directory is identical to that among other businessess in the Directory.

As we have defined a Chinese ethnic business as one owned and operated by Chinese, we used the last names of the chief executives—owner, CEO, president, chairman, general manager, director—to identify Chinese businesses. The assumption is that Chinese companies usually have Chinese executives. Chinese last names based on spellings commonly adopted in Hong Kong, mainland China, Taiwan, and Vietnam were employed in the identification process. Where the contact person with a Chinese last name was listed as branch manager or director, we called to find out the ethnicity of the owner. Where last names such as Lee, Cho, Dunn, or Young are shared by non-Chinese, we also called the business to find out if the owner is Chinese. This process reduced our initial sample by almost one-fifth, and gave us a final sample of 633 Chinese businesses from a total of 644,761[3] listings in the Directory for the entire Toronto CMA.

## RESEARCH FINDINGS

The rich information in the Dun & Bradstreet Directory allows us to examine three specific attributes of Chinese businesses: sectoral composition, size distribution, and geographic distribution. As previously mentioned, only Chan and Cheung (1985), and Marger and Hoffman (1992) provide similar information about

Toronto's Chinese businesses, and thereby a glimpse into the changing Chinese ethnic economy. While we cannot compare our data directly with theirs due to incompatibility of data sources, their studies can serve as rough benchmarks against which we examine the current status of Chinese businesses in Toronto.

## Sectoral composition

All businesses are classified by four-digit standard industrial classification codes. These four-digit codes can be aggregated into 77 two-digit industrial groupings which can be further generalized into ten broad industry sectors: agriculture/forestry/ fisheries (primary hereafter), mining, construction, manufacturing, transportation/ communication/utilities (TCU hereafter), whole trade, retail trade, finance/ insurance/real estate (FIRE hereafter), services, and public administration (see Table 4.1). For example, while the four-digit code 2515 refers to the production of bedsprings and mattresses and 2591 refers to the making of venetian blinds and shades, the two-digit code 25 (the first two digits) denotes the manufacturing sub-sector of furniture and fixtures and codes 20 to 39 include all manufacturing sector businesses. Using these codes, we can examine the representation as well as the relative concentration of Toronto's Chinese businesses.

In 1996, the base year for Dun & Bradstreet's 1997 compilation, Chinese businesses in Toronto were represented in all sectors except mining and public administration, although there was only one Chinese firm in the primary sector (Table 4.1). Of the 77 industrial groupings listed in Table 4.2, Chinese businesses were present in 66 percent of them, and of the 65 groupings outside the primary and public administration sectors, Chinese businesses were absent in only 14, yielding a 78 percent representation rate. The areas in which they were not represented included non-depository credit institutions; security and commodity brokers and exchangers; museums, art galleries, botanical/zoological gardens; rail and air transportation, postal and utility services; and the manufacturing of tobacco, petroleum, leather and transportation equipment. Many of these industries are publicly incorporated or regulated, with very stringent rules for entry.

As Table 4.1 shows, four industrial sectors accounted for over 80 percent of the Chinese businesses in 1996. In order of magnitude, they were retail trade (24.64% of total), wholesale trade (22.91%), manufacturing (20.85%), and services (18.48%). While the overall distribution may evidence some diversification of Chinese businesses in the Toronto economy, it does not immediately dispel the myth that immigrant or ethnic minority businesses concentrate heavily on retail trade and personal services. Fortunately, Dun & Bradstreet Canada's (1997, Table on Standard Industrial Classification Codes) report on the total number of busi-nesses in each industrial sector allows us to compare the percentage of Chinese businesses in each sector to the percentage of Toronto businesses in the same sector. The comparison yields the indices of concentration shown in Table 4.1, column 6. While an index value of one means an equal representation of Chinese businesses in a given sector, a value exceeding one indicates that Chinese busi-nesses are over-represented in that sector, and a value of less than one implies that

Chinese businesses are under-represented. Contrary to conventional expectation, Chinese retail businesses were similarly represented, service businesses were under-represented, yet manufacturing and wholesale trade businesses were over-represented by a large margin, in comparison to all Toronto businesses in their respective sectors. As in the service sector, Chinese businesses were only mildly under-represented in TCU and FIRE. Apart from the primary industrial sectors, the only area with weak Chinese representation was the construction sector.

Table 4.2 lists all two-digit industrial groupings in each of the ten sectors and underscores those where Chinese businesses were either lacking or in relative abundance. As mentioned earlier, there was a concentration of Chinese manufacturing and wholesale businesses in Toronto. Chinese firms covered 16 of the 20 standard classifications in the manufacturing category. The dominant types were apparel, industrial/commercial machinery, electronic and electrical equipment, food and kindred products, and printing and publishing. Together they accounted for 64 percent of all Chinese manufacturing firms. Chemical and allied products, and rubber and plastic products were fairly well represented within the manufacturing sector. The wholesale trading sector is of interest too. Of 145 firms in that sector, half deal with durable goods and the other half with non-durable goods.

*Table 4.1* Representation of Chinese firms in the Toronto CMA

| Industrial sector | Chinese firms | | All firms | | Concentration index |
|---|---|---|---|---|---|
| | N (A) | % (B) | N (C) | % (D) | (B/D) |
| Agriculture, forestry, and fisheries | 1 | 0.16 | 16,041 | 2.49 | 0.06 |
| Mining | 0 | | 7,113 | 1.10 | |
| Construction | 11 | 1.74 | 74,299 | 11.52 | 0.15 |
| Manufacturing | 132 | 20.85 | 59,707 | 9.26 | 2.25 |
| Transportation, communication and utilities | 25 | 3.95 | 34,643 | 5.37 | 0.74 |
| Wholesale trade | 145 | 22.91 | 63,596 | 9.86 | 2.32 |
| Retail trade | 156 | 24.64 | 163,270 | 25.32 | 0.97 |
| Finance, insurance, and real estate | 46 | 7.27 | 73,479 | 11.40 | 0.64 |
| Services | 117 | 18.48 | 152,613 | 23.67 | 0.78 |
| Public administration | – | | – | | |
| | 633 | 100.00 | 644761 | 100.00 | |

Source: Dun & Bradstreet Canada (1997). Compiled by authors.

Notes: Concentration index of a Chinese industrial sector = [(number of Chinese firms in Toronto in the sector / total number of Chinese firms in Toronto) / (number of Toronto firms in the sector / total number of Toronto firms)].

*Table 4.2* Number of Chinese firms in each industrial sector and sub-sector

| | | | |
|---|---|---|---|
| **Agricultural, forestry and fisheries** | **1** | **Wholesale trade** | **145** |
| **Mining** | **0** | Durables | 73 |
| **Construction** | **11** | Non-durables | 72 |
| General contractor | 5 | **Retail trade** | **156** |
| Heavy construction contractor | 1 | Auto dealers & gasoline service | |
| Special trade contractor | 5 | stations | 8 |
| **Manufacturing** | **132** | Apparel & accessory stores | 4 |
| Apparel & other made from | | Building mat., hardware, garden supp. | 0 |
| fabric | 25 | Eating & drinking places | 68 |
| Chemical & allied | 8 | Food stores | 17 |
| Electronic & electrical equipment | 15 | Furniture & home furnishing | 13 |
| Fabricated metal products | 2 | General merchandise | 1 |
| Food & kindred products | 14 | Misc. retail | 45 |
| Furniture & fixture | 5 | **Finance, insurance & real estate** | **46** |
| Ind./com. machinery & equipment | 18 | Combined real estate | 0 |
| Leather & leather products | 0 | Depository institutions (banking) | 3 |
| Lumber & wood products | 2 | Holding & investment offices | 12 |
| Measuring, analyzing, & controlling | | Insurance carrier | 4 |
| instr. | 4 | Insurance agents, brokers & | |
| Paper & allied products | 5 | services | 3 |
| Petroleum refining, coal & | 0 | Nondepository credit institution | 0 |
| related ind. | | Real estate | 24 |
| Primary metal industry | 1 | Security & commodity brokers/ | 0 |
| Printing, publishing & allied | 13 | dealers | |
| Rubber & plastic products | 8 | **Services** | **117** |
| Stone, clay, glass, & concrete | | Amusement & recreational | |
| products | 1 | services | 4 |
| Textile mill products | 5 | Auto repair services, parking & garage | 6 |
| Tobacco | 0 | Business services | 63 |
| Transportation equipment | 0 | Educational services | 5 |
| Misc. | 6 | Health services, nursing care, hospital | 8 |
| **Transportation, communication &** | | Hotels, lodgings, camps etc. | 9 |
| **utilities** | **25** | Legal services | 1 |
| Air transportation | 0 | Motion pictures | 1 |
| Communications | 3 | Museums, art galleries, botanical | |
| Electrical, gas & sanitary services | 0 | gardens | 0 |
| Local passenger | 1 | Non-profit membership organizations | 2 |
| Pipeline transportation | 0 | Personal services | 5 |
| Postal services | 0 | Misc. industrial repair | 2 |
| Railroad transportation | 0 | Misc. services | 11 |
| Transportation services | 16 | **Public administration** | **0** |
| Trucking & warehousing | 4 | | |
| Water transportation | 1 | | |

Source: Dun & Bradstreet Canada (1997). Compiled by authors.

Notes: (1) The agricultural, forestry and fisheries sector contains five standard industrial categories: agricultural production, agricultural products, agricultural services, forestry and fisheries, and there is one single Chinese firm in agricultural services. (2) The mining sector again consists of five industrial categories where Chinese presence is not found in any.

While 24.6 percent of the Chinese firms were in the retail sector, compared to 25.3 percent of all firms in the Toronto CMA, the Chinese retail sector was heavily biased towards the provision of eating and drinking places, which accounted for 44 percent of all Chinese retail firms. There was also considerable miscellaneous retail (such as drug stores, bookstores, florists, and newsstands) in addition to food; furniture and home furnishing; auto dealership and service stations; and apparel accessories. The Chinese retail sector lacked stores that sell general merchandise, hardware, building materials, and garden supplies. This corresponds to the under-representation in construction.

The data show that Chinese firms were mildly under-represented in three sectors: services, TCU, and FIRE, with sectoral concentration indices ranging between 0.64 and 0.78. However, we doubt the usefulness of the indices for these three sectors. The Dun & Bradstreet Business Directory listed many public administration and government-regulated industries. For example, listings in the service sector included public educational institutions and hospitals; those in the FIRE sector included local bank branches; and those in the TCU sector contained major land, air, and water transportation and utility service providers. These listings, unlikely to be owned and headed by Chinese directors or managers, were included as businesses in the overall Toronto sample. If they were excluded, Chinese businesses in the service, TCU, and FIRE sectors might not be under-represented.

Among Chinese businesses in the service sector, business services dominated, followed distantly by hotels and lodging, health care, auto repair, and miscellaneous services that include accounting, auditing, engineering, and architecture services. In the FIRE sector, real estate firms and holding companies predominated. Finally, in the TCU sector, the provision of transport services such as freight forwarding and packing and crating prevailed.

Two interesting observations emerge here. First, the evidence shows that Chinese businesses have entered a new era. They are diversifying and branching into terri-tories formerly untapped by or inaccessible to visible minority immigrants. Chinese businesses are represented in almost every sector. There is remarkable relative concentration in manufacturing, especially of machinery and electrical/electronic equipment. This diversification implies that contemporary Chinese businesses are no longer dominated by retail and service activities. Nor are they restricted to serving Chinese co-ethnics or other ethnic minorities. It also dispels the myth that immigrant and/or minority businesses can only be enclave or ethnic in nature. Second, while Chinese businesses show signs of diversification and integration, their industrial representation still evidences concentration. Industrial niches are present, but they do not necessarily reflect traditional perceptions of ethnic niches.

## Size distribution

We have used three measures here to examine the firm size distribution of Toronto's Chinese firms: employment size, volume of sales, and functional nature of the firm.

Most firms in the Toronto economy (and, by implication, in the Canadian economy) are small. However, there is no consistent definition as to what is small, medium, or large. For example, Industry Canada (Entrepreneurship and Small Business Office) considers manufacturing firms of less than 100 employees and non-manufacturing firms of less than 50 employees to be small and firms of over 300 to be large for both manufacturing and non-manufacturing firms, whereas Storey (1988) regarded less than 20 employees in manufacturing as small and over 500 as large, and the Quebec Ministry of Industry and Commerce (GAPMER 1994) took a firm size of 50 to 199 to be medium. Because of this incongruity, Shearmur and Coffey (1996) preferred to group firms into eight unequal size classes ranging from less than 5 to over 500. We have used a similar progressive scale. Table 4.3 shows the size distribution of Chinese firms in Toronto.

Dun & Bradstreet Canada (1997) does not include the very small firms commonly found in ethnic business directories. The Chinese firms in the Dun & Bradstreet sample ranged in size from 9 to 750 employees. Although the overall size distribution is negatively skewed and the majority of firms (56.55%, to be precise) employed less than 20 workers, Table 4.3 illustrates that slightly over 13 percent of the firms had a payroll of over 50 people and close to 2 percent hired more than 200 workers.

While it is not possible in this study[4] to compare the number of Chinese firms to the number of Toronto firms in each of the employment classes specified in Table 4.3, the Dun & Bradsheet Directory ranks the top 1,000 Toronto firms which employ at least 200 workers (Dun & Bradstreet Canada 1997: E1-E26). Eleven of these top firms, or 1.1 percent, are Chinese. This is significant, given that the overall Chinese sample accounted for only 0.1 percent of the total Toronto sample of 644,762. The 11 Chinese firms covered a range of business types including wholesale, manufacturing, realty, and hotel accommodation. In particular, the three manufacturing firms respectively dealt with industrial/commercial machinery, electronic/electrical equipment, and apparel. The largest was ATI Technologies Inc. It had a workforce of 750 and a sales volume of $360 million in 1996. It

*Table 4.3* Employee size of Chinese firms

| Employee range | Number of firms | Percent of firms | Cum. percent of firms |
|---|---|---|---|
| 9–10 | 160 | 25.3 | 25.3 |
| 11–19 | 198 | 31.3 | 56.6 |
| 20–29 | 95 | 15.0 | 71.6 |
| 30–39 | 65 | 10.3 | 81.8 |
| 40–49 | 32 | 5.1 | 86.9 |
| 50–74 | 36 | 5.7 | 92.6 |
| 75–99 | 11 | 1.7 | 94.3 |
| 100–149 | 18 | 2.8 | 97.1 |
| 150–199 | 7 | 1.1 | 98.3 |
| 200–299 | 5 | 0.8 | 99.1 |
| 300–399 | 2 | 0.3 | 99.4 |
| 400–499 | 3 | 0.5 | 99.8 |
| 500–750 | 1 | 0.2 | 100.00 |

Source: Dun & Bradstreet Canada (1997). Compiled by authors.

ranked among the top 200 firms in the overall Toronto business listing. It is also the third largest computer firm in Canada and the world's biggest maker of computer graphic chips (Wong 2000). The company was founded by two Chinese immigrants. One of them, Kwok-Yuan Ho, who immigrated from Hong Kong in 1985, has been ATI's CEO since its inception and was voted the Canadian entrepreneur of the year in 1998 (Acharya 1998).

An alternative measure of firm size is volume of sales. Table 4.4 lists the distribution of Chinese firms in each sales class. Only two firms, or less than half a percent in the sample, had sales of less than $100,000, whereas nearly 25 percent made between $1 million and $2 million. In particular, 10 percent had sales exceeding the $10 million mark. Apart from a holding company with annual sales totaling $1,700 million and a 52nd rank in the overall Toronto listing, the large Chinese firms were engaged in wholesale trade, machinery manufacturing, real estate, and business and transport services. The 1,000th largest firm in Toronto made $49.9 million sales in 1996. Ten Chinese firms made more than that amount, and they together accounted for 1 percent of the top sales of the 1,000 firms in Toronto.

*Table 4.4* Volume of sales of Chinese firms

| Sales range (Can $) | Number of firms | Percent of firms | Cum. percent of firms |
|---|---|---|---|
| 50,000–99,999 | 2 | 0.3 | 0.3 |
| 100,000–499,999 | 45 | 7.5 | 7.9 |
| 500,000–999,999 | 109 | 18.3 | 26.1 |
| 1,000,000–1,999,999 | 145 | 24.3 | 50.4 |
| 2,000,000–2,999,999 | 78 | 13.1 | 63.5 |
| 3,000,000–4,999,999 | 87 | 14.6 | 78.1 |
| 5,000,000–9,999,999 | 69 | 11.6 | 89.6 |
| 10,000,000–49,999,999 | 53 | 8.9 | 98.5 |
| 50,000,000–99,999,999 | 5 | 0.8 | 99.3 |
| 100,000,000–499,999,999 | 3 | 0.5 | 99.8 |
| 500,000,000–2,000,000,000 | 1 | 0.2 | 100.0 |

Source: Dun & Bradstreet Canada (1997). Compiled by authors.

Note: 36 firms did not report sales figures.

Generally speaking, among Chinese firms, those engaged in manufacturing and FIRE are the largest and those in construction are the smallest. To illustrate this, Table 4.5 records the distribution of Chinese firms by employee size in each industrial sector. While over 80 percent of the construction firms employed less than 20 workers, only 39 percent of the manufacturing firms and 48 percent of the FIRE companies were in this category. About 30 percent of the firms in services and wholesale and retail trades hired between 20 and 50 workers. Twenty-five percent of the manufacturing firms, 18 percent of those in FIRE, and 16 percent of those in TCU hired more than 50 workers.

While our data do not allow a size comparison between the average Chinese firm and the average Toronto firm, we note that while the Chinese economy was only

Table 4.5 Distribution of Chinese firms in each employee range by industrial sector

| Employee range | All | Construction | Manufacturing | Transp/Comm/Utility | Wholesale trade | Retail trade | FIRE | Services |
|---|---|---|---|---|---|---|---|---|
| 9–10 | 25.3 | 36.4 | 15.2 | 24.0 | 25.5 | 29.5 | 28.3 | 29.1 |
| 11–19 | 31.3 | 45.5 | 24.2 | 36.0 | 37.2 | 30.8 | 19.6 | 34.2 |
| 20–29 | 15.0 | 9.1 | 15.2 | 8.0 | 18.6 | 14.7 | 17.4 | 12.0 |
| 30–39 | 10.3 | 9.1 | 15.2 | 12.0 | 6.9 | 11.5 | 13.0 | 6.0 |
| 40–49 | 5.1 | | 5.3 | 4.0 | 2.8 | 5.8 | 4.3 | 7.7 |
| 50–74 | 5.7 | | 9.1 | 12.0 | 4.1 | 5.1 | 10.9 | 1.7 |
| 75–99 | 1.7 | | 6.1 | | | | 2.2 | 1.7 |
| 100–149 | 2.8 | | 6.1 | 4.0 | 3.4 | 1.3 | | 1.7 |
| 150–199 | 1.1 | | 1.5 | | 0.7 | 1.3 | | 1.7 |
| 200–299 | 0.8 | | 0.8 | | 0.7 | | 2.2 | 1.7 |
| 300–399 | 0.3 | | 0.8 | | | | | |
| 400–499 | 0.5 | | | | | | 2.2 | 0.9 |
| 500–750 | 0.2 | | 0.8 | | | | | 1.7 |

Source: Dun & Bradstreet Canada (1997). Compiled by authors.

0.1 percent of the overall Toronto economy, Chinese firms accounted for 1 percent of the largest 1,000 firms in Toronto in terms of both employee size and sales size. The Chinese ethnic economy has a more than proportionate share of the largest businesses in Toronto.

In addition, 82 percent of the Chinese businesses in the same sample were single location establishments, 6 percent were branch locations, and 12 percent were headquarters. The presence of branch locations and headquarters serves as another indicator of the growing size of Chinese firms in Toronto. The branch establishments were mostly restaurants, drugstores, or insurance franchisees such as McDonald's Restaurants and Shoppers Drugmarts. The head offices were for supermarkets, restaurants, real estate firms, and travel agencies. Most of their branch locations were not listed in the Directory. This functional structure suggests that there may be a higher proportion of Chinese establishments in the Toronto area than the data show. It also suggests that contemporary Chinese businesses are expanding in both scale and locale.

## Geographic distribution

The above discussion points to the shifting of Chinese businesses away from the small enclave that traditionally characterizes ethnic minority business. A detailed examination of their geographic distribution confirms the shift.

Chinese businesses in Toronto, like the Chinese people in the census metropolitan area (CMA), are urban bound and have decentralized. Nearly all Chinese businesses in our 1996 sample were located in the urbanized part of the Toronto CMA (Figure 4.1). The distribution of the sample is as follows: 27 percent in the urban core (Toronto), 33 percent in the inner suburbs (East York, Etobicoke, North York, Scarborough, and York), and 40 percent in the outer suburbs (remainder of the urbanized area in Figure 4.1). On a finer geographical scale (i.e., at the scale of census subdivision), the former city of Toronto contained 27 percent of the Chinese businesses, followed by 20 percent in Scarborough, 15 percent in Markham, 13 percent in Mississauga, 8 percent in North York, and 6 percent in Etobicoke (Table 4.6). When this distribution was compared to the 1996 Chinese population distribution in the Toronto CMA, it seems that the location of Chinese businesses was tied to the Chinese neighborhoods since 90 percent of the Toronto CMA's Chinese also resided in Scarborough, Toronto, North York, Markham, Mississauga, and Richmond Hill (Statistics Canada 1999; Lo and Wang 1997). The delineation below will show that this is not true. In fact, it shows that the overall spatial pattern of Chinese businesses is a dispersed one, but with identifiable pockets of concentration in the Toronto downtown core, Markham and Scarborough, municipalities that have high concentrations of Chinese population.

Figures 4.1 and 4.2 show that the population distribution pattern in 1996 was more compact than the business pattern in the same year. For example, while Mississauga contained 9 percent of the Chinese population and 13.4 percent of the Chinese businesses in the Toronto CMA, most Chinese firms were found in the industrial area close to the Pearson International Airport rather than in the residential

*Table 4.6* Municipal share of Chinese population and Chinese businesses

| Municipality | Relative share of Chinese business (A) | Relative share of business employment (B) | Relative share of Chinese population (C) | Concentration index | |
| --- | --- | --- | --- | --- | --- |
| | | | | Business (A/C) | Employment (B/C) |
| Aurora | 0.32 | 0.17 | 0.13 | 2.46 | 1.31 |
| Brampton | 1.58 | 1.27 | 1.45 | 1.09 | 0.88 |
| Caledon | 0.16 | 0.05 | 0.03 | 5.33 | 1.67 |
| East York | 0.16 | 0.51 | 2.03 | 0.08 | 0.25 |
| Etobicoke | 5.52 | 7.41 | 1.85 | 2.98 | 4.01 |
| Markham | 14.83 | 20.09 | 13.28 | 1.12 | 1.51 |
| Mississauga | 13.41 | 12.68 | 8.99 | 1.49 | 1.41 |
| Newmarket | 0.32 | 0.25 | 0.40 | 0.80 | 0.63 |
| North York | 7.57 | 6.88 | 15.25 | 0.50 | 0.45 |
| Oakville | 0.95 | 0.57 | 0.81 | 1.17 | 0.70 |
| Pickering | 0.79 | 0.55 | 0.48 | 1.65 | 1.15 |
| Richmond Hill | 4.42 | 2.33 | 6.24 | 0.71 | 0.37 |
| Scarborough | 19.72 | 19.83 | 28.03 | 0.70 | 0.71 |
| Toronto | 26.97 | 24.18 | 17.98 | 1.50 | 1.34 |
| Vaughan | 2.84 | 2.98 | 1.83 | 1.55 | 1.63 |
| York | 0.47 | 0.24 | 1.24 | 0.38 | 0.19 |

Sources: Dun & Bradstreet Canada (1997); Canada Census 1996.

Notes: See Table 4.1 for formula on concentration index.

areas to the southwest of the airport (see Figure 4.3). Similarly, with Markham accommodating 13.3 percent of Toronto's Chinese population and 14.8 percent of its Chinese businesses, the Markham businesses were concentrated in the industrial parks along the 404/Steeles area rather than in the Unionville residential neighborhoods to the east. In addition, there were a fair number of Chinese businesses found in Vaughan, Brampton, Etobicoke, and the south side of Scarborough, all of which housed many fewer Chinese. Comparing each municipality's share of Chinese businesses and their employee force to its share of Chinese population, Table 4.6 does not indicate a direct correspondence between Chinese business development and Chinese residential patterns. The concentration indices show that Caledon, Etobicoke, Vaughan, Mississauga, and Toronto had an above average share of Chinese businesses, while East York, North York, Newmarket, Richmond Hill, Scarborough, and York had a below average share. This finding is not surprising, given that nearly 50 percent of the Chinese firms are in the producer categories (i.e., construction, manufacturing, transportation/communication/ utilities, and wholesale trade). Whereas retail and commercial firms serving consumers are commonly found close to residential areas, producer industries serving other producers are likely to be away from residential locations. Chinese industrial firms do not target Chinese consumers and do not necessarily deal with other Chinese producers, and therefore have different locational requirements from

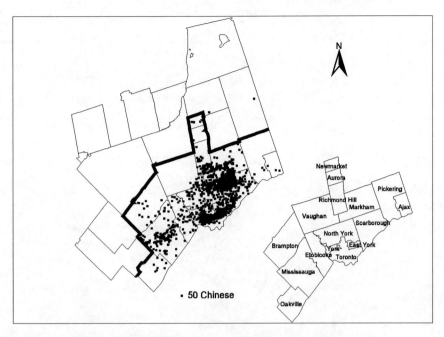

*Figure 4.1* Distribution of the Chinese population in the Toronto CMA, 1996.

Chinese enclave businesses. By the nature of their business, they are often restricted to areas designated as industrial under municipal land use plans. Industrial and business parks are separated from residential areas, and they are void of inhabitants. On population distribution maps such as Figure 4.1, industrial areas are conspicuous by the absence of population within the census tracts that they occupy, and therefore are represented as empty polygons. Some of those empty polygons show up in Figure 4.2 covered by Chinese firms. Figure 4.3 illustrates the separation between Chinese businesses locating in the industrial areas off the Pearson International Airport and the concentration of Chinese residences in Mississauga. It confirms that while ethnic population settlement can prescribe the development of retail/commercial businesses, it is often unrelated to the development of producer businesses, which are normally not co-ethnic in orientation.

The dispersion of Chinese businesses in Toronto can be further illustrated by the distribution patterns of the Chinese manufacturing and retail trade sectors. The latter are typical of traditional perceptions of ethnic business, and the former are more characteristic of the new ethnic economy. First, as outlined earlier and in Table 4.1, Chinese businesses in comparison to all Toronto businesses were over-represented in the manufacturing sector. Their spatial distribution, compared to other sectors, was fairly concentrated. Eighty-two percent of Chinese manufacturing firms were in Mississauga, Vaughan, Markham, Scarborough, and the former City of Toronto, which together housed slightly less than 70 percent of the CMA's Chinese population (see Figure 4.4). Second, the data indicate that Chinese retail

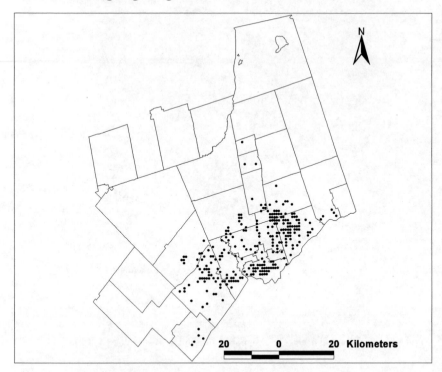

*Figure 4.2* Location of Chinese businesses in the Toronto CMA, 1996.

Source: Dun & Bradstreet Canada (1997).

trade was distributed similarly to the Toronto retail trade sector. While Figure 4.5 indicates pockets of concentration corresponding to settlement, it also illustrates that Chinese retail operations were all over the urbanized portion of the Toronto CMA. Due to their large size, some were located away from immediate Chinese residential areas to obtain other externalities. The dispersed pattern is evidenced by the statistics that while the former City of Toronto and Etobicoke respectively held 18 percent and 2 percent of the CMA's total Chinese population in 1996, they housed respectively 34 percent and 6 percent of the Chinese retail establishments (alternatively, 30 percent and 5 percent of the labor force in Chinese firms), proportions that are much above what the local Chinese population would need. The Chinese manufacturing and retail sectors both reflect the corresponding Toronto sectoral patterns, with the proviso that manufacturing spaces are essentially more segregated from residential areas than are retail spaces.

On average, businesses located in the outer suburbs of the Toronto CMA generated higher sales than those in the core or in the inner suburbs ($14 million per establishment compared to $4.7 and $4.4 million respectively, or $421,285 per employee compared to $161,309 and $124,705 respectively), although there was no significant difference in terms of employee size (28% in the core versus 32% in the suburbs). This may be explained by the nature of their businesses. While

N

Pearson Int'l
Airport

• **Chinese business**
**Chinese population**
0 - 30
31 - 90
91 - 180
291 - 455

2    0    2 **Kilometers**

*Figure 4.3* Distribution of Chinese population and Chinese businesses in Mississauga.
Source: Canada Census 1996; Dun & Bradstreet Canada (1997).

58 percent of the fringe businesses belonged to the high value-added manufacturing, transportation, and wholesale sectors, a similar percentage (57%) of businesses in the urban core were retail and service oriented. Moreover, branch establishments and single location firms were more likely to locate in the core, whereas head offices were almost evenly split between the core and the fringe.

## SUMMARY AND DISCUSSION

In order to fill a gap in contemporary research on the Chinese ethnic economy in Toronto, we embarked on this study to understand the nature and structure of medium-sized and large ethnic businesses and to examine their industrial and spatial representation in an era of mass global flow of people and capital. We used three attributes—sectoral composition, size distribution, and geographic distribution—to examine these questions. Our findings and their implications are summarized below.

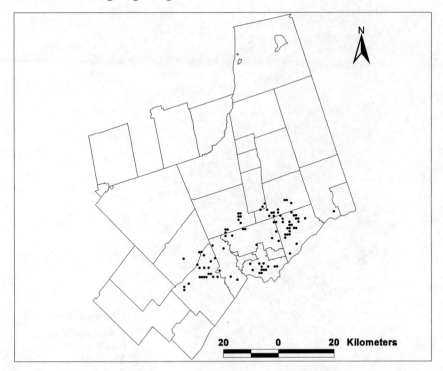

*Figure 4.4* Location of Chinese manufacturing businesses in the Toronto CMA, 1996.

Source: Dun & Bradstreet Canada (1997).

First, Chinese businesses have diversified. The Chinese sub-economy has moved away from its traditional focus on consumer goods and services to one that covers nearly the whole array of industrial activities, including producer and professional services. While many are still of a retail and service nature and, by their location, presumably serving a Chinese clientele, a fair proportion have succeeded in going beyond the enclave market and middleman status, as their standard industrial classifications indicate.

Second, Chinese firms are no longer small and family oriented; they are expanding, and multi-plant establishments have surfaced. On the one hand, this growth reflects the size of the Chinese ethnic economy. On the other hand, it implies significant changes in both the internal organizational structure and the external marketing strategy of Chinese firms. The sheer number of employees and the spatially distinct headquarters and branch locations of some firms necessitate an organizational structure significantly different from the "mom-and-pop" operation of small businesses, and bring it closer to one embodying a formal administrative hierarchy with numerous department heads supervising the rank and file and reporting directly to chief executives (CEOs and CFOs), who then report to a board of directors. In terms of organizational behavior, it is likely that these firms utilize non-ethnic resources that include formal bank financing arrangements and the hiring

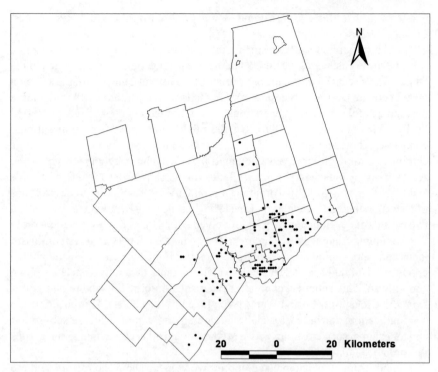

N

20      0      20 **Kilometers**

*Figure 4.5* Location of Chinese retail trade businesses in the Toronto CMA, 1996.

Source: Dun & Bradstreet Canada (1997).

of non-co-ethnic workers. They are also likely to employ different marketing strategies in search of new markets, such as advertising in mainstream media and trade journals, or participating in regional or international trade shows (Jones and McEvoy 1996; Nee *et al*. 1994).

Third, the locations of Chinese businesses, while shifting from the urban core, are both concentrated and dispersed. In some cases, such as retail trade, business activities coincide with spatially defined and culturally distinctive Chinese residential concentrations. In other cases, such as manufacturing, increasing numbers are found outside residential and commercial enclaves. For particular types of industry, these two patterns may co-exist, elucidating the complex processes underlying the contemporary pattern of Chinese firms.

Diversification in composition, size, and space illustrates the functional and structural as well as economic integration of Chinese businesses in Toronto. It underscores the macro changes in the world system. We have reason to believe that the local Chinese ethnic economy in the Toronto CMA has changed in response to global economic and political changes, and that its expansion in scale and structure is in part shaped by globalization and transnational networking. While we have not been able to substantiate the linkage, the diversity of Chinese immigrants to Toronto in terms of origins and immigration classes reported elsewhere is a testament to this claim (Lo and Wang 1997; Citizenship and Immigration Canada 2002).

In addition, our findings have larger implications that deserve further exploration. First, Chinese businesses are tiered. On the one hand, although not recorded in the Dun & Bradstreet Directory, the prevalence of very small Chinese firms is a known fact. There are over 60 Chinese shopping malls in the Toronto CMA and a large percentage of their business operations occupy limited floor space and are staffed by few personnel (Wang 1996). On the other hand, apart from transnational companies, some immigrants and/or their descendants have established fairly large enterprises, some of which have ventured into the technology/knowledge sector. A recent survey indicates 33 percent Chinese ownership of all computer wholesale and manufacturing firms in Toronto (Fairchild TV 1998). Similar to descriptions of New York and Los Angeles by Lin (1995), Tseng (1994), and Saxenian (1999), two circuits of development may have evolved within the Chinese ethnic economy. Popular opinion among local Chinese tells that there is a lower circuit of immigrant labor and petty capitalist incorporation, mostly from China and Vietnam, and an upper circuit of flight capital and high-skill immigrants, generally from Hong Kong and Taiwan. This belief is supported by statistical information about immigrants from these locations (Lo and Wang 1997; Lo and Wang 2004). This phenomenon has implications for internal social cohesion among various Chinese sub-groups and for external social relations between Chinese and other ethnic/immigrant groups in Toronto.

Second, from an economic standpoint, we wonder about the role of Chinese businesses in the larger restructured Toronto economy. As contemporary Toronto is embedded in a knowledge-based economy, the fact that Chinese businesses are over-represented in manufacturing may have implications, not least from a political economy perspective. Are immigrant and ethnic businesses still secondary to the general economy? Is ethnic succession still the rule in business development as in residential location?

Finally, contemporary locational patterns of ethnic enterprises are complex. Whereas enclaves in the past were explained in terms of social exclusion and discrimination, what social forces explain today's spatial patterns? Are they the outcomes of social history (for example, assimilation) or economic strategy (for example, agglomeration economies)? Zhou (1998) argued that ethnic enterprises relying heavily on ethnic networks are possibly confined to ethnic enclaves, whereas those with little such dependence may not cluster spatially at all. However, her theory based on transaction costs does not explain the diverse location patterns pertaining to a single industry such as the Chinese retail trade sector. In particular, we are asking about the role of space in ethnic business development. In the case of Toronto, is space a defined resource for ethnic business development, or an added resource interplaying with other factors such as the sectoral composition and maturity of an ethnic economy (Kaplan 1998)?

Ethnic economies are an interesting phenomenon and have captured much attention, in the past as well as the present. Examining a contemporary data set, we have raised a number of questions that we cannot address yet. They are important questions, dealing with social dynamics and economic succession, and hinging upon the notion of spatiality. Further research is warranted.

## Notes

1 The term Toronto can be referred to different spatial entities. In decreasing order of scale, they are the Census Metropolitan Area of Toronto (Toronto CMA), the Mega City of Toronto formed in 1998 through an amalgamation of the six municipalities (East York, Etobicoke, North York, Scarborough, Toronto, and York) formerly comprising Metropolitan Toronto, and the former City of Toronto. This chapter refers to Toronto in its largest context, the Toronto CMA. Where clarity is needed, former City of Toronto or Metro Toronto will be specified.
2 These figures were adapted from Table 2 in Marger and Hoffman (1992) and adjusted according to the standard industrial classification scheme. The manufacturing figure includes food processing; and import/export is grouped with wholesale/supply.
3 The Directory contains 648,258 listings in total. The additional 3,497 entries are public administrative services operated by various international, federal, provincial, and municipal governments.
4 Dun & Bradstreet did not produce an electronic copy of the Toronto directory in 1997. Research funding did not allow us to go through the directory of nearly 650,000 firms to categorize Toronto firms in each of the employment classes.

## References

Acharya, M. (1998) Turning a vision into a reputation: ATI chief built high-tech dream in tough niche, *Toronto Star* (October 9), D1, D5.
Anderson, K.J. (1991) *Vancouver's Chinatown: Racial Discourse in Canada 1875–1980*. Montreal: McGill-Queen's University Press.
Bates, T. (1994) An analysis of Korean-immigrant-owned small-business start-ups with comparisons to African-American- and minority-owned firms, *Urban Affairs Quarterly*, 30, pp.227–48.
Chan, J.B.L. and Cheung, Y-W. (1985) Ethnic resources and business enterprise: a study of Chinese businesses in Toronto, *Human Organization*, 4, pp.142–54.
Chin, K-S., Yoon, I-J., and Smith, D. (1996) Immigrant small business and international economic linkages: a case study of the Korean wig business in Los Angeles, 1968–1977, *International Migration Review*, 30, pp.485–510.
*Chinese Consumer Directory of Toronto 1997*. Toronto: World Journal.
*Chinese Yellow Pages 1997*. Toronto: Tele-Direct Services Inc. and Ming Pao Daily News.
Citizenship and Immigration Canada (2002) *Facts and Figures*.
Dun & Bradstreet Canada (1997) *1997 Regional Business Directory: Toronto*. Mississauga: Dun & Bradstreet Canada.
Entrepreneurship and Small Business Office, Industry Canada. *Small Business Quarterly*. http:// strategis.ic.gc.ca.
Evans, M.D.R. (1989) Immigrant entrepreneurship: effects of ethnic market size and isolated labor pool, *American Sociological Review*, 54, pp.950–62.
Fairchild TV (1998) Background materials (sourced through www.canada.yellowpages.com and telephone surveys) prepared for a special program on the Chinese ethnic economy in Canada.
Groupe d'Analyse sur les PME et les Régions (GAPMER) (1994) *Les PME au Québec: Etat de la Situation 1992–1993*. Québec: Ministère de l'Industrie, du Commerce, de la Science et de la Technologie.

Jones, T. and McEvoy, D. (1996) Commerce and context: South Asian retailers in Britain and Canada. Paper presented at the annual meeting of the Association of American Geographers, Charlotte, North Carolina, April.

Kaplan, D. (1998) The spatial structure of urban ethnic economies, *Urban Geography*, 19, pp.489–501.

Li, P. (1992) Ethnic enterprise in transition: Chinese business in Richmond, B.C. 1980–1990, *Canadian Ethnic Studies*, 24, pp.120–38.

Li, W. (1998) Los Angeles' Chinese ethnoburb: from ethnic service center to global economy outpost, *Urban Geography*, 19, pp.502–17.

Lin, J. (1995) Polarized development and urban change in New York's Chinatown, *Urban Affairs Review*, 30, pp.332–54.

—— (1998) *Reconstructing Chinatown: Ethnic Enclave, Global Change*. Minneapolis, MN: University of Minnesota Press.

Lo, L. and Wang, S. (1997) Settlement patterns of Toronto's Chinese immigrants: convergence or divergence? *Canadian Journal of Regional Science*, 20, pp.49–72.

Lo, L. and Wang, L. (2004) A political economy approach to understanding the economic incorporation of Chinese sub-ethnic groups, *Journal of International Migration and Immigration*, 5, pp.107–40.

Marger, M.N. and Hoffman, C.A. (1992) Ethnic enterprise in Ontario: immigrant participation in the small business sector, *International Migration Review*, 26, pp.968–81.

Nee, V., Sanders, J.M., and Sernau, S. (1994) Job transitions in an immigrant metropolis: ethnic boundaries and the mixed economy, *American Sociological Review*, 59, pp.849–872.

Olds, K. (1996) *Developing the Trans-Pacific Property Market: Tales from Vancouver via Hong Kong*. Research on Immigration and Integration in the Metropolis, Vancouver. Working paper 96–02.

Portes, A. and Jensen. L. (1989) The enclave and their entrants: patterns of ethnic enterprise in Miami before and after Mariel, *American Sociological Review*, 54, pp.929–49.

Razin, E. (1988) Entrepreneurship among foreign immigrants in the Los Angeles and San Francisco metropolitan regions, *Urban Geography*, 9, pp.283–301.

—— (1992) Paths to ownership of small businesses among immigrants in Israeli cities and towns, *Review of Regional Studies*, 22, pp.277–96.

Rhyne, D. (1982) *Visible Minority Business in Metropolitan Toronto: An Exploratory Analysis*. Report to the Race Relations Division, Ontario Human Rights Commission. Toronto: Institute for Behavioural Research, York University.

Saxenian, A. (1999) *Silicon Valley's New Immigrant Entrepreneurs*. San Francisco, CA: Public Policy Institute of California.

Shearmur, R.G. and Coffey, W.J. (1996) Establishment size and employment growth in the Canadian urban system 1991–1994: an exploratory analysis. *Canadian Journal of Regional Science*, 14, pp.303–31.

Statistics Canada (1999) *Custom Tabulation of 1996 Census Data*, Toronto Regional Office.

Storey, D. (1988) The role of small and medium-sized enterprises in European job creation. In M. Giaoutzi, P. Nijkamp, and D. Storey (eds.), *Small and Medium Size Enterprises and Regional Development*. London: Routledge.

Tait, D., Castles, S., Gibson, K., Collins, J., and Alcorso, C. (1989) Understanding ethnic small business: a case study of Marrickville, *Australian Journal of Social Issues*, 24, pp.83–197.

Teixeira, C. (1998) Cultural resources and ethnic entrepreneurship: a case study of the Portuguese in real estate industries in Toronto, *The Canadian Geographer*, 42, pp.267–81.

Thompson, R.H. (1989) *Toronto's Chinatown: The Changing Social Organization of an Ethnic Community*. New York: AMS Press.

Tseng, Y-F. (1994) Chinese ethnic economy: San Gabriel Valley, Los Angeles County, *Journal of Urban Affairs*, 16, pp.169–89.

Wang, S. (1996) *New Development Patterns of Chinese Commercial Activity in the Toronto CMA*. Toronto: Centre for the Study of Commercial Activity, Ryerson Polytechnic University.

Wong, T. (2000) ATI shares take a hit despite higher profits: leader chip maker sees future in set-top box, *Toronto Star* (January 14), E3.

Zhou, M. (1992) *Chinatown: the Socioeconomic Potential of an Urban Enclave*. Philadelphia, PA: Temple University Press.

Zhou, Y. (1996) "Ethnic Networks as Transactional Networks: Chinese Networks in the Producer Service Sectors of Los Angeles." Ph.D. Dissertation, University of Minneapolis.

—— (1998) Beyond ethnic enclaves: location strategies of Chinese producer service firms in Los Angeles, *Economic Geography*, 74, pp.228–51.

# Part II

# Transnational linkages and Chinese ethnic businesses

# 5 Globalization, transnationalism, and Chinese transnationalism

*Ivan Light*

An earlier generation of scholars meant by the term *diaspora* a handful of identifiable ethno-national communities, scattered around the globe, which remained in continuous, long-term contact with one another as well as with their real or putative homeland (Armstrong, 1976; Cohen, 1997: 185). That homeland constituted the hub of ethnic *diasporas*. Settlements abroad were the spokes. Thus understood, a diaspora was a geographical structure that characterized middleman minorities, not all minorities or all immigrants (Cohen, 1971). Middleman minorities are historic trading peoples that undertake commercial functions wherever they reside, who resided in host societies for generations without assimilation, and who maintained their ethno-national identity and separateness (Light and Gold, 2000: 6–8). Earlier scholars thought that only middleman minorities had or could have diasporas because only middleman minorities had the cohesiveness to endure diasporas without assimilation into host societies (Kieval, 1997). Recently, the term diaspora has been widened to include groups that have no historical identification as middleman minorities. Current research on transnationalism (Lever-Tracy and Ip, 1996; Lie, 1995; Chik, 2000) returns to many of the concerns that animated older research on historical diasporas, but, by emphasis upon globalization, opens the field of study to groups that are not historic middleman minorities.

The recent discovery of transnationalism has wrought this change in the meaning of the term diaspora. Glick Schiller *et al*. (1992) define *transnationalism* as "processes by which immigrants build social fields that link together their country of origin and their country of settlement." Immigrants who build diasporas are now dubbed "transmigrants." *Transmigrants* are resident in at least two societies between which they shuttle frequently enough to remain active participants in both, but encapsulated participants in neither. This lifestyle enables transmigrants to become and to remain comfortably bi-cultural, escaping assimilation because the springs of their foreign identity are constantly replenished and refreshed by living abroad. Proponents acknowledge that transnationalism is not new, but, they persist, in an era of globalization, transnationalism is easier to maintain than it was earlier (Foner, 2000: 176). Therefore, more people can attach themselves to the bi-cultural lifestyle formerly reserved to middleman minorities[1] (Cohen, 1997: 176). Before globalization, immigrants just assimilated to host societies; in the United

States, assimilation meant English mono-lingualism within three generations.[2] Assimilation was not an entirely free choice. In the first two decades of the twentieth century, campaigns of Americanization vilified immigrants who retained foreign languages, cultures, and identities (Higham, 1988). In the current era of multi-cultural goodwill, it is argued, immigrants are authorized to acculturate more slowly than earlier. Nonetheless, in the United States, resisting acculturation still means resisting English mono-lingualism, the terminus to which three generations of uninterrupted residence still normally lead (Portes and Hao, 1998). So long as transnationalism exists, non-middleman minorities, like the Sudanese or the Filipinos, can have a diaspora that was previously available only to middleman minorities like the Jews, Armenians, or Chinese (Gold, 1997: 410). Immigrant entrepreneurship has become much more common than it was in the past (Kloosterman and Rath, 2003).

In the historic past, as Max Weber long ago noted (1927: section 6C), diasporic communities routinely exploited the opportunities for international business that their dispersion afforded (Cohen, 1971; Light *et al.*, 1993: 38–43; Moallem, 1996; Laguerre, 1998). Middleman minorities were frequently international traders as well as local merchants. This international involvement arose because bi-lingual, bi-cultural people, who have, additionally, international social networks, have serious natural advantages in trade promotion (Collins, 1998: vol. 2, 398–9; Lever-Tracy *et al.*, 1991: xi, 113; Pécoud, 2002). First, such people more easily notice the business opportunities that cultural frontiers generate. For example, movie theaters in China until recently did not serve popcorn, which is not a traditional Chinese food. Noticing an opportunity, Chinese students abroad initiated the exportation of popcorn to China, whose movie theaters now sell popcorn.[3] Second, middleman minorities have the international social capital that supports international business (Fukuyama, 1995; Walton-Roberts and Hiebert, 1997; Wong, 1998: 95).[4] Precisely because conducted at long range, and out of the oversight of national legal institutions, international trade requires that buyers and sellers trust one another's probity and understand one another's financial standing. International social networks can provide this business service on the strength of their social capital. Finally, a diaspora's people maintain multilingual fluency that permits them to communicate in the customer's language when abroad, but in their own language when addressing co-ethnic merchants scattered around the globe. Coupled with relationships of trust, this linguistic resource solves the baffling communication problems that otherwise stymie international trade (Head and Ries, 1998: 48).

Globalization now offers diasporas to transnationals who are *not* historic middle-man minorities, thus expanding the share of immigrants who can notice and exploit international trading opportunities, making use of their international social capital (Levitt, 2001: 62; Cohen, 1997: 176; Massey *et al.*, 1993: 446). Portes *et al.* (2002) addressed the international trade business that is now conducted by overseas Dominicans, Salvadorans, and Colombians, finding that their newly acquired trans-nationalism immensely expanded the Central Americans' entrepreneurship. In their samples, transnationals represented only 5 percent of all the Central American immigrants, quite a small minority, but 58 percent of the self-employed immigrants were transnational (p. 285). None of these Hispanic immigrant groups were historic middleman minorities; but all now behave to some extent like middleman minorities. Because they were transnationals, Hispanics had social relationships of trust widely dispersed throughout their diaspora. As transnationals they also had the advantages in commerce that bi-culturalism conveys. They could communicate with Americans in English, but with co-ethnic merchants abroad in Spanish. In sum, the Central American immigrants capitalized upon the possibilities for international business that their bi-culturalism and social networks afforded, effectuating thereby a huge increase in their self-employment rate.

## RATE OF SELF-EMPLOYMENT

In a way, this result vindicates the middleman minority literature, which always insisted that diasporas afforded superior opportunities for entrepreneurship. However, middleman literature presumed that only a few groups could have diasporas because only exceptional immigrant communities could escape assimilation. Although immigrants in general have advantages in international trade, they lose their advantages when they assimilate (Head and Ries, 1998: 48). Assimilation simply wipes out diasporas by eliminating bi-culturalism. Bi-culturalism was essential if middleman merchants were to exploit the economic opportunity that diasporas afforded. On the other hand, possibly the globalization-induced extension of transnationalism to immigrants in general spells the obsolescence of the middleman minority theory because and to the extent that virtually every immigrant group now maintains a diaspora. Maintaining a diaspora, they can operate transnational business enterprises.[5] In that case, there is no longer anything unique about middleman status; and cultural heritage and ethnic resources, which were its core, no longer matter. All that matters is transnationalism.

Reviewing current literature on Chinese transnationalism, this chapter addresses that possibility, arguing that transnationalism *reduces the difference* between middleman minorities and other transnationals, but does not obliterate old distinctions. More generally, cultural heritages and ethnic resources continue to differentiate the entrepreneurship of transnational groups in contemporary diasporas and will probably continue to do so for the foreseeable future. Therefore, *Chinese* transnationalism is not identical with transnationalism in general. Transnationalism does not homogenize diverse cultural backgrounds nor create a one-size-fits-all ethnocategory called transnational. Convergences undeniably exist, but homogenization does not occur.

The scientific problem is to identify what is generically globalized about Chinese transnationalism, and what about Chinese transnationalism continues to reflect unique and distinctive Chinese cultural traditions, history, and resource endowments. Addressing that problem, this chapter examines several sources of evidence in order to initiate this kind of dialogue. The first evidence concerns inter-group differences in self-employment rates. If transnationalism equalizes entrepreneurship, all transnational groups should have comparable self-employment rates in the same diaspora whether they have or lack a middleman minority's past. In fact, this expectation proves sometimes true. Comparing Chinese and Koreans in the United States, Light and Gold (2000: 33) reported higher self-employment rates among the Koreans, Asian Indians, and Japanese, who are not historical middleman minorities, than among the Chinese, who are. Apparently, non-middleman groups can sometimes catch up with middleman minorities in this respect. On the other hand, comparing Chinese self-employment with that of Dominicans and Salvadorans, they found (p. 34) Chinese self-employment rates appreciably higher than for either newly transnational Hispanic population. Additionally, comparing Chinese-speaking and Spanish-speaking immigrants' impact upon American imports and exports, a classic middleman niche, Light (2001) found a statistically significant impact of both—but the Chinese coefficient was much larger than the Spanish. This result meant that, net of control variables, Chinese-speaking immigrants increased American trade with sending countries appreciably more than Spanish-speaking immigrants increased American trade with their own provenance. We may conclude that both Spanish-speaking immigrants and Chinese-speaking immigrants had diasporas, and these diasporas provided both with superior opportunities for entrepreneurship in international trade. Here is a convergence. Nonetheless, the historical middleman group outperformed the merely transnational group in this category "as if" the cultural legacy of business acumen added to and expanded the Chinese entrepreneurship net of the transnational status that they shared with Spanish-speaking immigrants.

## ETHNIC NICHES

If transnationalism alone governed entrepreneurship, then all transnational groups should share the same industrial niches in a host country. Again, to some extent, this expectation does materialize. After all, middleman minorities classically concentrate in international trade. Using as a measure of transnationalism, bi-lingual ability, Light (2001) found that transnational immigrants from 80 nations generally promoted the exports of the United States to their homelands in the period 1985–95. That is, when immigrant cohorts contained large proportions of bi-lingual individuals, those cohorts were associated after a five-year lag with increased exports (but not imports) to their homeland. It appears that international trade offers a convenient niche for transnationals from non-English-speaking homelands. In that sense, globalization produces another common effect among all the nations. However, comparison of the industrial niches in which transnationals cluster reveals differences that are not explained by transnationalism as well as similarities that are. Transnationals have different cultural histories, and these cultural histories affect their industrial niches abroad. The Chinese in North America and Europe are doctors of Oriental medicine, now practicing acupuncture to clienteles who are increasingly non-Chinese (Katz, 2003; Thuno, 1998: 182). Other Chinese are herbalists, supplying medication for Chinese doctors. For obvious cultural reasons, transnational Hispanics do not and cannot supply doctors of acupuncture or of Chinese pharmacy, any more, it should be added, than Chinese abroad can provide Cuban cigars. In these health-related occupations, Chinese transnationals exploit their traditional medicine, long unknown outside China, to develop a unique occupational niche that other transnational groups cannot duplicate for obvious reasons. True, Chinese transnationals also make essential use of their knowledge of and familiarity with American culture to market their medical service and pharmacological products to American patients. Chinese doctors who were *not transnational* long ago had all the medical skills required to treat American patients, but they could not do so because they lacked the ability to communicate in English, and their patients lacked understanding of Chinese medicine. Hence, being transnational is an essential part of what is required of Chinese medical personnel who now break out into new service niches. But, for all that, the Chinese medicine they provide is still an unavoidably and distinctively Chinese service that non-Chinese transnationals cannot offer.[6] Being Chinese makes the difference in this case.

In the last two decades, Chinese have developed a niche specialization in international trade in computer hardware. This trade utilizes and coordinates Chinese-language networks that distribute computer hardware, some made in China or Taiwan, all over the globe. South Asians also have developed a specialization in this niche; but all transnational immigrant groups have not done so. Evidently, transnationalism as such does not explain why the Chinese and South Asians alone among the transnationals developed *this particular niche*. Comparing the transnational Chinese with the transnational Hispanics, whom Portes *et al.* (2002) studied, one immediately confronts the divergent educational status of the various transnational groups. Chinese transnationals have engineering degrees that permit them to enter high-technology trading niches that Central American transnationals cannot (Leung, 2002). Evidently, more is required to understand the Chinese high-technology cluster than merely the fact, correct as far as it goes, that transnational and bi-cultural Chinese can market technology effectively to English speakers. Hispanic transnationals speak English too, but they do not occupy this niche.

A related argument addresses the role of real property developers in Chinese immigration. Working in tandem with Chinese and Chinese American banks, Chinese-born real property developers built and promoted Chinese suburbs in Los Angeles (Light, 2002; Chee *et al.*, 2001). The settlement of Chinese in the San Gabriel Valley, beginning in the 1970s, depended upon Chinese immigrant property developers, who identified neighborhoods available for Chinese take-over, promoted them in Taiwan and Hong Kong, and borrowed Chinese capital to effectuate their development schemes (Tseng and Zhou, 2001: 242). Here the globalization of capital requires transnational point men on the scene locally to support the successful investment policy. An equivalent property development apparatus did not develop among Hispanic immigrants in Los Angeles even though many Hispanics are transnationals too. The reasons for this inter-ethnic discrepancy are not hard to understand. Co-ethnics' concern about *feng shui* gave Chinese realtors, who understood this science, a decisive advantage over non-Chinese, when it came to selling houses to Chinese. Additionally, thanks to the economic development of Chinese societies, international Chinese banks needed local point operatives who could identify promising real estate investments in Los Angeles, interface with English-speaking local governments, and operate effectively in the American political system (Tseng, 2000: 15). While Central American trans-nationals were sufficiently bi-cultural to have performed this function for Central American banks which wanted to invest in Los Angeles real estate, no such niche developed in Central American real estate. Possibly there were no Central American banks eager to invest in Los Angeles real estate, in which case, one would conclude, Central American societies lacked the capital resources that supported transnational real property investment. For this reason, Chinese transnationals were in a position to exploit opportunities in real estate development and promotion that Central American transnationals were not. We need not linger over why Central American banks were not interested in Los Angeles real estate investments. It is not material. The essential fact is, however, that their lack of interest affected the occupational chances of Central American transnationals abroad, who could not duplicate the kind of role that Chinese real property entrepreneurs played in Los Angeles.

A similar conclusion applies to the garment manufacturing industry of Los Angeles in which Chineses provided entrepreneurs, and Hispanics provided workers. Differentially endowed with resources of education and capital, the two groups, Hispanic and Chinese, gravitated to different levels within the same industry (Light *et al.*, 1999). Transnationalism might explain why both groups found niches in this international industry, but it cannot explain why they found niches at different socio-economic levels. To explain that, we need to invoke the resource availability of the transnational cohorts, and that availability, in turn, requires us to examine the unequal development status of homelands as well as the actual migration dynamics at work in them.

## DISCUSSION

Comparing Hispanic and Chinese transnationalism, one finds points of similarity that support the inference that transnationalism trumps cultural history and home-land development. Many immigrants look somewhat transnational now. But one finds also points of substantial difference. On the one hand, their new trans-nationalism has increased the self-employment rate of Central Americans and landed them in international trade, a niche long characteristic of middleman minorities. In this sense, transnationalism has reduced the difference between the behavior of overseas Chinese and overseas Central Americans. The Central Americans have become more like the Chinese, concentrating in international business as the Chinese have long done. There is preliminary evidence too that the Chinese have moved toward bi-culturalism to an extent that greatly exceeds what was true two generations ago. Currently, Chinese transnationals and Central American transnationals can talk to one another in English, a facility that would not have been so widespread a generation ago. At this point, transnationalism has caused some convergence of Chinese and Central Americans.

On the other hand, the Chinese transnationals' occupational profile in North America displays distinctiveness born of economic conditions in Chinese societies (international banks, high technology), social background of the overseas Chinese (educational levels), and even distinctive Chinese cultural traditions (acupuncture, herbal pharmacology). It is also plausible, but not proven, that overseas Chinese entrepreneurship still obtains a boost from cultural traditions that antedate the modern era. This proposition implies that overseas Chinese entrepreneurship is greater now than overseas Central American entrepreneurship net of the independent contribution of homeland banks and personal human capital. To that extent, the cultural legacy of middleman minority status might have some continued relevance.

## CONCLUSION

Transnationalism endows more groups with bi-cultural competence today than has been possible in the past. Overseas bi-culturals resist assimilation into American society with its attendant reduction of the immigrant population to English mono-lingualism within three generations. Unlike assimilated mono-linguals, who have only their adopted homeland for living space, bi-cultural immigrants create and enjoy diasporas that permit them to move comfortably in at least two, often more, localities around the globe. As long as they can defer assimilation, bi-cultural people can perceive and exploit opportunities in international trade that were previously reserved to middleman minorities. From this point of similarity, one might suppose that transnationalism has trumped cultural heritage, economic development status, and even personal resources. But a review of evidence suggests that while transnationalism has indeed prompted some convergence in the behavior of divergent groups, it has not trumped older sources of inter-group difference. Chinese transnationalism today bears some natural resemblance to other trans-nationalisms, such as Central American, but Chinese transnationalism is still endowed with distinctive features that reflect distinctive Chinese cultural, social, and economic conditions. Evidently, transnationalism homogenizes the form of diaspora, but it leaves untouched the diaspora's specific cultural content.

## Notes

1   "Globalization has enhanced the practical, economic, and affective roles of diasporas, showing them to be particularly adaptive forms of social organization" (Cohen, 1997: 176).
2   Lieberson (1971) finds bi-lingualism in Montreal a long-term product of French and English coexistence rather than a step toward mono-lingualism.
3   The author thanks Dr. Zhong Deng for this observation.
4   "Trust and cultural affinities facilitate involvement in transnational ethnic businesses. The moment of business encounter is not solely determined by formal rationalized rules, but also by the presence of cultural codes favoring the process of trust building in business transactions. In small-scale transnational entrepreneurial activities, culture can both promote and limit business opportunities. In this context, formal and rationalized

market structures are subordinated to the economic culture of the social agents" (Moallem, 1996: 12).

5   "A transnational ethnic enterprise is defined here as a business . . . which entails separate operational components of the enterprise being located in different countries and the transmigration of the owners in order to operate it" (Wong and Ng, 2002: 514).

6   This situation may not last forever. The author knows several young Americans who are now studying traditional Chinese medicine in Beijing.

# References

Armstrong, J.A. 1976. "Mobilized and Proletarian Diasporas." *American Political Science Review* 9: 393–408.

Chee, Maria, Gary Dymski, Wei Li, and Yu Zhou. 2001. "Banking on Social Capital in the Era of Globalization: Chinese Ethnobanks in Los Angeles." *Environment and Planning A* 33: 1923–48.

Chik, Frances. 2000. "Hong Kong Chinese Immigrant Women in Business: The Impact of Transnational Networks." Paper presented at the Fifth Annual Metropolis Conference, Vancouver, Nov. 14.

Cohen, Abner. 1971. "Cultural Strategies in the Organization of Trading Diasporas." Pp. 266–84 in *The Development of Indigenous Trade and Markets in West Africa*, edited by Claude Meillassoux. London: Oxford University Press.

Cohen, Robin. 1997. *Global Diasporas*. Seattle: University of Washington Press.

Collins, Jock. 1998. "Cosmopolitan Capitalism: Ethnicity, Gender and Australian Entrepreneurs." Vols 1 and 2, PhD diss., University of Wollongong.

Foner, Nancy. 2000. *From Ellis Island to JFK: New York's Two Great Waves of Immigrations*. New York: Yale University Press and Russell Sage Foundation.

Fukuyama, Francis. 1995. "Social Capital and the Global Economy." *Foreign Affairs* 74: 89–103.

Glick Schiller, Nina, Linda Basch, and Cristina Blanc-Szanton. 1992. "Transnationalism: A New Analytic Framework for Understanding Migration." Pp. 1–24 in *Towards a Transnational Perspective on Migration*, edited by Nina Glick Schiller, Linda Basch, and Cristina Blanc-Szanton. New York: New York Academy of Science.

Gold, Steven. 1997. "Transnationalism and Vocabularies of Motive in International Migration: The Case of Israelis in the United States." *Sociological Perspectives* 40: 409–27.

Head, Keith, and John Ries. 1998. "Immigration and Trade Creation: Econometric Evidence from Canada." *Canadian Journal of Economics*, 31: 47–62.

Higham, John. 1988 [1956]. *Strangers in the Land: Patterns of American Nativism, 1860–1924*, 2d edition. New Brunswick, NJ: Rutgers University.

Katz, Marian. 2003. "Skilled and Professional International Migration and the Professionalization of Acupuncture and Oriental Medicine in Southern California." Paper presented at the Conference on the Human Face of Global Mobility, held at the University of California, Los Angeles, May 17.

Kieval, Hillel J. 1997. "Middleman Minorities and Blood: Is There a Natural Economy of the Ritual Murder Accusation in Europe?" Ch. 8 in *Essential Outsiders: Chinese and Jews in the Modern Transformation of Southeast Asia and Central Europe*, edited by Daniel Chirot and Anthony Reid. Seattle and London; University of Washington Press.

Kloosterman, Robert, and Jan Rath. 2003. "Introduction." Ch. 1 in *Immigrant*

*Entrepreneurship: Venturing Abroad in the Age of Globalization*, edited by Robert Kloosterman and Jan Rath. Oxford: Berg.

Laguerre, Michel. 1998. "Rotating Credit Associations and the Diasporic Economy." *Journal of Developmental Entrepreneurship* 3: 23–34.

Leung, Maggi W.H. 2002. "Get IT Going: New Ethnic Chinese Business. The Case of Taiwanese-owned Computer Firms in Hamburg." *Journal of Ethnic and Migration Studies* 27: 277–94.

Lever-Tracy, Constance, and David Ip. 1996. "Diaspora Capitalism and the Homeland: Australian Chinese Networks into China." *Diaspora* 5: 239–71.

Lever-Tracy, Constance, David Ip, Jim Kitay, Irene Phillips, and Noel Tracy. 1991. *Asian Entrepreneurs in Australia*. Canberra: Australian Government Publishing Service.

Levitt, Peggy. 2001. *The Transnational Villagers*. Los Angeles: University of California.

Lie, John. 1995. "From International Migration to Transnational Diaspora." *Contemporary Sociology* 24: 303–6.

Lieberson, Stanley. 1971. "Bilingualism in Montreal: A Demographic Analysis." *American Sociological Review* 41: 289–307.

Light, Ivan. 2001. "Globalization, Transnationalism, and Trade." *Asian and Pacific Migration Journal* 10: 53–80.

—— 2002. "Immigrant Place Entrepreneurs in Los Angeles." *International Journal of Urban and Regional Research* 26: 215–28.

Light, Ivan, and Steven J. Gold. 2000. *Ethnic Economies*. San Diego, CA: Academic.

Light, Ivan, Parminder Bhachu, and Stavros Karageorgis. 1993. "Migration Networks and Immigrant Entrepreneurship." Pp. 25–50 in *Immigration and Entrepreneurship*, edited by Ivan Light and Parminder Bhachu. New Brunswick, NJ: Transaction.

Light, Ivan, Richard B. Bernard, and Rebecca Kim. 1999. "Immigrant Incorporation in the Garment Industry of Los Angeles." *International Migration Review* 33: 5–25.

Massey, Douglas S., Joaquin Arango, Graeme Hugo, Ali Kouaouci, Adela Pellegrino, and J. Edward Taylor. 1993. "Theories of International Migration: A Review and Appraisal." *Population and Development Review* 19: 431–66.

Moallem, Minoo. 1996. "Transnationalism, Migrancy, and Entrepreneurship." Beatrice M. Bain Research Group and Sociology Department, University of California, Berkeley.

Pécoud, Antoine. 2002. "'Weltoffenheit schafft Jobs': Turkish Entrepreneurship and Multiculturalism in Berlin." *International Journal of Urban and Regional Research* 26: 494–508.

Portes, Alejandro, and Lingxin Hao. 1998. "E Pluribus Unum: Bilingualism and Loss of Language in the Second Generation." *Sociology of Education* 71: 269–94.

Portes, Alejandro, William J. Haller, and Luis Eduardo Guarnizo. 2002. "Transnational Entrepreneurs: An Alternative Form of Immigrant Economic Adaptation." *American Sociological Review* 67: 278–98.

Thuno, Mette. 1998. "Chinese in Denmark." *The Chinese in Europe*, edited by Gregor Benton and Frank N. Pieke. Pp. 168–96. New York: St. Martin's Press.

Tseng, Yen-Fen. 2000. "Immigrant Firms and Transnational Embeddedness: Chinese Entrepreneurs in Los Angeles." Pp. 1–20 in *Embeddedness and Corporate Change in a Global Economy*, edited by Rueyling Tseng and Brian Uzzi. New York: Peter Lange.

Tseng, Yen-Fen, and Yu Zhou. 2001. "Immigrant Economy in a Pacific Rim Context: Chinese Business in Los Angeles." Pp. 239–51 in *The Chinese Triangle of Mainland China, Taiwan, and Hong Kong: Comparative Institutional Analyses*, edited by Alvin So, Nan Lin, and Dudley Poston. Westport, CT: Greenwood Press.

Walton-Roberts, Margaret, and Daniel Hiebert. 1997. "Immigration, Entrepreneurship, and the Family: Indo-Canadian Enterprise in the Construction of Greater Vancouver." *Canadian Journal of Regional Science* 20: 119–40.

Weber, Max. 1981 [1927]. *General Economic History*. New Brunswick, NJ: Transaction.

Wong, Bernard. 1998. *Ethnicity and Entrepreneurship: The New Chinese Immigrants in the San Francisco Bay Area*. Boston: Allyn & Bacon.

Wong, Lloyd L., and Michele Ng. 2002. "The Emergence of Small Transnational Enterprise in Vancouver: The Case of Chinese Entrepreneur Immigrants." *International Journal of Urban and Regional Research* 26: 508–30.

# 6 Business social networks and immigrant entrepreneurs from China

*Janet W. Salaff, Arent Greve, and Siu-Lun Wong*

## INTRODUCTION

This chapter looks at the businesses started by a number of recent immigrants to Toronto from the People's Republic of China (PRC). These immigrants arrived as a wave of skilled workers seeking professional work. Some had established enterprises in China, others wished to start businesses in Toronto because of problems in the Canadian job market. We show the ways social networks helped them get resources to start businesses.

In recent years, researchers have singled out the importance of social networks in the business successes of diasporic Chinese (Chen, 2000; Faist, 2000; Kiong & Kee, 1998; Peng, 2000). Before emigrating, they often had family businesses, or partnerships with professional colleagues. Abroad, they draw on networks within the ethnic community, and links to their home countries. But there are limits to social network support (Chu, 1996; Portes, 1998). It takes some time for cohesive communities to emerge among immigrants, and for new immigrants to connect to such networks (Zhou *et al.*, 2002). Social networks in immigrant communities may lack a broad business base. They may be unable to connect business networks at home and abroad (Light, 1992; Rodriguez, 2000). Without these supportive networks, immigrant entrepreneurs have a narrow scope, which especially limits professional businesses.

Our study draws on a data base of 100 skilled PRC workers whom we studied over time. They immigrated to Toronto at the end of the 1990s, armed with technical and professional credentials, yet bereft of social ties. We first describe types of entrepreneurial networks and how they work. We outline the entrepreneurial backgrounds in China which can help them do business abroad. The historical patterns of Chinese immigration to Canada provide some understanding of how newcomers can build useful local business networks. We then explore the forms of entrepreneurship and the social networks our respondents use.

## ENTREPRENEURIAL NETWORKS

In contrast to earlier explanations of entrepreneurs as brave, ambitious, achieving individuals, recent entrepreneurship research focuses on the connections between founders and their communities (Aldrich, 1999). Four sorts of social networks figure in business start-ups: family, collegial, transnational, and ethnic, and Chinese participate in most of them (Wellman *et al.*, 2002; Wong & Salaff, 1998).

### Four types of entrepreneurial networks

Entrepreneurship runs in the family in many countries (Hamilton, 1991; Hsiung, 1996). Parents of nearly half of the business founders in a six-nation study ran firms of their own (Aldrich *et al.*, 1991; Greve & Salaff, 2003). One-third of Korean immigrant businessmen in Atlanta, Georgia, had relevant family firm experience before immigrating (Min, 1988: 74). Family businesses are informal teachers of running a business. They also pool funds, materials, labor, and social support, experience, and contacts for second-generation self-employment (Sanders & Nee, 1996). The efficient workings of the Chinese family economy enabled many migrants from Shanghai in the 1950s to start businesses again in Hong Kong (Hamilton & Kao, 1990; Wong, 1988). Young emigrant members of the Indian business community apprentice in a compatriot's firm abroad before starting their own (Poros, 2001).

Colleagues can give even more useful help than family for those who sell professional goods and services (Birley, 1985; Marger, 1992; Westhead, 1995). Friends and colleagues from school or earlier jobs not only can provide new business entrants with expertise, lines of credit, and links to suppliers and customers (Leonard & Tibrewal, 1993; Waldinger, 1986), but also share specialized knowledge. North American Chinese-owned IT businesses were located in a handful of communities, suggesting the clustering of knowledge (Fong, 1994).

Immigrants often draw on business communities from their home country and from the receiving country, referred to as transnational networks, our third kind of business network. The rapid development of telecommunications and business travel spurs transnational networks. Hong Kong Chinese immigrant entrepreneurs mobilize their Hong Kong-based enterprises to start businesses in British Columbia (Wong & Ng, 1998). Salvadoreans make use of their home ties to establish businesses in North American co-ethnic communities (Landolt, 2001). These transnational entrepreneurs reinvest in firms back home while remaining abroad. Other migrants may return to their original country, bringing with them new business connections. After the IT bubble burst, many Taiwanese and East Indian engineers who had worked in California's Silicon Valley returned home to invest in new software firms, armed with knowledge and contacts from their North American jobs (Mahroum, 2000; Misra, 2001; Tseng & Jou, 2000).

Migration creates momentum. As migrants pass along their experiences, other emigrants follow suit. They often congregate with co-ethnics with whom they feel comfortable, forming ethnic enclaves, a fourth kind of business network support.

An enclave has been described as a self-enclosed immigrant community (Wilson & Portes, 1980). However, Wellman (1999) argues that communities should be seen as a network which need not necessarily take a spatial form. Since an immigrant network can cross different geographical locations, we will use the term ethnic economy instead of ethnic enclave. Established migrants become newcomers' social resources in starting businesses. An immigrant community creates demand for ethnic products (Aldrich & Zimmer, 1986). The supporting ethnic community draws together resources for investment. Employers can find new employees, and customers can find the ethnic products they seek more easily (Bates, 1994; Bonacich, 1973; Light, 1992; Park, 1990; Peterson & Roquebert, 1993; Sanders & Nee, 1996; Waldinger, 1994; Zhou, 1992). Thus, the Chinese who are concentrated in New York and Los Angeles, where there are large coethnic communities, have a greater likelihood of becoming self-employed than Chinese in the United States overall (Portes & Zhou, 1999: 157).

## Structural features in business networks

By relying on network relations to help them pull together what they need to start their firms, the structure of the network affects the essential resources entrepreneurs mobilize (Gereffi, 1998). Social networks are composed of ties that people have with each other. A central feature of direct ties is their extent of overlap. Two people can share economic, friendship, or kinship roles, and thereby form multiplex networks (Granovetter, 1985; Portes & Sensenbrenner, 1993). Multiplex networks are likely to be overlaid with trust and can enforce social control. Those in densely networked circles of relations may feel obligated to meet a request for advice or funds and trust the borrower to return the favor. People may call on someone they know in a totally different context to help with a business. For these reasons, multiplex ties are useful in business. However, densely clustered social networks restrict the resources to what those in the circle can offer.

In contrast, single-stranded social networks are larger and contain more indirect ties. People often know others from different contexts, who may not know each other but still may be able to draw on each other's contacts. For instance, people with few business contacts themselves may have a friend who can introduce them to other entrepreneurs (Aldrich, 1999). Such people can reach further to get help. When networks do not connect, we say that there are structural holes between them. Those who can connect two otherwise unconnected networks bridge structural holes (Burt, 1992).

New entrepreneurs go between their different networks to start a business (Greve & Salaff, 2003). They get ideas from diverse contacts, bridging structural holes and combining resources in novel ways, which is essential to starting a profitable business (Burt, 1992). Next, to get their start-up resources, they are likely to draw on multiplex ties to obtain capital and partners, and employees who are committed to them (Greve, 1995). Finally, to develop the business further, businesspeople widen their contacts by bridging to other business circles. Business formation depends closely on structural properties of the entrepreneur's networks.

## Immigrants' business networks

In these ways, it is often thought that immigrants who take part in the ethnic economy, where their social networks are underlaid by multiplex interpersonal ties, can easily start a business. Coethnics may know the same people. Concentrated ethnic communities make social connections even more visible. Even if coethnics do not personally know each other, those who are connected through multiplex ties may share perspectives and trust, and make things easy for each other, which Light and Bonacich (1988) refer to as ethnic facilitation. Newcomers intending to do business may draw on multiplex relations for advice, information about business opportunities, access to credit, and customers, central to entrepreneurship (Aldrich, 1999; Light, 1972, 1992). For these reasons, the ethnic economy draws heavily on multiplex networks.

Ethnic bridging further widens immigrants' networks. Diverse networks can reveal structural holes and help immigrants do business. For instance, immigrants can join together previously unconnected direct and indirect ties in their countries of origin and destination (Landolt, 2001). From these historical examples and conceptual bases, researchers predict that the newest skilled immigrants from China will use social networks to start their own firms.

However, new immigrants often do not have the right kinds of contacts for setting up businesses relevant to the local scene. They are likely to face a dense network of established relations in old and mature markets, where supplier and vendor networks are institutionalized (Burt, 1992). There may be no structural holes for outsiders to fill. New immigrants who do not have contacts with non-ethnics may only be able to set up firms in their own community but not outside it. In the end, newcomers who want to go beyond the ethnic community and build contacts in the local business community cannot get in: this creates problems for professional entrepreneurs who do not sell ethnic goods.

Entrepreneurs' contacts must be embedded in a business environment (Granovetter, 1985). The challenge for new immigrants is finding social resources to start a business in a new and foreign land. Some draw on the social networks they developed before emigration to connect the new business to transnational networks. Others combine resources in the new country with those of the home country in order to create a business that appeals to the local market. If they do not expand their networks more widely, entrepreneurship remains limited to the ethnic economy.

## THE DEVELOPMENT OF PROFESSIONAL
## ENTREPRENEURIAL NETWORKS IN CHINA

Entrepreneurs draw on diverse networks at different stages of their business start-ups. Let us first consider the kinds of social networks which these professionals and skilled men and women, drawing from the societal structure and their personal life course, were likely to mobilize in China before they emigrated to Canada.

# FROM STATE-SECTOR CAREERS TO MARKET ECONOMY IN CHINA

For those from a post-Socialist country, with a short history of private enterprise, getting business inputs is particularly problematic. Since the market for labor, capital, or land is incompletely institutionalized, new entrepreneurs developed personal networks to get a wide range of inputs that elsewhere might be gotten through the market (Keister, 2000, 2001). Hence, PRC businesses today rely on social networks to pull together the needed resources for business.

Before the 1980s, people looked down upon entrepreneurs as parasites. They could not run their own firms and, at worst, former businessmen were physically attacked during successive political campaigns. While it is true that prior to the 1980s, the poorest members of the population resorted to self-foraging, petty social exchanges, and a black market to sustain a living, little of this entrepreneurial activity was considered respectable or legal.

The Chinese educational system had produced well-trained technicians and professionals, but private business was allowed only after 1978. When young professionals graduated from college, they were assigned to state-sector jobs, finished their apprenticeships, became certified, and moved up the organizational ladder. They enjoyed security and expected lifetime employment (referred to as the "iron rice bowl") in this prestigious sector. They had many perks, albeit a modest wage (Walder, 1986). State-sector employment was congruent with a tradition that valued officials and intellectuals (Li, C., 2000).

The restructuring of the Chinese economy loosened fetters on business ventures. Peasants, industrial workers, or urban youth "sent down" to villages and towns during the Cultural Revolution formed the first business enterprises. Small-scale private enterprises emerged early in manufacturing, construction, and transportation industries, followed by the professional services sector. By 1998, there were an estimated two million registered private enterprise owners. This includes enterprises of seven or more employees; smaller enterprises need not register (Unger, 1996: Zhou, 2000: 326).

Joint ventures gave the biggest push to the private sector. A joint venture is a company set up by two other firms, usually a cooperation between a private foreign firm and a Chinese public-sector firm. In this cooperative venture, joint ventures provide capital, machinery, and new products. State firms supply organizational and political networks, local know-how and labor (Pearson, 1997). State firms also second engineers and other skilled employees to joint ventures with which they have contracts.

In this manner, technocrats who had started their careers in large bureaucracies entered private enterprises as extensions of their organizational networks (Foster, 2002; Gipouloux, 2000). As joint ventures brought China into the global capitalist economy, new career opportunities emerged. State firms, joint ventures, and transnational firms sent employees abroad for meetings, contract negotiations, and training, giving many their first chance to travel outside China. Professionals got a positive view of the private sector, and were keen to develop themselves further.

As the market developed, occupational preferences changed as well. For instance, the importance of getting sales experience and business degrees for the new market economy became apparent. No longer disdaining business, many professionals left state or joint venture enterprises to start their own companies to meet new market needs. In many cases joint ventures created these niches. However, although it became easier to start private firms offering professional services in general, entrepreneurship was uneven, flourishing in some cities, for instance in Shanghai, but not Harbin (Hsu, 2002; Yeung & Li, 1999).

In this historical context, we may ask which forms of business networks entrepreneurs engage in. Upon which can they draw when they go abroad? We earlier identified four types of immigrant entrepreneur social networks: (1) family entrepreneurship, (2) collegial, organizational, and work ties, (3) transnational networks, and (4) ethnic "enclave" or ethnic community networks. The first two types are rooted in social structures in China. The third type of network connects the two countries. Participating as an ethnic minority in a foreign land, the fourth, is chiefly an immigrant scenario.

Family entrepreneurship is historically recent. Young professionals and skilled workers are not likely to get training, contacts, or funds from family firms. However, in the few years during which private enterprises were launched, many entre-preneurs left state firms, agencies, or joint ventures to start a business of their own (Pearson, 1997). They retain close ties with, and get licenses, orders, materials, and funding through, these organizational and political networks (Wank, 1999). Often, small entrepreneurs mobilize colleagues to share the financing risks, since it is hard to raise loans from state banks. They hire those with whom they had once worked, and get accounts from former clients as well. Having worked in the field alerts them to shortages of many commodities and services, and they bridge structural holes to provide them. Chinese professionals mainly start businesses through such organizational, career-based, and collegial networks.

In the third form of social support for entrepreneurship, Chinese businesses are starting to network internationally (Chen, 2000; Yeung, 2000; Zhou, 2000). Even state firms are beginning to work with private enterprises abroad.

The social structure of business in China fosters particular business combinations for those selling professional goods and services. Family firms are least common, and entrepreneurs establish firms based on networks from their prior employers and professions. Private firms may set up international links. Young emigrants in our study who draw on China-based ties to assist them with entrepreneurship abroad are likely to choose one of these three main forms.

## WAVES OF CHINESE IMMIGRATION TO CANADA

The structure of ethnic community networks shapes how new immigrants establish businesses. Coethnics may extend or withhold help. We pinpoint two key elements in the structure of the immigrant community: first, whether community members identify with each other; second, the ethnic economy in which they hope to participate. These variables affect how much help the Toronto Chinese community can extend to men and women who wish to set up businesses after immigrating from the PRC.

## The ethnic community

The timing of migration, the social class of the migrants, and their dialect, or sub-ethnic backgrounds, shape the cohesiveness of the ethnic community (Benton & Gomez, 2000). Chinese immigration in Canada has a particularly varied history. There have been breaks and sharp shifts in Chinese migration. As a result, Chinese do not form a single diaspora. They come from diverse dialect groups and places, and even those from the same original area came at different times and represent different cohorts (Luk & Li, 1996; Wong, 1999). Such diverse backgrounds affect how helpful the local community is, and whether it will reach out to these newest immigrants from China who want to start a business.

Limited by Canadian racial-based policies, mainland Chinese trickled into Canada in the middle of the twentieth century. Entry was virtually halted by the Pacific War, the break in political relations between the People's Republic of China and the United States, and subsequent Chinese isolation (Boyd & Vickers, 2000; Li, 2002; Zhao, 2002). After the end of WWII, there was a modest increase in immigration as families reunited. Until this point, Chinese immigrants from the mainland were the longest-residing Chinese in Canada. However, after the 1949 Chinese revolution, those who had arrived prior to the 1950s were separated from their homeland. For those who came afterwards, mainland China was not their last place of residence.

The introduction of the points system in Canadian immigration policies in 1967 was a turning point for skilled Chinese without Canadian kin, who became eligible to immigrate. Hong Kong residents were the earliest and most numerous of the Chinese populations to take advantage of the broadened immigration criteria. Through 1998, numerous Hong Kong students studied in Canadian institutions and many graduates found jobs and later became citizens. Many Hong Kong Chinese in the skilled worker and business categories immigrated surrounding the 1997 political reversion of Hong Kong to China. Hong Kong Chinese have since built up a number of dense residential communities with varied businesses (Li, 1993).

The June 4, 1989, Tiananmen incident sparked a new influx from the mainland. An estimated 6,000 Chinese students already in Canada were permitted to remain (Zweig & Chen, 1995). However, this policy was short-lived. The current influx of educated Chinese from the PRC marks a new flow of immigrants from mainland China. In the mid-1990s, China relaxed the residential permit system, allowed freedom of movement, and eased restrictions on passport applications. When Canadian regulations permitted independent applicants from the PRC to apply like any other population, numbers swelled. By 1998, mainland Chinese had become the largest body of migrants. The urban educated with tertiary schooling who enter as independent immigrants are most typical (Liang, 2001). The professionals in this study are part of this flow.

As a result of starts and stops in Chinese migration, the experiences and statuses of Chinese residents in Toronto are highly varied (Benton & Gomez, 2000; Luk, 1999). PRC immigrants do not share a common language, education, or other cultural background with those from Hong Kong or Taiwan. They may live nearby and shop at the same Chinese stores, but they do not share the same social space. They do not share a common identity with their Hong Kong brethren. Peter Li (1993) concludes that local Chinese businesses in Canada have diversified beyond the narrow catering business of fast food outlets and restaurants into diverse sectors. Nevertheless, while Chinese from Hong Kong may extend PRC professionals a place in their firms as workers, it will take more time for them to take them in as partners. Their unequal resources may lead to exploitative exchanges (Kwong, 1998). Although there is limited research, we suspect that Chinese networks in Toronto are not multiplex. Mutual help may not be forthcoming.

Mainland refugees from the June 4th Tiananmen incident and recent PRC immigrants do share an identity. However, their needs differ. Nor do the earlier compatriots have a lot of resources. Sympathetic, they are unable to give much help in starting a business to newly arrived professionals from China (Li, 2000).

## Social networks of professional businesses

Building a professional business requires helpful ties, that arise from widely ranging diverse circles. We stress here mainly business networks. Professionals usually call upon colleagues and organizations more than kinship. Coethnic ties are less likely to support entrepreneurship. Professional ties are also built up over time, through a wide range of historical contacts. Families' friends or professional schoolmates may come forward with resources useful to the entrepreneurial. Newcomers to a country cannot count on easily locating such ties.

Apart from business networks, the theme of this chapter, we also note that establishing a firm based on a profession requires more than personal ties. Social structures must fit the immigrants' needs. Key professional associations routinely exclude those who trained and qualified internationally. Hence new immigrants from these professions have to jump hurdles to become certified, creating further burdens to some businesspeople (Salaff *et al.*, 2002). Bank loans may not be forthcoming. Lines of supply and demand are well established, and hard for newcomers to break into.

Even older Chinese immigrants may not be well integrated into local professional institutions. How then can newcomers access diverse networks of professionals? The difficulty of newcomers in making inroads into local professional sectors is a central dilemma.

Current PRC skilled worker immigrants are pioneers. Forging their own paths, they rely little on established migration chains, although they may produce them. Entry to Canada is a defining event that unifies them, but may not provide enough support for business start-ups. To whom do new, skilled immigrants who want to start a business in Canada turn for help? Can their networks provide resources to start a business?

## SAMPLE AND METHODS

We studied 100 immigrants (50 married couples) from the People's Republic of China (PRC) with high education and skills. Our interviews focus on how they go about re-establishing their careers in Canada.

When we met them, respondents were between the ages of 25 and 50, with young families, and had arrived since the late 1990s. We selected this demographic group because we wanted to learn how people with modest financial resources (they were not business immigrants) and who had to earn a living found work. We recruited most of our sample soon after they arrived, and traced the business and employment experiences of our sample from point of landing to the point at which they become citizens.

We drew half of our sample from the rosters of a large non-governmental organization (NGO) in Toronto serving new immigrants and half by snowball sampling. We recruited half from the NGO, and these respondents in turn introduced us to others who were eligible for our study.

In this chapter we discuss solely those who have done business in China or Canada. We define an entrepreneur as a person who establishes, runs, and assumes the risk of an enterprise by either investing or registering a firm (Aldrich *et al.*, 1989; Wilken, 1979). This definition follows the North American research tradition, as well as Revenue Canada tax rules. Those in the preparatory stage, working on a business plan, are not considered entrepreneurs in this chapter.

We conducted semi-structured interviews with each couple (each lasting from two to three hours), collecting work and family histories. We followed up one and two years later to learn of their progress in the job and business markets.

The immigrants in our sample embody considerable human capital, reflecting the requirements of Canadian immigration policy. In 46 of the couples, husbands were the chief applicants. They had relatively more technical education and skills than their wives, and were also more keen on emigrating.

The men had technical and professional degrees, mostly in engineering and science subjects. A minority had studied in non-engineering fields. Almost all held university degrees, with many having M.Sc. and Ph.D. degrees. Wives were also educated, and majored in diverse fields such as accounting, library science, nursing, medicine, and foreign languages.

It might be useful to consider the biases of this sample. These immigrants embody considerable human capital, reflecting the Canadian immigration policy. They turned to the NGO primarily for help developing their résumé and job-finding skills. The agency's rosters are undoubtedly slanted towards those who have few contacts who can furnish them with job leads, suggesting their limited social networks. Certainly those most frustrated in their job search had most reason to sign up for a workshop. Nevertheless, while we do not claim that the sample represents the entire new arrivals from China, they can help us to learn how those with slim social resources start businesses in a new land.

**RESULTS**

## Doing business in China

Having trained as professionals and technically skilled workers, these men and women had more varied careers than before in Chinese history. After graduation, most respondents took jobs in their fields of study in state organizations. At the time they entered the labor force and developed their careers, these structures were undergoing change, and they could chart new courses. By the time they left China, 38 men and 15 women worked in joint ventures or private firms. Although private business is new in China, 12 men went on to begin full-time businesses of their own.

Their occupation, location, and organizational contacts prompted opportunities to open a business. Engineers were among the earliest to take jobs in joint ventures, after which some started firms of their own. Non-professionals in marketing and sales jobs who were also exposed to the private sector opened firms of their own early on. Eventually, professional and technically skilled employees in a wide range of occupations saw a chance to become entrepreneurs.

It should be pointed out that the majority did not entertain running businesses. Doctors, teachers and professors, and scientists, among other professionals, preferred careers in large state and private-sector organizations. However, as restructuring gained momentum, state-sector firms downsized. Soon state concerns privatized, and their employees entered the private sector.

Leaving the iron rice bowl was risky and couples wanted a fixed income on which to depend (Lee, 2000). Wives earned good livings in state positions. Since they also had to take care of children, including education, and husbands and other kin, they were willing to remain in the less arduous state sector. Only men could work long hours establishing a market-based firm (Salaff & Greve, 2001).

## Entrepreneurship networks in China

None of our respondent couples' families had mature businesses. Nevertheless, within a few years after our couples entered the labor market, as many as 16 had parents or siblings who became entrepreneurs. Private enterprise was in the air, stimulating both generations. Most of their parents' businesses were linked to agriculture or village crafts. For instance, the father of a bank employee in China was a petty trader, buying coal, processing it, and selling it as coke to village vendors. This type of business did not attract our educated respondents.

Only one couple's parents ran a modern manufacturing firm. The firm's founder, who had a B.Sc. in chemistry, went from a state to a joint venture, and on to his own factory making paint solvent. He hired both his children, including his daughter, an accountant with an overseas MBA, and her husband with an M.Sc. in biochemistry, who were our respondents. Our respondent couple left their first jobs in order to manage a branch of the family firm. They then emigrated to Canada, to help arrange suppliers and buyers for the products of the parent firm. At the same time, the husband took an M.Sc. in computer science, and the wife a second accounting degree. Subsequently, the founder had a heart attack and the husband returned to Guangzhou and assumed a central role in his father-in-law's business. Unusual in our sample, these transnational activities may presage future activities of others.

Rather than following the lead of family firms, most of our graduates in engineering, computer science, and others started businesses within their professional fields. They partnered with colleagues. They designed, manufactured, assembled, or marketed products in such diverse fields as pharmaceuticals, computer software, water-treatment chemicals, and rugs. One entered the property business to get quick returns. They drew their employees or clients and ideas of products from earlier jobs. Those who knew about their earlier achievements gave financial backing.

## Case study

Shanghai businesses became connected to the global market early on, and many found dynamic opportunities around them to do business (Gu & Tang, 2002). On graduation from a two-year college course in English in Shanghai, Jin was slated to become a teacher. He instead sought a more dynamic job in Shanghai's large transportation industry. Jin's parents were managers in state-sector firms, and knew many people. The husband of Jin's mother's colleague told Jin of an opening in the state transportation firm where he worked. Jin's strength in English fitted its business development needs and he passed the interview. This big company provided opportunities for further training, and Jin moved from sea freight to air cargo. The unit was transferred to a newly set-up joint venture, and Jin became department manager. As opportunities opened up, Jin thought he could progress faster on his own. He and two colleagues set up a transportation company, each in charge of air, sea, and sales operations. Unable to get a bank loan, Jin borrowed 2 million rmb (Chinese dollars) to start up from a dozen of his friends. "They all knew that it was a sure win since I had the contacts and was not starting from scratch." Drawing from the customer pool he had built, he had recruited 30 staff by the time he emigrated. We asked, "Do you need *guanxi* [networks] to set up your business?" "Of course you need *guanxi*. You always find friends of friends to help. It's subtle. I myself didn't even need to reach out to ask. Sometimes they come to you to initiate the help. I didn't need to pay or bribe them. We just ate and entertained together and talked, and things got done afterwards." Profits were high and he repaid the loan in a short time. However, as business became more competitive, Jin considered expanding in another direction. "Why emigrate? The biggest transportation business is in North America. I always wanted to develop something in the North American market. I was quite enthusiastic about coming." Although Jin emigrated to increase the avenues of his firm, he became an ordinary employee. He was still in his area of expertise, in a seven-person department working on Asian shipping orders for a European shipping company. His manager was a long-term Hong Kong immigrant and the rest were mainland immigrants. He did not reveal that he owned a company. "Of course I wouldn't tell since I just applied for a low position. I said I was a manager in my company." He spent a month becoming familiar with the local standards by doing daily operations. In a small way, he links his original business to his present one. "Now the Shanghai company uses us as transportation agency in Canada. But the Canadian company only knows that I used to work there . . ." He did not have any future business plan for the time being. By becoming an employee, Jin can only suggest areas in which one firm can become a client of another. As Jin's case suggests, it is a long process to link businesses together.

In China, our professional and skilled employees started up businesses through career-based networks. They developed markets for products whose need was suggested by their jobs, and drew on colleagues for wide-ranging help. To start a firm of their own in Canada is harder.

## Doing business in Canada

There is considerable interest in doing business in Canada, and many couples take a hand at it, and this point is crucial. But without local networks, these new-comers cannot set up businesses in their professional career lines. Whereas in China, colleagues helped co-finance their business, previous clients provided markets, and they hired their co-workers from earlier jobs, in Canada, few can still tap those social networks. Nor do newcomers have the local contacts they need to set up a business, making it hard to build new social networks that might aid entrepreneurship.

### *Poverty of local networks*

Immigrants in the skilled worker category arrive through their own efforts. They do not need jobs or kin in Canada to be admitted. As a result, being newcomers, our respondents are not embedded in multiplex relations that are committed to help with business.

Eleven couples knew no one at all in North America before landing. Close kin (the husband's father, the wife's sister) preceded only two couples to Toronto. The remaining 38 couples had one or more acquaintances in Canada. Some had known them in China. Others asked around after deciding to emigrate until they located distant acquaintances in Toronto.

Contacts who came in the late 1980s extended some help. One respondent's engineering professor, now behind the counter of a small corner grocery store, hired our respondent couple at weekends. An employee of IBM in China, who contacted former IBM employees, had more recent contacts before arriving, who gave him job searching advice. Former classmates from a Shanghai MBA program formed a social group. More distant links brought them: someone a neighbor knew, a daughter's primary school classmate's parents, the wife's father's friend. Others contacted complete strangers through the Internet: the listserv of PRC Chinese students at the University of Toronto turned up people who met them at the airport and found them a temporary place to live. By helping the newer immigrants in small ways, their own countrymen started building a community.

Few respondent couples have local contacts that can serve as business resources. First, few of these were involved in reciprocal relationships that might underwrite a business venture (Faist, 2000). Moreover, well known or not, not many are well placed to help them in their professional ventures. Most acquaintances also arrived recently, and had little time to establish themselves. These contacts were not embedded in local networks that could provide resources for our respondents' business ventures.

## *Types of businesses*

Lacking helpful business networks, there is little continuity between running a business in China and Canada. In most cases, neither the product, the persons, nor the underlying business networks are the same or complementary.

Of those who currently do business in Toronto full time:

- nine work as individuals;
- four husband and wife couples run ventures together, in the kitchen and behind the counter of fast food and corner stores, as marketers for consumer products.

We have not included in our count:

- two men who remain in China running their business full time, while their wives and children live and work in Toronto. They are colloquially called "astronauts," because they fly so often between their families and their businesses;
- two in the early planning stages of setting up transnational firms between China and North America in their original professions;
- several part-timers who sell on their own account, while working full time for another firm;
- and two have closed down their failing registered companies.

*Who does business?* There is little continuity between running a business in China and Canada. Although several had hoped to expand their business abroad, they have not done so. Local knowledge of product niches, and the variety of contacts needed to start businesses, are barriers.

This lack of continuity is seen when comparing those who ran businesses in China with Canadian entrepreneurs. Six former businessmen immigrated with the idea of connecting markets in China to those in Canada, but have not succeeded in rebuilding their professional networks like those who had supported their business in China. Three of the 12 who had done business in China also run businesses in Toronto, but their products changed completely. Ten new entrepreneurs had not intended to open businesses, but after several bad labor jobs, they started small stores.

*What they do.* In contrast to China, where our professional entrepreneurs in China made and sold products and services that were based on their professions, in Canada most businesses depart from their owners' professional education.

*Their business networks.* Most do business as sole proprietors who registered their own firms. This contrasts with China, in which most had partnerships with colleagues. Lacking backers, they choose products with low start-up costs. The majority engage in marketing and sales ventures affiliated with larger companies. For instance, they are concentrated in work as multi-level marketers affiliated with an American-based firm selling health products. Finally, four independent business-people sell insurance, stocks, and other financial products affiliated with a large North American insurance corporation. These ventures do not need much capital to get started, and ease of entry makes this the largest group.

Other proprietorships which include property and equipment, such as an office, bedrooms, or fixtures, cost more and are harder to enter. Among our sample, such sole proprietors include two hostels that rent rooms to new immigrants, and four small food industry outlets. For instance, two former engineers, whose wives were accountants, are now in the catering business. Selling stir-fry vegetables in small malls has little to do with their training. "We did not even cook much at home," said one wife from behind the counter in her fast food outlet. They trained for a month to learn the ropes from their former proprietor.

Three draw on transnational professional contacts to run a business in their line of training. A chemical saleswoman started training programs for PRC chemists to support the clients of the multinational employer for which she had worked. A former engineer raises capital from former colleagues to invest in the steam machinery company in which he is employed in Toronto. The founder of a chemical company in China sought new contacts abroad through his daughter and son-in-law's immigrant status. In transnational enterprises like these small ventures, they did not need to advance much capital. However, without international contacts, few as yet have such opportunities.

The rest start businesses serving the ethnic community. They draw on their ethnic cultural capital, not professional achievements. They sell products identified with their community; their supply lines or clients are Chinese. Their small businesses are on the margins of the economy and employ only family members. To launch the business, they borrow capital from kin and draw on their own savings, supplemented by small business loans. For these highly trained professionals, such enterprises reflect desperation, not choice.

To establish a professionally meaningful business in Toronto, new PRC immigrants must find a niche, or bridge structural holes. Three accounts reveal some of the difficulties doing so: (1) an engineer acted as a broker between suppliers and vendors in water treatment equipment in China, but could not broker networks in Canada; (2) a former pediatrician in China, who cannot practice in Ontario, opened a hostel and also sells cosmetics and health products to new immigrants; (3) a former saleswoman of pharmaceutical products is meeting the need for professionals in the PRC to get training in Toronto.

## (1) An engineer doing business in China, without networks in Canada

Liu, an engineer and former businessman, desired to start his own firm in Canada. Graduating from a hydroelectric institute, Liu was first assigned to a state-owned power plant, then transferred to its research institute as project manager. He worked closely with an official in the state power bureau. When the bureau joined a joint venture (JV) that supplied equipment to water treatment projects, the official appointed Liu to head its technical department. The department dealt with American suppliers of chemical water treatment products. When Liu and his colleague quit the JV to set up their own company, they became a dedicated agent to one of them. "There is a kind of connection with my former experience . . . During our work, we found no people doing business in this field, so we thought we'd found a gap and could try . . . But although the products were the same, the work was not. Our company sells chemicals for water treatment, it's different from doing engineering projects." They rented an office with a downstairs warehouse. Former colleagues from his first two jobs directed prospective customers from other companies to them. "Our biggest problem was that we had little experience dealing with the tax department and the industrial and trading departments. We solved it by asking people who knew those things to help us lobby. We looked for acquaintances—whoever we could find. In China, you must have some acquaintances."

As an immigrant, this former self-employed engineer looked in vain for ways to extend his former firm to Canada. Liu became a process design assistant in a small Canadian-owned company that handles water treatment. "I've thought of setting up my own business in Canada, but not all the conditions exist and it seems impossible. First is language. You must communicate very well with others . . . Then you should know how people here do business, and if there is a market here . . . Relationships are important, of course." In China, a setting abundant in structural holes, Liu established connections to new companies that needed to set up supplier–vendor relations. He turned his rich relations to the task of finding and bridging structural holes. In Canada, Liu was hired because of his experience, but without the same rich fabric of ties, he could not find a niche to start up on his own. Newcomers face a business setting with supplier–vendor relations that are already institutionalized, and which they do not know how to access. In the end, Liu may be satisfied to remain an employee in his field.

## (2) Transformation of professional to entrepreneur

The credentials of Lei Min, a pediatrician, and her husband, a mechanical engineer, were not recognized in Canada. After several manual labor jobs, they ended as unskilled clerical workers in a large warehouse. The couple devoted themselves to the PRC immigrant community. Volunteering in local agencies gave them a large network of friends who became their support. Lei Min started her entrepreneurial career by opening their roomy house to rent rooms to new immigrants, a natural fit to their volunteer work. Their enterprise drew on family labor and money from the kin group. Well-off kin in China lent them small sums for the down payment and renovations of their house. Their 13-year-old daughter spent her summer holiday answering phone calls and greeting guests. Guests, who learn about the hostel from their home page, Internet ads, and articles in local Chinese papers, are met at the airport. After the new immigrants eat their first breakfast of familiar rice congee, Lei Min passes on a detailed checklist of how to apply for a social insurance number, bank account, and provincial health card, and gives them transportation tokens and a city map. In their first few months of operation, they received 20 guests from China. "We believe we can be of some help to the new immigrants by owning a house."

Next, Lei Min became an agent selling dietary supplements and household products for an American multi-level marketing company. She markets the products mainly to Chinese immigrants. Drawing on her medical know-how, she advises clients to balance their personal regimen. Cultural norms and trust surround this unregulated arena and she promotes her medical skills to the ethnic community. Lei Min finds dual purpose in helping Chinese immigrants adjust to Canadian life and earning her living from their success. "It's not that I'm making friends because I want to do business. It is because we are friends that I share business with them." Lei Min's Canadian-Chinese grass-roots social networks start enterprises that draw on knowledge from but do not build a career in medicine.

### (3) Establishing a transnational business

Cathay, also a newcomer to business, could not find good employment in Canada until she opened a business to train Chinese colleagues in Canadian firms. After her BS, Cathay worked in a state-owned enterprise in the pharmaceutical industry, then in a Sino-Belgian pharmaceutical firm, where she marketed non-prescription drugs wholesale to hospitals and other large organizations. After Cathay and her husband emigrated to Canada, the company contacted her to undertake trans-national training. They desired professionals from China to take short courses from Canadian experts in China and Canada. The University of Toronto School of Medicine ran a workshop to market their services. From them, Cathay learned how to find medical practitioners, others in the field of pharmaceuticals, and those making policy on new drugs to run workshops for Chinese professionals. She is one of the few in our study who has used her connection with her field in China to start a new transnational business, an example of spanning a structural hole (Burt, 1992). Cathay is a respondent who has opened a business based on her past training. Is this the future of entrepreneurship for our Chinese respondents? Or is she an unusual case?

Their stories reveal the importance of social connections in entrepreneurship. Most of the PRC immigrants we met through our study who have started a business provide low value added, non-professional services on the periphery of the Canadian market. Without broad-ranging social contacts that match their professional skills and interests, they cannot set up a business in their line of work in Canada.

## DISCUSSION AND CONCLUSIONS

We explore how those starting businesses use four forms of business social networks. In China, some had exposure to entrepreneurship, starting businesses that drew on professional contacts. In Canada, excluded from their professions, and without social networks built over past years, most work outside their professions. They instead tap into the ethnic market. Such endeavors are small scale, arduous, and do not have a chance to develop far into the future.

Doing business proved daunting for these professionals and skilled immigrants. Those who had formerly provided professional services could neither move their Chinese-based resources to Canada, nor graft their businesses onto Canadian roots. Consequently, there is little continuity between those who tried entrepreneurship, their businesses, and the social networks that underlay these in China and Canada.

These attempts at starting new businesses in Canada underscore how networks contain resources. Most of our respondents' Canadian networks support firms that are easily set up and dismantled. To establish viable professional businesses in the new country, immigrant entrepreneurs need professional certification and recognition, and they need to become integrated into local business networks, and build trust and legitimacy. Without connections to local business networks, they have trouble finding structural holes to bridge different network clusters.

## References

Aldrich, Howard. 1999. *Organizations Evolving*. Thousand Oaks, CA: Sage.

Aldrich, Howard and Zimmer, Catherine. 1986. "Entrepreneurship through social networks." Pp. 3–23 in D. Sexton and R. Smiler (eds.), *The Art and Science of Entrepreneurship*. New York: Ballinger.

Aldrich, Howard E., Kalleberg, Arne, Marsden, Peter, and Cassell, James. 1989. "In pursuit of evidence: Sampling procedures for locating new businesses." *Journal of Business Venturing*, 4: 367–86.

Aldrich, Howard, Birley, Sue, Dubini, Paolo, Greve, Arent, Johannisson, Bengt, Reese, Pat R., and Sakano, Tomoaki. 1991. "The generic entrepreneur? Insights from a multinational research project." Paper presented at the Babson Conference on Entrepreneurship.

Bates, Timothy. 1994. "Social resources generated by group support networks may not be beneficial to Asian immigrant-owned small businesses." *Social Forces*, 72: 671–89.

Benton, Gregor and Gomez, Edmund Terence. 2000. "Chinatown and transnationalism." Paper presented at "International Conference on Immigrant Societies and Modern Age Education," Singapore.

Birley, Sue. 1985. "The role of networks in the entrepreneurial process." *Journal of Business Venturing*, 1(1): 107–17.

Bonacich, Edna. 1973. "The theory of middleman minorities." *American Sociological Review*, 38: 983–44.

Boyd, Monica and Vickers, Michael. 2000. "100 years of immigration in Canada." *Canadian Social Trends*, 58: 2–12. Statistics Canada.

Burt, Ronald. S. 1992. *Structural Holes: The Social Structure of Competition.* Cambridge, MA: Harvard University Press.

Chen, Xiangming. 2000. "Both glue and lubricant: Transnational ethnic social capital as a source of Asia-Pacific subregionalism." *Policy Sciences*, 33(3–4): 269–87.

Chu, Priscilla. 1996. "Social network models of overseas Chinese entrepreneurship: The experience in Hong Kong and Canada." *Revue Canadienne des Sciences de l'Administration/Canadian Journal of Administrative Sciences*, 13: 358–65.

Faist, Thomas. 2000. *The Volume and Dynamics of International Migration and Transnational Social Spaces*, Oxford: Clarendon Press.

Fong, Timothy P. 1994. *The First Suburban Chinatown: The Remaking of Monterey Park, California.* Philadelphia, PA: Temple University Press.

Foster, Kenneth W. 2002. "Embedded within state agencies: Business associations in Yantai." *China Journal*, 47: 41–65.

Gereffi, Gary. 1998. "Commodity chains and regional divisions of labor: Comparing East Asia and North America." Paper presented at the International Sociological Association (ISA) conference (Montreal).

Gipouloux, Francois. 2000. "Network and guanxi: Towards an informal integration through common business practices in Greater China." In Chan Kwok Bun (ed.), *Chinese Business Networks: State, Economy and Culture*: 57–70. Singapore: Prentice Hall and Nordic Institute of Asian Studies.

Granovetter, Mark. 1985. "Economic action and social structure: The problem of embeddedness." *American Journal of Sociology*, 91: 481–510.

Greve, Arent. 1995. "Networks and entrepreneurship—an analysis of social relations, occupational background, and the use of contacts during the establishment process." *Scandinavian Journal of Management*, 11(1): 1–24.

Greve, Arent and Salaff, Janet W. 2003. "Social networks and entrepreneurship." *Entrepreneurship: Theory and Practice*, 28(1): 1–22.

Gu, Felicity Rose, and Tang, Zilai. 2002. "Shanghai: Reconnecting to the global economy." In Saskia Sassen (ed.), *Global Networks, Linked Cities*. New York: Routledge: 273–307.

Hamilton, Gary (ed.). 1991. *Business Groups and Economic Development in East Asia.* Hong Kong: Centre of Asian Studies, University of Hong Kong.

Hamilton, Gary and Kao, Chengshu. 1990. "The institutional foundations of Chinese business: The family firm in Taiwan." *Comparative Social Research*, 2: 135–51.

Hsiung, Ping-Chun. 1996. *Living Rooms as Factories: Class, Gender, and the Satellite Factory System in Taiwan.* Philadelphia, PA: Temple University Press.

Hsu, Carolyn. 2002. "Interpreting the new business class in market socialist China: The narrative construction of GETIHU in Harbin." Paper delivered at Annual Meeting of the American Sociological Association, Chicago, 2002.

Keister, Lisa A. 2000. "The social basis of economic structure: Capital structure and the emergence of China's financial market 1980–1989." Paper delivered at Annual Meeting of the American Sociological Association.

———. 2001. "Exchange structures in transition: Lending and trade relations in Chinese business groups." *American Sociological Review*, 66: 336–60.

Kiong, Tong Chee and Kee, Yong Pit. 1998. "Guanxi bases, xinyong and Chinese business networks." *British Journal of Sociology*, 49(1): 75–96.

Kwong, Peter 1998. *Forbidden Workers: Illegal Chinese Immigrants and American Labor.* New York: New Press.

Landolt, Patricia. 2001. "Salvadoran economic transnationalism: Embedded strategies for household maintenance, immigrant incorporation, and entrepreneurial expansion." *Global Networks*, 1: 217–41.

Lee, Ming-kwan, 2000. "The decline of status in China's transition from Socialism," *Hong Kong Journal of Sociology*, 1(1): 53–82.

Leonard, Karen and Tibrewal, Chandra. 1993. "Asian Indians in southern California: Occupations and ethnicity." In I. Light and P. Bhachu (eds.), *Immigration and Entrepreneurship: Culture, Capital, and Ethnic Networks*: 141–62. New Brunswick, NJ: Transaction Publishers.

Li, Cheng. 2000. "'Credentialism' versus 'entrepreneurism': Interplay and tension between technocrats and entrepreneurs in the reform era." Pp. 86–111 in Chan Kwok Bun (ed.), *Chinese Business Networks: State, Economy and Culture*. Singapore: Prentice Hall and Nordic Institute of Asian Studies.

Li, Peter S. 1993. "Chinese investment and business in Canada: Ethnic entrepreneurship reconsidered." *Pacific Affairs*, 66: 219–43.

——. 2000. "Overseas Chinese network: A reassessment." Pp. 261–84 in Chan Kwok Bun (ed.), *Chinese Business Networks: State, Economy and Culture*. Singapore: Prentice Hall and Nordic Institute of Asian Studies.

——. 2002. *Destination Canada: Immigration Debates and Issues*. Toronto: Oxford.

Liang, Zai. 2001. "Demography of illicit emigration from China: A sending country's perspective." *Sociological Forum*, 16: 677–701.

Light, Ivan Hubert. 1972. *Ethnic Enterprise in America; Business and Welfare among Chinese, Japanese, and Blacks*. Berkeley, CA: University of California Press.

——. 1992. *Immigrant Networks and Immigrant Entrepreneurship*. Los Angeles: Institute for Social Science Research, University of California, Los Angeles.

Light, Ivan Hubert and Bonacich, Edna. 1988. *Immigrant Entrepreneurs: Koreans in Los Angeles, 1965–1982*. Berkeley, CA: University of California Press.

Luk, Bernard and Li, Fatima. 1996: "*The Chinese Expansion and the World Today: North American Experience*," Proceedings of an International Symposium of the Centre for Area Studies, Keio University, December 2–3, 1994.

Luk, Chiu-Ming. 1999. "Ethnic succession in suburban Toronto: The case of the Chinese." Pp. 196–232 in Yen-Fen Tseng, Chilla Bulbeck, Lan-Hung Nora Chiang, and Jung-Chung Hsu (eds.), *Asian Migration: Pacific Rim Dynamics*. Monograph 1. Interdisciplinary Group for Australian Studies, National Taiwan University, Taipei, Taiwan.

Mahroum, Sami. 2000. "Highly skilled globetrotters: Mapping the international migration of human capital." *R&D Management*, 30(1): 23–31.

Marger, Martin N. 1992. "Ethnic enterprise in Ontario: Immigrant participation in the small business sector." *International Migration Review*, 26: 968–81.

Min, Pyong Gap. 1988. *Ethnic Business Enterprise: Korean Small Business in Atlanta*. New York: Center for Migration Studies.

Misra, Nikki. 2001. "IT firms fire workers in the US but shift jobs to India." *Indus Business Journal*, 1(5): 1–11.

Park, Kyeyoung. 1990. "The Korean American dream: Ideology and small business in Queens." Ph.D. thesis, Dept. of Anthropology, City University of New York.

Pearson, Margaret. 1997. *China's New Business Elite*. Berkeley, CA: University of California Press.

Peng, Dajin. 2000. "Ethnic Chinese business networks and the Asia-Pacific economic integration." *Journal of Asian and African Studies*, 35: 229–50.

Peterson, Mark F. and Roquebert, Jaime. 1993. "Success patterns of Cuban-American enterprises: Implications for entrepreneurial communities." *Human Relations*, 46: 921–37.

Poros, M. 2001. "The role of migrant networks in linking global labor markets: The case of Asian Migration to New York and London." *Global Networks*, 1(3): 243–59.

Portes, Alejandro. 1998. "Social capital: Its origin and applications in modern society." *Annual Review of Sociology*: 1–24.

Portes, Alejandro and Sensenbrenner, Julia. 1993. "Embeddedness and immigration: Notes on the social determinants of economic action." *American Journal of Sociology*, 98: 1320–50.

Portes, Alejandro and Zhou, Min. 1999. "Entrepreneurship and economic progress in the 1990s: A comparative analysis of immigrants and African Americans." Pp. 143–71 in Frank D. Bean and Stephanie Bell-Rose (eds.), *Immigration and Opportunity: Race, Ethnicity, and Employment in the United States*. New York: Russell Sage Foundation.

Rodriguez, Margarita. 2000. "Different paths, same destination: U.S.-bound Nicaraguan and Cuban migration in a comparative perspective." Abstract: *Dissertation Abstracts International, A: The Humanities and Social Sciences*, 2000, 60, 10, Apr, 3805-A.

Salaff, Janet W. and Greve, Arent. 2001. "Women that move: Migration from the PRC to Canada and gendered job opportunities." Paper delivered at Conference on Family and Migration, Singapore National University of Singapore.

Salaff, Janet W., Greve, Arent, and Xu, Lynn. 2002. "Paths into the economy: Structural barriers and the job hunt for skilled PRC migrants in Canada." *International Journal of Human Resource Management*, 13: 450–64.

Sanders, Jimmy M. and Nee, Victor. 1996. "Immigrant self-employment: The family as social capital and the value of human capital." *American Sociological Review*, 61: 231–49.

Tseng, Yen-Fen, and Jou, Su Ching. 2000. "Taiwan–Taiwanese American linkages: A transnationalism approach to return migration." Paper presented at the 95 Annual Meeting of the American Sociological Association, Washington, DC, 14 August.

Unger, Jonathan. 1996. "'Bridges': Private business, the Chinese government, and the rise of new associations." *China Quarterly*, 147: 795–819.

Walder, Andrew. 1986. *Communist Neo-traditionalism*. Berkeley, CA: University of California Press.

Waldinger, Roger. 1986. *Through the Eye of the Needle: Immigrants and Enterprise in New York's Garment Trades*. New York: New York University Press.

——. 1994. "The making of an immigrant niche." *International Migration Review*, 28: 3–30.

Wank, David. 1999. *Commodifying Capitalism: Business, Trust and Politics in a Chinese City*. Cambridge, MA: Cambridge University Press.

Wellman, Barry. 1999. "The network community: An introduction." Pp. 1–48 in Barry Wellman (ed.), *Networks in the Global Village*. Boulder, CO: Westview Press.

Wellman, Barry, Chen, Wenhong, and Dong, Weizhen. 2002. "Networking guanxi." Pp. 221–41 in Thomas Gold, Douglas Guthrie and David Wank (eds.), *Social Networks in China: Institutions, Culture and the Changing Nature of Guanxi*. Cambridge University Press.

Westhead, Paul. 1995. "Survival and employment growth contrasts between types of owner-managed high-technology firms." *Entrepreneurship: Theory and Practice*, 20(1): 5–27.

Wilken, P.H. 1979. *Entrepreneurship: A Comparative and Historical Study*. Norwood, NJ: Ablex.

Wilson, K. and Portes, Alejandro. 1980. "Immigrant enclaves: An analysis of the labor market experiences of Cubans in Miami." *American Journal of Sociology*, 86: 295–315.

Wong, Lloyd L. and Ng, Michele. 1998. "Chinese immigrant entrepreneurs in Vancouver: A case study of ethnic business development." *Canadian Ethnic Studies/Études Ethniques au Canada*, 30(1): 64–85.

Wong, Shuguang. 1999. "Chinese commercial activity in Toronto CMA: New development patterns and impacts." Pp. 167–98 in Yen-Fen Tseng, Chilla Bulbeck, Lan-Hung Nora Chiang, and Jung-Chung Hsu (eds.), *Asian Migration: Pacific Rim Dynamics*. Monograph 1. Interdisciplinary Group for Australian Studies, National Taiwan University, Taipei, Taiwan.

Wong, Siu-Lun. 1988. *Emigrant Entrepreneurs: Shanghai Industrialists in Hong Kong*. Hong Kong: Hong Kong University Press.

Wong, Siu-lun and Salaff, Janet W. 1998. "Network capital: Emigration from Hong Kong." *British Journal of Sociology*, 49: 258–74.

Yeung, Henry Wai-chung. 2000. "Economic globalization, crisis and the emergence of Chinese business communities in Southeast Asia." *International Sociology*, 15: 266–87.

Yeung, Yue-Man and Li, Xiaojian. 1999. "Bargaining with transnational corporations: The case of Shanghai." *International Journal of Urban and Regional Research*, 23: 513–33.

Zhao, Xiaojian. 2002. *Remaking Chinese America: Immigration, Family and Community, 1940–1965*. New Brunswick, NJ: Rutgers University Press.

Zhou, Min. 1992. *Chinatown: The Socioeconomic Potential of an Urban Enclave. Philadelphia*. Philadelphia, PA: Temple University Press.

Zhou, Min, Bankston, Carl L. III, and Kim, Rebecca Y. 2002. "Rebuilding spiritual lives in the new land: Religious practices among Southeast Asian refugees in the United States." Pp. 37–70 In Pyong Gap Min and Jung Ha Kim (eds.), *Asian America: Building Faith Communities*. Walnut Creek, CA: AltaMira.

Zhou, Yongming. 2000. "Social capital and power: Entrepreneurial elite and the state in contemporary China." *Policy Sciences*, 33: 323–40.

Zweig, David and Chen, Changgui. 1995. *China's Brain Drain to the United States: Views of Overseas Chinese Students and Scholars in the 1990s*. Berkeley: Institute of East Asian Studies, University of California, Berkeley, Center for Chinese Studies.

# 7 From battlers to transnational ethnic entrepreneurs?

## Immigrants from the People's Republic of China in Australia

*David Ip*

### INTRODUCTION

In North America, Western Europe and Britain there is an established and substantial literature on ethnic enterprise. (For overviews see Waldinger *et al*. 1985; Boissevain *et al*. 1986; Min 1987; Light and Karageorgis 1994; Portes 1997; Light 1998.) This literature has long argued that as alien immigrant groups were blocked from opportunities for getting ahead in the society of settlement, many were left only with the restricted options of finding work in the ethnic enclave economy, or were herded into a narrow ethnic business niche, the most obvious being the provision of goods and services to co-ethnics (themselves employed in undesirable jobs in the mainstream economy). The literature also argued that in so doing, immigrant groups frequently relied on the use of cultural resources, i.e., their skills, values, networks and solidarities, some of which were transmitted intact from the country of origin and the reactive resources developed within the country of settlement.

The literature, however, does not end with the concept of ethnic niche. In more recent times, empirical studies have demonstrated that in some circumstances some ethnic firms, using ethnic finance and labor and servicing community needs, could emerge over time as established businesses in the wider business environment (Waldinger *et al*. 1985: 593; Nee *et al*. 1994). Studies of Chinese ethnic business concentration in California, in San Gabriel Valley by Tseng (1994) and Li (1998), and in Monterey Park by Fong (1994), give just such a picture of expansion and diversification, moving out of Chinatown into a much wider range of activities and producer services. Most significant, however, is that these studies have also drawn our attention to the fact that although the size of many of these businesses is small, their activities are often transnational. They insert themselves not only into the mainstream or national economy but also into a global economy. This is particularly evident among the capital-linked migration of transmigrant entrepreneurs from places like Hong Kong and Taiwan, who bring already well-established transnational activities which can link up with and transform the established ethnic and even national economies (Lever-Tracy *et al*. 1991; Tseng 1995).

The transnational perspective has recently earned a significant place in studies of ethnic enterprises (Menkhoff and Gerke 2002). Increasingly immigrants are reconceptualized as *transmigrants* and their businesses as *transnational projects and social fields*. Many scholars are also quick to conclude that the traditional notion of immigrant or "ethnic" enterprises should be abandoned, as many immigrant enterprises are deeply embedded in a web of transnational networks that not only strengthens their economic solvency, solidifies their social networks, and augments their social status back home, but also challenges the place-bound notion of local economic activity.

While transnationalism has emerged as the new frontier for further development and research in ethnic enterprises, one needs to remain cautious in determining whether transnationalism is so common that it has become the dominant mode of operation for ethnic business and the theories of old should be totally relegated to the recycling bin.

Based on a study of 45 ethnic Chinese entrepreneurs from the People's Republic of China (PRC) in Brisbane and Sydney[1] who arrived in Australia between 1988 and 1989, this chapter seeks to demonstrate that although they came from a middle-class background similar to that of entrepreneurs from Taiwan and Hong Kong, the PRC entrepreneurs were separated from the capital-linked migration that characterized many in the other two groups. In tracing the patterned obstacles and opportunities presented by Australian society, and the resources or lack thereof, we found their business trajectories less ready to arrive at a transnational business enclave (Rogers 1992) or at a global economic outpost.

## PATTERNED OBSTACLES

In this study, 45 ethnic Chinese entrepreneurs from the PRC were interviewed in depth, 34 in Brisbane and 11 in Sydney. These interviews were conducted between July 1997 and June 1999 by the researcher and two Chinese research assistants, using snowballing introductions. The method led to enterprises of diverse types, established at different times throughout the city and suburbs, and to people of different ages from different regions and speaking different dialects. Broadly, the informants were found to concur with the profile provided by the census data, covering much of the range of variability to be found in the community.

Unlike the recent immigrants from Hong Kong and Taiwan, the majority of these PRC informants first arrived in Australia on their own without their spouses or families. None of them had any transnational links, in terms of either personal (relatives or friends) or business networks. This was because, on the one hand, the White Australian policy in the past had prohibited many Chinese from staying on and living in Australia, and on the other, as one of the Brisbane informants explained, "during the Cultural Revolution, we were forced to denounce anyone who had foreign capitalist connections. For this reason, few would maintain family networks overseas until the recent changes in political climate." Fewer still had any transnational business networks prior to coming to Australia because "none of us would ever have thought of being a private entrepreneur when the risk of being denounced as a capitalist was still high."

Not surprisingly, the 45 informants interviewed were graduates of tertiary institutions, four possessing a master's degree and one a doctorate. Many held professional positions (see Table 7.1) and earned good incomes before they departed for Australia to study English in the late 1980s when Australia decided to turn education into a commodity for export. Nonetheless, close to 90 percent admitted they had borrowed heavily to study and that upon arrival, most had financial resources to live in Australia for only six months.

Without exception, these informants had believed that they could find employment easily once they arrived in Australia, especially in Chinatown if nothing was available elsewhere. However, they soon found out that they lacked all the resources to do well transnationally. With poor English language proficiency, many had difficulties communicating even on the most basic level in the new social environment. Given that China had been isolated from the global academic system for a long period, their educational and professional qualifications were found internationally irrelevant for job applications. Many found that they had little option but to look for jobs in Chinatown. To their surprise, they discovered not only deep divisions between themselves and other Chinese migrant groups, but also that, as "mainlanders," they were considered "backward" and "unsophisticated," suited to only menial jobs in Chinese restaurants, groceries, and garment workshops. Many were offered remuneration much lower than the minimum wage.

Typically, an informant recalled that he was paid "10 lousy dollars for working in the kitchen all day" because the restaurant owner knew he was desperate for a job. Another informant was offered 5 dollars for sewing a shirt by hand by the owner of a Chinese garment workshop who knew he needed money to pay fees for studying fashion design. With little knowledge of the mainstream job market, no money, no personal social or support network, and practically no previous experience of working and living in a foreign country, nearly all the informants were left with little option but to take low-status, non-skilled employment in factories, garment workshops, restaurants, or cleaning offices and motels, or working as casual labourers (see Table 7.1). About two-thirds of them had to take on additional jobs to supplement their incomes. It was common, say, to work as a kitchen hand during the day and fix electric appliances on the side at night, or clean toilets in offices and motels after midnight. Out of desperation and determination to secure some stability in her life, a Sydney informant went as far as marrying an Anglo-Australian man for the sake of securing "a meal ticket and to gain permanent residence."

## RESOURCES

Waldinger *et al*. (1990) and Boissevain *et al*. (1990) observed that in migrant businesses, resource mobilization was intimately bound up with the dynamics of ethnic identity, close ties and social networks within the migrant community itself. This may no longer be necessary for the ethnic Chinese immigrants from Hong Kong and Taiwan with their transnational ties and capital. However, for the PRC

*Table 7.1* PRC immigrant entrepreneurs: present business and previous occupations

| Present business | Previous occupation |
| --- | --- |
| Restaurant | Electrical Engineer |
| | Bank Accountant |
| | Editor |
| | Professional Singer |
| Computer Retail | Electrical Engineer |
| | Lecturer in Physics |
| | Postgraduate Researcher |
| | High School Teacher |
| Grocery/Convenience Store | Electronic Technician |
| | Postgraduate Student |
| | Housewife |
| Fashion Designer | Public Service |
| Color Photocopying | Medical Doctor (GP) |
| Discount Warehouse Store | Tertiary Student |
| Chinese Herbalist | Medical Doctor |
| | Lecturer (Biochemistry) |
| Fish and Chip Shop | Lecturer in Marine Biology |
| Parquet Flooring | Civil Engineer |
| Furniture Maker | Agricultural Mechanics |
| | Post-secondary Student |
| Shop Fitting and Specialized Joinery | Bank Clerk |
| Uniform/Logo Embroidery | Undergraduate Student |
| Cleaning Contractor & Financial Service | Mining Engineer |
| Real Estate Agency | Metallurgy Engineer |
| Exporter | Diplomatic Staff |
| Property Management | Lecturer in English |
| Importer/Exporter | Postgraduate Student |
| | Foreign Trade Officers |
| | Army |
| | Import/Export Manager |
| Rug Wholesaler | Master Weaver in Rug Factory |
| | Lecturer (Social Sciences) |
| Builder (Property Development) | Electrical and Civil Engineer |
| Carpet Cleaning | High School Teacher |
| Education Export | Professor in English Literature |
| Trade Consultant | Mechanical Engineer |
| Quilting Service | Para-medic |
| Travel Agent | Electric Engineer |
| Printing | Technician |
| Migration Consultant | Civil Engineer |
| Garment Making | Factory Manager |
| Technology Consultant | Foreign Trade Representative |
| Accountant | Accountant |
| Public Relations | Official Cadre |
| Cab Driver/Owner | Civil Engineer |

immigrants, these remained the most important resources they had for immediate survival and for establishment of their businesses at a later stage. Almost two-thirds of informants reported that they found their social networks in Australia in the language schools where they had their first classes. These institutions provided a convenient setting where they met and found immediate cultural and group affinity. A Brisbane informant remembered that it did not take him long to identify his compatriots because they shared similar looks, age, (middle) class, and vocabulary:

> When you heard someone using the same peculiar vocabularies characteristic of people who were sent to remote villages for re-education during the Cultural Revolution, you quickly developed an intense personal bonding with him.

Similarly, a Sydney informant found that:

> when you realized that you were made to feel inferior by Chinese from Hong Kong or Taiwanese, you just wanted to band together with people of your own kind.

Of course, their group affinity was necessitated by the fact that few had any pre-existing friendship or kin networks when they first arrived. These ties were also necessary for social and economic support. A Brisbane informant recalled how he survived his most difficult times through a group of friends whom he met on only the first day of classes:

> I made a stopover in Hong Kong before I arrived in Australia. Unfortunately, someone stole all of my money when I went out and I had only a hundred Australian dollars left in my pocket upon my arrival in Brisbane. I had to take a cab to the language school but the cab driver took me to the wrong place. By the time I got to where I was enrolled to study, I had less than sixty dollars. I had no place to live, and I didn't know where to go. I finally broke down, but to my good fortune this person came to my rescue. He took me home and allowed me to share his tiny room with three other students without asking me to pay any rent because he knew I was also from the PRC . . . You don't forget friends who saved your life . . .

Over time, as over half the Brisbane informants stated, they developed friendship groups not only to pull together resources but also to share information about employment and eventually business opportunities when some of them decided that the only way to get ahead was to "be your own boss" and "run your own business."

There were few similar stories reported from Sydney. One informant there speculated that Sydney was much too impersonal and too competitive as a metropolis. Another commented that "those who chose to settle in Sydney were more competitive in the first place and they wouldn't like to help others," while still another thought that PRC entrepreneurs in Sydney were "simply too proud to acknowledge that they had help from others."

In either case, about half the Brisbane informants and one-third of the Sydney informants found jobs outside Chinatown, because they could get better wages there, though not better positions. Indeed, with few exceptions, a majority felt humiliated and resentful at having to accept unskilled and laboring jobs. An ex-mining engineer in Brisbane, for example, found it difficult to do cleaning. Similarly, another two engineers, one in electrical and one in civil engineering, had to sweep and clean floors in a timber mill and in a restaurant kitchen. Not surprisingly, they were full of resentment. It was only later that they realized these experiences were "their necessary apprenticeship in knowing the Australian economy." In particular, as one Brisbane informant observed, "This made me look at the Australian economy from the ground up and helped me to realize that plenty of other business opportunities were actually located outside the Chinese enclave." The mining engineer is now running a cleaning business with multiple contracts from offices, hotels and motels. The civil engineer currently operates a successful parquet flooring business, while the electrical engineer is owner of a pan-Asian restaurant. Similarly, a bank clerk who first settled in Sydney, after working in another timber yard for a number of years, moved to Brisbane and is running a business specializing in shop fitting and joinery.

Frequently the start-up capital involved was considerable. A computer repair business required about $20,000, while a restaurant or grocery could need as much as $60,000. It would be misleading to conclude that the owners could achieve this easily. In fact, given that most informants in the study had little previous experience in running a business, many actually began in a much more humble manner. At least half a dozen informants in both Sydney and Brisbane gained their first business experiences from "having a go at the weekend flea markets," selling trinkets and clothing imported from China, involving only very modest capital outlay. Over half the respondents secured their start-up capital largely through their own savings, while six also borrowed money to supplement their own from trusted acquaintances they had met in Australia.

In cases where local ties and capital were inadequate to help them in setting up their own business, home ties were the most common recourse. About one-third had turned to their family members, parents or siblings, or to friendship networks they had established through work or education in their place of origin. Several respondents reported they had borrowed as much as 90 percent of their establishment costs, while others indicated that it was more common to obtain about 30 percent of the required capital from these sources.

Although in many cases accessible capital was cited as the most essential resource for establishing a business, many respondents also believed that personal and social networks, transnational or otherwise, were equally valuable. The owner of a sushi bar in Brisbane credited his friends' advice and information, not the capital they lent him, for making it possible to start his business, because "it was they who saw the business opportunity and insisted that I took advantage of it." Informed by friends about the availability of a color photocopying business in a shopping centre, a Brisbane informant plunged into self-employment because only then did he realize that he could become his own boss, with encouragement and support from his friends. Similarly, another respondent in Brisbane decided to buy a grocery business only after his friends told him about the opportunity and offered him a careful analysis of its viability.

Transnational networks were likewise instrumental in international trade. For example, a wholesale rug trader and the owner of a discount store selling Chinese products in Brisbane benefited enormously from having an extended six-month credit arrangement rather than the usual three months when they imported commodities from the state enterprises where they used to work.

> I called up my old colleagues. They were immediately helpful not only because they knew me personally, but also because they were under pressure to export more. They thought I was also doing them a favor. In return, they offered me extended credit. This certainly helped my business to stay liquid. On the other hand, they also benefited from increased export sales. We both benefit from eating from the socialist rice bowl!

Similarly, a seafood trader in Sydney spent up to two years in China renewing old contacts she had made in school, workplace and local organizations. She was convinced that her friendship networks in China gave her business not only favorable prices but, more importantly, a sense of stability. With similar friendship networks in China, the consultant in Brisbane could also circumvent bureaucratic red tape and offer his Australian clients better services in negotiating trade, migration and education contracts in China. His business has been so successful that he now simultaneously runs a kindergarten for children of expatriates living in Ningbo. As well, another Sydney trader claimed that her connections with the local Chinese government have been instrumental in her completing a deal sourcing animals from South Africa for a theme park in Shunde. Equally significant for yet another export trader in Sydney was her social network in Guangzhou. Her tripe-export venture only became prosperous when her mainland Chinese contacts helped her set up a sales and distribution system.

Despite their use of transnational ties to achieve business successes, none of these informants considered their business to be "transnational," as they believed that their financial capital, clientele, market and operation were still rather localized. As our Brisbane education consultant explained:

> I don't think we can compare our business successes with those migrants from Taiwan or Hong Kong because what they do is truly transnational. They set up production in China, Vietnam and other Southeast Asian countries, but many of our businesses are still dealing with import and export. Their capital sources are diverse, coming from their friends or relatives in North America, Southeast Asia and Europe. Most of our businesses are still relying heavily on our own family resources. Their businesses have an international or global market, but all we can do now is still branching out to the Australian market. To achieve what they have accomplished, we'll need much more—networks, experience, capital, and above all, time.

# FROM BATTLERS TO TRANSNATIONAL ETHNIC ENTREPRENEURS?

Along with the Hong Kongers and Taiwanese, the PRC migrants were considered part and parcel of the "new Asian immigration" sweeping Australia in the latter half of the 1980s and early 1990s (Ip 2001). In numerical terms, Hong Kong became the top source of Australia's immigrants during this time (Inglis 1999; Walmsley *et al.* 1999), and the Taiwanese formed the largest immigrant group entering Australia through the Business Migration Program in the early 1990s (Inglis and Wu 1991; Wu *et al.* 1998; Chiang and Hsu 2000). Not surprisingly, they became objects worthy of academic research, as their capital-linked migration and visible presence brought into question models of immigrant social mobility and settlement typical of Australian post-war immigration (Coughlan and McNamara 1997; Hon and Coughlan 1997; Anstee 1995; Inglis *et al.* 1992; Inglis and Wu 1994; Ip *et al.* 1998a–c; Kee and Skeldon 1994; Lary *et al.* 1994). The class resources they brought, often including well-established transnational business, capital and social networks, and their frequent movements between Australia and their place of origins, have also prompted quick recognition that the traditional notions of place-specific immigration and ethnic enterprises should be rethought and refashioned. Historically, immigrant entrepreneurial activities have been seen as a stepping-stone towards economic incorporation and assimilation into the mainstream society. The findings that many Hong Kong and Taiwanese immigrant enterprises are deeply embedded in a web of transnational networks (Lever-Tracy *et al.* 1991; Lever-Tracy and Ip 2005) have seen many authors redirecting their attention to studying the continuing links migrants have with their country of origin (Lever-Tracy *et al.* 2002). Some are even beginning to suggest that ethnic enclave economies should be viewed in a broader globalized context.

Separated from the capital-linked migration, the PRC migrants in Australia, dubbed by the press as "Generation Exodus" (Marsh 1999), nonetheless offer us a reminder of the danger of over-simplifying the complexities of the Australian Chinese ethnic economy. As migrants who held high education and training credentials (Zhou 2000a, 2000b; Yan 2004) but not the financial resources that came readily with most Hong Kong and Taiwanese migrants (Kee and Skeldon 1994; Pitt 1996; Ip *et al.* 1998a; Ip 1999, 2001; Zhou 2000b) to shield themselves from hardships, their trajectories to self-employment and entrepreneurship have been remarkably different.

Entering Australia during a period of ongoing economic recession with little finance capital, few established networks, business or otherwise, and hardly any prior business experience, they became not only convenient objects of mirth among their Hong Kong and Taiwanese compatriots (Ye 1996), but also stigmatized by the broader Australian community as potential "dole cheats," a new ethnic underclass trapped within their own "enclave" and heavily reliant upon government handouts (Birrell 1993; Birrell and Evans 1996; Marsh 1998; Healy 1994). In this context, they typified more the image of a battler than that of a well-seasoned transnational entrepreneur. Their road to self-employment resembled more the conventional scenario of "blocked mobility" where they were forced into self-employment, albeit in narrow niches that often pose no threat to or are considered undesirable by the mainstream society. Unlike the Taiwanese or Hong Kong settlers, who were more apt to use migration as an opportunity to extend their business projects transnationally (King 1991), the PRC migrants still see their businesses more as a means for economic and social survival in their settlement. In their entrepreneurial efforts, they sought an array of cultural endowments in the form of personal and kinship networks, transnational or otherwise, to facilitate resource mobilization as well as business development (Bonacich and Modell 1980; Boissevain 1984; Light and Bonacich 1988; Li 1993), but their business orientation remained largely localized.

Numerous researchers have insisted that ethnic businesses usually have only limited success and only within an ethnic economic enclave (Auster and Aldrich 1984; Waldinger *et al.* 1990; Aldrich and Waldinger 1990). Furthermore, others have also been concerned that the enclave economy could become a mobility trap for migrants, as ethnic exploitation was found to be widespread among immigrant employers (Sanders and Nee 1987; Nee *et al.* 1994). The experiences of the PRC migrant entrepreneurs in Brisbane and Sydney have demonstrated that these assumptions may not always hold true. In fact, although a significant number of PRC migrants began work in Chinatown, many ventured out of the Chinatown enclave to seek better wages and work conditions and discovered new niches in the mainstream economy. For this reason, there has been a growing diversity among the PRC migrant-owned businesses, and frequently they are catering to the mainstream rather than the exclusively ethnic market. In this context, the traditional concept "ethnic" businesses, implying their entrapment in an ethnic "enclave economy," is inadequate. As the case of the PRC migrants has indicated, "ethnic business" as a term fails to describe the full range of activities of businesses operated by immigrants. Given their determination to use employment in the enclave economy *as a transition*, many PRC migrants were successful in overcome their mobility trap.

Nonetheless, it is still too early for researchers to include the PRC migrant business with those operated by their Hong Kong and Taiwanese compatriots as globalized transnational projects. In many cases, the PRC migrant enterprises are still localized, although some have embarked on a path of internationalization and transnationalization after attaining the necessary financial, social and cultural capital. Until the time when the bulk of these businesses become what Li (1998) termed "global economy outposts," the heterogeneity of ethnic Chinese enterprises should be closely observed.

## Notes

1   This study involves in-depth interviews with 45 PRC business owners in Brisbane (34) and Sydney (11) conducted between July 1997 and June 1999. Informants were selected through a snowballing technique. Funding for this research was supported by the Chiang Ching-Kuo Foundation for International Scholarly Exchange and an ARC (Australia Research Council) Small Grant. Inputs from Dr. Dong Zun-qi, Xu Ming-xian, Dr. Chi-Wai Lui and Dr. Yan Ru are much appreciated.

# References

Aldrich, H. and Waldinger, R. (1990) "Ethnicity and Entrepreneurship," *Annual Review of Sociology*, 16: 111–35.

Anstee, M. (1995) "From Paw Paws to Palm Urns: Immigrant Agency and Southside Postsuburbia in Brisbane." Unpublished Honours Thesis, Department of Anthropology and Sociology, University of Queensland.

Auster, E. and Aldrich, H. (1984) "Small Business Vulnerability, Ethnic Enclaves and Ethnic Enterprise," in Ward, R. and Jenkins, R. (eds.) *Ethnic Communities in Business: Strategies for Economic Survival.* Cambridge, MA: Cambridge University Press.

Birrell, R. (1993) "Unemployment Dependency amongst Recently Arrived Migrants," *People and Place*, 1(1): 19–23.

Birrell, R. and Evans, S. (1996) "Recently-Arrived Migrants and Social Welfare," *People and Place*, 4(2): 1–11.

Boissevain, J. (1984) "Small Entrepreneurs in Contemporary Europe," in Ward, R. and Jenkins, R. (eds.) *Ethnic Communities in Business: Strategies for Economic Survival.* Cambridge, MA: Cambridge University Press.

Boissevain, J., Blaschke, J., Joseph, I., Light, I., Sway, M. and Weber, P. (1986) *Ethnic Communities and Ethnic Entrepreneurs*, Euromed Working Paper, No. 44, November.

Boissevain, J. Blaschke, J., Grotenberg, H., Joseph, I., Light, I., Sway, M., Waldinger, R. and Werbner, P. (1990) "Ethnic Entrepreneurs and Ethnic Strategies," in Waldinger, R., Aldrich, H., Ward, R. and associates (eds.) *Ethnic Entrepreneurs: Immigrant Business in Industrial Societies*, pp. 131–54. Newbury Park, CA: Sage.

Bonacich, E. and Modell, J. (1980) *The Economic Basis of Ethnic Solidarity.* Berkeley, CA: University of California Press.

Chiang, L.H. and Hsu, J.C. (2000) "Location Decisions and Economic Incorporation of Taiwanese Migrants in Sydney," *Journal of Geographical Science*, 27: 1–20.

Coughlan, J. and McNamara, D.J. (eds.) (1997) *Asians in Australia: Patterns of Migration and Settlement*, pp. 120–70. South Melbourne: Macmillan Education Australia.

Fong, T.P. (1994) *The First Suburban Chinatown: The Remaking of Monterey Park, California.* Philadelphia, PA: Temple University Press.

Healy, E. (1994) "Unemployment Dependency Rates amongst Recently-Arrived Migrants: An Update," *People and Place*, 2(3): 47–54.

Hon, C.H. and Coughlan, J.E. (1997) "The Chinese in Australia: Immigrants from the People's Republic of China, Malaysia, Singapore, Taiwan, Hong Kong and Macau," in Coughlan, J.E. and McNamara, D.J. (eds.) *Asians in Australia: Patterns of Migration and Settlement*, pp. 120–70. South Melbourne: Macmillan Education Australia.

Inglis, C. (1999) "The Chinese in Australia," in Pan, L. (ed.) *The Encyclopaedia of the Overseas Chinese.* Cambridge, MA: Harvard University Press.

Inglis, C. and Wu, C. (1991) "Business Migration to Australia." Paper presented at the International Conference on International Manpower Flows and Foreign Investment in Asia, September 9–12, Nihon University and the East West Centre, Honolulu.

——. (1994) "The Hong Kong Chinese in Sydney," in Skeldon, R. (ed.) *Reluctant Exiles? Migration from Hong Kong and the New Overseas Chinese*, pp. 197–214. Armonk, New York: M.E. Sharpe.

Inglis, C., Gunasekaran, S., Sullivan, G. and Wu, C.T. (eds.) (1992) *Asians in Australia: The Dynamics of Migration and Settlement.* St Leonards: Allen & Unwin.

Ip, D. (1999) "Network as Capital: PRC Immigrant Entrepreneurs in Brisbane," in Tseng, Yen-Fen, Bulbeck, Chilla, Chiang, Lan-Hung Nora and Hsu, Jung-Chung (eds.) *Asian*

*Migration: Pacific Rim Dynamics*, pp. 149–164. Taipei: Interdisciplinary Group for Australian Studies (IGAS), National Taiwan University.

Ip, D. (2001) "A Decade of Taiwanese Migrant Settlement in Australia: Comparisons with Mainland Chinese and Hong Kong Settlers," *Journal of Population Studies*, No. 23, December: 113–45.

Ip, D., Anstee, M. and Wu, C. (1998a) "Cosmopolitanisation of Australian Suburbia: Asian Immigration in Sunnybank," *Journal of Population Studies*, No. 19, October: 55–79.

Ip, D., Wu, C. and Inglis, C. (1998b) "Gold Mountain No More: Impressions of Australian Society among Recent Asian Immigrants," in Sinn, E. (ed.) *The Last Half Century of Chinese Overseas*, pp. 347–70. Hong Kong: University of Hong Kong Press.

Ip, D, Wu, C.T. and Inglis, C (1998c) "Settlement Experiences of Taiwanese Immigrants in Australia," *Asian Studies Review*, March: 79–97.

Kee, P. and Skeldon, R. (1994) "The Migration and Settlement of Hong Kong Chinese," in Skeldon, R. (ed.) *Reluctant Exiles? Migration from Hong Kong and the New Overseas Chinese*, pp. 183–96. Armonk, New York: M.E. Sharpe.

King, A. (1991) Kuan-hsi (*Guanxi*) and Network Building: A Sociological Interpretation, *Daedalus*, 120 (2): 63–84.

Lary, D., Inglis, C. and Wu, C.T. (1994) "Hong Kong: A Case Study of Immigration and Settlement," in Adelman, H. *et al.* (eds.) *Immigration and Refugee Policy: Australia and Canada Compared*, Vol II, pp. 405–46. Melbourne: Melbourne University Press.

Lever-Tracy, C. and Ip, D. (2005) "Diversification and Extensible Networks: The Strategies of Chinese Businesses in Australia," *International Migration*, 43(3): 73–97.

Lever-Tracy, C., Ip, D., Kitay, J. and Tracy, N.I. (1991) *Asian Entrepreneurs in Australia: Ethnic Small Business in the Chinese and Indian Communities of Brisbane and Sydney*. Canberra: Office of Multicultural Affairs, Australian Government Publishing Service.

Lever-Tracy, C., Ip, D. and Tracy, N. (2002) "From a Niche to a World City: Barriers, Opportunities and Resources of Ethnic Chinese Businesses in Australia," in T. Menkhoff and S. Gerke (eds.) *Chinese Entrepreneurship and Asian Business Networks*, pp. 267–92. London and New York: RoutledgeCurzon.

Li, P.S. (1993) "Chinese Investment and Business in Canada: Ethnic Entrepreneurship Reconsidered," *Pacific Affairs*, 66(2): 219–43.

Li, W. (1998) "Los Angeles's Chinese Ethnoburb: From Ethnic Service Center to Global Economy Outpost," *Urban Geography*, 19(6).

Light, I. (1998) "Afterword: Maturation of the Ethnic Enclave Economy Paradigm," *Urban Geography*, 19(6).

Light, I. and Bonacich, E. (1988) *Immigrant Entrepreneurs*. Berkeley, CA: University of California Press.

Light, I. and Karageorgis, S. (1994) "The Ethnic Economy," in Smelser, N. and Swedberg, R. (eds.) *Handbook of Economic Sociology*. New York: Russell Sage.

Marsh, J. (1998) "New Aussie Battler: Asian and Dirt Poor," *The Sydney Morning Herald*, September 19: 3.

——. (1999) "Generation Exodus", *The Sydney Morning Herald*, Spectrum, 29 May.

Menkhoff, T. and Gerke, S. (eds.) (2002) *Chinese Entrepreneurship and Asian Business Networks*. London and New York: RoutledgeCurzon.

Min, P.G. (1987) "Factors Contributing to Ethnic Business: A Comparative Synthesis," *International Journal of Comparative Sociology*, 253: 3–4.

Nee, V., Sanders, J.M. and Sernau, S. (1994) "Job Transitions in an Immigrant Metropolis: Ethnic Boundaries and the Mixed Economy," *American Sociological Review*, 59: 849–72.

Pitt, H. (1996) "Northern Exposure: The New Chinese," *The Sydney Morning Herald*, February 12: 14–15.

Portes, A. (1997) "Immigration Theory for a New Century: Some Problems and Opportunities," *International Migration Review*, 31(4): 799–825.

Rogers, A. (1992) "The New Immigration and Urban Ethnicity in the United States," in Cross, M. (ed.) *Ethnic Minorities and Industrial Change in Europe and North America*, pp. 226–49. New York: Cambridge University Press.

Sanders, J.M. and Nee, V. (1987) "Limits of Ethnic Solidarity in the Enclave Economy," *American Sociological Review*, 52: 745–73.

Tseng, Y.F. (1994) "Chinese Ethnic Economy: San Gabriel Valley, Los Angeles County," *Journal of Urban Affairs*, 16: 169–89.

——. (1995) "Beyond Little Taipei: The Development of Taiwanese Immigrant Businesses in Los Angeles," *International Migration Review*, 29(1): 33–58.

Waldinger, R., Ward, R. and Aldrich, H. (1985) "Trend Report: Ethnic Business and Occupational Mobility in Advanced Societies," *Sociology*, 19(4): 586–97.

Waldinger, R., Aldrich, H. and Ward, R. (1990) "Opportunities, Group Characteristics and Strategies," in Waldinger, R., Aldrich, H., Robin, W. and Associates, *Ethnic Entrepreneurs, Immigrant Business in Industrial Societies*, pp. 13–48. Newbury Park, CA: Sage Publications.

Walmsley, J., Roley, F. and Hugo, G. (1999) *Atlas of the Australian People 1996 Census: National Overview*. DIMA, Canberra.

Wu, C., Ip, C. and Inglis, D. (1998) "Settlement Experiences of Recent Chinese Immigrants in Australia," in Sinn, E. (ed.) *The Last Half Century of Chinese Overseas*, pp, 391–422. Hong Kong: University of Hong Kong Press.

Yan, R. (2004) "Settlement Stress and Health Needs of Migrant Women from the People's Republic of China in Brisbane." Unpublished doctoral thesis. Brisbane: Griffith University.

Ye, S. (1996) *The Year the Dragon Came*. Brisbane: University of Queensland Press.

Zhou, Z. (2000a) *Community Profiles 1996 Census Hong Kong Born*. Canberra: ABS.

——. (2000b) *Community Profiles 1996 Census China Born*. Canberra: ABS.

# 8 The cemetery of Huang Xiulang

## Transnationalism and the Overseas Chinese in the early twentieth century[1]

*Michael A. Szonyi*

Understanding the transnational linkages between migrant sending and receiving countries is complicated by, among other reasons, the very terms that are commonly used to characterize the migrants themselves. Much of the vocabulary traditionally used in Overseas Chinese and Chinese migration studies implicitly seeks to locate Overseas Chinese subjects in terms of a single nation-state. Terms such as sojourner, immigrant, or return migrant reflect efforts to situate individuals in relation to either host country or home country—to see them as either here or there. Adam McKeown points out that the use of such language has the effect of obscuring the transnational activities of Chinese migrants and their descendants.[2] To what extent does use of terms "Chinese ethnic economy" or "Chinese ethnic business" have a similar effect? In one of its two commonly used formulations, that of the ethnic enclave, the first term does seem to localize individuals to a single defined territory, in which certain economic sectors, occupations, or neighborhoods are monopolized or dominated by a particular ethnic group. But the term "Chinese ethnic economy" is also increasingly used in a second sense, to describe the economic activities of Chinese firms operating across national boundaries, in transnational, dispersed, or deterritorialized ways. In this usage, the term offers a useful corrective to analyses of Chinese migrants restricted to a single locale. Even in this sense, however, the term should still be used with care to avoid over-simplification. While the transnational linkages between ethnic Chinese business firms have attracted considerable scholarly attention, the transnational activities of Chinese migrants and their descendants are rarely solely economic. They involve circulation and flows not only of goods and capital, but also of human beings, and of ideas. They are shaped by a broad set of ideas and values, for example, by discourses of Chinese identity and authenticity, nationalism, and modernity, to name just a few. Moreover, this transnational element to the Chinese ethnic economy is not a new phenomenon which can be understood purely as a product of the current phase of globalization. It has been shaped by a long history. This chapter discusses some of the multiple forms of transnationalism engaged in by one of the most prominent figures in the history of the Overseas Chinese in the Philippines, Huang Xiulang (1859–1925). Its purpose is to explore the interconnections between transnational flows in the Chinese ethnic economy in the early twentieth century and imaginings of the meaning of Chinese identity. Then, as now, wealthy Overseas Chinese were targeted by political leaders as potential contributors to the grand project of building the Chinese nation. Ties of blood, heritage, and patriotism were invoked to persuade the Overseas Chinese to play their appointed roles. But beneath the enthusiasm lay profound ambivalences about the project of nation-building and modernization, and specifically about motivations and possible consequences of the involvement of Overseas Chinese in that project. The early-twentieth-century discourses of Chinese transnationalism, and of the relationship between the Chinese ethnic economy and China, resemble in many ways those of the present day.

Huang Xiulang was a native of the small coastal port of Shenhu, in Jinjiang County, Quanzhou, a famous homeland of Overseas Chinese (*qiaoxiang*). His life story is a familiar trope of Overseas Chinese entrepreneurial success. Orphaned at an early age, Huang went to the Philippines to seek his fortune, and by 1899 had become a rich man. In that year, he returned to China and using funds remitted from the Philippines established a merchant house and native bank (*qianzhuang*) in Xiamen. Business was good, and branches were later set up in Tianjin, Shanghai, and Hong Kong. Huang's social activities after his return to China, like his business activities, were typical of his generation of merchant capitalists, spanning the continuum of Chinese philanthropic practices. He paid for the repair of roads and the reconstruction of the lineage ancestral hall in his home village; donated funds for the repair of the magnificent stone towers of the Kaiyuan monastery in Quanzhou; participated in late Qing efforts to construct railways in Fujian; and also earned a medal from Sun Yat-sen for contributions to the revolutionary cause.[3] But his was hardly a simple case of a return migrant. He and his family continued to live a transnational life. His eldest son, Huang Zuyi (1879–1929), followed Xiulang to the Philippines, and after his father's return to China remained in Manila looking after the family business interests there. In 1928, Zuyi was elected to the position of Chairman of the Manila Overseas Chinese Commercial Association. The very composition of Huang Xiulang's household reflected his continued engagement with multiple locales—his wives and concubines, five in all, came from China, Hong Kong, the Philippines as well as Japan. The magnificent home that he constructed on Xiamen's Gulangyu Island is yet another example of how his life was shaped by social and cultural fields that transcended national borders. The Sea Heaven Hall (*Haitian Tang*), built in 1905, was the first major example of what would become an architectural trend in Xiamen, the creative mixture of Eastern and Western styles, combining traditional elements like the tiled sloped roof with new elements like exterior balconies and staircases which displayed the owner's wealth and power where the more traditional courtyard structure had concealed them. James Cook describes the house as "a western foundation and structure all covered by a Chinese cap and gown."[4]

The most interesting illustration of how different types of transnational flows generated by the Chinese ethnic economy were intertwined in Huang's activities is the Gubo Estate (*Gubo shanzhuang*), a cemetery built by Huang in his ancestral village of Gubo between 1912 and 1915, at a cost of 250,000 *yuan*. Today the cemetery is gated and surrounded by a high concrete wall, and entrance is only possible if one of the nearby residents is available with the key. Passing under memorial arches, with inscriptions by Sun Yat-sen and Chen Baochen (1848–1935), Senior Tutor and adviser to the last emperor, Pu Yi, the visitor enters a large, rectangular open space. In the centre of the space is a decorative pool, overrun with lotus leaves. On the grassy field behind the pool are a number of graves in traditional horseshoe style. The largest and most imposing of these is the tomb of Huang Xiulang himself, and that of his primary wife. In three of the four corners are small buildings, each built in imitation of a distinct architectural style. One is obviously intended to suggest Middle Eastern influence, one South Asian, and one European. Inside the latter is a remarkable trove of historical sources. Every wall is lined with inscribed stone tablets, more than a hundred in all, from many of the most prominent figures of early Republican China.[5]

To mark the completion of the cemetery, Huang Xiulang composed an essay, "Record on the Family Cemetery at Gubo Estate," the text of which is carved on the first inscription. Huang then distributed his essay widely to prominent Chinese of the time, and invited them to contribute essays, poems, and mottoes to commemorate the new cemetery. People began to respond almost immediately, and poems and essays continued to be written even after Huang's death and burial in 1925. By 1932, more than 190 responses had been received, from more than 180 individuals.[6] Prominent calligraphers were hired to copy the poems and essays, which were then inscribed on the stone tablets which now line the building on the cemetery grounds. Rubbings were taken of the stones, and these rubbings collected and published in a commemorative volume, the "Collected Commemorative Writings on the Gubo Cemetery" (*Gubo shanzhuang tiyong ji*). The contributors represent a cross-section of the local and national elite of the time. They include former Qing officials like Zheng Xiaoxu (1860–1938), later Premier of Manchukuo, and prominent Republican officials like Tang Shaoyi (1868–1938), the first Premier of the Republic, and Wang Jingwei (1883–1944), who would later become China's most famous collaborator with the Japanese, and who had a direct connection with the Overseas Chinese through his wife, a native of Penang. From the world of the arts came contributions from Mei Lanfang (1894–1964), the century's most prominent operatic performer, painter Li Ruiqing (1867–1920), and the literary scholar Lin Shu (1852–1924), translator of one of the early Chinese editions of the works of Shakespeare. Scholars who responded to Huang's invitation included the philosopher Kang Youwei (1858–1927); Huang Yanpei (1878–1965), a famous early advocate of vocational education; and the former anti-Manchu revolutionary Zhang Binglin (1868–1936), who by this time was devoting himself to research into ancient history. There are also contributions by the magistrate of Jinjiang County, where the cemetery is located, and Li Houji, the province's military governor. The majority of the contributors are Fujian natives. Some were famous men like Chen Baochen and Chen Yan (1856–1937), Professor at Xiamen and Beijing Universities and compiler of the mammoth *Gazetteer of Fujian*. But most are now unknown, local scholars, businessmen, and returned Overseas Chinese.

The contents of the volume present a fascinating window into how people of the time understood the relationship of the Overseas Chinese with the developing Chinese nation-state. Huang and the other contributors lived at a time when this relationship was a matter of wide interest. In gratitude for their financial contribution to early revolutionary efforts, Sun Yat-sen had famously bestowed on the Overseas Chinese the honorary title "Mother of the Revolution," and this title encapsulated one widely held view of the relationship. Capital generated in the ethnic Chinese economy abroad was to be remitted to China to serve the cause of national revolution and modernization, creating a strong, wealthy, and modern China.[7] In their contributions to the "Collected Commemorative Writings on the Gubo Cemetery," authors present their own views on the nature and significance of Overseas Chinese contribution to modernization efforts, and thus comment indirectly on the complex transnational linkages between participants in the Chinese ethnic economy and China. In the body of the chapter, I discuss the main views expressed by the contributors to Huang Xiulang's commemorative volume on several issues related to the larger concerns of the day. I focus especially on the less well known among the essayists, men who wrote merely as friends and acquaintances of Huang or as concerned and engaged citizens. For these authors, the issue of funerary practices was weighted with heavy symbolic meaning, a metaphor for the challenges confronting China. The Gubo cemetery was discussed as a prescription for how those challenges should be addressed, and Huang Xiulang as a model for the Overseas Chinese. But the views of the different authors, their ideas about how China should modernize and what role the Overseas Chinese should play in that modernization, were far from unified, so their interpretations of Huang and his cemetery also diverged widely. I discuss first the key issue raised explicitly in the documents, reform of funerary practice, and show how this issue was linked to a larger question confronting reformers, whether the basis for reform should be Western, Chinese, or some combination of the two. I then illustrate that this issue was understood in terms of a larger project of cultural transformation. How to secure Overseas Chinese participation in this larger project, and ensure that their contribution was a positive one, is the underlying, implicit focus of many of the essays carved on the walls of Huang's cemetery.

## ERADICATING SUPERSTITION, REVIVING TRADITIONAL CHINESE CULTURE, EMULATING WESTERN WAYS

Huang's own essay begins by tracing his ancestry back to a Song official whose descendants spread to various other villages in the vicinity, including his native village of Shenhu. Though his lineage had produced many prominent scholars, the location of their graves was unknown, so it was impossible to carry out grave-sweeping and sacrificial rituals. Huang hoped that by endowing this grand cemetery, he would ensure that his own grave would not be forgotten, thus "expressing his commitment not to forget one's origins." Huang frames his cemetery in terms of an attack on the widespread traditional practice of geomancy (*fengshui*), of which he was highly critical. "The people of my locale are extremely taken in by geomantic theories. I have written this so that the descendants of later generations will reflect on the careful planning of the [ancestors of] the descent line, and will not be taken in by the sayings of the geomancers and move the tombs in order to seek good fortune." Many contributions focus on this aspect of Huang's essay, and elaborate on his argument that the Gubo cemetery will have a salutary effect on local society, by setting a useful example in the fight against superstitious practices, particularly geomancy. "I have heard," writes one of them, "that the people of Quanzhou are all taken in by the theories of the geomancers (*xingjia*). For months and years, they delay the burial of their kin."[8] Wang Woqun of Jinjiang enumerates the effects of geomancy in more detail. "Since the spread of geomantic theory [*kanyu zhi shuo*], [people] are taken in by [ideas about ] Yin and Yang and seek to obtain good fortune. In some cases, they delay burial for a long time, or they bury [the dead] but then relocate the graves, or they bury [the dead] in distant places." The tragic consequence of these practices is that descendants neglect ancestral sacrifice, or even forget the location of the graves. "Superstition [*mixin*]," adds Wang, "can really fool people."[9]

Belief in geomancy is seen as a particular problem in South China. "The people of Fujian and Guangdong all rely on geomancy to pursue good fortune." Some suggest that this is related to the regional socioeconomic environment. "The people of Quanzhou live near the sea and labor as merchants. So their sentiments of attachment to their native place are weak and their sense of kinship light. Their desire for profit is strong and their ambition for good fortune great. So they lay great importance on geomancy and fortune-telling."[10]

In his own essay, Huang claims that his cemetery will replace funerary practices rooted in geomancy with traditions rooted in Chinese antiquity. He compares the Gubo estate to the "lineage cemetery [*zusang*] of the ancients," a reference to the *Zhouli* (*Institutes of Zhou*, a classic text dating from the fifth to third century BCE), which provides instructions for a collective cemetery for the descendants of a common ancestor. Many of the commentators pick up on this theme, elaborating on the comparison and commending Huang for reviving the spirit of traditional culture. Huang's project is described as "a legacy of the official system of the Zhou dynasty. The depth and profundity of his devotion [to the ancient ways] carries on the work of Sima Wen [i.e. Sima Guang (1019–86), the great Song dynasty scholar and statesman]." These essays quote extensively from the Confucian classics on the importance of filial piety and ancestral sacrifice as the foundation of social cohesion and harmony. "The ancients have already thought of the system of the lineage cemetery as implemented by Huang, and transmitted its regulations in texts."[11] Geomancy and other superstitions are represented as distortions of the pure Chinese culture of antiquity which have arisen since the Qin and Han dynasties.[12] Somehow, Huang Xiulang has managed to avoid being tricked by these seductive customs. "In his heart, the gentleman does not harbor the customs which have accumulated since the Qin and Han."[13] The Gubo cemetery is thus a revival of China's ancient glory, and of the purification of Chinese culture back to its original essence.

Other authors claim that the inspiration for the Gubo cemetery is not ancient China but the modern West, specifically the public cemeteries established by churches and colonial authorities in Chinese treaty ports and Southeast Asia, where many Overseas Chinese contributors had lived. As Jiang Zhiyou puts it, "since the beginning of trade with Westerners, [Western] sojourners [in Asia] grow ever more numerous. In the places they reside, they always have a place set aside as a public cemetery." Several authors suggest that Huang was impressed with these cemeteries in his travels abroad. "I learned that in the prime of life Huang travelled abroad and observed that Western cemeteries were well ordered and systematic. In his heart he truly wished to emulate this." Another author pointed out that with the spread of Western influence, many people admired and imitated different aspects of the West, "from minor things such as daily habits of food and drink to major matters such as politics, education, and customs." The Gubo cemetery thus became a symbol of the selective adoption of Western practices in China. Jiang Zhiyou went on to advocate the establishment of "public cemeteries" on the Western model in every part of China. But this argument clearly made some other authors uncomfortable. According to Huang Qitai, "It is said that Huang has journeyed abroad and observed that Westerners' cemeteries were well ordered. In his heart he admired this. I alone disagree. I observe that in his own record, his ambition was extremely high. But there is not a single mention of the West . . . So how can it be said that he is comparable to those fashionable people who imitate Western styles?"[14]

It occurred to a third group of writers that the Gubo cemetery was actually an organic integration of ancient Chinese and modern Western practice. Some suggested that Western modernity was somehow prefigured in China's long-past golden age. "Up to the present, the Way of Heaven has moved to the West. I have heard that there is more than one aspect of the institutions and standards of Europe which accords with the intentions of the *Zhouli*." Others saw Huang's accomplishment in terms of reconciling the two systems in a single whole. It did not matter, said one essayist, whether Huang's cemetery followed ancient practice or imitated Westerners. The key was that his approach accorded with reason.[15]

Together, these three approaches to the precedents behind Huang Xiulang's Gubo cemetery suggest the ambivalence widely felt at the project of cultural reform in the early twentieth century. For some, wholesale Westernization was the right approach. Others rejected Westernization, calling for the preservation and revival of a distinctly Chinese culture. This required identifying the essential elements of Chinese culture and eliminating its negative elements, which were often described in terms of accretions that had somehow attached themselves to the pure Chinese culture of ancient times. Still other writers tried to integrate the two possibilities, looking for selective Westernization that harmonized with the strengths of the Chinese cultural tradition, for modern cemeteries "with Chinese characteristics."

## A NEW CONFUCIAN MODERNITY AND A SPECIAL ROLE FOR OVERSEAS CHINESE

Many of the contributors identify a metaphoric element to Huang's project. It was about more than just how to build cemeteries. It was also about how to build China. The correct solution to the question of how China should deal with the modernizing challenge of the West had, of course, been a central preoccupation of Chinese intellectuals since the mid- to late-nineteenth century. By the early years of the Republic, attention was increasingly focusing on the need for cultural or spiritual transformation. The essays in the collection which place Huang Xiulang's cemetery within this larger project argue for a vision of a distinctly Chinese modernity that could rejuvenate their decaying civilization, one which would be based on traditional Confucian culture, and one in which the Overseas Chinese would play a special leadership role.

It was evident to all that Chinese society was in crisis. As Liang Xiaoxiong writes, "The world is changing dramatically. The European wind [*Ou-feng*] blows to the East, [causing] the destruction of the old altars to the virtuous sages of our country . . . The people consider degeneracy to be a virtue, and have personal profit as their ambition. Those who would heroically take it upon themselves to use the systems which survive from the ancients in order to effect a transformation are few indeed. Is not Mr. Huang one such man?"[16] What was at stake in the cemetery was more than just funerary customs, and more than just funerary customs in one village. The sentiments that lay behind the cemetery could be extended to Jinjiang County as a whole, and ultimately could be "extended to serve as guidance for the whole country," contributing to the cause of social unity (*datong*) for all of China.[17]

This argument made sense in the context of ancient but still vibrant notions of the homology between the family and the larger society. Creating appropriate relationships and patterns of behavior within the family, through education, ritual, and other means, was a crucial first step in creating social harmony and unity; indeed, the former would lead naturally to the latter. Writes one author, "To encourage filiality and submissiveness under Heaven [i.e. social harmony], nothing is more important than carefully attending to funeral rites and requiting one's origins [through ancestral sacrifice], treating one's kin as kin ought to be treated, and treating one's superiors as superiors ought to be treated. If one is able [to accomplish this] then the people's virtue will naturally deepen and all under Heaven will naturally be at peace."[18]

The link between funerary and ancestral sacrifice within the family and the national crisis went beyond vague homology. Funerary rituals and ancestral sacrifice had long been considered the basis for creating social cohesion among groups of kin.[19] As the magistrate of Jinjiang wrote in a proclamation forbidding encroachment on the property of the Gubo estate, such rituals served to generate "respect for the descent-line and to unite the agnates . . . This method is the height of excellence and profundity."[20]

Since the late nineteenth century, the social Darwinist notion that the strength of an ethnic or national group depended on the social cohesion of its members had become widespread among reform-minded Chinese.[21] Several essays suggest that the sense of cohesiveness between members of a single lineage could be the foundation for a modern national or civic virtue.[22] These authors were evidently influenced by the thought of Sun Yat-sen, who, as David Strand has shown, imagined the construction of a national polity based on the lineage, thereby completing the heretofore incomplete community of the Chinese people. Concern over the extinguishing of descent lines could be re-imagined in terms of the racial threat to the Chinese people, giving modern applications to traditional cultural practices.[23] Conceiving of national unity as an extension of lineage cohesiveness made it possible to find the roots of national salvation in the national past. Jiang Zhiyou compares China to the great nations of antiquity, Babylon, Egypt, Greece, India, and the Jewish nation. While all of these other nations have declined or disappeared, only China remains majestic. "For four thousand years it has been a powerful country. Its territory is ever increasing, and its population ever growing." What made China's historical trajectory different? The answer was the uniqueness of China's culture. At the heart of this uniqueness was lineage ideology and practice. "The people of the lineage follow the example of the ancestors and treat their kin as kin [ought to be treated]. This is the basis of transformation through education, and of social unity in the present."[24] Thus Jiang was arguing that China's route forward in the current crisis was not the wholesale rejection of Chinese culture, but rather its revival or renewal. The authors' attacks on Chinese tradition are selective. The purpose of eradicating geomancy was to strengthen, not to challenge, traditional orientations to the family and patriline. Unlike some May Fourth intellectuals, who argued that the Confucian emphasis on the family was an obstacle to Chinese modernization, the contributors to this volume sought to revive and refine this emphasis. Jiang Zhiyou and others like him were calling for a distinctly Chinese modernity, in which the unique characteristics of ancient Chinese culture played an essential role.

Cemeteries modelled on Gubo would seem to be equally suited to all parts of China. Widespread adoption of the practice would lead to the eradication of geomantic superstition and the promotion of lineage cohesiveness and in turn to a broader social unity. But numerous authors suggest that although there were comparable practices in the north, Huang's cemetery was uniquely suited to South China. The cemetery of Confucius' family in Qufu, Shandong, is frequently cited as a point of comparison, but most authors agree that Fujian and Shandong were not really comparable. For one thing, the population density is greater, and the terrain more variable, so disputes over graves are more frequent.[25] The key difference which made the salutary effects of the Gubo cemetery so well suited to South China, though, was the influence of the Overseas Chinese whose native place it was. Many essays identify a special role for them in the improvement of local society.

That the transformation of society will be the work of a select elite, that ordinary people will not bring about change themselves, is an assumption the authors do not really question. "Since the lineage cemetery [system of antiquity] has not been practiced, the poor have neglected the sacrifice and cleaning of the graves. They even move the tombs so that the location of the ancestral graves [is forgotten] and cannot be known again. The rich are taken in by geomancers, and delay burial to select a site, or get into disputes over grave sites leading to violent feuds. The diversity of problems is such that they cannot be fully enumerated." The question was who was most qualified to lead. The traditional elite were not the answer. Recall Liang Xiaoxiong's commentary on the degeneracy of the age. "Those who would heroically take it upon themselves to use the systems which survive from the ancients in order to effect a transformation are few indeed." The groups which traditionally saw social transformation as their responsibility were not up to the task. "The transformation of customs is the responsibility of the scholarly elite [*dafu*]," writes Chen Guolin. "But only those who recognize [the need] to eradicate bad customs can accomplish this. Those who [fall under the influence] of sentiment will generally be themselves transformed. At the extreme there are those who recognize the problem, but who are unable to tear themselves away from it. Observing closely, it is rarely the common people [who are guilty of this], but mainly the elite."[26] Thus it was precisely their lack of objective distance from the problematic cultural practices that made the traditional elite unable to change them.[27]

Overseas Chinese elites were the natural leaders in the movement to transform China. It was precisely their transnational activities, their exposure to modern ideas from the West, their ability to reflect critically on indigenous Chinese culture, and, not least, the wealth they had generated in the transnational Chinese ethnic economy that suited them for the task. Not surprisingly, many of the essays commemorating Huang Xiulang's project found ways to praise him and his background. Several point to the new knowledge that he obtained while abroad, or the breadth of his domestic and international experience prior to his return home.[28] Dan Zhen notes that Huang had long engaged in commerce abroad. "The ideas he has encountered and the things to which he has been exposed are indeed considerable." Chen Yan argues that it was precisely Huang's wealth that enabled him to purchase the site of the cemetery and establish his plan "without regrets." Wu Zhengkui goes so far as to propose that the knowledge and experience of the Overseas Chinese merchants meant that the whole traditional social order, which favored scholarship over commerce, had to be overturned. "The traditional elite [*shidafu*] ought to follow Mr. Huang's [example]."[29] This implied overcoming traditional prejudices and validating the Overseas Chinese not only as merchants and businessmen but also as national leaders.

The suitability of Overseas Chinese elites to lead national reform efforts was rooted in a logic of authenticity and cultural or racial purity. Overseas Chinese elites offered, to use Ong's phrase, "modernity without deracination." Their transnational activities had enabled them to acquire wealth as well as knowledge and skills, while managing to avoid becoming simply inferior versions of Westerners.[30] With the construction of his cemetery, Huang Xiulang had indeed demonstrated that the transnationalism of the Overseas Chinese did not threaten, but indeed strengthened, his Chinese identity. By reviving the pure Chinese culture of antiquity, and eliminating the distortion that had muddied the essential purity of that culture, Huang had proved himself more authentically Chinese than ordinary Chinese in China.

While several essays celebrate the Overseas Chinese merchant-scholar (*shenshang*) elite for their leadership in the development of China, a contradictory discourse reflects considerable ambivalence about their participation. Some authors suggest that Huang Xiulang was hardly representative of the Overseas Chinese generally. "His virtue and knowledge are not that which the average merchant is able to match." Most Overseas Chinese were only interested in personal profit, and had no concern for public good.[31] "Who would look to rich businessmen and

great merchants for knowledge? They rely on their wealth to travel around the world
. . . Mr. Huang became wealthy through commerce, but his learning is exceptional
in this age."[32] It was by no means certain that other Overseas Chinese were not
just as mired in backward customs as the people left behind. Moreover, their great
wealth made it possible for them to practice such customs with greater fervor. "Since
the opening of sea-[trade], many people from Quanzhou and Zhangzhou travel to
the Nanyang region to do business. When they become rich they return. Aside from
establishing fields and residences, they exert themselves to construct tombs, to serve
the way of requiting kin. This is as it ought to be. But owing to geomancy, they
frequently vie for personal profit. Lawsuits and disputes arise. They shame and
bankrupt themselves."[33]

Moreover, while Overseas Chinese may have had strong feelings about their
home villages and ancestral lineages, it was not clear that these parochial loyalties
could be transformed into national ones. Furthermore, the Overseas Chinese'
exposure to the West could potentially also have negative consequences, should
they become blinded to the values of Chinese culture. "Those who go to the West
[i.e. Overseas Chinese] strive to become more advanced [*kaitong*]. But sometimes
they go to extremes, violate prudence, and in the end their pursuit of what is far
off leads them to break with virtue. The sentiment of a filial son when taken to
extremes destroys the way of humanity."[34] Thus some authors worried, to use Ong's
language, that transnationalism had indeed deracinated the Overseas Chinese, that
their Chinese identity had been lost through exposure to the rest of the world.

Another set of arguments sought to resolve the contradictions about the Overseas
Chinese role. If the Overseas Chinese were to serve effectively the functions in
China's modernization which many of the essayists assign to them, they had to
promote a new kind of civic culture, which involved the selective integration of
East and West.[35] The problems of traditional Chinese culture should be identified
and eradicated, but not through blind adherence to Western values. Rather, it was
essential to distinguish vulgar customs from the national essence (*guocui*),
discarding the former while retaining the latter. This argument should be considered
in relation to those powerful intellectual movements of the early twentieth century
that rejected indiscriminate Westernization and called for the recovery and
preservation of the national heritage in the interest of preventing moral and
intellectual disintegration.[36] "Someone who is trapped by custom would not be able
to accomplish [what Huang has done]. Someone who is not trapped by custom but
unable to preserve the national essence also would not be able to do it."[37] The longest
sustained discussion of this issue comes in an essay by Dan Zhen, who introduces
the notion of patriotism (*aiguo*) as a valuable Western concept.

> Those who make contributions to the country, and who are connected to the
> changing fortunes of the country, are the model [patriots]. The so-called state
> funeral system is used to decorate them because they are not just people in a
> family but people of the nation. It is also to encourage other members of the
> country to try to devote their lives to the nation. If those who devote their
> lives to the nation grow more numerous, the nation flourishes.

Dan insists that patriotism is not equivalent to Westernization. Rather, the key is the ability to strike a balance between the two, something that the unique experiences of Overseas Chinese like Huang Xiulang made them well suited to do.

> He emulates the system of the Zhou official lineage cemetery while harmonizing with the system of Western public cemeteries. His ability to have a penetrating knowledge of East and West, to evaluate past and present, and to implement [his conclusions] without shortcomings is not just something that people of Fujian should take as a rule. Those who make plans for our nation, consider the great trends of the world, and reflect on what should be implemented in our country ought also to do so.[38]

It was thus the unique experience of the Overseas Chinese that enabled them to judge effectively how Western models might be appropriated to serve Chinese needs. The resulting synthesis should not simply be applied in the Overseas Chinese homeland of Fujian. Rather, it was the key to the broader cultural transformation of China as a whole. The Overseas Chinese had a patriotic responsibility to devote themselves to the cause of national renewal.

## CONCLUSIONS

Huang Xiulang's cemetery, a single project by a single Overseas Chinese, is now all but forgotten by history. But as we have seen, in its time "The Collected Commemorative Writings on the Gubo Cemetery" drew together a wide cross-section of elite contributors, who used the project to reflect on larger issues. For obvious reasons, none of the essays directly criticizes Huang Xiulang's cemetery project. But this does not mean the contents should be dismissed as mere conventional flattery. Rather, they provide valuable access to the contemporary discourses on the Overseas Chinese relationship with Chinese nationalism, modernization, and, indeed, Chinese identity itself.

Their arguments expressed considerable disagreement about the basis of Chinese modernity. This disagreement should be considered in terms of the broader debate on Westernization and China's future that within a few years would come to be referred to as the May Fourth Movement. The men who chose to contribute to the collection tended to fall on the more conservative side of this debate. But their attempt to reconcile modernity and nationalism was central to the debate as a whole. One thrust of the essays is to deny that Western ideas provided the universal, necessary basis for Chinese modernity.[39] Rather, they argue for alternative approaches to modernization according to Chinese principles, with Chinese characteristics.

The question also arose as to what was the appropriate role of the Overseas Chinese in this modernization. Much scholarship, perhaps influenced by the history of Overseas Chinese support for Sun Yat-sen's revolutionary efforts, stresses that their contribution was primarily financial. But with the Gubo cemetery, Huang

Xiulang was staking a claim to play some role in the broader task of modernization and cultural renewal. A few of the essays anticipate the arguments of scholars such as Watson and Woon, suggesting that the greater wealth of the Overseas Chinese enabled them more easily to fulfill traditional Chinese ideals, and therefore they were part of the problem, not the solution.[40] This was a delicate position to take in the context of a commemorative record celebrating an Overseas Chinese endeavor. The more common perspective was that Overseas Chinese were to serve as the leaders of a Confucian modernity, centered on South China, in which their capitalist endeavors in the global economy were to be celebrated, not criticized.

At the same time, there was tension over the focus of Overseas Chinese loyalty. The bulk of their remittances went to support their immediate family, and their charitable efforts were usually linked to their lineage or home village. For this model of Overseas Chinese as leaders of a national modernity to work, their loyalties had to be redirected towards the nation. Running through the essays is a desire to overcome the parochial loyalties of the Overseas Chinese and reorient them. To do so, elites in China appealed not only to Overseas Chinese self-interest but also to their ties of blood and heritage, and to their patriotism, making use of a variety of "political and rhetorical mechanisms [to] exchange symbolic values in order to secure material support." This was a difficult task, not always successfully accomplished in practice.[41] The transnationalism of the Overseas Chinese also created considerable ambivalence towards them. It was necessary to domesticate and capture their transnationalism if they were to serve as the leaders of a new China.[42]

After the interval of the Maoist period, China itself has once again become an important node in the flows of people and capital of the transnational Chinese ethnic economy. Many of the discourses that structure these flows today are remarkably similar to those of a century ago. In the late nineteenth and early twentieth centuries, economic and other forms of integration with the developed world caused dislocation in China, and contributed to a heightened sense among Chinese intellectuals of China's relative backwardness. Some looked to discourses about Chinese tradition and racial or cultural difference as tools to promote national unity and development, and define a distinctive route to modernity. Today, these same discourses are once again being invoked, and once again, the Overseas Chinese are seen as having a special role to play. As Aihwa Ong's work seeks to show, Confucianism, now defined in terms of features like entrepreneurialism, thrift, and commitment to the family and to social and political order, is used by many actors to try to reinforce the linkages between the Overseas Chinese ethnic economy and Chinese identity.[43] A contradictory set of discourses continues to express ambiguity and ambivalence about the Overseas Chinese contribution to national goals. The contributors to Huang's volume were concerned that Overseas Chinese loyalties were not appropriately focused on the nation, being either too parochial or too transnational, and hence deracinated. Today, while senior officials call on the Overseas Chinese to contribute their capital to the grand project of nation-building, Overseas Chinese remittances continue to fund local education, the revival of lineage and religious activities, and further emigration from their native places.[44] At the same time, complaints about the treatment of Chinese labor in Overseas

Chinese-owned factories or the cheap sale of state-owned assets to Overseas Chinese entrepreneurs by corrupt cadres expose the contradictions in claims that the Overseas Chinese Confucian form of capitalism is a more humane and moral variant, and that the Overseas Chinese represent a more authentic Chinese identity.[45]

As the other essays in this volume illustrate, terms such as Chinese ethnic economy or Chinese ethnic business can be very useful in conceptualizing the transnational links between ethnic businesses, just as they are helpful in drawing attention to the transnationalism of Overseas Chinese subjects. In both cases the terms highlight deterritorialized networks and spheres of activity, and linkages that defy state regulation. But regardless of whether the object of analysis is the firm or the individual, such terms are used most productively when considered not just in terms of economic circulation, but also in relation to the cultural logics and discourses which underlie and structure such circulation. Implicit in some formulations of the Chinese ethnic economy is the notion that Chinese-owned firms operate according to certain logics beyond that of the perfect market, but these logics are all too often expressed in terms of essentialized, timeless cultural characteristics. Identifying these logics, and situating them historically, is an important task for research on Chinese ethnic business as well as Chinese identity generally. This essay has tried to illustrate the discourses underlying a specific aspect of Overseas Chinese transnationalism, the relationship with their place of origin and with China. For over a century, ideas of Chinese identity, authenticity, patriotism, and nationalism have shaped the linkages between the Overseas Chinese and their putative place of origin. These ideas continue to be deployed in the service of particular interests among the Overseas Chinese, in China itself, and not least in other places in which the Chinese ethnic economy operates. Just as the very notion of a distinctly Chinese modernity, integrating outside elements in a way that accords with "Chinese characteristics," remains disputed, the place of the Overseas Chinese in that modernity continues to generate complex tensions. Similar tensions underlie the construction of the Chinese ethnic economy in which many of these Overseas Chinese participate.

## Notes

1   An earlier version of this chapter appeared in *Asian and Pacific Migration Journal*, 10.1 (2001).
2   Adam McKeown, *Chinese Migrant Networks and Cultural Change: Peru, Chicago, Hawaii, 1900–1936* (Chicago: University of Chicago Press, 2001). A related set of problems appear in the field of Chinese studies, which has often treated Overseas Chinese communities either as a sort of "residual China" or as minorities that are less "authentically" Chinese. See Ong and Nonini, "Introduction," in their *Ungrounded Empires*, 5–9.
3   On Huang Xiulang's life, see *Quanzhou shi Huaqiao zhi* (1996), 385–6. This account is also based on "Huang Xiulang yu Gubo shanzhuang jianjie" (mimeograph, no date) which I obtained at the Gubo cemetery.
4   See Gong Jie, *Gulangyu Jianzhu congtan* (Xiamen: Lujiang, 1997), 112–14; James Cook, "Bridges to Modernity: Xiamen, Overseas Chinese, and Southeast Coastal Modernization, 1847–1937" (PhD Thesis, University of California at San Diego, 1998), 139–41.

5 Gubo today is a sleepy village, largely bypassed by the prosperity of much of Jinjiang County. Few of the new multi-storey homes that are ubiquitous elsewhere in the county have been built; the villagers mostly make their living from a combination of agriculture and piecework assembly of umbrellas for a nearby (Overseas Chinese-invested) manufacturer.

6 A few individuals made multiple contributions in different genres: essays, poems, and felicitious phrases.

7 The sociologist Chen T'a would later try to expand the nature of this contribution, arguing that by introducing Western ideas about education, politics, social welfare, and even architecture to their home villages, emigrants had a modernizing effect on Chinese society. Chen T'a, *Emigrant Communities in South China* (Shanghai: Kelly & Walsh, 1939).

8 Yu Chunyan, Preface (*xu*), in *Gubo shanzhuang tiyong ji*, 13a. Unless otherwise noted, all subsequent references are from this source.

9 Wang Woqun, Preface, 14a.

10 Liang Xiaoxiong, Preface, 22a.

11 Chen Guolin, Preface, 20; Jiang Zhiyou, Preface, 28a.

12 Because of the cultural transformations of the period following the fall of Han, including the spread of Buddhism and the presence of many "barbarian" rulers in North China, the expression "after the Qin and Han" became a trope for the adulteration of Chinese culture by foreign elements. It was frequently invoked in the face of Westernization in the nineteenth and early twentieth centuries.

13 Huang Guisong, Preface, 69a; Zhou Dianzhong, Preface, 17a.

14 Jiang Zhiyou, Preface, 28a; Wu Zhengkui, Preface, 15a; Dan Zhen, Preface, 72a; Huang Qitai, Preface, 23a.

15 Wu Zhengkui, Preface, 15b; Zheng Zhao, Preface, 77b. Interestingly, none of the essayists mentions as a possible source of inspiration the famous Chinese cemetery of Manila, with which Huang must have been familiar. With its grand houses and furnishings for the dead, the Manila cemetery would have been difficult to square with the essayists' efforts to portray Huang as a modernizer opposed to superstition.

16 Liaong Xiaoxiong, Preface, 36a.

17 Chen Guolin, Preface, 36a. "Admiring [Huang's cemetery], the people of this locality will imitate it. From one locality, it will be implemented throughout the country." Chen Xiuyu, 55a.

18 Huang Guizhuo, Preface, 21a.

19 Kai-Wing Chow, *The Rise of Confucian Ritualism in Late Imperial China* (Stanford: Stanford University Press, 1994).

20 Zhang Zujun, "Jinjiang xian gongzhi shi," 3b. Another example is Zheng Xingsi, Preface, 75a. "The natural trend is that after the passage of only a few generations, the descendants of a single father become like strangers to one another. In order to prevent this . . . the Zhou system of official burials and lineage cemeteries [should be used]."

21 See Frank Dikotter, *The Discourse of Race in Modern China* (Hong Kong: Hong Kong University Press, 1992), ch. 4.

22 The cemetery will serve to "deepen the virtue of the people and encourage harmony under Heaven." Huang Guizhuo, Preface, 21b. A similar argument appears in Zheng Xingsi, Preface, 75a. I discuss this argument, which appeared frequently in the political discourse of the time, in more detail in "Practicing Kinship: Descent and Lineage in Late Imperial China" (Stanford: Stanford University Press, 2002), 202–3.

23 Sun Yat-sen, 1: 60–6; David Strand, "Community, Society, and History in Sun Yat-sen's *Sanmin zhuyi*," in Theodore Huters, R. Bin Wong, and Pauline Yu, eds., *Culture and State in Chinese History: Conventions, Accommodations, and Critiques* (Stanford: Stanford University Press, 1977).

24 Jiang Zhiyou, Preface, 28a ff.

25 Chen Yan, Preface, 60a.

26 Jiang Chunlin, Preface, 36a; Chen Guolin, Preface, 20a.

27  Song Zengyou also laments the recent decline of traditional Chinese scholarship. "Since the gradual spread of westernization to the east, elderly scholars have had to seek out practical learning." Classical scholarship is mocked, and there are many corrupt scholars. Preface, 37a.

28  For example, Huang Qitai, Preface, 23a; Zhang Cheng, Preface, 61a.

29  Dan Zhen, Preface, 72b; Chen Yan, Preface, 60a; Wu Zhengkui, Preface, 15b.

30  Aihwa Ong, *Flexible Citizenship: The Cultural Logics of Transnationality* (Durham, NC: Duke University Press, 1999), 52.

31  Zhou Dianzhong, Preface, 17a; Liang Xiaoxiong, Preface, 22a.

32  Song Zengyou, Preface, 37a.

33  Lin Han, Preface, 44a. These remarks invite comparison with the work of anthropologists such as James Watson and Yuen-fong Woon, who suggest that by enabling working-class men to fulfill traditional patriarchal ideals, emigration actually encouraged conservatism and the maintenance of traditional institutions. James Watson, *Emigration and the Chinese Lineage: The Mans in Hong Kong and London* (Berkeley: University of California, 1975); Yuen-fong Woon, *Social Organization in South China, 1911–1949* (Ann Arbor: Center for Chinese Studies, 1984).

34  Wang Woqun, Preface, 14a.

35  For a good discussion of the content of this culture, see Cook (1998), ch. 7. For comparable contemporary arguments, see Edward Friedman, "Reconstructing China's National Identity: A Southern Alternative to Mao-Era Anti-Imperialist Nationalism," *Journal of Asian Studies*, 53.1 (1994): 78–87.

36  On arguments about national essence, see Laurence Schneider, "National Essence and the New Intelligentsia," and Martin Bernal, "Liu Shih-p'ei and National Essence," in Charlotte Furth, ed., *The Limits of Change: Essays on Conservative Alternatives in Republican China* (Cambridge, MA: Harvard University Press, 1976).

37  Wang Woqun, Preface, 14a.

38  Dan Zhen, Preface, 72b.

39  Partha Chatterjee explores similar arguments in Indian history in *The Nation and Its Fragments: Colonial and Postcolonial Histories* (Princeton: Princeton University Press, 1993).

40  Watson (1975); Woon (1984).

41  Prasenjit Duara, "Nationalists among Transnationals: Overseas Chinese and the Idea of China, 1900–1911," in Donald Nonini and Aihwa Ong, eds., *Ungrounded Empires: The Cultural Politics of Modern Chinese Nationalism* (New York: Routledge, 1997), 38. As Madeline Hsu has written of magazines for Taishan (Toisan) emigrants, "it was easier to promote and nurture allegiances when they already existed, as in the case of communities defined by native place in the form of country, district or village, or by kinship and shared surname. In contrast, the magazines could do little to instill new loyalties in their readers, and so the relatively abstract notion of China the modern nation had much less appeal for the pockets of overseas Taishanese." Madeline Hsu, "Migration and Native Place: *Qiaokan* and the Imagined Community of Taishan County, Guangdong, 1893–1993," *Journal of Asian Studies* 59.2 (May 2000): 326.

42  I borrow the expression "domesticating transnationalism" from Duara.

43  Ong, 59.

44  In the words of Vice Premier Qian Qichen to a 1999 conference, "Overseas Chinese, although they live in different parts of the world, have always been the most supportive and enthusiastic about the opening up of China, the economic, scientific, and cultural exchanges of China with the world and about the economic growth of China." "Overseas Chinese urged to enlarge role," *China Daily*, 07/13/99. On remittances to lineage and native place, see Graham Johnson, "Family Strategies and Economic Transformation in Rural China: Some Evidence from the Pearl River Delta," in Deborah Davis and Stevan Harrell, eds., *Chinese Families in the Post-Mao Era* (Berkeley: University of California Press, 1993), 132–3.

45  Ong, 41.

# Part III

# Chinese businesses, local urban structures, and homogenization

# 9 Chinese ethnic economies within the city context

*Eric Fong and Linda Lee*

## INTRODUCTION

In recent years, sociologists have shown growing interest in the economic consequences of participation in the ethnic economy in general. However, the understanding of this topic is decidedly mixed. On the basis of the segmented labor market and ethnic solidarity theories, Portes and his associates (Portes and Bach 1985; Portes and Jensen 1989, 1992; Wilson and Portes 1980) argued that the ethnic economy provides an alternative avenue for minority members, especially for those with limited English ability, to achieve socioeconomic advancement. Since there are few jobs available for people with low proficiency in English, the ethnic economy provides employment opportunities to ethnic group members who would otherwise be competing for these jobs. The ethnic community fosters the development of social capital, which in turn offers access to additional resources for ethnic group members and their businesses to survive and, in some cases, prosper. These additional resources include extended credit (Portes and Sensenbrenner 1993), pooled financial resources (such as the credit rotation associations suggested by Light (1972)), and lower labor costs (such as the informal support of family members studied by Sanders and Nee (1996)). Consequently, the economic returns of human capital resources such as education and work experience for those participating in the ethnic economy correspond closely to those for people working in the broader economy. This positive and benign understanding of the ethnic economy has been documented by a series of studies based on Cubans in Miami (Portes and Bach 1985; Portes and Jensen 1989), and Chinese in New York (Zhou and Logan 1989).

Another perspective on the economic consequences of participating in the ethnic economy portrays a pessimistic and discouraging picture. This group of researchers suggest that ethnic solidarity can be negative as well as positive. To ignore the negative consequences of ethnic solidarity is to fail to paint the full picture of the ethnic economy. In their study of the Chinese in San Francisco and a reanalysis of Cubans in Miami, Sanders and Nee (1987) found that the ethnic enclave economy is only of benefit to entrepreneurs, not to workers. They argued that the different earning patterns of entrepreneurs and workers in the ethnic economy reflect its true nature. The ethnic economy can support only so many entrepreneurs. Therefore, the success of small businesses in the ethnic economy depends to a great extent on maintaining a large pool of low-paid workers. To keep wages low, entrepreneurs recruit workers through kinship and ethnic ties and bind them in a web of ethnic obligations. This notion of negative consequences to participation in the ethnic economy is further reinforced by Bonacich's (1973) "middleman minority theory." Bonacich argued that large capitalist firms use ethnic entrepreneurs to exploit their ethnic group members through ethnic bonds in order to reduce labor costs. Later research on the Chinese in New York (Kwong 1979) and Koreans in Chicago (Hurh and Kim 1979; Min 1996) and Los Angeles (Bonacich and Light 1988) supported this pessimistic view.

To explain these seemingly confusing findings, we suggest that earlier studies have been limited in several key respects. First, previous research on this topic compares the earning of individuals participating inside and outside the ethnic economy, focusing primarily on the role of individual human capital (Portes and Bach 1985; Portes and Jensen 1989, 1992; Sanders and Nee 1987; Wilson and Portes 1980; Zhou and Logan 1989). These studies ignore the effect of the broader city context, especially the larger economy, and treat the ethnic economy as self-contained and self-sustaining. The economic returns of those participating in the ethnic economy are largely treated as insulated from the effects of the broader city labor market.[1] However, the ethnic economy is an integral part of and has a close connection with the larger economy (Nee *et al.* 1994), which can be shaped by globalization. Changes in the city contexts definitely will have effects on the economic returns to those participating in the ethnic economy. Therefore, we must go beyond the effect of human capital and incorporate the effect of the city context, with the perspective of how they are related to globalization, to obtain a more complete picture of the economic returns to individuals participating in the ethnic economy.

Another limitation of previous studies on the economic consequences of participating in the ethnic economy relates to the analytical strategy. Many of these studies were not designed to take into account the possibility of selectivity problems, which can arise from two sources. First, observed earning patterns of those participating inside and outside the ethnic economy may be related to the selection of individuals with distinctive expectations and orientations towards their jobs because of the unique occupational structures and environments inside and outside ethnic economies. In turn, their earning potential may be affected (Park 1997; Waldinger 1986). The second source of selectivity is the non-random selection of entrepreneurs and salaried workers. There may be personality differences between entrepreneurs and salaried workers; entrepreneurs may be more willing to take risks and may be more aggressive in personality. These personal characteristics may have substantial influence on their earning potential and the return of human capital resources. Therefore, to understand fully the economic consequences of participating in the ethnic economy and to avoid the possibility of biased estimation, one must consider the relationship of earning and human capital resources jointly with selection in participating in the ethnic economy and self-employment.

The third limitation of most studies on the economic consequences of participating in the ethnic economy is that they focus on a single city (e.g., Miami, New

York). Although some studies include more than one city, the earnings of ethnic group members who participate in the ethnic economy are analyzed in separate models for each city (Sanders and Nee 1987; Zhou and Logan 1989) or the focus on ethnic entrepreneurs only (Light and Rosenstein 1995; Evans 1989). Studies seldom provide a pooled multi-city analysis to discuss general patterns of the economic returns of participating in the ethnic economy for both entrepreneurs and workers. Although research devoted to discovering general patterns may lose detailed differences among cities, it can uncover patterns that may be overlooked by single case studies. As well, it can study the effects of city structural contexts, affected by different levels of globalization, in relation to the economic consequences of participating in the ethnic economy.

In this article, we go beyond prior studies by dealing with these limitations. First, we model the economic consequences of participating in the ethnic economy by incorporating city structural contexts in addition to individual human capital. We disentangle the effects of the relative importance of the two sets of factors. Second, we use a bivariate probit selection regression model to deal with the double selectivity issues, namely self-employment and participating in the ethnic economy. Finally, we include 16 cities in the analysis, which allows general patterns to emerge, to study the economic returns of Chinese participating inside and outside the ethnic economy.

## THEORETICAL FRAMEWORK

Most discussions of the economic consequences of participating in the ethnic economy emphasize the comparative economic return for those participating inside the ethnic economy and those participating outside. Most studies have revealed a general pattern that immigrants with a higher level of education, better English, and more work experience usually have higher earnings, regardless of whether they are entrepreneurs or workers in the ethnic economy (Light and Rosenstein 1995; Portes and Bach 1985; Portes and Jensen 1989, 1992; Sanders and Nee 1987; Wilson and Portes 1980). However, these studies have been inconclusive about the relative importance of human capital resources on the economic returns for those participating inside and outside the ethnic economy. Some studies found that the economic returns of human capital resources are comparable (Portes and Bach 1985; Portes and Jensen 1989, 1992; Wilson and Portes 1980). However, other findings suggest that the economic returns of human capital resources are comparable only between entrepreneurs inside and outside the enclave economy, but not between workers (Park 1997; Sanders and Nee 1987). Yet others found that the differences are related to gender (Hurh and Kim 1979; Zhou and Logan 1989). Taking into consideration all these results, we hypothesize that the *rates of return of human capital resources are different between entrepreneurs and workers participating inside and outside the ethnic economy*.

This focus on individual characteristics provides inconsistent results and suggests that a broader perspective is needed which incorporates both human capital resources and embedded city structural contexts. As Nee, Sanders, and Sernau observed, "contemporary ethnic economies are deeply embedded in the metropolitan economy in which they are located" (Nee *et al.* 1994: 850–1). It is especially important to situate the economic returns of participation in ethnic economy in the metropolitan context. Some unique contexts that may affect the economic returns of participating in the ethnic economy are closely tied to the considerable transformation that has resulted from globalization.

In the following section, we discuss four key city structural contexts related to globalization that are likely to affect the economic consequences of working inside and outside the ethnic economy. The literature concerning globalization, the labor market, and economic achievement suggests that these city structural contexts related to globalization have substantial influence on individual earnings. We do not presume that the variables discussed in this chapter include all the factors that may influence the economic consequences of participating inside and outside the ethnic economy. However, we argue that the discussion includes variables that are likely to be important determinants.

(1) *City structural context: Relative size of the minority group in the city:* Globalization stimulates labor migration. This dynamic, in conjunction with changes in immigration policies in the 1970s, led to an increase in the size of minority groups in some cities. Over the past several decades, the effect of the relative size of the minority group on the economic achievements of its members has been investigated. The basic thesis is that a larger relative size of minority group is associated with a higher level of discrimination against the minority group in the city (Lieberson 1980). This discrimination originates from a fear in the majority group that their own social and economic welfare will be affected as the relative size of the minority group increases. This hypothesis has received substantial empirical support (Fossett and Kiecolt 1989; Jiobu and Marshall 1971; Lieberson 1980; Parcel 1979; Quillian 1995). Although most of these studies focus on the relationship between whites and blacks, some studies that focused on other racial and ethnic groups found similar results (Tienda and Lii 1987).

In this study, we compare the effect of the relative size of the minority group on the economic returns of those working in the ethnic economy and those working outside it. As their relative size increases through international migration, members of the group become more "visible" to the majority group. As their labor pool increases, they have more intense contact and direct competition with other groups in the labor market. Members of the minority group working outside the ethnic economy who want to avoid the stiff competition and hostile working environment may turn to the ethnic economy for opportunities.[2] Although the ethnic economy can be a "protected market," and ethnic group members participating in it can be shielded from direct competition with other groups (Aldrich *et al.* 1985), the competition from within it will increase as participation in the ethnic economy rises and the ethnic economy is not large enough to absorb the surplus labor (Lieberson 1980). In turn, the economic returns to employees in the ethnic economy will be affected. Thus, *the relative effect of group size on the economic returns of the minority group is hypothesized to be negatively related to the earnings of workers inside the ethnic economy.*

(2) *City structural context: Level of residential segregation:* As the minority group population increases due to immigration, neighborhood clustering emerges. Although research suggests the effect of residential patterns on economic achievement of groups (Tienda 1991; Wilson 1996), the findings of the effects of residential segregation on the economic returns of those participating in the ethic economy are mixed. Although the residential concentration of Chinese in New York (Zhou and Logan 1989) and San Francisco (Sanders and Nee 1987) or Cubans in Miami (Portes and Jensen 1989) facilitates economic activity within those ethnic communities, the residential concentration of other Southeast Asian groups, such as the Cambodian community in the Long Beach area of Los Angeles County or the Hmong around Fresno, does not necessarily create more economic activity within those ethnic communities (Rumbaut 1995).

One possible means of explaining these seemingly mixed results is to understand how the interaction of residential patterns and group size affects the economic returns of those participating in the ethnic economy. The Chinese populations in New York and San Francisco and the Cubans in Miami have considerable size due to international migration from their countries of origin. When a large number of group members are clustered in concentrated ethnic communities, the residential ecology of a critical mass will foster the development of a more formal structure and more business opportunities among ethnic group members (Evans 1989). They are more likely to make use of these ethnic organizations and businesses to satisfy their needs, such as food, medical care, and entertainment, which in turn creates the "institutional completeness" of the ethnic group (Breton 1964). Both entrepreneurs and salaried workers in the ethnic economy benefit from the context, as they have the advantage of serving a large number of their own members with minimal competition from other groups. Therefore, in a large and segregated ethnic community, ethnic entrepreneurs can expect a large volume of sales and possibly higher profit, and ethnic workers can expect a high demand for their labor and consequently higher earnings.

A smaller ethnic population, even with high levels of residential concentration, can only support a limited number of businesses. After all, most ethnic business attracts mainly ethnic customers. A small pool of potential customers considerably limits the growth and opportunities of ethnic business. Suttles' study in the Addams area of Chicago found that the small number of Puerto Ricans and Mexicans in the community did not support many shops dealing with African-American ethnic products (Suttles 1968: ch. 3). In such situations, entrepreneurs cannot expect as high earnings, and ethnic workers cannot expect as much demand for their labor, which then implies possibly lower wages. We therefore hypothesize that *the interaction of a higher level of residential segregation of the minority group and a higher proportion of ethnic group members in the city is positively related to the earnings of both entrepreneurs and workers participating in the ethnic economy.*

(3) *City structural context: Relative employment rates among racial and ethnic groups:* Employment differentials among racial and ethnic groups have been well

documented (Cohn and Fossett 1995). They can be related to various factors, such as the presence of foreign investments that may benefit certain racial and ethnic groups, the differences in the human capital resources of groups, the absence of unions that prevent unequal employment of groups, and the preferential treatment of certain groups (Portes and Sensenbrenner 1993). Consequently, members of some groups are less likely to secure jobs even when vacancies are available. Since ethnic group members are usually "positively typified" (Portes and Sensenbrenner 1993) in the ethnic economy, ethnic employers prefer to hire workers from their own ethnic labor pool. Ethnic group members are offered job opportunities that are not available outside the ethnic economy. If one controls for all factors, more ethnic members will be employed when more jobs are offered in the ethnic economy. Although more ethnic businesses are opened, partly because of the increase in foreign investment from home countries which has resulted from an easier flow of international capital, a higher number of ethnic businesses leads to stiff competition. Ethnic business owners maintain their profits by minimizing costs in all aspects of their business operation, including keeping wages low. Subsequently the economic returns for workers in the ethnic economy will be affected. Therefore, we hypothesize that *the economic returns for ethnic group workers in the ethnic economy will be less than the returns for ethnic group workers outside the ethnic economy when the level of relative employment rate is high.*

(4) *City structural context: High unemployment rate in the city:* The economy of most cities is linked to the global market at different levels, while employment opportunities for groups are strongly influenced by the state of the city economy through the queuing process (Hodge 1973; Lieberson 1980). In this process, ethnic groups are ranked according to various dimensions, such as ethnic stereotypes or statistical discrimination. Employers first hire the top-ranked groups and then continue to hire groups from successively lower ranks in the queue. This hiring process substantially affects the employment opportunities of those who are ranked at the end of the queue, usually minority groups, when the unemployment rate is high. The disadvantage in the labor market encourages some ethnic group members to seek self-employment while others will consider the ethnic economy as an alternative avenue for jobs. Given the increase in migration, the pool of potential business owners as well as the labor supply within the ethnic economy can increase. Workers compete for jobs and ethnic businesses compete against one another for clientele. This can substantially affect the earnings of both workers and employers. We hypothesize that *the earnings of entrepreneurs and workers in the ethnic economy will be lowered when there is a high unemployment rate in the city.*

In short, we argue that any understanding of the economic returns of participating inside and outside the ethnic economy should take into consideration both human capital resources and city structural contexts. Drawing from the literature on the labor market and economic achievement, we further suggest that the economic returns for those participating in the ethnic economy are closely related to the city structural contexts that are shaped by globalization. In relation to financial capital and migration due to economic globalization, we have discussed how four possible city structural contexts (the size of the minority group, the interaction of the level of residential segregation and the size of the group, the relative employment rate between groups, and the unemployment rate) may have substantial effects on the economic returns to both entrepreneurs and employees participating in the ethnic economy.

## DATA

The data are drawn from the 1990 5 percent Public Use Microdata Sample File (PUMS). We selected Chinese immigrants of both sexes in 16 primary metropolitan statistical areas (PMSAs) where the Chinese population is over 10,000.[3] The Chinese in the 16 PMSAs represent 90 percent of the Chinese in urban America. We restricted the study to people between the ages of 18 and 65, to ensure that respondents were eligible to participate in the labor force. The Chinese were chosen in this study because this group has grown rapidly in the last few decades and Chinese ethnic economies can be found in most major cities.

However, caution should be used when interpreting these data, because the Chinese represent a heterogeneous group. The majority of Chinese immigrants who arrived in the last few decades were from mainland China, Taiwan, and Hong Kong. Immigrants from these three areas may differ in their expectations and adaptation experiences due to the diverse social and political systems in these places of origin.

The objective of this study is to compare how human capital and city structural contexts affect the earnings of entrepreneurs and workers inside and outside the ethnic economy. The dependent variable is individual earnings, and it is logged for the purpose of computation. The transformed dependent variable allows for the interpretation of estimated coefficients of the model as the percentage change in earnings by a unit change in the predictor.

The first set of independent variables is human capital. It is measured by education level, language ability, and years of work experience. Educational level is measured by two dummy variables that designate the highest level of education as "with some university education" and "with university degree." The reference group is those individuals who "completed high school or less." Language ability is also indicated by two dummy variables: "speaks English well" and "speaks English not well." The reference category for language ability is "does not speak English." "Years of work experience" is approximated by subtracting years of schooling and six pre-school years from the age at the time of data collection. We also included the square of the number of years of work experience for the possibly non-linear relationship between years of work experience and earnings.

The second set of independent variables is city structural contexts. In accordance with the earlier discussion, we included four city ecological factors. First, there is a variable to capture the relative size of the Chinese population in the metropolitan areas. It is indicated by the proportion of Chinese in the metropolitan area. The second variable is the segregation level of the Chinese. It is measured by the commonly used dissimilarity index:

$$D = \frac{1}{2} \sum_{i=1}^{k} \left| \frac{p_{1i}}{p_1} - \frac{p_{2i}}{p_2} \right|$$

where $p_{1i}$ is the proportion of Chinese in census tract $i$, $p_{2i}$ is the total non-Chinese population in census tract $i$, $k$ is the number of census tracts in the city, and $p_1$ and $p_2$ are the total Chinese population and total non-Chinese population in the city respectively. The index ranges from 0 to 1. A large value indicates a higher level of uneven distribution of Chinese from other groups.

The third variable is the relative employment rate between the Chinese and other groups. It is measured by the ratio of the odds of employment for non-Chinese to the odds of employment for Chinese (Cohn and Fossett 1995). In other words, it is $(N_e/N_n)/(C_e/C_n)$, where $N_e$ is the number of employed non-Chinese, $N_n$ is the number of unemployed non-Chinese, $C_e$ is the number of employed Chinese, and $C_n$ is the number of unemployed Chinese. Consistent with previous analyses, only individuals between the ages of 18 and 65 are included in the analysis. A higher score suggests higher employment inequality for the Chinese. For example, a score of 4 means that the odds of employment for non-Chinese are four times higher than the odds of employment for Chinese.

The last city structural variable is the unemployment rate. It is measured by the proportion of total unemployment in the labor market. A higher unemployment rate suggests a weaker labor market.

Our earning specification also controls for a set of variables that may confound the effects of human capital and city structural contexts on individual earnings. They are marital status, gender, immigration period, hours of work, and industry involved. Controlling for marital status recognizes the possible positive effect of the presence of a spouse. As Sanders and Nee (1996) succinctly pointed out, family can be viewed as an important form of social capital in the pursuit of economic advancement. Family members not only provide unpaid labor, but also develop trust and mutual obligations among themselves that enable any family business to economize on costs of production and operation. The model also controls for gender and duration in the country because previous research has documented that the economic returns of human capital resources are insignificant among females working in the ethnic economy (Zhou and Logan 1989), and that the economic returns of human capital resources improve as individuals stay in the country longer (Alba *et al.* 2001). We controlled for hours of work because respondents who work long hours usually earn more than those who work less, *ceteris paribus*. Finally, we created a set of categorical variables to control for those who are working in finance/business, trade, construction, manufacturing, and agriculture. The agricultural industry variable was set to contrast with other industries. Therefore, the results can be interpreted as the effects of human capital and city structural contexts, holding this set of variables constant, on earnings.

An additional task was to identify whether respondents are entrepreneurs or wage earners in the ethnic economy. To identify entrepreneurs, we used the census question on class of workers. Although we could identify entrepreneurs by the question on sources of self-employment earnings, they would also include individuals who are classified as salaried workers based on the "class of workers" question who have additional self-employment earnings (Light and Rosenstein 1995). These people are most likely salaried workers who are involved in self-employment projects after business hours, and, strictly speaking, they are not entrepreneurs. Their economic well-being does not depend entirely on the success of their business.

It is not easy to identify individuals in the ethnic economy. So many attempts have been made to operationalize the concept that even researchers deeply involved in the study of ethnic economy have lamented the confusion (Light *et al.* 1993; Nee *et al.* 1994). Ethnic economy usually refers to ethnic ownership or a co-ethnic working environment. The latter information, however, is not available in the census data. In this study, we used a working definition suggested by Logan *et al.* (1994), which was later used in other studies (Wilson 1999; Rosenfeld and Tienda 1999). The definition emphasizes specialization in industrial sectors, and it provides a proxy of co-ethnicity, a salient characteristic of the ethnic economy (Logan *et al.* 1994). If workers and entrepreneurs of a certain ethnic group are concentrated in a specific sector, there is a high likelihood that these people will be working in a co-ethnic environment. This definition obviously does not capture those ethnic businesses which are in industries with lower representation of the particular ethnic group. The following results, therefore, should be interpreted with caution, taking this limitation into account.

According to the operationalized definition of the ethnic economy, we identify an industry as being over-represented by an ethnic group whenever the number of ethnic group members involved is at least 1.5 times greater than the chances for either entrepreneurs or workers. For a formal presentation, an industry is defined as over-represented whenever one of the two following conditions is fulfilled: (1) the odds ratio for Chinese entrepreneurs in an industry $(f_1/f_2)/(f_5/f_6)$ is 1.5 or above, where $f_1$ is Chinese entrepreneurs, $f_2$ is non-Chinese entrepreneurs in the industry, $f_5$ is Chinese in all other industries, and $f_6$ is non-Chinese in all other industries; (2) the odds ratio for Chinese salaried workers in an industry $(f_3/f_4)/(f_5/f_6)$ is 1.5 or above, where $f_3$ is Chinese salaried workers, and $f_4$ is non-Chinese salaried workers in the industry. The cut off point is consistent with previous studies, thus allowing for direct comparison.

## METHODS

The outcome of interest in this study is individual earnings. According to the literature review above, individual earnings are a function of human capital resources, city structural contexts, entrepreneurial status, and working inside ethnic economies. The formal expression of the model is:

$$Y = \beta X + \alpha K + \omega W + \tau E + \mu \tag{1}$$

where Y is current earnings, X is a vector of individual characteristics, K is the vector of city structural contexts, W is another dummy variable representing working in ethnic economies (1 for working in ethnic economies and 0 for working outside ethnic economies), E is a dummy variable indicating entrepreneurs (1 for entrepreneurs and 0 for workers), and $\mu$ is the error term. ß, $\alpha$, $\omega$ and $\tau$ are estimated parameters of X, K, W, and E respectively.

Since entrepreneurial status and working in ethnic economies may interact with individual characteristics and city structural contexts, individual earnings may in turn be affected. Taking into consideration these concerns, model 1 can be refined as:

$$Y_1 = ß_1 X + \alpha_1 K + \mu_1$$
$$Y_2 = ß_2 X + \alpha_2 K + \mu_2$$
$$Y_3 = ß_3 X + \alpha_3 K + \mu_3$$
$$Y_4 = ß_4 X + \alpha_4 K + \mu_4 \qquad (2)$$

where $\mu_j$ denotes the specific error term for each earning prospect. This set of models allows for consideration of four earnings prospects ($Y_j$): workers working in ethnic economies ($j=1$), workers working outside ethnic economies ($j=2$), entrepreneurs working in ethnic economies ($j=3$), and entrepreneurs working outside ethnic economies ($j=4$).

To capture the decisions of being entrepreneurs and working inside or outside the ethnic economies in the metropolitan areas selected for this study, $D_1$ denotes working inside or outside the ethnic economies, and $D_2$ denotes working in the salaried or self-employed class:

$$D_1 = 1, \text{ if } Y_1^* = \gamma X_1 + \mu_1 > 0$$
$$\phantom{D_1} = 0, \text{ if } Y_1^* = \gamma X_1 + \mu_1 < 0 \qquad (3)$$

where

$$D_2 = 1, \text{ if } Y_2^* = \rho X_2 + \mu_2 > 0$$
$$\phantom{D_2} = 0, \text{ if } Y_2^* = \rho X_2 + \mu_2 > 0. \qquad (4)$$

$Y_1^*$ and $Y_2^*$ are unobserved continuous variables. They can be interpreted as the respective indices of the propensity to self-employment and to working in the ethnic economies. $X_1$ and $X_2$ are observed individual characteristics that affect the two decisions. $\mu_1$ and $\mu_2$ reflect the unobserved components that relate to the decisions. $\gamma$ and $\rho$ are estimated parameters of $X_1$ and $X_2$ respectively.

Cases where $D_1=0$ and $D_2=0$ include workers outside the ethnic economies. When $D_1=0$ and $D_2=1$, they are workers working in the ethnic economies. Entrepreneurs working in the ethnic economies are represented by cases where $D_1=1$ and $D_2=1$. Finally, entrepreneurs outside the ethnic economies are included when $D_1=1$ and $D_2=0$.

To consider the double selection of being an entrepreneur and participating in the ethnic economies in these analyses, we used a two-stage estimation approach suggested by Tunali (1986). In the first stage, we used two criterion variables, entrepreneurial status $(D_1)$ and participating in ethnic economies $(D_2)$, and estimated a bivariate probit model. We constructed two lambda terms $(\lambda_1$ and $\lambda_2)$ from the results of the bivariate probit model. In the second stage, we used OLS techniques to estimate equation (1) with these two lambda terms. The two lambda terms are double selection analogs similar to the inverse Mills ratio of Heckman's single selection model. The inverse Mills ratio is a non-linear function obtained from the probit analysis of the selection (Stolzenberg and Relles 1997). The final model of the estimation will be:

$$Y = \beta X + \alpha K + \phi\lambda_1 + \rho$$

where $\phi$ and $\rho$ are additional coefficients to be estimated.

## RESULTS

Table 9.1 displays the earnings of entrepreneurs and salaried workers participating inside and outside the ethnic economies within the 16 PMSAs with the largest number of Chinese. The first two rows of the table indicate that the average earnings of those participating in ethnic economies in the 16 cities are lower than the average earnings of those who do not. The average earnings of those participating outside the ethnic economies are on average $3,371 higher than the average earnings of those inside the ethnic economies (last column). There are three possible explanations for the earning advantage of those working outside ethnic economies: the differences in human capital resources between those participating inside and

*Table 9.1* Average earnings of immigrant Chinese in five major PMSAs by status of entrepreneurship and participation in ethnic economies, 1990

|  | Los Angeles | New York | Oakland | San Francisco | San Jose | Average |
|---|---|---|---|---|---|---|
| Participating in the ethnic economy | 27,969 | 15,665 | 28,471 | 19,749 | 36,341 | 25,132 |
| Not participating in the ethnic economy | 26,983 | 26,180 | 29,583 | 27,660 | 37,603 | 28,503 |
| Entrepreneurs in the ethnic economy | 46,644 | 23,895 | 45,598 | 33,486 | 38,877 | 39,330 |
| Entrepreneurs not in the ethnic economy | 36,152 | 34,124 | 31,168 | 42,853 | 46,567 | 38,345 |
| Workers in the ethnic economy | 24,586 | 14,764 | 25,633 | 17,974 | 35,896 | 22,930 |
| Workers not in the ethnic economy | 25,866 | 25,580 | 29,495 | 26,029 | 37,172 | 27,704 |

Source: 1990, 5 percent PUMS.

outside ethnic economies, the differential effects of city structural contexts on earnings in the two categories, or the differential returns of human capital resources between the two categories.

A closer look at the results shows substantial intercity variations in the earning differences between those who participate and those who do not participate in ethnic economies. For example, the difference in earnings is $10,515 in New York, but only $1,112 in Oakland. This wide variation suggests that the differences in earnings may be related to city structural contexts.

Since the earnings of individuals may be related to their employment class (entrepreneur or salaried worker), rows 3 to 6 of Table 9.1 indicate the earnings of people participating inside and outside ethnic economies, controlling for being entrepreneurs. Once this status is controlled, the pattern becomes blurred. First, the results suggest that there are no consistent patterns of earnings for those participating inside and outside ethnic economies. In New York, San Francisco, and San Jose, entrepreneurs participating outside ethnic economies earn more than the other three groups. However, in Oakland and Los Angeles, earnings are highest for entrepreneurs in ethnic economies. In addition, employees working outside ethnic economies earn levels similar to those of entrepreneurs in ethnic economies in New York and San Jose.

Second, the results show no consistent pattern of earning differentials for entrepreneurs who participate in ethnic economies compared to those who do not participate. In Los Angeles and Oakland, entrepreneurs participating in the ethnic economy earn $10,492 and $14,430 more, respectively, than entrepreneurs who do not participate. However, the earnings of entrepreneurs participating in the ethnic economy in New York, San Francisco, and San Jose are $10,229, $9,367 and $7,690 less, respectively, than those who do not participate.

Finally, comparisons of earnings of workers participating in ethnic economies with workers participating outside also reveal substantial variations among cities. The earning difference between workers in the ethnic economy and those who do not participate is $10,816 in New York, but only $1,280 in Los Angeles. The results point to the possible effects of city structural contexts on the economic returns of participating inside and outside ethnic economies.

In summary, the results portray a complex pattern of the earnings of entrepreneurs and salaried workers participating inside and outside the ethnic economies, and substantial variations in earning patterns among cities with different levels of globalization. To understand fully the economic consequences of participating in ethnic economies, these results clearly suggest that the analysis should include the effects not only of human capital but also of city structural contexts on the economic returns of entrepreneurs and salaried workers.

To begin the disentanglement of the economic consequences of participating in ethnic economies, Table 9.2 presents the information on human capital resources and other individual characteristics of entrepreneurs and salaried workers inside and outside ethnic economies. Although the four groups do show variation in their human capital resources, the differences are not substantial. For example, the proportion having completed college education is between 0.41 and 0.53 among

*Table 9.2* Labor market characteristics of immigrant Chinese in 16 major PMSAs by status of entrepreneurship and participation in ethnic economies, 1990

| Variables | Entrepreneurs | | Workers | |
|---|---|---|---|---|
| | Ethnic economy | Outside the ethnic economy | Ethnic economy | Outside the ethnic economy |
| **Individual characteristics** | | | | |
| *Human capital resources* | | | | |
| Education | | | | |
| Completed college | 0.449 | 0.466 | 0.414 | 0.526 |
| Some college | 0.300 | 0.317 | 0.274 | 0.305 |
| Completed high school or less | 0.251 | 0.217 | 0.312 | 0.169 |
| Language | | | | |
| Speaks English well | 0.675 | 0.678 | 0.594 | 0.734 |
| Speaks English not well | 0.247 | 0.240 | 0.253 | 0.169 |
| Speaks no English | 0.078 | 0.182 | 0.153 | 0.091 |
| Work experience | 22.696 | 21.333 | 19.005 | 16.963 |
| *Other individual characteristics* | | | | |
| Married | 0.874 | 0.821 | 0.729 | 0.682 |
| Male | 0.684 | 0.687 | 0.520 | 0.526 |
| Hours of work | 2,422.2 | 2,229.7 | 1,938.52 | 1,907.4 |
| Immigration period | | | | |
| 1985–1990 | 0.102 | 0.141 | 0.244 | 0.199 |
| 1980–1984 | 0.259 | 0.252 | 0.276 | 0.251 |
| 1970–1979 | 0.384 | 0.363 | 0.308 | 0.337 |
| 1960–1969 | 0.177 | 0.159 | 0.131 | 0.168 |
| Before 1960 | 0.077 | 0.085 | 0.041 | 0.045 |
| Industry | | | | |
| Manufacturing | 0.102 | 0.053 | 0.302 | 0.222 |
| Trade | 0.610 | 0.338 | 0.375 | 0.209 |
| Financial/Business | 0.098 | 0.214 | 0.099 | 0.195 |
| Professional | 0.138 | 0.174 | 0.158 | 0.159 |

Source: 1990, 5 percent PUMS.

the four groups, and the proportion not knowing English differs by only 0.1 across the four groups. Thus, the results suggest that the earning differences among the four groups may not be related to their differences in human capital resources.

In addition, the results show that the variations in the earning differences among the four groups in different cities do not correspond to the variations in human capital resources in these cities. For example, we should expect the human capital resources of entrepreneurs participating in ethnic economies to be different from those of entrepreneurs outside ethnic economies because Table 9.1 shows that the earnings of entrepreneurs in the ethnic economies are considerably different from those of entrepreneurs outside the ethnic economies. However, Table 9.2 shows no substantial differences in human capital resources between the two groups.

Since the earning differences among the four groups do not reflect their human capital resources, the variations may be related to the differential returns of human capital resources (for individuals working as entrepreneurs or workers, participating inside or outside ethnic economies), or the effects of the structural contexts of different cities. In the following analysis, we study the returns of human capital and the effects of city structural contexts on entrepreneurs and workers participating inside and outside ethnic economies.

## Decisions to be entrepreneurs and to participate in ethnic economies

Table 9.3 presents two sets of estimates, predictions about individuals being entrepreneurs and participating in ethnic economies. They are the results of the first step of a bivariate probit selection regression model, which estimates simultaneously the effects of independent variables on entrepreneurial status and participation in ethnic economies. Included at this stage of the analysis is a set of individual human capital resources to predict entrepreneurial status and participation in ethnic economies.[4] Previous results suggest that human capital resources, such as education, language, and work experience, are negatively related to entrepreneurship and participation in the ethnic economies (Maxim 1992).

In addition, we controlled for a set of individual characteristics, including marital status, gender, immigration period, number of family members, living in the same city five years ago, and number of weeks worked the previous year. We expect entrepreneurs to be more likely to be married males with larger families. Ethnic entrepreneurs with limited resources can rely on help from family members, usually with minimal pay, in the daily operation of their ethnic business. We also expect entrepreneurs to have been in the country for a longer period of time, since it takes time to accumulate enough financial capital and to become familiar with the market. Finally, those who were active in the labor market the previous year are more likely to be entrepreneurs, as indicated by the weeks worked in the last year. For participation in ethnic economies, we expect that recent immigrants, those who were living in the same city five years ago, and those who worked more weeks the previous year would be more likely to participate in the ethnic economies. Although newcomers may bring with them financial capital and labor from their countries of origin, recent immigrants with limited knowledge about the country and recent arrivals to the city who do not know the local market well are more likely to seek jobs in places such as ethnic economies where they have relatively more information.

The results demonstrate how human capital and city structural contexts are related to entrepreneurial status and participation in ethnic economies. To focus our discussion on understanding the economic consequences of participating in ethnic economies, we will concentrate on the findings pertinent to that topic.

The first column shows the effects of human capital endowment on entrepreneurial status. Consistent with previous research (Borjas and Bronars 1989; Maxim 1992), the results indicate that education and language have a negative impact on the likelihood of individuals becoming entrepreneurs. Individuals who

*Table 9.3* Bivariate probit coefficients for the effects of human capital resources and other selected independent variables on being entrepreneurs and on participating in the ethnic economy: immigrant Chinese in 16 major PMSAs, 1990

| Variables | Entrepreneurship | Participation in the ethnic economy |
| --- | --- | --- |
| **Individual characteristics** | | |
| *Human capital resources* | | |
| Education | | |
|    Completed college | –0.197** | –0.263** |
|    Some college | –0.105** | –0.258** |
|    Completed high school or less | o.c. | o.c. |
| Language | | |
|    Speaks English well | –0.121** | –0.147** |
|    Speaks English not well | –0.074 | 0.002 |
|    Speaks no English | o.c. | o.c. |
| Work experience | 0.017** | 0.008** |
| Work experience (squared)[a] | –0.000** | 0.0000 |
| *Other individual characteristics* | | |
| Married | 0.183** | – |
| Male | 0.233** | – |
| Immigration period | –1.309** | |
|    1985–1990 | –0.955** | 0.332** |
|    1980–1984 | –0.838** | 0.328** |
|    1970–1979 | –0.837** | 0.245** |
|    1960–1969 | –0.084** | 0.133** |
|    Before 1960 | o.c. | o.c. |
| Living in the same city | – | 0.004 |
| Number of persons in family | –0.006 | 0.030** |
| Weeks worked in 1989 | –0.009** | 0.001 |
| Rho | | 0.181** |
| Log-likelihood | | –18858 |
| Number of cases | | 18793 |

Source: 1990, 5 percent PUMS.
*p<0.05; **p<0.01;
o.c.: Omitted category.
[a] Decimal point is moved three places to the right.

have lower levels of education and lower levels of English ability are more likely to be entrepreneurs. In other words, these findings support previous assertions that entrepreneurship is an alternative avenue of economic participation for members of a minority group who have less capital endowment (Portes and Bach 1985; Portes and Jensen 1989). The results also show that other individual characteristics relate to entrepreneurial status. Chinese who are male or married are more likely to be entrepreneurs. Chinese immigrants who arrived in the country after 1960 are less likely to be entrepreneurs. This may simply reflect that entrepreneurship requires financial capital. The longer one stays in the U.S., the more capital one accumulates.

Consequently, those who arrived earlier are more likely to become self-employed. Finally, individuals who spent fewer weeks at work are less likely to be entrepreneurs.

The model of participation in ethnic economies (column 2) also shows that Chinese who speak English well and have higher education levels are less likely to participate in ethnic economies. These findings, like those about entrepreneurs, indicate that participation in ethnic economies is an alternative means to achieving economic success for those who have less human capital.

As for other individual characteristics, periods of immigration are related to the likelihood of participating in the ethnic economies. Contrary to the effects of immigration period on the likelihood of self-employment, Chinese who arrived in the U.S. in recent years are more likely to participate in the ethnic economies. This may be related to the fact that the socioeconomic and demographic backgrounds of the Chinese who arrived in the U.S. before the change in immigration policies (the contrast category is those who arrived before 1960) are different from those of recent Chinese immigrants. In addition, length of time in the city and number of weeks worked in previous years are not related to the participation in ethnic economies. However, family size is positively related to participation in the ethnic economies. The results may indicate that members of a larger family may seek work wherever it is available for economic survival.

Finally, a statistically significant positive rho of the model indicates the dependence of participating in ethnic economies and entrepreneurial status. Participation in ethnic economies increases the likelihood of being an entrepreneur. In short, the results indicate that entrepreneurship or participating in ethnic economies are alternative and related paths to economic pursuits for Chinese with limited human capital.

## Earnings of entrepreneurs and participation in ethnic economies

Table 9.4 presents the results of using individual characteristics and city contextual factors to predict the earnings of individuals. In addition, the model corrects the selectivity of entrepreneurial status and participation in ethnic economies, which is captured by the two lambdas in the model. Our discussion will first focus on the effects of human capital resources on the economic returns of individuals participating inside and outside ethnic economies after controlling for city contextual factors. Then we will discuss the effect of city structural contexts on the economic returns of various groups.

The first two columns provide the estimates of individual human capital and city structural variables in relation to the earnings of entrepreneurs participating inside and outside the ethnic economies. The findings indicate that virtually all human capital resources and individual characteristics, except gender, are not related to the earnings of entrepreneurs inside and outside the ethnic economies.

The third column shows the earnings estimates for workers participating in the ethnic economies. Differing from those of entrepreneurs, the earnings of employees

*Table 9.4* Effects of human capital resources, selected individual characteristics, and city structural contexts on the earnings of entrepreneurs and of workers participating in and outside the ethnic economy: immigrant Chinese in 16 PMSAs, 1990

| Variables | Entrepreneurs | | Workers | |
|---|---|---|---|---|
| | Ethnic economy | Outside the ethnic economy | Ethnic economy | Outside the ethnic economy |
| **Individual characteristics** | | | | |
| *Human capital resources* | | | | |
| Education | | | | |
| Completed college | −0.142 | 0.474 | −0.715 | 1.202** |
| Some college | −0.242 | 0.177 | −1.009** | 0.938** |
| Completed high school or less | o.c. | o.c. | o.c. | o.c. |
| Language | | | | |
| Speaks English well | −0.225 | 0.252 | −0.506 | 0.495** |
| Speaks English not well | −0.208 | −0.005 | −0.051 | −0.182** |
| Speaks no English | o.c. | o.c. | o.c. | o.c. |
| Work experience | 0.088 | 0.058 | 0.102** | 0.022** |
| Work experience (squared)[a] | −0.002 | −0.002 | −0.002** | −0.001** |
| *Other individual characteristics* | | | | |
| Married | 0.532 | 0.462 | 0.425** | 0.289** |
| Male | 0.759* | 0.844* | 0.640** | 0.438** |
| Hours of work (in 1,000) | 0.146* | 0.198* | 0.406** | 0.532** |
| Immigration periods | | | | |
| 1985–1990 | −3.264 | −3.279 | −2.431** | −3.627** |
| 1980–1984 | −2.435 | −2.353 | −1.704* | −3.123** |
| 1970–1979 | −1.954 | −2.048 | −1.625* | −2.527** |
| 1960–1969 | −1.948 | −1.732 | −1.947* | −2.034** |
| Before 1960 | o.c. | o.c. | o.c. | o.c. |
| Industry | | | | |
| Manufacturing | 0.225 | 0.019 | −0.108 | 0.028 |
| Trade | −0.102 | −0.058 | −0.250** | −0.160** |
| Financial/Business | 0.335* | 0.150 | 0.063 | −0.016 |
| Professional | 0.556** | 0.044 | −0.042 | −0.030 |
| Agricultural | o.c. | o.c. | o.c. | o.c. |
| **City structural factors** | | | | |
| Proportion of Chinese | −0.298 | −0.336 | −0.029* | 0.070* |
| Segregation | −0.849 | −1.289 | −0.045 | −0.644** |
| Relative employment of Chinese | −0.574 | −0.706 | 0.490 | −0.609** |
| Unemployment rate | −0.138** | −0.131 | −0.050** | 0.033** |
| Segregation*proportion of Chinese | 0.638 | 0.761 | 0.012** | −0.095 |
| Participation in ethnic economy ($\lambda$) | 1.511 | −1.058 | 6.772** | −4.813** |
| Being entrepreneurs ($\lambda$) | 2.627 | 1.947 | 6.405** | 3.779** |
| Adjusted $R^2$ | 0.286 | 0.275 | 0.589 | 0.587 |
| Number of cases | 1,443 | 603 | 9,319 | 7,428 |

Source: 1990, 5 percent PUMS.
*p<0.05; **p<0.01.
o.c.: Omitted category.
[a] Decimal point is moved two places to the right.

working in ethnic economies are statistically related to human capital resources and other individual factors. If one controls for possible selectivity and city contextual factors, Chinese married male workers in the ethnic economies who arrived in the country before 1960 with lower levels of education and more work experience have increased earning potential. The findings indicate that the economic returns for workers in the ethnic economies are strongly related to most of their human capital resources and other individual factors. However, the results may be affected by the large sample size. These conclusions, nevertheless, are consistent with the findings of Zhou and Logan (1989) based on the experiences of Chinese in New York and Portes and Jensen's (1989) study of Miami-Hialeah.

The last column of the table shows the earnings of employees outside the ethnic economies. All individual characteristics are statistically related to the economic returns for employees working outside the ethnic economies. Comparing these effects on the earnings for employees working inside and outside the ethnic economies, the economic returns on the human capital resources of the two groups are very similar.[5]

The results also demonstrate that city structural contexts have significant and strong effects on the earnings of individuals participating inside and outside ethnic economies, especially workers. This finding suggests that previous studies that focused on individual characteristics neglected a set of determinants that are critical to the economic returns of those participating outside the ethnic economies, and which subsequently affect the relative importance of economic returns among groups.

As predicted, the earnings of entrepreneurs in ethnic economies substantially decrease when the unemployment rate increases. A weak economy encourages ethnic group members to seek opportunities in ethnic economies. Given the increase in migration, more ethnic members are more likely to participate in ethnic economies, which in turn increases competition and considerably affects the earnings of those working in the ethnic economy. The strong effect strongly supports the notion of the significance of city structural contexts for the earnings of entrepreneurs in ethnic economies. It is important to mention that though other city structural factors are not significantly related to the earnings of entrepreneurs in the ethnic economies, the effects are in the expected direction. Among entrepreneurs outside the ethnic economies, none of the city structural factors are related to earnings, although all relationships are in the expected direction.

With regard to workers in the ethnic economies, their earnings are strongly related to city structural contexts. The significant negative effect of the size of the Chinese population in the city suggests that too large a population of Chinese drives down the earnings of workers in the ethnic economy. The state of the economy also has a significant impact on the earnings of workers participating in ethnic economies. As suggested, a weak economy encourages more ethnic group members to seek jobs within the ethnic economies. Since the migration increases the pool of potential workers, more competition among ethnic group members can be created. In turn, the economic returns for workers participating in the ethnic economies are adversely affected.

The results also suggest that the level of residential segregation of Chinese from other groups does not necessarily relate to the economic returns for workers participating in ethnic economies. However, the interaction effects of the segregation level and proportion of Chinese are positive and statistically significant. The results confirm our hypothesis that segregation itself is not a necessary condition to advance economic returns for those participating in ethnic economies. A segregated ethnic community with a larger ethnic group helps the development of business opportunities for individuals working inside ethnic economies.

Among workers outside the ethnic economies, the results show strong and significant effects of city structural factors. Earnings of workers outside the ethnic economies increase when the city's proportion of Chinese increases, the segregation level decreases, the relative employment rate between Chinese and others decreases, and the unemployment rate increases. The seemingly contradictory relationship between the city unemployment rate and the earnings of workers outside the ethnic economies suggests that those who still hold jobs outside ethnic economies with the mentioned city structural environments have high earnings.

Finally, the earnings of workers inside and outside the ethnic economies are significantly related to both selection factors of being an entrepreneur and participating in the ethnic economies. The selection coefficients suggest that being a worker participating inside an ethnic economy significantly affects earnings. Similarly, being an entrepreneur or a worker can affect earnings.

## CONCLUSION

In this chapter, we have broadened the understanding of the economic returns of participating inside and outside ethnic economies by situating the issue in a context that has been shaped by globalization. We have treated ethnic economies as being deeply embedded and closely intertwined with the larger city economy. We also suggested that the larger context can be shaped by the international flow of financial capital and migration due to globalization. Therefore, we have argued that the economic returns for individuals participating inside and outside ethnic economies are affected by individual human capital resources and the embedded city structural contexts where the ethnic economies are located. In addition, we have suggested that the understanding of the economic returns of participating inside and outside ethnic economies should take account of two selectivity processes: being an entrepreneur and participating in an ethnic economy. Being an entrepreneur reflects the possible non-random selection of individuals with certain characteristics, which in turn may affect their earning potential. Those participating inside and outside the ethnic economy can be related to the selection of individuals with distinctive expectations and orientations towards their jobs because of the unique occupational structure of ethnic economies, which differs from that of the broader city economy. Subsequently, their earnings will be affected.

The analysis was based on 1990 census data on Chinese immigrants in 16 major cities. The results show that, controlling for city structural contexts, economic returns for entrepreneurs inside and outside the ethnic economies in these cities are weakly related to their human capital resources. For employees, economic returns are strongly related to human capital resources whether inside or outside the ethnic economies. Controlling for the city structural contexts, the economic returns on the human capital resources of employees participating in the ethnic economies are comparable to those for employees working outside the ethnic economies.

The results also document that city structural factors have significant effects on the economic returns of groups. Earnings of entrepreneurs in ethnic economies are significantly related to the city unemployment rate. A higher unemployment rate in the city is associated with lower economic returns for workers in the ethnic economies. The earnings of employees working both inside and outside the ethnic economies are significantly related to most of the city structural contexts.

The results clearly reveal several avenues of inquiry for understanding the economic returns of the ethnic economies. First, the strong impact of city structural factors indicates the importance of including city structural contexts in any understanding of the economic returns of participating inside the ethnic economies, especially for workers. The results support the concept of the interconnection of the ethnic economies and the broader city economy. The economic returns of those participating in ethnic economies are affected by these wider economic and social contexts. Since the city contexts are at different levels of association with globalization, a larger picture of how globalization interacts with local contexts can shape the economic returns of those participating in the ethnic economies should be included.

Second, the results show that the earnings of workers inside and outside the ethnic economy are significantly related to selection factors. Potential earnings of workers are affected not only by their human capital resources and urban contexts, but also by the selectivity effect of being entrepreneurs and participating in the ethnic economy. Therefore, future research on earnings inside and outside the ethnic economy should control for both of these selectivity effects.

Third, the relationship of city structural factors and the economic returns of participating inside ethnic economies points to the fact that ethnic economies are affected by the volatility of the larger economy. Our analysis has demonstrated that those who have lower levels of human capital are more likely to be involved in the ethnic economies. Taken together, economic returns are insecure and are subject to various city conditions that are beyond the control of minority members, although the development of the ethnic economies creates opportunities for them to achieve economic success, especially for those who are less competitive. Therefore, participation in ethnic economies cannot be viewed simply as a safe haven for ethnic group members. There is a considerable cost of uncertainty.

Fourth, the results suggest a paradoxical structure within ethnic economies. Opportunities in the ethnic community are largely created because of a demand for ethnic services and businesses that stems from the size of the ethnic group. However, the same factor can also hamper the economic returns of those participating in it. Since the supply of labor in the ethnic economies can support only a finite number of businesses, the economic returns of those participating in it will be adversely affected when the pool of participants increases due to various conditions in the larger labor market, including international migration due to the increasing connectedness of the economies of various countries.

In sum, the findings of this study indicate the importance of including city structural contexts in any analysis of the economic returns of participating in ethnic economy. We have also shown that city structural contexts can be shaped by the larger economic forces of globalization. Although this research has distinguished the effects of individual human capital and city structural contexts on the economic returns of participation inside and outside the ethnic economies, we have not attempted to develop a comprehensive theory for understanding the dynamics of ethnic economies. Indeed, the results of this analysis should be considered preliminary at best. More research on the interplay between individual factors and urban contexts is needed in order to provide a more complete understanding of ethnic economies.

## Notes

1  Two studies indirectly or partially dealt with the relationship between the city context and the economic returns of entrepreneurs and workers participating in the ethnic economy. Model (1997) documented the change in economic returns to employees working inside and outside ethnic economy industries over time. Although the discussion implicitly acknowledges the effects of city contexts on earnings in the ethnic economy, Model did not go further to delineate how these changes occurred or to analyze the effect of city contexts on these changes. Light and Rosenstein (1995) considered the city effect in their analysis, but their study focuses on ethnic business owners rather than on both owners and employees.

2  Most historical studies have found that one of the important factors in the development of Chinatowns before the turn of the twentieth century was the desire of the Chinese to avoid the extreme hostility of Caucasian workers (Fong and Markham 1991).

3  These PMSAs include Anaheim-Santa Ana, Boston, Chicago, Dallas, Houston, Los Angeles-Long Beach, Middlesex-Somerset-Hunterdon, Nassau-Suffolk, New York, Newark, Oakland, Philadelphia, Riverside-San Bernandino, San Francisco, San Jose, and Seattle.

4  There were some concerns about including similar sets of variables in the first and second stages of estimation. However, research in econometrics has pointed out that the restriction of at least one independent variable in the first stage of estimation that is different from the independent variables in the second stage is sufficient to identify ß (Cosslett 1991). The issue of variables included in both stages of the analysis is about the identification problem. Tunali's method, the model we employed in the analysis, takes care of the problem by imposing certain restrictions on the set of equations (for details, see Tunali 1983, pp. 17–24). These restrictions make it very difficult to find a linear combination of the equations that is similar to the original equation.

5  T-test results suggest that the differences between coefficients of all human capital variables of workers inside and outside the ethnic economy are not statistically significant at $p<0.01$.

## References

Alba, Richard, Amy Lutz, and Elena Vesselinov. 2001. "How Enduring were the Inequalities among European Immigrant Groups in the U.S.?" *Demography* 38: 349–56.

Aldrich, Howard, John Cater, Trevor Jones, David McEvoy, and Paul Velleman. 1985. "Ethnic Residential Concentration and the Protected Market Hypothesis." *Social Forces* 63: 996–1009.

Bonacich, Edna. 1973. "A Theory of Middleman Minorities." *American Sociological Review* 38: 583–94.

Bonacich, Edna and Ivan Light. 1988. *Immigrant Entrepreneurs: Koreans in Los Angeles 1965–1982.* Berkeley, CA: University of California.

Borjas, George J. and Stephen G. Bronars. 1989. "Consumer Discrimination and Self-Employment." *Journal of Political Economy* 97: 581–605.

Breton, Raymond. 1964. "Institutional Completeness of Ethnic Communities and the Personal Relations of Immigrants." *American Journal of Sociology* 70: 193–205.

Cohn, Samuel and Mark Fossett. 1995. "Why Racial Employment Inequality is Greater in Northern Labor Markets: Regional Differences in White–Black Employment Differentials." *Social Forces* 74: 511–42.

Cosslett, Stephen B. 1991. "Semiparametric Estimation of a Regression Model with Sample Selectivity." Pp. 175–97 in *Nonparametric and Semiparametric Methods in Econometrics and Statistics: Proceedings of the Fifth International Symposium in Economic Theory and Econometrics.*

Evans, M.D.R. 1989. "Immigrant Entrepreneurship: Effects of Ethnic Market Size and Isolated Labor Pool." *American Sociological Review* 54: 950–62.

Fong, Eric and William T. Markham. 1991. "Immigration, Ethnicity, and Conflict: The California Chinese, 1849–1882." *Sociological Inquiry* 61: 471–90.

Fossett, Mark A. and K. Jill Kiecolt. 1989. "The Relative Size of Minority Populations and White Racial Attitudes." *Social Science Quarterly* 70: 820–35.

Hodge, Robert W. 1973. "Toward a Theory of Racial Differences in Employment." *Social Forces* 52: 16–31.

Hurh, Won Moo and Kwang Chung Kim. 1979. *Assimilation Patterns of Immigrants in the United States: A Case Study of Korean Immigrants in the Chicago Area.* Washington, DC: University Press of America.

Jiobu, Robert M. and Harvey H. Marshall Jr. 1971. "Urban Structure and the Differentiation between Blacks and Whites." *American Sociological Review* 36: 638–49.

Kwong, Peter. 1979. *Chinatown, New York: Labor and Politics, 1930–1950.* New York: Monthly Review Press.

Lieberson, Stanley. 1980. *A Piece of the Pie.* Berkeley, CA: University of California Press.

Light, Ivan. 1972. *Ethnic Enterprise in America: Business and Welfare among Chinese, Japanese, and Blacks.* Berkeley, CA: University of California Press.

Light, Ivan and Carolyn Rosenstein. 1995. *Race, Ethnicity, and Entrepreneurship in Urban America.* New York: Aldine de Gruyter.

Light, Ivan, George Sabagh, Mehdi Bozorgmehr, and Claudia Der Martirosian. 1993. "Internal Ethnicity in the Ethnic Community." *Ethnic and Racial Studies* 16: 581–97.

Logan, John R., Richard D. Alba, and Thomas L. McNulty. 1994. "Ethnic Economies in Metropolitan Regions: Miami and Beyond." *Social Forces* 72: 691–724.

Maxim, Paul S. 1992. "Immigrants, Visible Minorities and Self-Employment." *Demography* 29: 181–98.

Min, Pyong Gap. 1996. *Caught in the Middle.* Berkeley, CA: University of California Press.

Model, Suzanne. 1997. "An Occupational Tale of Two Citites: Minorities in London and New York," *Demography* 34(4): 539–50.

Nee, Victor, Jimy M. Sanders, and Scott Sernau. 1994. "Job Transitions in an Immigrant Metropolis." *American Sociological Review* 59: 849–72.

Parcel, Toby L. 1979. "Race, Regional Labor Markets and Earnings." *American Sociological Review* 44: 262–79.

Park, Kyeyoung. 1997. *The Korean American Dream: Immigrants and Small Business in New York City.* Ithaca, NY: Cornell University Press.

Portes, Alejandro and Robert L. Bach. 1985. *The Latin Journey: Cuban and Mexican Immigrants in the United States.* Berkeley, CA: University of California Press.

Portes, Alejandro and Leif Jensen. 1989. "The Enclave and the Entrants: Patterns of Ethnic Enterprise in Miami before and after Mariel." *American Sociological Review* 54: 929–49.

——. 1992. "Disproving the Enclave Hypothesis." *American Sociological Review* 57: 418–20.

Portes, Alejandro and Julia Sensenbrenner. 1993. "Embeddedness and Immigration: Notes on the Social Determinants of Economic Action." *American Journal of Sociology* 98: 1320–50.

Quillian, Lincoln. 1995. "Population, Perceived Threat, and Prejudice in Europe." *American Sociological Review* 60: 586–611.

Rosenfeld, Michael J. and Marta Tienda. 1999. "Ethnic Concentrations and Labor-Market Opportunities." Pp. 64–105 in *Immigration and Opportunity; Race, Ethnicity, and Employment in the United States,* edited by Frank D. Bean and Stephanie Bell-Rose. New York: Russell Sage Foundation.

Rumbaut, Ruben G. 1995. "Vietnamese, Laotian, and Cambodian Americans." Pp. 232–70 in *Asian Americans: Contemporary Trends and Issues,* edited by Pyong Gap Min. Thousand Oaks, CA: Sage.

Sanders, Jimy M. and Victor, Nee. 1987. "Limits of Ethnic Solidarity in the Enclave Economy." *American Sociological Review* 52: 745–67.

——. 1996. "Social Capital, Human Capital, and Immigrant Self-Employment." *American Sociological Review* 61: 231–49.

Stolzenberg, Ross M. and Daniel A. Relles. 1997. "Tools for Intuition about Sample Selection Bias and Its Correction," *American Sociological Review* 62: 494–507.

Suttles, Gerald D. 1968. *The Social Order of the Slum.* Chicago, IL: University of Chicago Press.

Tienda, Marta. 1991. "Poor People and Poor Places: Deciphering Neighborhood Effects on Poverty Outcomes." Pp. 244–62 in *Macro–Micro Linkages in Sociology,* edited by Joan Huber. Newbury Park, CA: Sage.

Tienda, Marta and Ding-Tzann Lii. 1987. "Minority Concentration and Earnings Inequality: Blacks, Hispanics, and Asians Compared." *American Journal of Sociology* 93: 141–65.

Tunali, Insan. 1983. "A Common Structure for Models of Double Selection." Social Systems Research Institute, University of Wisconsin, Workshop Series No. 8304.

——. 1986. "A General Structure for Models of Double-Selection and an Application to a Joint Migration/Earnings Process with Remigration." *Research in Labor Economics* 8 (Part B): 235–82.

Waldinger, Roger. 1986. *Through the Eye of the Needle: Immigrants and Enterprise in New York's Garment Trade.* New York: New York University.

Wilson, Franklin D. 1999. "Ethnic Concentrations and Labor-Market Opportunities." Pp. 106–40 in *Immigration and Opportunity; Race, Ethnicity, and Employment in the United*

*States*, edited by Frank D. Bean and Stephanie Bell-Rose. New York: Russell Sage Foundation.

Wilson, Kenneth L. and Alejandro Portes. 1980. "Immigrant Enclaves: An Analysis of the Labor Market Experiences of Cubans in Miami." *American Journal of Sociology* 86: 305–19.

Wilson, William J. 1996. *When Work Disappears: The World of the New Urban Poor*. New York: Alfred A. Knopf.

Zhou, Min and John R. Logan. 1989. "Returns on Human Capital in Ethnic Enclaves."

# 10 Business owners and workers

## Class locations of Chinese in Canada

*Peter S. Li*

A recurring theme in the study of the Chinese diaspora is why Chinese overseas have an apparent tendency towards entrepreneurship and self-employment. The historical position of the Chinese, as middleman minorities in Southeast Asia and as marginalized minorities in North America, provides the context for understanding Chinese entrepreneurship. More recently, globalization is believed to have reinforced ethnic transnationalism, which in turn has enabled Chinese overseas to mobilize ethnic ties to promote business opportunities. Thus far, the preferred explanation is a cultural resilience argument which stresses the ability of ethnic Chinese to convert family values and affinal relations to instrumental networks for business development. There has been little empirical research to explore the more fundamental question of whether Chinese overseas are indeed more inclined towards business ownership than are other groups. This chapter is an attempt to use the case of Chinese in Canada to study the recent changes in the class locations of Chinese Canadians, and to assess whether they have a greater propensity to business ownership than other Canadians.

## CHINESE ENTREPRENEURSHIP AND BUSINESS OWNERSHIP

Many terms have been used to characterize the apparent business success of the ethnic Chinese outside of Hong Kong, Taiwan and mainland China, which were estimated to be around 35 million in number distributed in 134 countries (Poston and Yu, 1992). Examples of terms used include the Chinese trade diaspora (Cohen, 1997: 83–94), Chinese diaspora capitalism (Lever-Tracy *et al.* 1996: 21–40), Chinese entrepreneurial familism (Wong, 1988: 163–87), networked society (Redding, 1993: 95–114), transnational Chinese business culture (Goldberg, 1983: 13–23) and bamboo network (Tanzer, 1994). Despite a difference in emphasis, these concepts stress several widely accepted features of the ethnic Chinese: the strength of Chinese familism, the extensity of Chinese networks and the success of a distinctive form of capitalism premised upon familial entrepreneurship.

Taken together, the literature offers an interesting explanation of Chinese diasporic entrepreneurship in the context of cultural resilience, which may be summarized as follows. Despite the dispersion of ethnic Chinese in different societies away from their original homeland, they manage to maintain a common allegiance to Confucianism and familism which enables diaspora Chinese to convert familial values and kinship cohesion to social networks that are instrumental to business success. In turn, the ability to develop extensive ethnic networks and to apply them to business development has become a defining feature of Chinese diaspora capitalism (Lever-Tracy *et al.*, 1996; Redding, 1993; Hamilton, 1996). This line of thinking has produced a robust literature that stresses the importance of *guanxi*, or Chinese network, and its central role in Chinese entrepreneurship in the diaspora (Bian, 1994; Chan and Chiang, 1994; Chan, 2000; Clegg and Redding, 1990; Greenhalgh, 1984; King, 1991; Lever-Tracy *et al.*, 1996; Wong, 1988).

The above theoretical perspective on the Chinese diaspora is in fact premised on the assumption that ethnic Chinese in various countries outside China are particularly inclined towards entrepreneurship and business ventures. Undoubtedly, there are historical examples which show that selective waves of Chinese emigration were prompted by a clear trade motive, as in the case of Chinese merchant settlement in Manila in the late sixteenth century, and in Batavia in the seventeenth century (Wang, 1991, 79–101). There are many other forms of Chinese emigration: artisans, laborers and settlers to Southeast Asia in the eighteenth and nineteenth centuries, and immigrants to industrial countries in the twentieth century (Cohen, 1997: 83–93; Pan, 1998). The end result is that Chinese communities in the diaspora are occupationally diverse and structurally multifaceted (Pan, 1998).

In North America, since the publication of Light's *Ethnic Enterprise in America* in 1972, there have been some heated debates about the reason for Asian entrepreneurship. Light's original thesis focuses on the cultural endowment of Chinese and Japanese immigrants in their ability to pool resources for business investment despite historical discrimination in the labor market (Light, 1972). However, other studies have stressed blocked mobility as the antecedent factor accounting for the emergence of immigrant enterpreneurship, and highlighted the absence of competition from the dominant group in marginal immigrant businesses as the explanation for minority owners' success (Aldrich *et al.*, 1989; Blalock, 1967; Li, 1998; Loewen, 1971; Min, 1984; Rinder, 1958–9). The difference is one of emphasis, and there has been a growing consensus that both market disadvantages and ethnic resources are useful in explaining the development of immigrant entrepreneurship (Bonacich and Modell, 1980; Light, 1979; Light and Bonacich, 1988; Light and Rosenstein, 1995; Waldinger *et al.*, 1990; Ward and Jenkins, 1984). In their effort to integrate the two approaches, Light and Gold (2000: 207) distinguish between group labour market disadvantage and group resource disadvantage and suggest that high entrepreneurship, as found among middleman minorities, emerges when the former is present and the latter absent.

Despite the theoretical advances, the debate has not paid much attention to a more fundamental question of whether Chinese in various adopted countries are indeed more inclined than other groups towards business ownership. Using Canadian census data, this chapter first explores the class locations of Chinese Canadians to see how entrepreneurship has changed, and then compares the class locations of those of Chinese origin in the Canadian labour force to the class location of other Canadians to determine whether the Chinese were more likely to be business owners than others.

## HISTORICAL BACKGROUND

The Chinese in Canada have a history dating back to 1858. During the first 90 years, the Chinese were essentially second-class citizens, denied many civil rights which other Canadians took for granted (Li, 1998). Their marginal economic and social positions can be largely explained by the type of Chinese immigrants who immigrated to Canada in the latter half of the nineteenth century and the first part of the twentieth century, the conditions under which Chinese labor was recruited, and their subsequent institutional exclusion. Occupational data from the 1921 and 1931 censuses indicate that about 80 percent of Chinese in Canada were laborers or workers in menial jobs; shop owners and business operators accounted for roughly 20 percent of those in the labor force (Li, 1998: 52). Most Chinese business owners in the 1920s and 1930s were in limited retail services such as restaurants, laundries, and retail stores (Li, 1998).

The removal of discriminatory laws against the Chinese in Canada after the Second World War, and the granting of political and civil rights, enabled them gradually to move into other lines of work. As well, the law banning Chinese from entering Canada was lifted in 1947, ending 24 years of Chinese exclusion and allowed limited Chinese immigration to Canada annually. It was only as a result of the changes in immigration policy in 1967, when a universal points system for selecting immigrants was instituted, that Chinese immigrants were evaluated and admitted on the same grounds as immigrants of other national or racial origins. Throughout the 1970s and 1980s, Canada witnessed a surge of immigration from Hong Kong, and to a lesser degree from Taiwan, especially in the ten years prior to the return of Hong Kong to China in 1997. Between 1968 and 1994, over half a million immigrants were admitted to Canada from Hong Kong, Taiwan and mainland China; about 68 percent were from Hong Kong (Li, 1998: 99). The admission of many Chinese immigrants with professional skills and investment capital from the late 1970s to the 1990s greatly expanded the Chinese-Canadian population, and accelerated the growth of the Chinese-Canadian middle class (Li, 1990, 1998). Chinese businesses in Canada also proliferated in number and diversity (Li, 1993).

By the time of the 1996 census, there were 921,585 individuals, or 3.2 percent of Canada's total population, who claimed to be of Chinese origin (Statistics Canada, 1999: 11). This number is 7.4 times the estimated Chinese-Canadian population of 124,600 in 1971, 3.2 times the population of 285,800 in 1981, and about 1.5 times the population of 633,933 in 1991 (Li, 1998: 104). It is certain that immigration has played a large role in expanding the Chinese-Canadian population since the 1970s.

## RECENT CHANGES IN CLASS LOCATIONS OF
## CHINESE CANADIANS

The class locations of Chinese Canadians can be estimated from various Canadian censuses, using the theoretical formulation of Wright based on ownership and control over money capital, physical capital and labour (Wright, 1977, 1978, 1979).[1] Using Wright's (1978: 1370) criteria of ownership of the means of production and control over others' labor, five classes may be constructed. The first two classes, employers and petit bourgeois, pertain to business owners, while the remaining three classes, managers, professionals and workers, are employees or wage earners.

Specifically, those who are self-employed with paid help are classified as "employers," and those self-employed without paid help are categorized as "petit bourgeoisie."[2] Both employers and petit bourgeois own and control money capital and physical capital of production, but employers also control the labor of others. Those "employed" are subdivided into three groups, according to how much inferred autonomy and control they have over capital and labor. Employees in managerial positions occupy a contradictory class location because, in acting on employers' behalf, they have some control over money capital, physical capital and labor. Employed "professionals" form another contradictory class position in that, unlike other workers, they have a certain autonomy over their work, and therefore some control over their labor. Employees not in managerial and professional occupations are classified as "workers," on the basis of their lack of control over capital and labor.

Using the above formulation, Table 10.1 shows the class locations of Chinese Canadians in the 1981, 1986 and 1996 censuses. The data (col. 3) indicate that in 1981 about 6 percent of the Chinese were employers and 3.4 percent belonged to the petit bourgeoisie, making a total of slightly less than 10 percent in business ownership. The class structure did not change much between 1981 and 1986. However, by 1996, the proportion of Chinese Canadians engaged in business ownership (employers and petit bourgeois) had increased to 14 percent (col. 9). The increase in the petit bourgeoisie is particularly noticeable among foreign-born Chinese Canadians: it expanded from 3.6 percent in 1981 to 7.4 percent in 1996. Several factors probably explain the increase in Chinese entrepreneurship in Canada in the late 1980s and early 1990s: the high rate of immigration of affluent Chinese from Hong Kong during this period, the expansion of Canada's business immigration program, and the burgeoning transnational business opportunities in the nascent market economy of mainland China (Li, 1993, 1998, 2003).

## CLASS LOCATIONS OF CHINESE CANADIANS AND OTHER
## CANADIANS

Despite the increase of Chinese entrepreneurship from 1981 to 1996, do the data in the 1996 census show the Chinese to be more inclined to business ownership than other groups? Table 10.2 compares the class locations of Chinese Canadians

Table 10.1 Class locations of Chinese Canadians, by nativity, 1981, 1986, and 1996

| Class locations | Chinese Canadians | | | | | | | | |
| --- | --- | --- | --- | --- | --- | --- | --- | --- | --- |
| | 1981 | | | 1986 | | | 1996 | | |
| | Native born [1] % | Foreign born [2] % | Total [3] % | Native born [4] % | Foreign born [5] % | Total [6] % | Native born [7] % | Foreign born [8] % | Total [9] % |
| Employers | 3.6 | 6.3 | 5.9 | 2.9 | 6.5 | 5.9 | 2.8 | 7.6 | 6.9 |
| Petit bourgeoisie | 2.3 | 3.6 | 3.4 | 2.6 | 4.1 | 3.8 | 5.0 | 7.4 | 7.1 |
| Managers | 8.3 | 5.7 | 6.1 | 10.2 | 6.3 | 6.9 | 6.5 | 5.8 | 5.9 |
| Professionals | 15.3 | 17.0 | 16.8 | 18.8 | 15.1 | 15.7 | 26.1 | 19.6 | 20.6 |
| Workers | 70.5 | 67.4 | 67.8 | 65.6 | 68.1 | 67.7 | 59.7 | 59.5 | 59.5 |
| Total percent | 100.0 | 100.0 | 100.0 | 100.1 | 100.1 | 100.0 | 100.0 | 100.0 | 100.0 |
| (Number of cases) | 23,550 | 144,550 | 168,100 | 38,350 | 194,450 | 232,800 | 64,656 | 385,992 | 450,648 |

Source:
Compiled from 1981 Census of Canada, Public Use Sample Tape for Individuals, 1986 and 1996 Census of Canada, Public Use Microdata File on Individuals. The 1981 and 1986 data are based on a 2.0 percent probability sample, and the 1996 data, a 2.8 percent probability sample of the population, excluding persons under 15 years of age, persons not in the labor force, and non-permanent residents. The 1986 and 1996 data also exclude those in the Atlantic provinces and territories where Chinese origin is unavailable in microdata. The Chinese origin is based on single origin response to the ethnic origin question in the 1981 data, and on single and multiple origin responses in the 1986 and 1996 data. Cell frequencies have been weighted to arrive at population estimates.

*Table 10.2* Class locations of Chinese Canadians, other visible minority Canadians, and majority Canadians, 1996

| Class locations | Chinese Canadians | Other visible minority Canadians | Majority Canadians | All Canadians |
|---|---|---|---|---|
| | [1] % | [2] % | [3] % | [4] % |
| Employers | 6.8 | 4.4 | 5.0 | 5.0 |
| Petit bourgeoisie | 7.0 | 5.1 | 8.0 | 7.7 |
| Managers | 5.9 | 4.3 | 6.6 | 6.4 |
| Professionals | 20.7 | 17.5 | 18.2 | 18.3 |
| Workers | 59.6 | 68.7 | 62.1 | 62.6 |
| Total percent | 100.0 | 100.0 | 99.9 | 100.0 |
| *(Number of cases)* | *457,272* | *1,112,868* | *12,519,540* | *14,089,680* |

Source:
Compiled from 1996 Census of Canada, Public Use Microdata File on Individuals, based on a 2.8 percent probability sample of the population, excluding persons under 15 years of age, persons not in the labor force, and non-permanent residents, and excluding those in the Atlantic provinces and territories where Chinese origin was unavailable. Cell frequencies have been weighted to arrive at population estimates.

to those of other visible minority Canadians, as well as those of majority Canadians.[3] The data show that 6.8 percent of Chinese Canadians were employers, and 7 percent petit bourgeois. In short, about 14 percent of Chinese Canadians may be considered as business owners, compared to 9.5 percent of other visible minorities, and 13 percent among majority Canadians.

Managers comprised about 6 percent of the Chinese-Canadian population, 4.3 percent of other visible minority population, and 6.6 percent of the majority Canadian population. The percentage of Chinese in the professional class location (20.7%) tended to be slightly higher than for other visible minorities (17.5%) and majority Canadians (18.2%). Finally, about 60 percent of Chinese Canadians were workers, compared to 69 percent of other visible minorities and 62 percent of majority Canadians. In sum, Table 10.2 clearly shows that Chinese Canadians were similar to majority Canadians in class locations, and on the basis of the data, Chinese Canadians cannot be said to have a higher propensity to business ownership than majority Canadians.

When gender is considered along with racial origin, Table 10.3 shows further that, with minor exceptions, Chinese-Canadian men and women were also very similar to their majority counterparts. For example, about 17 percent of Chinese-Canadian men and 10.6 percent of Chinese-Canadian women were employers and petit bourgeois, compared to 16 percent of majority Canadian men and 9 percent of majority Canadian women. However, Chinese-Canadian men (22.6%) were more inclined to belong to the professional class than majority Canadian men (15.2%), but Chinese-Canadian women (18.6%) were slightly less inclined to belong to the professional class than majority Canadian women (21.7%).

*Table 10.3* Class locations of Chinese Canadians, other visible minority Canadians, and majority Canadians, by gender, 1996

| Class locations | Chinese Canadians | | Other visible minority Canadians | | Majority Canadians | |
| --- | --- | --- | --- | --- | --- | --- |
| | Male [1] % | Female [2] % | Male [3] % | Female [4] % | Male [5] % | Female [6] % |
| Employers | 8.4 | 5.1 | 5.8 | 2.7 | 6.9 | 2.9 |
| Petit bourgeoisie | 8.4 | 5.5 | 6.4 | 3.6 | 9.4 | 6.4 |
| Managers | 7.8 | 4.0 | 5.3 | 3.2 | 8.0 | 4.9 |
| Professionals | 22.6 | 18.6 | 16.3 | 18.9 | 15.2 | 21.7 |
| Workers | 52.8 | 66.8 | 66.1 | 71.6 | 60.5 | 64.1 |
| Total percent | 100.0 | 100.0 | 99.9 | 100.0 | 100.0 | 100.0 |
| (*Number of cases*) | *236,232* | *221,040* | *590,040* | *522,828* | *6,702,912* | *5,816,628* |

Source:
Compiled from 1996 Census of Canada, Public Use Microdata File on Individuals, based on a 2.8 percent probability sample of the population, excluding persons under 15 years of age, persons not in the labor force, and non-permanent residents, and excluding those in the Atlantic provinces and territories where Chinese origin was unavailable. Cell frequencies have been weighted to arrive at population estimates.

Table 10.4 shows the additional effect of nativity, along with gender and origin, on class locations. The data indicate some differences in the composition of native-born and foreign-born population among the three defined groups. Over 85 percent of Chinese-Canadian men and women were foreign born, similar to the pattern among other visible minorities (Table 10.4, last row). However, only 13 percent of majority men and 12 percent of majority women were foreign born. These differences reflect the immigration history of Canada, which historically had favored the immigration of Europeans but began admitting immigrants from Asia and Africa on the same grounds after 1967. Thus, the vast majority of visible minorities, including the Chinese, were recent immigrants who tended to have moved to Canada after the late 1960s.

Table 10.4 shows some differences in class locations when nativity and gender are considered along with racial origin. Native-born Chinese-Canadian men (col. 1) and foreign born Chinese-Canadian men (col. 2) were less likely to be employers and petit bourgeoisie than their majority Canadian counterparts (cols. 9 and 10 respectively). Similarly, native-born Chinese-Canadian women (col. 3) and foreign-born Chinese-Canadian women (col. 4) were less inclined to be employers and petit bourgeoisie than majority men and women (cols. 11 and 12 respectively). In contrast, native-born Chinese-Canadian men (55.7%) were less likely to be in the class location of "workers" than native-born majority men (61.8%), but foreign-born Chinese-Canadian women (67.2%) were more inclined to be workers than foreign-born majority women (61.8%). Despite these differences, the data are unequivocal in suggesting that Chinese-Canadian men and women do not have

Table 10.4 Class locations of Chinese Canadians, other visible minority Canadians, and majority Canadians, by gender and nativity, 1996

| | Chinese Canadians | | | | Other visible minority Canadians | | | | Majority Canadians | | | |
| | Male | | Female | | Male | | Female | | Male | | Female | |
| Class locations | Native born [1] % | Foreign born [2] % | Native born [3] % | Foreign born [4] % | Native born [5] % | Foreign born [6] % | Native born [7] % | Foreign born [8] % | Native born [9] % | Foreign born [10] % | Native born [11] % | Foreign born [12] % |
|---|---|---|---|---|---|---|---|---|---|---|---|---|
| Employers | 4.2 | 9.2 | 1.3 | 5.8 | 3.0 | 6.4 | 1.3 | 3.0 | 6.4 | 9.9 | 2.7 | 4.8 |
| Petit bourgeoisie | 4.9 | 9.1 | 5.1 | 5.7 | 5.1 | 6.6 | 3.3 | 3.6 | 9.0 | 12.2 | 6.2 | 7.9 |
| Managers | 7.8 | 7.8 | 5.1 | 3.8 | 5.2 | 5.2 | 3.4 | 3.2 | 7.9 | 9.1 | 4.9 | 5.1 |
| Professionals | 27.5 | 21.6 | 24.6 | 17.5 | 15.6 | 16.3 | 18.6 | 19.2 | 14.9 | 17.0 | 21.9 | 20.4 |
| Workers | 55.7 | 52.3 | 64.0 | 67.2 | 71.1 | 65.5 | 73.4 | 71.0 | 61.8 | 51.8 | 64.4 | 61.8 |
| Total percent | 100.1 | 100.0 | 100.1 | 100.0 | 100.0 | 100.0 | 100.0 | 100.0 | 100.0 | 100.0 | 100.1 | 100.0 |
| (Number of cases) | 33,372 | 199,296 | 31,284 | 186,696 | 78,696 | 494,460 | 74,736 | 435,060 | 5,812,272 | 875,664 | 5,104,620 | 699,372 |
| (% Foreign-born) | | 85.7 | | 85.6 | | 86.3 | | 85.3 | | 13.1 | | 12.0 |

Source:
Compiled from 1996 Census of Canada, Public Use Microdata File on Individuals, based on a 2.8 percent probability sample of the population, excluding persons under 15 years of age, persons not in the labor force, and non-permanent residents, and excluding those in the Atlantic provinces and territories where Chinese origin was unavailable. Cell frequencies have been weighted to arrive at population estimates.

a higher propensity for business ownership than do majority Canadian men and women, even controlling for nativity.

## CHARACTERISTICS OF CHINESE CANADIANS' CLASS LOCATIONS

If propensity to business ownership does not distinguish Chinese Canadians from majority Canadians, are there other characteristics which can be identified? Table 10.5 shows the distribution of industry by class locations for Chinese Canadians and majority Canadians, and the data indicate some marked differences between the two groups. Chinese-Canadian employers (col. 1) were heavily concentrated in wholesale, retail and accommodation and food services, which together accounted for about 48 percent of all Chinese-Canadian employers. In contrast, only 27 percent of majority Canadian employers were in these industries (col. 2), but 12 percent of them were in agriculture and primary industries, with another 15 percent in the construction industry. These patterns suggest the continued importance of retail and food services in Chinese-Canadian business ownership, since historically Chinese in Canada typically established themselves in these lines of ethnic businesses as a means of self-preservation (Li, 1979, 1993).

Among the Chinese-Canadian petit bourgeoisie (col. 3), retailing accounted for 16.5 percent, finance and real estate for 11 percent, and business services made up another 18 percent. These percentages tend to be higher than those found among majority Canadians (col. 4), who were more heavily concentrated in agriculture, primary industries and construction than were the Chinese-Canadian petit bourgeois. In short, the data on the petit bourgeoisie reflect the concentration of self-employed Chinese Canadians in business and financial services, as well as in retailing.

Chinese-Canadian managers and majority Canadian managers tended to be similar in location in various industries, except that the former were more likely to be in finance, and real estate, accommodation and food services, and the latter more inclined towards government services.

In the professional class location, over 50 percent of majority Canadians were in educational, health and social services (col. 8), compared to only 33 percent of Chinese Canadians. However, about 19 percent of Chinese-Canadian professionals were in business services, compared to only 10 percent of majority Canadians. As well, Chinese-Canadian professionals were more inclined to be in manufacturing than were their majority Canadian counterparts.

Finally, Chinese-Canadian workers (col. 9) were more likely to be in manufacturing, accommodation and food services than were majority Canadians (col. 10). About 20 percent of Chinese-Canadian workers were in accommodation and food services, compared to only 9 percent of majority Canadian workers. This difference suggests the continued importance of the traditional food service industry as a major sector of employment which hired as much as one-fifth of Chinese-Canadian workers. The fact that another 22 percent of Chinese Canadians were in

Table 10.5 Class locations by industry, for Chinese Canadians and majority Canadians, 1996

| | Employers | | Petit bourgeoisie | | Managers | | Professionals | | Workers | |
| | Chinese Canadians [1] % | Majority Canadians [2] % | Chinese Canadians [3] % | Majority Canadians [4] % | Chinese Canadians [5] % | Majority Canadians [6] % | Chinese Canadians [7] % | Majority Canadians [8] % | Chinese Canadians [9] % | Majority Canadians [10] % |
|---|---|---|---|---|---|---|---|---|---|---|
| Agriculture & Primary | 1.3 | 11.9 | 1.5 | 19.1 | 0.4 | 1.5 | 1.1 | 2.0 | 1.5 | 5.3 |
| Manufacturing | 7.8 | 6.8 | 5.5 | 4.7 | 11.2 | 13.1 | 12.2 | 7.5 | 22.4 | 17.3 |
| Construction | 5.3 | 14.9 | 5.2 | 11.7 | 3.1 | 3.8 | 1.3 | 1.1 | 1.7 | 6.3 |
| Transportation & Storage | 1.0 | 3.3 | 1.0 | 4.1 | 1.9 | 2.7 | 1.5 | 1.7 | 2.5 | 5.2 |
| Communication & Utilities | 0.2 | 0.6 | 0.8 | 1.0 | 2.4 | 3.7 | 3.3 | 3.0 | 2.9 | 3.5 |
| Wholesale Trade | 10.7 | 4.7 | 9.5 | 3.2 | 9.7 | 8.2 | 4.0 | 1.8 | 6.6 | 5.8 |
| Retail Trade | 17.9 | 15.7 | 16.5 | 9.7 | 15.6 | 17.5 | 4.0 | 2.0 | 13.4 | 15.2 |
| Finance, Insurance & Real Estate | 5.6 | 3.5 | 10.9 | 3.8 | 16.1 | 10.4 | 8.1 | 3.5 | 9.2 | 5.8 |
| Business Services | 13.0 | 13.3 | 18.2 | 14.9 | 9.4 | 5.6 | 19.2 | 9.8 | 5.0 | 4.2 |
| Government Services | | | | | 4.1 | 10.3 | 7.1 | 8.6 | 2.1 | 6.3 |
| Educational Services | 1.2 | 0.7 | 3.5 | 1.8 | 2.8 | 5.2 | 17.4 | 25.7 | 1.9 | 3.2 |

| | | | | | | | | | | |
|---|---|---|---|---|---|---|---|---|---|---|
| Health & Social Services | 9.3 | 8.3 | 5.9 | 7.6 | 3.7 | 4.8 | 16.0 | 25.9 | 3.9 | 5.7 |
| Accommodation & Food Services | 19.0 | 7.0 | 9.4 | 2.5 | 14.8 | 7.6 | 0.4 | 0.7 | 19.8 | 9.0 |
| Other Services | 7.6 | 9.3 | 12.1 | 15.9 | 4.9 | 5.6 | 4.5 | 6.7 | 7.2 | 7.4 |
| Total | 99.9 | 100.0 | 100.0 | 100.0 | 100.1 | 100.0 | 100.1 | 100.0 | 100.1 | 100.2 |
| (Number of cases) | 31,248 | 629,820 | 32,076 | 1,002,240 | 27,072 | 824,688 | 94,428 | 2,282,148 | 272,448 | 7,780,644 |

Source:
Compiled from 1996 Census of Canada, Public Use Microdata File on Individuals, based on a 2.8 percent probability sample of the population, excluding persons under 15 years of age, persons not in the labor force, and non-permanent residents, and excluding those in the Atlantic provinces and territories where Chinese origin was unavailable. Cell frequencies have been weighted to arrive at population estimates.

*Table 10.6* Class locations of Chinese Canadians by nativity and period of immigration, 1996

| Class locations | Native born [1] % | Foreign born | | | |
| | | Immigrated before 1968 [2] % | Immigrated 1968–77 [3] % | Immigrated 1978–87 [4] % | Immigrated 1988–96 [5] % |
| --- | --- | --- | --- | --- | --- |
| Employers | 2.8 | 11.9 | 8.5 | 6.4 | 7.3 |
| Petit bourgeoisie | 5.0 | 10.2 | 7.5 | 5.8 | 8.1 |
| Managers | 6.5 | 6.6 | 8.4 | 5.1 | 5.1 |
| Professionals | 26.1 | 21.3 | 26.7 | 16.8 | 17.9 |
| Workers | 59.7 | 50.0 | 48.9 | 65.8 | 61.6 |
| Total | 100.1 | 100.0 | 100.0 | 99.9 | 100.0 |
| *(Number of cases)* | *64,656* | *20,808* | *80,964* | *109,584* | *174,492* |
| *(% Native born & foreign born)* | *14.4* | *4.6* | *18.0* | *24.3* | *38.7* |

Source:
Compiled from 1996 Census of Canada, Public Use Microdata File on Individuals, based on a 2.8 percent probability sample of the population, excluding persons under 15 years of age, persons not in the labor force, and non-permanent residents, and excluding those in the Atlantic provinces and territories where Chinese origin was unavailable. Cell frequencies have been weighted to arrive at population estimates.

manufacturing also suggests the rising importance of blue-collar jobs for Chinese-Canadian workers, even though historically they tended to be denied these employment opportunities.

Chinese who immigrated to Canada in different time periods also show some differences in class locations (Table 10.6). In terms of business ownership, about 22 percent of Chinese who immigrated before 1968 were employers and petit bourgeoisie, compared to only about 12 percent of those who came between 1978 and 1987, 15 percent who immigrated between 1988 and 1996, and only 8 percent of those born in Canada. These differences suggest that business ownership was a principal means of economic survival for Chinese who came before 1968, when economic opportunities tended to be more restrictive for racial minorities, and that business ownership was less important for later Chinese immigrants, who also tended to come with more educational and professional skills. Table 10.6 (last row) also shows that over 80 percent of Chinese Canadians immigrated to Canada after 1968.

Chinese Canadians in various class locations also differ from other Canadians in university education. Table 10.7 indicates that 31 percent of Chinese-Canadian men and 24 percent of Chinese-Canadian women had a university degree, compared

*Table 10.7* Percentage of Chinese Canadians, other visible minority Canadians, and majority Canadians with a university degree, by class locations and gender, 1996

| Class locations | Male | | | Female | | |
|---|---|---|---|---|---|---|
| | Chinese Canadians | Other visible minority Canadians | Majority Canadians | Chinese Canadians | Other visible minority Canadians | Majority Canadians |
| | [1] % | [2] % | [3] % | [4] % | [5] % | [6] % |
| Employers | 35 | 38 | 24 | 28 | 28 | 18 |
| Petit bourgeoisie | 34 | 26 | 15 | 27 | 24 | 19 |
| Managers | 43 | 41 | 33 | 36 | 36 | 28 |
| Professionals | 65 | 57 | 48 | 58 | 43 | 42 |
| Workers | 13 | 12 | 5 | 14 | 14 | 6 |
| Total | 31 | 24 | 16 | 24 | 21 | 16 |

Source:
Compiled from 1996 Census of Canada, Public Use Microdata File on Individuals, based on a 2.8 percent probability sample of the population, excluding persons under 15 years of age, persons not in the labor force, and non-permanent residents, and excluding those in the Atlantic provinces and territories where Chinese origin was unavailable. Cell frequencies have been weighted to arrive at population estimates.

to 16 percent of majority Canadian men and women. Within each class location, a larger percentage of Chinese-Canadian men and women had a university degree in comparison to their majority Canadian counterparts.

Taken together, Tables 10.2 to 10.7 show that Chinese Canadians were not more inclined to business ownership than majority Canadians. However, Chinese-Canadian employers and petit bourgeois concentrated in different industries than majority Canadian business owners. In particular, wholesale, retail and food services accounted for about 47 percent of Chinese-Canadian employers. Finance and business services accounted for about 29 percent of the Chinese-Canadian petit bourgeoisie, and another 26 percent were in retail and wholesale business.

## ECONOMIC CONSEQUENCE OF CHINESE CANADIANS' CLASS LOCATIONS

In view of both similarities and differences in class locations between Chinese Canadians and other Canadians, do these patterns produce different economic outcomes?

Table 10.8 provides the results of a regression model used to estimate the actual (gross) and adjusted (net) earnings for Chinese-Canadian men and women and for other Canadian men and women in various class locations.[4] The dependent variable used in the analysis is "annual earnings from employment and self-employment,"

Table 10.8 Actual and adjusted labor market earnings in deviations above (+) or below (−) the national average ($27,065), for Chinese Canadians, other visible minority Canadians, and majority Canadians, by class locations and gender, 1996

| | Actual earnings | | | | | | Adjusted earnings | | | | | |
| | Male | | | Female | | | Male | | | Female | | |
| Class locations | Chinese Canadians | Other visible minority Canadians | Majority Canadians | Chinese Canadians | Other visible minority Canadians | Majority Canadians | Chinese Canadians | Other visible minority Canadians | Majority Canadians | Chinese Canadians | Other visible minority Canadians | Majority Canadians |
| | [1] | [2] | [3] | [4] | [5] | [6] | [7] | [8] | [9] | [10] | [11] | [12] |
|---|---|---|---|---|---|---|---|---|---|---|---|---|
| Employers | $4,999 | $8,885 | $17,011 | −$2,472 | −$3,301 | −$256 | $770 | $4,119 | $11,964 | −$3,703 | −$4,853 | −$2,479 |
| Petit bourgeoisie | −$1,490 | −$5,767 | −$3,802 | −$8,871 | −$12,890 | −$12,365 | −$4,458 | −$8,409 | −$5,063 | −$9,462 | −$12,510 | −$11,393 |
| Managers | $13,497 | $15,286 | $29,676 | $4,925 | $1,505 | $8,881 | $7,656 | $9,573 | $22,363 | $527 | −$1,351 | $4,504 |
| Professionals | $11,205 | $10,039 | $15,786 | $3,099 | $464 | $3,104 | $4,993 | $4,440 | $9,989 | −$24 | −$3,243 | $251 |
| Workers | −$6,590 | −$6,239 | $610 | −$10,632 | $11,766 | −$10,123 | −$4,206 | −$4,993 | $1,859 | −$7,964 | −$8,544 | $6,569 |

Source:
Compiled from 1996 Census of Canada, Public Use Microdata File on Individuals, based on a 2.8 percent probability sample of the population, excluding persons under 15 years of age, persons not in the labor force, and non-permanent residents, and excluding those in the Atlantic provinces and territories where Chinese origin was unavailable. Cell frequencies have been weighted to arrive at population estimates.

Note:
Actual earnings are gross earnings before variations in education, language ability and other individual human capital-related factors, and labor market features of work have been adjusted for. Adjusted earnings are earnings after variations in other variables have been taken into account. Variables controlled for include education, ability to speak English or French, years in Canada for immigrants, years of work experience, experience squared, number of weeks worked, part-time or full-time work, and industry of work.

which is the sum of gross wages and salaries, and net self-employment income before individual income taxes.[5] The independent variables measuring individual variations in human capital and work-related features include years of schooling,[6] experience estimated by subtracting from age the years of schooling and the six years before schooling began, experience squared, knowledge of the official languages, the number of weeks worked in 1995 (1 to 52), the nature of work in terms of whether the weeks worked were full-time or part-time,[7] and the industry of work (14 categories).[8] In addition, a variable "years since landing in Canada" is used as a proxy for Canadian experience for immigrants.[9]

Table 10.8 shows that Chinese-Canadian men (col. 1) who were employers, managers and professionals had earnings above the national average, but petit bourgeoisie and workers earned less than the average. This pattern persists even when variations in other variables have been taken into account (col. 7). However, compared to majority Canadian men (col. 3), Chinese Canadians in every class location earned less, except for Chinese-Canadian petit bourgeois, who, despite their sub-national average income, earned more than the majority Canadian petit bourgeois. The difference in earnings between Chinese-Canadian managers and majority Canadian managers was $16,179 a year, but this disparity became $14,707 a year when differences in other variables were controlled for (cols. 7, 9).

Chinese-Canadian women (col. 4) earned less than the national average, with the exception of managers and professionals. In particular, Chinese-Canadian female workers earned more than $10,000 less than the national mean. Chinese-Canadian female employers and managers also earned less than their majority Canadian female counterparts (cols. 4, 6), but the Chinese-Canadian female petit bourgeois earned more, even though both groups had earnings below the national average. When differences in other variations were adjusted for (cols. 10, 12), Chinese-Canadian women earned less than majority women in every class location.

The results in Table 10.8 suggest that Chinese Canadians and majority Canadians did not receive the same remuneration in every class location, even when adjusting for differences in human capital and other work-related characteristics. In general, Chinese-Canadian men and women earned less than their majority Canadian coun-terparts in every class location, except for the Chinese-Canadian petit bourgeoisie.

## CONCLUSIONS

The literature on the Chinese diaspora has generally assumed that Chinese overseas are more inclined towards business ownership than are other groups, and has then proceeded to explain why this is so. Globalization in trade and commerce as well as the liberalization of the market economy in mainland China since the late 1970s and early 1980s are believed to have contributed to the growth of entrepreneurship in the Chinese diaspora (Lever-Tracy *et al.* 1996). There is some evidence that entrepreneurship has increased in Canada since the 1980s and early 1990s, and it is likely that such an increase is related to globalization, the opening of China and Canada's business immigration program.

The analysis of the most recent census data from Canada suggests that Chinese Canadians were not more likely than majority Canadians to be employers and petit bourgeois. Nevertheless, there are marked differences in certain features of Chinese-Canadian class locations. First, Chinese-Canadian employers and petit bourgeois tended to concentrate in different industries from their majority Canadian counterparts. Wholesale, retail and food services remained important areas of concentration for Chinese-Canadian employers, while finance and business services accounted for about 29 percent of the Chinese-Canadian petit bourgeoisie. Second, over 80 percent of Chinese Canadians immigrated to Canada after 1967, and those who came before 1968 tended to be more inclined towards business ownership. Finally, Chinese Canadians and majority Canadians received unequal economic returns in almost all class locations, despite controlling for difference in other variables.

These findings suggest that there are distinguishing features between Chinese Canadians and majority Canadians that arise from class location, gender relations and race relations. The preoccupation with explaining overseas Chinese entrepreneurship probably has resulted in many finer differences between Chinese overseas and other groups being overlooked. One such difference is the effect of race and gender on the life chances of Chinese overseas. The case of the Chinese in Canada also suggests that economic globalization and new economic opportunities in the opening of China may have contributed to the growth of Chinese entrepreneurship in recent years, but the ethnic Chinese in Canada are not more entrepreneurial than majority members. Indeed, the analysis suggests that Chinese entrepreneurship may be distinguished from the entrepreneurship of other groups not necessarily in the propensity to business ownership, but in the nature and type of business undertaken. Many factors probably contribute to these qualitative differences, including historical factors, changing economic and employment opportunities, as well as forces of globalization.

## Notes

1   In subsequent writings, Wright (1985) reformulates the typology of class locations in capitalist societies. His reformulation involves the notion of exploitation based on ownership of production assets, organizational assets and credential assets to produce 12 class locations. However, the new typology lacks the theoretical and operational elegance of the original formulation. For a debate on Wright's reformulation, see Carchedi (1987) and Wright (1989).

2   Wright explains the importance of the self-employed and why they should be classified as the petit bourgeoisie: "Of particular importance . . . is simple commodity production: the production and sale of goods by self-employed individuals who employ no workers. In terms of the three dimensions of social relations of production . . ., such 'petty bourgeois' class locations involve control over money capital and physical capital but not over labor (since no labor power is employed within production)" (Wright, 1980: 329–30).

3   In the 1996 Canadian Census, a new question (Question 19) was included to ask respondents to specify which of the following groups they belong to: White, Chinese, South Asian, Black, Arab/West Asian, Filipino, South East Asian, Latin American, Japanese and Korean. Membership in "visible minorities" includes those who did not choose "white." Since the variable "visible minority" in the 1996 Census was based on direct

answers and previous censuses constructed this variable with inferences from the "ethnic origin" question, Statistics Canada suggests that caution be used in comparing visible minority data from the 1996 Census with previous censuses. See Statistics Canada, 1996 Census Questions, and Statistics Canada, 1996 Census Public Use Microdata File on Individuals, Documentation. In this chapter, "majority Canadians" refers to those who are not Chinese Canadians or visible minority Canadians.

4   Multiple classification analysis (Andrews *et al.*, 1976) is used to analyze the gross and net differences in earnings of the 30 groups (class by origin by gender). The statistical procedure is essentially a linear least squares solution which treats the dependent variable as a linear combination of a set of categorical and interval variables. For each interval variable in the equation, multiple classification analysis calculates the unstandardized multiple regression coefficient. For categorical variables, the analysis produces a regression coefficient for each category and expresses it as a deviation from the grand mean of the dependent variable. The actual or gross deviations measure the effects when variations in other independent variables have not been adjusted for; the adjusted or net deviations are effects when inter-group variations in other independent variables have been taken into account.

The statistical model used is: $Y_j = \alpha + \sum (\beta_{ij}, \delta_{ij}, \phi_{ij})$, where $Y_j$ is the labor market-related earnings of individual $j$, $\alpha$ is the grand mean of $Y_j$, $\beta_{ij}$ is a list of dummy variables in which $j$ varies from 1 to 30 measuring membership in the 30 groups, $\delta_{ij}$ are variables that relate to individual human capital, experience and language ability, and $\phi_{ij}$ are work-related characteristics such as industry of work, and part-time or full-time work.

5   In reporting income data, Statistics Canada applies upper and lower limits to individual earnings to ensure confidentiality. There were 837 individuals with wages and salaries and 403 individuals with self-employment income in the census microdata to whom these positive or negatives limits applied. Assuming these were unique individuals in the labor force, they made up at most 0.3 percent of the labor force in the sample (Statistics Canada, 1999, Table 7). Wages and salaries are always positive, but net self-employment income can have a negative value. Earnings in dollars are retained for easy interpretation, but a slightly better regression "fit" is obtained when using the natural logarithm of earnings as a dependent variable. Portes and Zhou (1996) argue that the statistically superior log-linear model risks sacrificing outliers in order to normalize the distribution of residuals, and further argue that there are solid grounds for retaining actual earnings in performing the analysis.

6   The "years of schooling" is constructed from several variables. For individuals with post-secondary education, the category "years of schooling" is the sum of years of university or non-university education, whichever is higher, and 12 years of elementary and secondary grades. For those with secondary school graduation, the number of years of schooling is coded as 12. For those with less than secondary school graduation, the highest grade coded is 11 even though higher grades may be reported. Individuals with only "grade 5–8" education are coded as having an average of 6.5 years of schooling, and those with "less than grade 5" are coded as having an average of 2 years of schooling.

7   "Full-time" refers to those who worked mainly full-time weeks in 1995, and "part-time" refers to those who worked mainly part-time weeks in 1995. A full-time week is 30 hours or more in one week (Statistics Canada, 1999).

8   The microdata file of the 1996 Census uses 16 classifications of industry based on the 1980 Standard Industrial Classfication. In this analysis, agriculture and other primary industries are collapsed into one category, and federal government services and other government services are recoded into one group.

9   The variable is measured as the number of years since an individual has immigrated to Canada, and native-born Canadians are coded as 0.

# References

Aldrich, Howard, John Cater, Trevor Jones and David McEvoy 1989. "From periphery to peripheral: The South Asian petite bourgeoisie in England." *Research in Sociology of Work* 2: 1–32.

Andrews, Frank M., James N. Morgan, John A. Sonquist, and Laura Klem 1976 *Multiple Classification Analysis*. Ann Arbor, Michigan: Institute for Social Research, University of Michigan.

Bian, Yanjie 1994 *Work and Inequality in Urban China*. Albany, New York: State University of New York Press.

Blalock, Herbert, M. Jr. 1967 *Towards a Theory of Minority Group Relations*. New York: John Wiley.

Bonacich, Edna and John Modell 1980 *Economic Basis of Ethnic Solidarity*. Berkeley and Los Angeles: University of California Press.

Carchedi, Guglielmo 1987 *Class Analysis and Social Research*. Oxford and New York: Basil Blackwell.

Chan, Kwok Bun 2000 *Chinese Business Networks: State, Economy and Culture*. Singapore: Prentice Hall.

Chan, Kwok Bun and Claire Chiang 1994 *Stepping Out: The Making of Chinese Entrepreneurs*. Singapore: Prentice-Hall.

Clegg, Stewart and Gordon S. Redding, eds. 1990 *Capitalism in Contrasting Cultures*. Berlin and New York: Walter de Gruyter.

Cohen, Robin 1997 *Global Diasporas*. Seattle, WA: University of Washington Press.

Goldberg, Michael A. 1983 *The Chinese Connection: Getting Plugged In to Pacific Rim Real Estate, Trade and Capital Markets*. Vancouver, WA: University of British Columbia Press.

Greenhalgh, Susan 1984 "Networks and their nodes: Urban society on Taiwan." *China Quarterly* 99 (Sept.): 529–52.

Hamilton, Gary G., ed. 1996 *Asian Business Networks*. Berlin and New York: Walter de Gruyter.

King, Ambrose Yeo-chi 1991 "Kuan-his and network building: A sociological interpretation." *Daedalus* 120 (2): 63–84.

Lever-Tracy, Constance, David Ip and Noel Tracy 1996 *The Chinese Diaspora and Mainland China*. London and New York: Macmillan Press and St. Martin's Press.

Li, Peter S. 1979 "A historical approach to ethnic stratification: The case of the Chinese in Canada, 1858–1930." *Canadian Review of Sociology and Anthropology* 16(3): 320–32.

—— 1990 "The emergence of the new middle class among Chinese in Canada." *Asian Culture* 14 (April): 187–94.

—— 1993 "Chinese investment and business in Canada: Ethnic entrepreneurial reconsidered." *Pacific Affairs* 66 (summer): 219–43.

—— 1998 *The Chinese in Canada*. Second edition. Toronto: Oxford University Press.

—— 2003 *Destination Canada: Immigration Debates and Issues*. Toronto: Oxford University Press.

Light, Ivan 1972 *Ethnic Enterprise in America*. Berkeley and Los Angeles: University of California Press.

—— 1979 "Disadvantaged minorities in self-employment." *International Journal of Comparative Sociology* 20: 31–45.

Light, Ivan and Edna Bonacich 1988 *Immigrant Entrepreneurs*. Berkeley and Los Angeles: University of California Press.

Light, Ivan and Carolyn Rosenstein 1995 *Race, Ethnicity, and Entrepreneurship in Urban America*. New York: Aldine de Gruyter.

Light, Ivan and Steven J. Gold 2000 *Ethnic Economies*. San Diego, CA: Academic Press.

Loewen, James W. 1971 *The Mississippi Chinese: Between Black and White*. Cambridge, MA: Harvard University Press.

Min, Pyong Gap 1984 "From white collar occupations to small business: Korean immigrants' occupational adjustment." *The Sociological Quarterly* 25: 333–52.

Pan, Lynn 1998 *The Encyclopedia of the Chinese Overseas*. Singapore: Archipelago Press and Landmark Books.

Portes, Alejandro and Min Zhou 1996 "Self-employment and the earnings of immigrants." *American Sociological Review* 61: 219–30.

Poston, Dudley L., Jr. and Mei-Yu Yu 1992 "The distribution of overseas Chinese". Pp. 117–48 in D.L. Poston, Jr. and D. Yaukey, eds., *The Population of Modern China*. New York: Plenum Press.

Redding, Gordon S. 1993 *The Spirit of Chinese Capitalism*. Berlin and New York: Walter de Gruyter.

Rinder, Irwin D. 1958–9 "Stranger in the land: Social relations in the status gap." *Social Problems* 6: 253–60.

Statistics Canada 1999 *Documentation for 1996 Census, Public Use Microdata File on Individuals*.

Tanzer, Andrew 1994 "The bamboo network." *Forbes* July 18: 138–45.

Waldinger Roger, Howard Aldrich, Robin Ward and Associates 1990 *Ethnic Entrepreneurs: Immigrant Business in Industrial Societies*. Newbury Park, CA: Sage.

Wang, Gungwu 1991 *China and the Chinese Overseas*. Singapore: Times Academic Press.

—— 1998 "Introduction." Pp. 10–13 in Lynn Pan, ed., *The Encyclopedia of the Chinese Overseas*. Singapore: Archipelago Press and Landmark Books.

Ward, Robin and Richard Jenkins, eds. 1984 *Ethnic Communities in Business*. Cambridge, MA: Cambridge University Press.

Wong, Siu-lun 1988 *Emigrant Entrepreneurs: Shanghai Industrialists in Hong Kong*. Hong Kong: Oxford University Press.

Wright, Erik Olin 1977 "Marxist class categories and income inequality." *American Sociological Review* 42: 32–55.

—— 1978 "Race, class, and income inequality." *American Journal of Sociology* 83: 1368–97.

—— 1979 *Class Structure and Income Determination*. New York: Academic Press.

—— 1980 "Varieties of Marxist conceptions of class structure." *Politics and Society* 9(3): 323–70.

—— 1985 *Classes*. London: Verso.

—— 1989 *The Debate on Classes*. London: Verso.

# 11 The global–local nexus and ethnic business location

*Chiu Luk*

## INTRODUCTION

The year 2003 bore witness to the proliferation of the deadly virus known as SARS (Severe Acute Respiratory Syndrome), which originated from Asia and eventually spread to Canada and other parts of the world. The diffusion of SARS is typically hierarchical, with large cities such as Beijing, Hong Kong, Taipei, Singapore, and Toronto as highly infected nodes. Spread to smaller communities followed. However, the most intriguing part of the spread of SARS is the global extent and the rapidity of its proliferation, serving as another reminder that our world today is highly interconnected. The flows of people that criss-cross countries in the form of tourists, business contacts, or migrants are testimony to the globalization process that has gathered momentum since the 1990s.

Globalization can be observed everywhere and in almost every domain. *Crouching Tiger, Hidden Dragon*, the Oscar award winner for foreign films in 2001, is an excellent example of a globalized product. The film script had Chinese martial arts as background, was directed by a Taiwanese and shot in mainland China, yet it had international financing, including American capital investment. The main cast consisted of well-known movie stars from Hong Kong and Malaysia. Its production team was composed of a myriad of technical personnel from different countries. Its wide popularity at box offices around the world demonstrates its successful packaging as a global product that avoided exclusiveness of any aspect.

Widely accepted as the most important socio-economic-political change in the contemporary world, globalization can be observed through at least four lenses: extensive worldwide trade (as represented by the World Trade Organization), a world with high connectivity in communication (typified by the Internet), the emergence of regional blocs of previously independent countries (such as the European Community), and the growing cultural and environmental concerns that stem from penetration of American culture to all parts of the world (such as the spread of McDonald's restaurants, Starbucks Coffee, etc.).

This chapter will address the cultural concerns brought forth by globalized movements of people and their impact on the socio-cultural milieu of cities. I will look at how an immigrant group (the Chinese), when further subdivided into subethnic components, responds and is affected by global forces and the local scene.

Specifically, my focus is on the locational strategy of ethnic businesses adopted by different subgroups of Chinese, illustrating their unique ways of interacting in their locales. Two research objectives stand out. The first is to identify the links between the "global" and the "local" to break new ground for a fresh understanding on how ethnic business chooses its location. I argue for an integrative approach that enmeshes both global and local perspectives. The centrality of the geographic dimension is identified. My second objective is to argue against the simplistic observation that ethnic businesses of the same nature will appear everywhere as a result of globalization. The argument is substantiated with this examination on the finer divisions of ethnic Chinese and their businesses in Toronto.

The next section is an examination of pertinent literature on globalization, including geography's role, relationship to ethnic business research, and the global–local discourse as the conceptual framework for this study. Also, I shall also discuss the Chinese diaspora and its subgroups as central subjects of this research. The third section discusses the study area, data, and methodology, while the fourth section presents the findings. The final section presents a full discussion of the implications of the locational strategy within the context of a global–local nexus.

## LITERATURE REVIEW

### Globalization, geography, and ethnic business research

The literature on globalization is voluminous. Nevertheless, the main idea is to recognize that globalization is a process of change that encompasses economic, social, cultural, political, and demographic dimensions brought forth by increasing connectivity between nation states. Connectivity implies technological developments such as the emergence of telecommunications, widespread Internet usage and, not least, the ease of air travel that fosters extensive movements of people around the globe. The obvious result is "the intensification of world-wide social relations which link distant localities in such a way that local happenings are shaped by events occurring many miles away" (Giddens, 1990: 64). The complexity of the subject of globalization is reflected in its multi-disciplinary treatment by a variety of social sciences. For the sake of clarity, I intend to restrict my discussion to the geographic dimension as this is the basis of this research.

Geography as the study of the earth is intrinsically tied to any interest in global phenomena. Globalization is not merely a philosophical construct, but is expressed and observed on the ground to capture the attention of geographers. Its importance is demonstrated in a special issue entitled "Globalization and Geography" which appeared in *GeoJournal*, Vol. 45, No. 1–2, 1998. In that issue, papers cover two major focuses: one examines globalization as a process (cultural, political, or economic) with profound social consequences, while the other centers on the ways in which globalization relates to the discipline of geography as a whole. The "shrinking" of our globe suggests the need for fresh understanding of traditional geographic concepts of *distance*, *scale*, and *spatial differentiation*. Globalization may bring forth a decline in the importance of distance as almost everything proliferates out with unprecedented speed. Globalization expresses itself most strongly at the "global scale" far more often than at other local scales that geographers employ in examining other phenomena. Spatial differentiation regarding the varying responses that societies have to global changes may induce new efforts to comprehend the dissimilar impacts that globalization may have on the human organization of this world.

The richness of the geographic perspective is further demonstrated in the widely employed concepts of *space* and *place* to which this research addresses. First and foremost is *space* (expressed in absolute or relative ways), defined in terms of the areal extent in which human or physical objects occupy the earth's surface. Patterns of concentration or dispersion are often the concern. With globalization, the rise of new urban spaces within global cities is a popular subject of inquiry (Yeoh, 1999: 609). From an empirical standpoint, globalization induces the need to reinvent old neighborhoods or even leads to the rise of new ones on the urban scene (Mele, 1996). My study will discuss the ways that globalization forces lead to the rise of ethnic business clusters as ecological niches of optimal spatial arrangements. I shall also advance a unique way to examine how global *and* local forces interact to enable distinct subethnic "neighborhoods" to appear as a new kind of urban space.

The concept of *place* refers to the geographic area occupied by a person that involves built-in attachment feelings to justify its value of existence. Attachments to a place are often related to the culture with which the place is tied. Two review articles on the geographic literature on immigration appeared recently (Gober, 2000 and Hiebert, 2000). The former touches more on the U.S., while the latter concentrates on the Canadian scene. Both devote sections to the social and cultural changes observed in cities that experience a growing intensity of immigration. Implicit in these papers is the emergence of distinct immigrant identities as a new sense of place attachment to such host areas. Borrowing Appadurai's (1990) idea of "ethnoscapes" that represent new social landscapes generated by immigrants settling in their new host societies, McNeill (1999) discusses the possibility of a European scenario. All in all, globalization is now closely tied with urban development, with interconnections with immigration, race, and the construction of new identities based on their previous cultures (Liu, 2000). My present study, therefore, expands the discourse on place for an immigrant society affected by globalization, through examination of dissimilar subethnic "landscapes" arising from subethnic populations who share the same ethnic source.

This study employs both *space* and *place* concepts in articulating the geographic dimension. The distributional aspect of ethnic business is clearly an analysis within a *spatial* framework to detect possible formation of ecological niches. On the other hand, the discussion of attachment to former places of origin ties the *place* perspective to the identity issue of immigrants newly interpreted within the framework of globalization.

Traditionally, most studies of ethnic business have focused on three interrelated issues: self-employment participation patterns (e.g., Light and Rosenstein, 1995), economic returns of participating in the ethnic economy (e.g., Portes and Zhou, 1996), and social networks among ethnic businesses (e.g., Saunders and Nee, 1996). Central to these attempts are assessments of how the *structural* context (such as causes, conditions, and mechanisms of individual participation in ethnic business) affects individual economic achievements (Fong, Luk, and Ooka, 2005). A major drawback of such studies is the lack of attention given to the *spatial* context which articulates the environment in which such businesses are located and which in turn strongly affects the dynamics and survival of the businesses. The locational advantages of a successful business are often demonstrated in the flow of customers, competitiveness, or even potential business investments.

To date, the literature on the spatial aspects of ethnic business is sparse. Fortunately, there are a few writings that point to the significance of this approach. Rekers and van Kempen (2000) offer an overview discussion of the utility of the spatial approach. The work by Fong, Luk, and Ooka (2005) provides an empirical examination of the spatial distribution of suburban ethnic business. Among the three critical spatial factors noted by Rekers and van Kempen, demographic change (such as the varying lifestyles of different Chinese subgroups across space) and urban environmental variables (such as differential local policies) are particularly relevant to my research. The first relates to urban consumers, the present case being Chinese immigrants; or, to be specific, subgroups of Chinese. The second factor is concerned with the neighborhoods in which they congregate. Both factors vary across geographic space, pinpointing the centrality of the geographic dimension for ethnic business. Beyond such considerations are the unique links to be established between global and local forces in the study of location patterns of ethnic business.

## The global–local nexus discourse

Early discussions on the topic of globalization have been skewed towards the over-whelming impact of global forces at the expense of local conditions. The implicit understanding is that local societies have no ability to challenge globalization, seen to be permeating to every corner of the world. Recent literature advances the idea that each locality still has a value to contest globalization forces. This is particularly the viewpoint of Appadurai (1990, 1996), who formulates interactions between people, media, technology, finance, ideology, etc., at the local scene as "-scapes", representing globalized cultural and economic flows. Surely, global and local forces co-exist, although their relative importance might not be equal.

The relationship between the global and the local is often portrayed as their being antithetical to each other. More and more evidence points to the contrary. A good example is the worldwide spread of McDonald's restaurants as the epitome of modernity, leading to the promulgation of the "McDonaldization" thesis by Ritzer (1996). This represents an acknowledgment of the homogenization thesis, the idea that places are becoming more and more similar with globalization. However, there are stories of McDonald's offering meals that reflect local tastes in an effort to further strengthen its market penetration. Hence, rice meals are sold in Taipei

(*Taipei Times*, Dec. 16, 2002) and all-vegetarian burgers are offered in New Delhi (*CNN*, July 14, 2002). Another interesting case is the strategic alliance between Coca-Cola (the multinational soft-drink giant) and Ten Ren Tea (the Taiwanese tea guru) to initiate a new market for Chinese tea in aluminum cans in Taiwan (*China Times*, August 11, 2003). Such innovative market strategies demonstrate the meshing of the twin concepts of global and local in a "*glocalized*" situation.

There are various formal academic discourses on the global–local nexus. Examples include the concepts of "heritage landscape" (Cartier, 1998), "heritage tourism" (Chang *et al.*, 1996), cyberspace manifestation (Prichard, 1999), local development (Ettlinger, 1999), social movements (Soyez, 2000), etc. As a proponent for globalization, the homogenization thesis is now challenged by advocates who favor greater attention to local conditions and the assertion of place identity amidst a globalized environment. Using urban heritage tourism as an example (Chang *et al.*, 1996), the global approach is top-down, focusing on exogenous forces such as global market demands and the likelihood of seeing homogeneous tourism cities and landscapes emerge as globalization intensifies. On the other hand, the local approach is bottom-up, placing high value on each urban site as unique. The endogenous forces have the potential to carry out local development on their own. Yet, the beauty of the nexus between the global and the local lies in what Oakes (1993: 47) calls "a dynamic cultural negotiation in which dominant structures (i.e., the global) are mediated by individual agency (i.e., the local)." An excellent articulation of this nexus is given by Urry's (1990) concept of "global division of tourism." When international tourism becomes commonplace in this increasingly globalized world, large numbers of tourists with varying tastes and preferences are generated. Different countries then emphasize certain tourist activities. The United Kingdom was cited as specializing in heritage tourism, Switzerland for those who love mountaineering activities, and Thailand for exotic adventurers. Specialization calls for the best utilization of local resources and full expression of the uniqueness of each locality. Site-specific considerations therefore play a crucial role in mediating the global impacts of tourism. This integrative approach, proven to be successful for urban heritage tourism, is also adopted in my present research.

A recent paper by Castles (2001) articulates well the relationship between globalization and migration within which the global–local dimensions are also applicable. One corollary of human migration is community formation that leads to social and cultural changes. Unlike older migrants in the past, migrants in the current era of globalization are more diverse in social and cultural characteristics. The transnational social space (Faist, 2000) that these migrants form is largely a product of globalization and also intrinsically tied to the locales in which they live. The interplay of factors involved in the generation of such unique transnational communities (empirically verified in this study as subethnic neighborhoods) clearly exhibits the negotiation of global and local factors in a dynamic way.

Much has been written on the global–local nexus, with diverse viewpoints on whether global forces or local conditions are more prevalent. The study on global production networks (such as automobile, electronics, etc.) by Palpacuer and

Parisotto (2003) suggests that globalization is the "stronger" force. The implications of such global enterprises for local industrial upgrading, jobs, and development policy are discussed. From their findings, they are skeptical of the ability of global enterprises to be a lever for local development. The disproportionate strength of large enterprises that involve global investment actually stifles the prospects of upgrading for small industrial firms at the local level. There are alternative views that place central importance on local conditions. A paper by Zhou and Tseng (2001) articulates the significance of localization in transnational space sustenance. The territorial division of labor and local community networks are found to be critically important for the operation of high-tech and accounting firms in Los Angeles. This finding is noteworthy, for it is widely agreed that globalized forces have had major impact on Los Angeles.

In addition to economic examples, the literature gives considerable attention to the socio-cultural realm. Researches have consistently pointed out that community networks in the host societies are highly useful for new immigrants to gain entry into the workforce (Poros, 2001; Salaff *et al.*, 2002). Such social networks are locally defined and sustained. These studies clearly point out the critical link between the local labor market and contemporary migrants, whose intention to migrate is accelerated by the increase in globalization (Castles, 2001). Credentials and skills acquired in their homeland many miles away have to be repackaged and re-evaluated to fit the established socio-structural context. In this chapter, I shall argue that subcultural Chinese elements (inherited from the homeland afar) are strongly expressed as a distinct socio-cultural milieu in the local setting whereby subethnic Chinese businesses can expand into valuable cultural resources for them to survive or excel. As a result, the global and local aspects reinforce each other to construct a cultural reproduction in a foreign land (Salamandra, 2002).

## THE CHINESE DIASPORA AND ITS SUBGROUPS

The Chinese have a long history of out-migration from China, especially from the coastal provinces. The diaspora has always been worldwide, with heavy con-centrations in Southeast Asia, now gradually developing with tremendous speed in Western countries such as Canada, U.S., Australia, etc. Social scientists are very interested in the recent rise of a new type of Chinese migrant. The distinction between them and earlier migrants is best summarized in two Chinese phrases by Wang and Wang (1998). The *luoye guigen* type refers to traditional Chinese migrants, who were simply sojourners in foreign lands who would eventually return to the former homeland; hence, "returning to their roots." In contrast, there is the *luodi shenggen* type, describing those new Chinese migrants who try hard to "plant as permanent roots" and assimilate to the host country. The latter type constitutes the recent wave of immigrants from Hong Kong, mainland China, and Taiwan into Canada. Special note should be made of Canada's multiculturalism policy that encourages immigrants to preserve their ethnic heritage as well as integrating with the mainstream. To the Chinese, this situation provides fertile soil for the rise of ethnic businesses that reflect elements of Chinese culture. To many Chinese Canadians, such businesses provide them with economic survival. To Canadian society as a whole, promotion of cultural diversity enhances inter-ethnic harmony.

Research on ethnic Chinese has long treated the Chinese as one single homogeneous group, labelling them as *haiwai huaren* (overseas Chinese). Crissman (1967) and his associates began to question the validity of doing so. The segmentary model of viewing Chinese communities was proposed, and further refined in subsequent writings (Crissman *et al.*, 1998; Sedgwick, 1998). The model suggests a more refined examination of overseas Chinese with regard to their places of origin. There should be subgroups for Hong Kong, mainland China, Taiwan, and perhaps Southeast Asia. The term "subethnicity" refers to these distinctions (Min, 1999). The rationale is to go beyond the primary ethnic group to unearth and clear away misconceived or misunderstood notions about subgroups. The work by Light *et al.* (1993) and Bozorgmehr (1997) regarding various types of Iranians is an effort in this direction. As for overseas Chinese, there is a welcome trend lately to look into subethnic Chinese differentiation in Australia (Wu *et al.*, 1998) and Great Britain (Parker, 1998).

Of the ethnic Chinese in Canada reported in the 2001 census, 40 percent live in Toronto, followed by 31.8 percent in Vancouver. Therefore, Toronto is an ideal place to study the new type of Chinese immigrants and their subgroups. The segmentary view of the Toronto Chinese community is evaluated here to enrich the pertinent literature on the Chinese diaspora within the context of globalization. In essence, this study contests the assumed notion that globalization would bring forth numerous ethnic businesses throughout the world without distinction of subethnic affiliation (consistent with the homogenization thesis of globalization).

Immigrant subgroups play an important role in helping their members adapt to the larger alien culture. In doing so, their respective identities are fundamental to bringing themselves together. This process of adaptation and identity formation functions under the umbrella of the larger culture to which such subgroups belong. Cultures as patterns of beliefs and values are essentially ways of life, often expressed in language, habits, and social or institutional structures which are internalized as natural by most individuals in that culture (Matthews, 1996). In other words, individual subgroup members share similar attributes of the "larger" culture, along with particular *sub*-cultural elements that prove to be distinctive identities. As discussed by Matthews (1996, 1997), the Hong Kong identity is the result of a complex mixture of diverse elements of the larger cultural milieu. Each individual has some degree of freedom to pick what he or she sees as most relevant from the "cultural supermarket" to form his or her own version of identity.

This present study ties together the concepts of subculture and identities. The cultural appeal in subethnic business titles could be treated as an expression of cultural identity, without which the businesses would not be able to survive in a foreign market. To be able to identify as a separate group is full expression of localism within a globalized environment. Also, such identities create the mentality of a safe haven for adjustment in the immigration settlement process, helping to alleviate the sense of rootlessness of group members. For some subgroups, such identities offer the opportunity to receive a "transplanted milieu" from place of origin to host country. Therefore, the business titles should bear strong resemblances to things which are well known in the homelands. A sense of being "at home" is the aspiration of everyone in the subgroup. These are the points to be addressed in the following analysis.

## STUDY AREA, DATA, AND RESEARCH METHODOLOGY

The study area for this chapter is the Greater Toronto Area, encompassing the metropolitan core of Toronto and its surrounding suburban communities (Map 11.1). Our prime concern is the former six municipalities of Metropolitan Toronto (amalgamated as the new City of Toronto in 1998), and the immediately adjoining municipalities to the north (Vaughan, Richmond Hill, Markham), and west (Mississauga).

The data used in this research includes information from the 1996 Canadian census and from Chinese businesses which have identifiable subethnic targets. In the Canadian census, an immigrant is defined as one who was foreign born. The measuring indicator is "place of birth." This is the only statistical indicator from the census which offers a subethnic breakdown of the Chinese community into

*Map 11.1* Principal municipalities in the Greater Toronto area under study.

those who were born in Hong Kong, mainland China, and Taiwan. This indicator is not perfect, as the following example shows. An immigrant family from Hong Kong may have parents who were born in mainland China and settled in Hong Kong early in their childhood, while their children were born in Hong Kong. With the "place of birth" indicator, each member of that family is categorized according to where they were born instead of being treated as a Hong Kong family. A better alternative would be to use the "country of last permanent residence" information from Citizenship and Immigration Canada. However, this department only keeps track of incoming immigrants and does not release statistical counts of the existing stock of past immigrants. Nor does it provide readily available data at the local level of a census tract. Without other viable alternatives, I used the "place of birth" indicator from the census as an acceptable surrogate to measure the general size of the three subethnic Chinese groups.

According to Statistics Canada, census tracts are small geographic units representing urban or rural neighborhood-like communities (Statistics Canada, 1997, 195–9). Their populations range from 2,500 to 8,000, with an average of around 4,000. In terms of socio-economic characteristics, they are relatively homogeneous. Hence, census tracts are used here to aggregate statistics related to different Chinese subgroups and are ideal for displaying significant spatial variation in map form. There is great variation in the population size of the three Chinese subgroups at the census tract level. To simplify computation work, only those tracts with more than 100 persons of a subgroup were selected for analysis. Although 100 is an arbitrary cut-off figure, it roughly represents a "critical mass" which helps to draw in sufficient customers to sustain a business. From a total of 804 tracts in the Toronto CMA, 183 tracts were selected for the Hong Kong subgroup, 209 for mainland Chinese, and only 26 for the Taiwanese. To measure the strength of the collective Chinese market in each tract, the summed populations of the three subgroups were computed as a percentage of the general population. These two statistical indicators are used to evaluate the ecological niches for each subgroup of Chinese businesses.

In this study, only businesses which express an identifiable subethnic Chinese target were selected for analysis. The principal source of information was from commercial advertisements found in the three major Chinese daily newspapers in Toronto: *Ming Pao* (most popular among immigrants from Hong Kong), *World Journal* (whose prime target is the Taiwanese audience), and *Sing Tao* (most welcome among people from mainland China). Observations were made on two days: one in early January and the other in late March, 2000. The selected business titles were supplemented by the latest *Chinese Yellow Pages*, by *Ming Pao*, as well as personal awareness of relevant individual businesses. Since the interest is *only* in those businesses which are highly expressive in targeting the three Chinese subgroups, the resultant selection should not be taken as a scientifically generated random sample. The work done here is not meant to be exhaustive. Therefore, extra care has been exercised in the interpretation of findings and only highly distinctive differences will be noted.

The selection and categorization of relevant Chinese businesses into the three subgroups of Hong Kong, mainland China, and Taiwan are based on careful inspection of their business titles, both English and Chinese. In some cases, additional information provided in the advertisement was used as well. The individual locations and appeal conveyed in the business titles are analyzed below. The central idea of such analyses is to prove the existence of the three diverse Chinese subgroups instead of just one.

## THE SUBETHNIC CHINESE BUSINESS COMMUNITIES OF TORONTO

### Locational analysis

Table 11.1 displays summary findings on the three sampled subethnic Chinese business groups of Toronto. Apparently, the Hong Kong (hereafter, HK) subgroup is largest in number (150), while the mainland Chinese (ML) and the Taiwanese (TW) subgroups are roughly the same size (39 and 33). This finding truly reflects the reality that Hong Kong immigrants have long dominated the Chinese community in Toronto, generating substantial demand for HK products and services. On the other hand, immigration from Taiwan has been phenomenal since the early 1990s, and thus there are relatively fewer businesses catering towards the TW market. The composition of the ML sector needs elaboration. Persons born in mainland China fall into this group, but there should be a further distinction of whether they were born before or after 1949. Those born before 1949 are likely to have immigrated first to Hong Kong/Taiwan, taking up residence there for quite some time before settling in Canada. Those born after 1949 most likely came directly to Canada from the People's Republic of China. These two types of ML differ considerably in socio-economic status. The pre-1949 subgroup has been settled in Canada for a much longer time period and presumably has reached a higher level on the social ladder. Those who are new immigrants (defined as those who immigrated five years ago or less) from the People's Republic are more likely to be less successful either economically or socially in integrating with the larger society. Hence, merging the "old" and the "new" ML sectors together in any discussion might conceal significant differences.

I shall begin by looking at the *location* aspects of the sample businesses and then provide an interpretation of different forms of appeal *attributes* expressed in their business titles. The methodology employed to inspect different locational strategies is map correlation analysis. Each business is geocoded and plotted as a point on a map of Toronto, signifying its specific location in geographic space. Areal data in terms of census tracts are used to represent either (1) the number of Chinese subgroup members (i.e., HK, ML, TW) or (2) the total percentage of Chinese in the tract. Clusters of points on the map corresponding to high values of areal data are considered to be a "niche" for the occurrence of a particular subethnic group's businesses.

Map 11.2 displays the locations of sampled HK, ML, and TW businesses against census tracts of their respective subgroup populations. Clearly, there is a suburban

*Table 11.1* Summary findings of the three subethnic Chinese business sample in Toronto

|  | Hong Kong | | Mainland | | Taiwan | |
|---|---|---|---|---|---|---|
|  | Count | Percent | Count | Percent | Count | Percent |
| *Category sets* | | | | | | |
| (Hong Kong) | | | | | | |
| Borrowed name | 9 | 6.0 | | | | |
| Chinese culture | 1 | 0.7 | | | | |
| Colloquial Cantonese | 16 | 10.7 | | | | |
| English title attraction | 1 | 0.7 | | | | |
| Hong Kong landmark | 11 | 7.3 | | | | |
| Lucky name | 32 | 21.3 | | | | |
| Prestigious symbol | 8 | 5.3 | | | | |
| Special offer | 1 | 0.7 | | | | |
| Specifying Hong Kong | 4 | 2.7 | | | | |
| Transplanted title | 67 | 44.7 | | | | |
| Total | 150 | 100.0 | | | | |
| | | | | | | |
| (Mainland) | | | | | | |
| Borrowed name | | | 1 | 2.6 | | |
| Chinese landmark | | | 11 | 28.2 | | |
| Chinese culture | | | 8 | 20.5 | | |
| *Pinyin translation* | | | 9 | 23.1 | | |
| Specifying Chinese | | | 6 | 15.4 | | |
| Transplanted title | | | 4 | 10.3 | | |
| Total | | | 39 | 100.0 | | |
| | | | | | | |
| (Taiwan) | | | | | | |
| Chinese culture | | | | | 2 | 6.1 |
| Specifying Taiwan | | | | | 7 | 21.2 |
| Taiwan landmark | | | | | 7 | 21.2 |
| Taiwanese culture | | | | | 9 | 27.3 |
| Wade-Giles translation | | | | | 8 | 24.2 |
| Total | | | | | 33 | 100.0 |
| | | | | | | |
| *Types of activities* | | | | | | |
| Auto-related | 2 | 1.3 | 0 | 0.0 | 0 | 0.0 |
| Eating establishments | 38 | 25.3 | 16 | 41.0 | 23 | 69.7 |
| Financial services | 25 | 16.7 | 2 | 5.1 | 2 | 6.1 |
| Labor-related | 4 | 2.7 | 0 | 0.0 | 0 | 0.0 |
| Malls | 12 | 8.0 | 1 | 2.6 | 0 | 0.0 |
| Others | 1 | 0.7 | 0 | 0.0 | 0 | 0.0 |
| Professional-related | 2 | 1.3 | 11 | 28.2 | 1 | 3.0 |
| Retail | 34 | 22.7 | 3 | 7.7 | 2 | 6.1 |
| Services | 32 | 21.3 | 6 | 15.4 | 5 | 15.2 |
| Total | 150 | 100.0 | 39 | 100.0 | 33 | 100.0 |

Data Source: Sample analysis from business advertisements, January and March, 2000.
Note: Only businesses with identifiable subethnic Chinese targets are selected here.

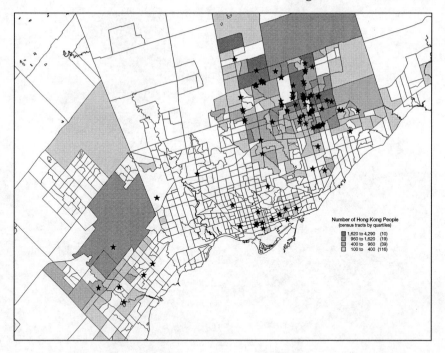

*Map 11.2A*  Hong Kong business location over census tracts with >100 Honkongese.

stretch of HK businesses in the north (Map 11.2A): in Scarborough (an inner sub-urb), and in Markham and Richmond Hill (outer suburbs). They correspond with high values of HK population to a great extent. The "niche" in these areas is clearly seen. On the other hand, the relatively loose cluster of such businesses in downtown Toronto is in contrast with that area having the least number of HK people. This simply means that the occurrence of HK business there has a very low corre-spondence of HK people residing there. At the extreme, there are a few places where HK businesses occur in areas with no HK people at all. Correspondence analysis with the total percentage of Chinese yields similar observations.

Map 11.2B portrays a different picture for ML business. More obvious clusters are observed in both downtown Toronto and northern Scarborough. They corre-spond nicely with high values of ML population in these areas, and similarly with the total percentage of Chinese. The distinction between "old" and "new" ML people helps explain some occurrence of ML businesses in central Markham, as apparently they are the "older" ML subgroup. In downtown Toronto, the high concentration of mainlanders, together with the cluster of ML businesses, testify to the dual function of Chinatown: as a residential community and an employment base. Also worthwhile to note is a possible re-succession of business in Chinatown: Previously catering to the HK market, it now is oriented towards the ML. The niche in downtown is always present, as Chinatown is always a hub of ethnic Chinese activities with tremendous tourist potential.

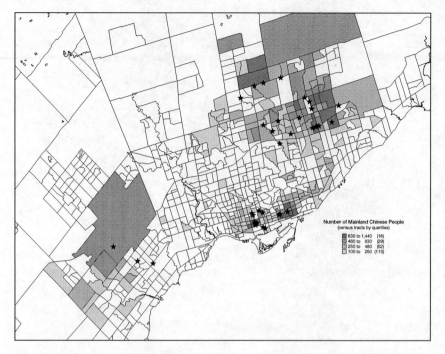

*Map 11.2B* Mainland Chinese business location over census tracts with >100 mainlanders.

The TW case is highly intriguing (Map 11.2C). Its cluster at the border of Markham and Scarborough does not coincide with a high concentration of TW people. The highest concentration of TW people in central North York is not met with a proportionate cluster of TW business. The situation is even worse for the cluster in downtown Toronto. These observations imply that the inner and outer suburbs serve as "bedroom communities" for the TW people. The downtown cluster is there to cater to the tourist market instead of serving its co-ethnics.

Using the "niche" perspective to inspect these three subgroups of Chinese business yields dissimilar results. The perspective best fit the HK subgroup, was a partial fit for ML businesses, and the least compliance was with the TW sector. Since the ML business sector is a late arrival, there is a possibility that it may follow the footsteps of its HK counterpart. Generally speaking, the existence of a strong Chinese community (represented by high values of Chinese population) is the incubator for subethnic business. This is obvious in downtown Toronto for ML and TW cases, and in Markham for HK and TW businesses. In other words, the "niche" concept is still important to explain the location of subethnic business. *Local conditions* are instrumental to the start and sustenance of such activities.

Nonetheless, there is evidence to the contrary. Map 11.3 shows the locations of sampled banks represented in each of the three types of subethnic Chinese business. The ML and TW cases have only two locations each, and they are exclusively centered in downtown Toronto. In marked contrast, the HK case shows a widely

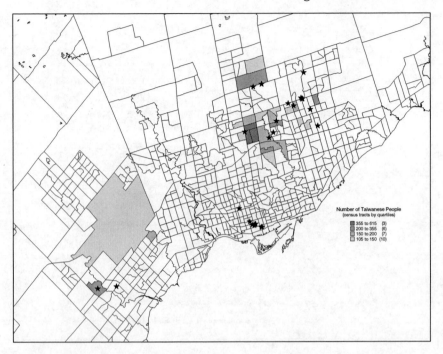

*Map 11.2C* Taiwanese business location over census tracts with >100 Taiwanese.

dispersed pattern. A partial explanation of the clustered pattern for ML and TW cases is their relatively "weaker" position in the financial market, apparently due to their smaller population. They tend to occupy the downtown area to take advantage of its central location. In contrast, the predominance of the HK community explains the abundance of its bank branches across Toronto. In fact, this locational strategy is to capture the "beachheads," thus maximizing the market share. In other words, the "niche" component for bank locations is not clearcut. A macro and holistic perspective is of more importance here. We shall critically examine this point again in the discussion section below.

## Attribute analysis

Table 11.1 presents a listing of the appeal category sets for the three subethnic Chinese business groups. These categories not only suggest the strategies that business owners used to appeal to their intended customers, but also reflect strongly the socio-cultural inclinations of each of the three subethnic Chinese groups. Almost 45 percent of the HK businesses have titles directly transplanted from Hong Kong. It should be noted that most of the titles are well known to everyone. Legally, this practice is not appropriate and might invite lawsuits. However, this is the easiest and most direct way to appeal to customers who originate from Hong Kong. Next on the list is the use of lucky names (21%). Whether or not this epitomizes the

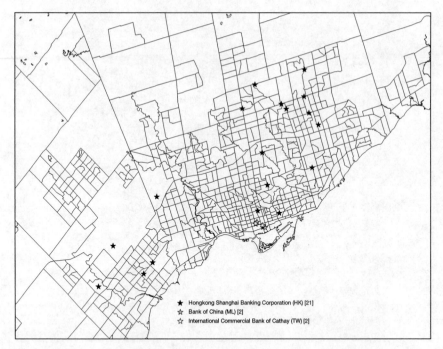

*Map 11.3* Distribution of Hong Kong, mainland Chinese and Taiwanese banks.

commercial nature of the HK people is subject to debate. The third place goes to the employment of colloquial Cantonese in business titles (11%). Needless to say, colloquial words are only effective with those who know and appreciate that local culture. The strong emphasis that the HK subgroup gives to such uses clearly demonstrates the superb utilization of objects of appeal to strengthen their sub-markets. *Reference to commercialism* is the key appeal structure for this subgroup.

The ML business titles present a very different story. Top on the list of appeal categories is the use of Chinese landmarks (28%). Real objects, geographic concepts, or concrete territories are used. For those with strong nationalist feelings, the use of Chinese landmarks is the most direct way to embrace elements of Chinese identity. The use of *pinyin translation* comes second (23%) and should appeal effectively to the "new" ML group of people, as it is the style of romanization practiced in the People's Republic. Last of all, reference to Chinese culture in general (21%) should have relevance for all people born in China, regardless of when they were born. In a word, *traces of Sinocentrism* could be detected in this subgroup.

It should not be difficult to observe a strong sense of *Taiwanese identity* when inspecting business titles for the TW subgroup. Expression of Taiwanese culture (27%) comes first, followed by the usage of the Wade-Giles system of translation (24%). History is the explanatory factor for the use of this traditional way of trans-lating Chinese words. For strong identification, the specification of Taiwan or the use of landmarks from the area comes third on the list (21%). Compared to the HK case, the level of abstraction employed here is higher, emphasizing higher cultured preferences and individual tastes.

Looking at the activity breakdowns in Table 11.1, there are clear commonalities and differences among the three subgroups of Chinese business. The prime activity is always eating establishments: 25 percent of the HK subgroup, 41 percent of ML, and 70 percent of TW. The reason is not difficult to understand: preparing food in the accustomed cuisine appeals most to people who are looking for a cultural identity. A traditional Chinese saying states, "The first and foremost issue for all is to enjoy eating," so to engage in the eating business is logical. The fact that the TW subgroup has a much higher concentration in the eating business (followed by ML) has a lot to do with the length of time in Canada. The short duration of settlement of the TW subgroup has not allowed a diversification of activities to emerge. The HK subgroup is exactly the opposite, with the top three activities almost equal in percentage. Evidently, this situation approaches a more mature scenario whereby much diversification of activities is achieved. The ML subgroup is situated somewhere in between.

A closer look at the HK subgroup yields more insight into its attributes. The much longer period of settlement in Toronto for this subgroup explains why its retail and service sectors have grown to such magnitude to cater to the needs of the HK immigrant market. When this stage of "institutional completeness" is reached, an increase in newcomers of this subgroup would most likely generate further demand for subethnic business activities. The almost negligible share of the professional category among the HK subgroup (as opposed to being second in importance in the ML subgroup) is worth noting. Being more established over time and more conversant in English, association with mainstream business is often the strategy, and so they were not captured in our sample.

## REVISITING THE GLOBAL–LOCAL DEBATE FOR ETHNIC BUSINESS LOCATION

This chapter has presented a unique piece of research on ethnic business location by employing a new framework interpreted in the broad context of globalization. The focus is on the geographic dimension of ethnic business expressed as new social relations over urban space. Such urban features could also be interpreted as special landscapes generated by the presence of subethnic Chinese business clusters. To the average person, this might only be part of the overall living environment where the hidden global dimension is often left unnoticed.

Here I shall critically examine the contributions made in this chapter. Three points are to be cited, related back to the two research objectives stated at the beginning and the special geographic attributes this study inherits. The first point concerns the *links between the "global" and the "local."*

I hereby advance the schematic model presented in Figure 11.1 as a conceptual guide for the present study. The "global" dimension is expressed in the continuous

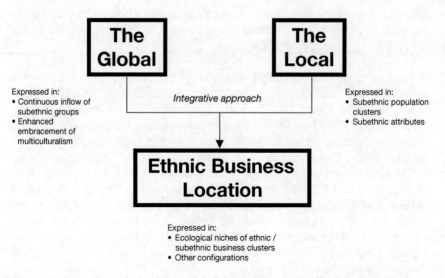

*Figure 11.1* A schematic model on global–local dimensions affecting ethnic business location.

inflow of immigrants from all parts of the world and the manifestation of multiculturalism in terms of their diverse *places of origin*. In other words, the widespread locations of immigrants and the global movements of such people (with their cultures) constitute the "global" dimension of this research. Each year, such global forces bring forth copious streams of foreign-born people into Canada, culminating in a socially diverse "mosaic" best characterized in the Toronto setting. The *Toronto Star* (October 2, 2003) reported on the Ethnic Diversity Survey conducted in 2002 by Statistics Canada and the Multiculturalism Program of the Department of Canadian Heritage, which pinpointed immigrants' strong sense of belonging to their international home cultures even after they have settled comfortably in a multicultural Canada. This suggests a "fertile soil" in which "global" elements could flourish well in harmony amongst multiethnic groups.

"Local" elements are represented in subethnic clusters of business, signaling the presence of favorable location factors at such locales. There are also subethnic attributes that can be traced back to *long-held traditions and values* of the homeland. Such attributes are definitely locally derived there, but expressed anew in the immigrant host society. As discussed earlier, each of the HK, ML, and TW subgroups have vastly dissimilar values to be explored. In other words, the "local" elements are of two types. One points to the specific local environs of different Toronto neighborhoods that accept such subethnic businesses. Another refers to the "local" elements transplanted from abroad and re-established in this new Toronto context.

In my view, the "global" and the "local" portions of the model should be integrated in order to explain specific ethnic business locations. Two situations may occur. First, subethnic businesses could develop either as specific clusters or in other configurations. Clearly, the HK and ML cases have expressed themselves in specific clusters over geographic space. These clusters could be referred to as ecological niches whereby local geographic factors could explain why such businesses occur and succeed in such locations. On the other hand, the case of HK banks, which have a dispersed distribution pattern, represents a departure from that norm. To me, this aggressive strategy to disperse rather than to congregate at a few clusters is only feasible when a truly "*glocalized*" situation is attained. In this case, when "global" and "local" elements are intrinsically tied to each other, the situation is conducive for some businesses to become more daring, seeking to capture "unclaimed lands" in the hope of capturing new markets. The Hongkong and Shanghai Banking Corporation (now HSBC) is a good example of a growing international business that capitalizes on its Hong Kong background. In this case, its global investment effort is complemented with true consideration of the local market conditions. Specifically, its locational strategy is to capture different parts of Toronto in recognition of the relatively "dispersed" location of Hong Kong Chinese. As suggested in its recent motto, "the world's local bank," it is truly a "*glocalized*" scenario.

In this study, the landscape where subethnic business clusters are present is a direct manifestation of a combination of "global" and "local" factors. While Oakes (1993) subordinates "local" elements to the dominant "global" structure, I prefer labeling the "global" as an overarching societal context that provides fertile ground in which the "local" factors can ferment. In other words, they complement each other when the right conditions (such as a congenial multicultural setting, as in Canada) appear. Here, the "local" conditions become more and more positive to foster the growth of subethnic business. These businesses are the very linkages that tie "global" and "local" elements together to allow "*glocalization*" to emerge.

The second contribution of this study is the *clear distinction made between the three subethnic Chinese groups of businesses*. Hence, the homogenization thesis as advanced from a globalization perspective is not supported, echoing previous studies such as Zhou and Tseng (2001). I observed no signs of the ubiquitous occurrence of a "homogeneous" type of ethnic business. Instead, multifarious situations abound, as demonstrated in the different attributes held by HK, ML, and TW business subgroups. Other attributes, such as their varying length of stay in Canada (subsequently affecting the diversity of business types), plus the vastly dissimilar cultural orientations suggested in their business titles, all point to diversity rather than unity. Perhaps the only commonality among these subgroups of businesses is their Chinese language. Recalling Matthews' (1997) "cultural supermarket" concept, the three subgroups could be treated as separate departments in a supermarket whereby diversity and unity might co-exist. Nevertheless, their (sub)cultural differentiation as expressed in a foreign land echoes the process of cultural reproduction advanced by Salamandra (2002).

Using a global–local framework, this study demonstrates *the value of utilizing a geographic viewpoint* to look at ethnic business. A variety of fundamental geographic concepts were shown to be useful in this endeavor. First of all, *globality* can be expressed locally: in this instance, how the varied sources of Chinese population come into play with the local Toronto scene. This situation corresponds well with what Faist (2000) termed "transnational social space," which links faraway places to the local setting. Second, subethnic Chinese businesses tend to occur in clusters, recognizing the existence of *spatial differentiation* over geographic space. Third, the central importance of tying *place* to one's identity is articulated through transplanted business titles that strongly suggest an immigrant's identification with the place where he or she once belonged. Last but not least, the kind of lifestyle associated with each of the three subethnic Chinese groups is reflective of the unique demographics of the people involved, constituting one of the important spatial factors affecting the occurrence of ethnic business as suggested by Rekers and van Kempen (2000).

Having discussed the achievements of this study, I now suggest several avenues for future research. First of all, in-depth examination of specific contexts in which globalization could further prosper would be a highly promising research direction. Second, by observing the systemic interconnections between global and local factors (such as policy and impact analyses), we will be able to identify the real dynamics between them. Last but not least, further refinement of the subethnicity concept regarding Chinese ethnic business will bring fresh insights into the "localness" on which "global" elements are continually making an impact.

In a nutshell, the global–local nexus is intrinsically tied to the occurrence of the three kinds of subethnic Chinese business we observe in Toronto. By expanding our viewpoint to include global elements in the explanation of how such businesses locate themselves, we go beyond the observation of such businesses as mere economic entities on their own. The locally embedded global dimension is expressed clearly in this case of subethnic differentiation as new urban space.

## References

Appadurai, A. (1990) "Disjuncture and Difference in the Global Cultural Economy". In Featherstone, M. (ed.) *Global Culture: Nationalism, Globalization and Modernity.* London: Sage.

—— (1996) *Modernity at Large: Cultural Dimensions of Globalization.* Minneapolis, MN: University of Minnesota Press.

Bozorgmehr, M. (1997) "Internal Ethnicity: Iranians in Los Angeles", *Sociological Perspectives*, 40(3):387–408.

Cartier, C. (1998) "Megadevelopment in Malaysia: From Heritage Landscapes to 'Leisurescapes' in Melaka's Tourism Sector", *Singapore Journal of Tropical Geography*, 19(2):151–76.

Castles, S. (2001) "Migration and Community Formation under Conditions of Globalisation". Paper presented to the Conference on Reinventing Society in the New Economy, University of Toronto, March 9–10, 2001.

Chang, T.C., Milne, S., Fallon, D., and Pohlmann, C. (1996) "Urban Heritage Tourism: The Global–Local Nexus", *Annals of Tourism Research*, 23(2):284–305.

Crissman, L.W. (1967) "The Segmentary Structure of Urban Overseas Chinese Communities", *Man*, 2(2):185–204.

Crissman, L.W., Beattie, G., and Selby, J. (1998) "The Chinese in Brisbane: Segmentation and Integration". In Hsu, F.L.K. and Serrie, H. (eds) *The Overseas Chinese: Ethnicity in National Context*. Lanham, MD: University Press of America, pp.87–113.

Ettlinger, N. (1999) "Local Trajectories in the Global Economy", *Progress in Human Geography*, 23(3):335–57.

Faist, T. (2000) "Transnationalism in International Migration: Implications for the Study of Citizenship and Culture", *Ethnic and Racial Studies*, 23(2):189–222.

Fong, E., Luk, C., and Ooka, E (2005) "Spatial Distribution of Suburban Ethnic Businesses", *Social Science Research*, 34(1):215–35.

Giddens, A. (1990) *The Consequences of Modernity*. Stanford, CA: Stanford University Press.

Gober, P. (2000) "Immigration and North American Cities", *Urban Geography*, 21(1):83–90.

Hiebert, D. (2000) "Immigration and the Changing Canadian City", *The Canadian Geographer*, 44(1):25–43.

Light, I. and Rosenstein, C. (1995) *Race, Ethnicity, and Entrepreneurship in Urban America*. Hawthorne, NY: Aldine de Gruyter.

Light, I., Sabash, G., Bozorgmehr, M. and Dar-Martirosian, C. (1993) "Internal Ethnicity in the Ethnic Economy", *Ethnic and Racial Studies*, 16(4):581–97.

Liu, Laura Y. (2000) "The Place of Immigration in Studies of Geography and Race", *Social and Cultural Geography*, 1(2):169–82.

McNeill, D. (1999) "Globalization and the European City", *Cities*, 16(3):143–47.

Matthews, A. (1996) "Names and Identities in the Hong Kong Cultural Supermarket", *Dialectical Anthropology*, 21(3/4):399–419.

—— (1997) "Heunggongyahn: On the Past, Present, and Future of Hong Kong Identity", *Bulletin of Concerned Asian Scholars*, 29(3):3–13.

Mele, C. (1996) "Globalization, Culture, and Neighborhood Change: Reinventing the Lower East Side of New York", *Urban Affairs Review*, 32(1):3–22.

Min, P.G. (1999) "Ethnicity: Concepts, Theories, and Trends". In Min, P.G. and Kim, R. (eds) *Struggle for Ethnic Identity: Narratives by Asian American Professionals*. Walnut Creek, CA: AltaMira Press, pp.16–46.

Oakes, T.S. (1993) "The Cultural Space of Modernity: Ethnic Tourism and Place Identity in China", *Environment and Planning C: Society and Space*, 11:47–66.

Palpacuer, F. and Parisotto, A. (2003) "Global Production and Local Jobs: Can Global Enterprise Networks be Used as Levers for Local Development?", *Global Networks*, 3(2):97–120.

Parker, D. (1998) "Emerging British Chinese Identities: Issues and Problems". In Sinn, E. (ed.) *The Last Half Century of Chinese Overseas*. Hong Kong: Hong Kong University Press, pp.91–114.

Poros, M.V. (2001) "The Role of Migrant Networks in Linking Local Labour Markets: The Case of Asian Indian Migration to New York and London", *Global Networks*, 1(3):243–60.

Portes, A. and Zhou M. (1996) "Self-Employment and the Earnings of Immigrants", *American Sociological Review*, 66:219–30.

Prichard, W. (1999) "Local and Global in Cyberspace: The Geographical Narratives of US Food Companies on the Internet", *Area*, 31(1):9–17.

Rekers, A. and van Kempen R. (2000) "Location Matters: Ethnic Entrepreneurs and the Spatial Context". In Rath, J. (ed.) *Immigrant Business: The Economic, Political and Social Environment*. New York: St. Martin's Press, pp.54–69.

Ritzer, G. (1996) *The McDonaldization of Society*. Revised edition. Thousand Oaks, CA: Pine Forge Press.

Salaff, J., Greve, A., and Xu, L.L.P. (2002) "Paths into the Economy: Structural Barriers and the Job Hunt for Skilled PRC Migrants in Canada", *International Journal of Human Resource Management*, 13(3):450–64.

Salamandra, C. (2002) "Globalization and Cultural Mediation: The Construction of Arabia in London", *Global Networks*, 2(4):285–9.

Saunders, J.M. and Nee, V. (1996) "Immigrant Self-employment: The Family as Social Capital and the Value of Human Capital", *American Sociological Review*, 61:231–49.

Sedgwick, C.P. (1998) "The Chinese in New Zealand: Persistence, Change and Innovation". In Hsu, F.L.K. and Serrie, H. (eds) *The Overseas Chinese: Ethnicity in National Context*. Lanham, MD: University Press of America, pp.87–113.

Soyez, D. (2000) "Anchored Locally—Linked Globally. Transnational Social Movement Organizations in a (Seemingly) Borderless World", *GeoJournal*, 52:7–16.

Statistics Canada (1997) *1996 Census Dictionary* (Catalogue 92-351-XPE). Ottawa: Statistics Canada.

Tickell, A.T. (1998) "Questions about Globalization", *Geoforum*, 29:1–5.

Urry, J. (1990) *The Tourist Gaze: Leisure and Travel in Contemporary Societies*. London: Sage.

Wang, L.C. and Wang, G. (eds) (1998) *The Chinese Diaspora: Selected Essays*. Volume 1. Singapore: Times Academic Press.

Wu, C.T., Ip, D., and Inglis, C. (1998) "Settlement Experiences of Recent Chinese Immigrants in Australia: A Comparison of Settlers from Hong Kong, Taiwan, and China". In Sinn, E. (ed.) *The Last Half Century of Chinese Overseas*. Hong Kong: Hong Kong University Press, pp.391–422.

Yeoh, Brenda S.A. (1999) "Global/Globalizing Cities", *Progress in Human Geography*, 23(4):607–16.

Zhou, Y. and Tseng, Y.F. (2001) "Regrounding the 'Ungrounded Empires': Localization as the Geographical Catalyst for Transnationalism", *Global Networks*, 1(2):131–54.

# 12 Going to malls, being Chinese?

## Ethnic identity among Chinese youths in Toronto's ethnic economy

*Emi Ooka*

## INTRODUCTION

Due to the influx of new immigrants of Chinese origin, there has been a dramatic revitalization in the past three decades of Chinese ethnic economy in the major North American cities, such as New York, Los Angeles, Vancouver, and Toronto (Fong 1994; Fong 2001a; P.S. Li 1998; Tseng 1994; Wang 1999; Zhou 1992). A prime characteristic of the latest expansion of Chinese ethnic economy is the emergence of "Chinese Malls" or "Asian Theme Malls" (Preston and Lo 2000) as a new genre of suburban commercial development. These malls function as the center of the newly developed *ethnoburb* (W. Li 1998).[1]

Well-educated and upwardly mobile immigrants have settled directly into the suburbs and have generated a strong demand for new commercial services in these areas. Immigrants with an entrepreneurial orientation and capital took advantage of such demand, which has resulted in the development of suburban shopping centers in immigrant gate cities (Fong 1994; Laguerre 2000; Preston and Lo 2000; Qadeer 1998).

Chinese malls are shopping centers in which each compartmentalized shop, rented or owned, sells ethnically specialized products and/or provides services in an ethnic language (Wang 1999). In most North American mainstream shopping malls, we will certainly find major brand shops such as Gap, Nike, and HMV, but they are not present in most of the Chinese malls yet. These malls have large-scale restaurants and grocery stores, as well as small-scale enterprises, which specialize in Asian products. They target a culturally distinctive niche market.

Recent studies have documented that business arrangements in such ethno-specific enterprises have become transnational under the influence of globalization (Wong and Ng 2002; Portes *et al.* 2002). Instead of relying on limited local co-ethnic networks in the receiving society, entrepreneurs in the era of globalization tend to depend more on transnational networks of suppliers, capital, and markets beyond nation-state borders. New technologies of communication and transport enable the immigrant entrepreneur to mobilize resources transnationally and manage business at multiple locations. In addition to traditional import–export enterprises, there has also been a great expansion in businesses with Asian production and North American distribution, and in retail chains with branch operations

(Wong and Ng 2002). As a consequence, suburban Chinese malls have emerged as new focal nodes for increasing transnational flows of commodities, culture, and labor that move across the Pacific Ocean (Tseng 1994; Wong 1997; Faist 2000).

As well as providing a working place for immigrant entrepreneurs and workers, these malls have become a physical, cultural, and symbolic center of the contemporary Chinese diaspora in North America. They are connected not only with the homeland but also with other diasporic enclaves. For youths of the second generation, they have offered emblematic "transnational spaces" where they grow up, and visit for after-school and/or weekend leisure activities (W. Li 1998; Lin 1998: 314). Various cultural materials and symbols are selectively brought into the malls by immigrant entrepreneurs. Frequent visits to such malls enable youths to keep up to date with the latest trends, mainly from Hong Kong, Taiwan, Japan, and Korea.

How do the existence of and frequent visits to transnational spaces such as ethnic malls influence the incorporation process of contemporary immigrant groups, especially among the second generation? Despite the existence of a rich body of literature on ethnic economy, most sociological studies have focused exclusively on the factors that facilitate the establishment of ethnic economy (Light 1972), the operation of small-scale ethnic business (Light and Bonacich 1988; Portes and Bach 1985), and its economic, social, and psychological influences on *first-generation* immigrants (Portes and Zhou 1996; Sanders and Nee 1996; Fong 2001b; Fong and Ooka 2002; Zhou and Logan 1989). Little attention has been paid to the influence of the increasingly globalized ethnic economy on the social incorporation process of the second generation. Existing studies on ethnic malls have been largely limited to their geographic patterns of development and their impact on urban planning (Preston and Lo 2002; Qadeer 1998; Wang 1999).

Given that shopping malls have become central components of today's youths' social world, and have become a significant space for identity construction, we need to pay more attention to the emerging Chinese malls and their relevance for second-generation incorporation (Anthony 1985; Vanderbeck and Johnson 2000). Public perception of Chinese malls sees them as rather a mixed blessing. Though some have appreciated the multicultural shopping opportunities provided by ethnic malls, most local residents believe that their emergence has only contributed to the "social isolation" of the Chinese community. The cultural distinctiveness embodied in the goods and customers of the malls has encouraged this view. Chinese malls have received a negative or even hostile depiction as a new form of "ethnic ghetto" (P.S. Li 1998: 146–8; Wang 1999: 32).

Do frequent visits to Chinese malls actually hinder the incorporation process of the second generation? In what way are frequent visits to Chinese malls associated with the patterns of ethnic self-identification and ethnic attachment among contemporary second-generation youths? This chapter takes the first step to more systematically addressing these questions beyond such casual and reactive observations. The study draws on a small-scale survey of Chinese youths in Toronto, which is one of the largest settlements of the contemporary Chinese diaspora.

We first discuss the limitations of the conventional assimilation framework for understanding the contemporary process of second-generation incorporation. Then, drawing on studies on the new second generation and transnationalism, this study suggests that paying frequent visits to ethnic malls does not automatically hinder the incorporation process. Instead of such a zero-sum relationship, we suggest that it may facilitate the proliferation of binational hybrid identities among the new second generation. Associations are then explored through recently collected data on Chinese second-generation youths growing up in Toronto. Studying the ethnic identity of the second generation with reference to ethnic malls will provide a unique linkage between studies on ethnic economy and the new second generation and will expand our theoretical understanding of immigrant incorporation in the global era.

## LITERATURE REVIEW

### Assimilation and transnationalism

Studies of immigrant incorporation have been largely influenced by the assimilation theory (Alba and Nee 1997). In the canonical assimilation framework, participation in ethnic structures such as ethnic businesses and community institutions has been theorized to block or at least delay the process of cultural, structural, and subjective assimilation into the mainstream society (Gordon 1964). As the theory of institutional completeness suggests, sustained involvement in ethnic structures has been assumed to weaken its members' need for integration and the mainstream society's forces of attraction (Breton 1964). Accordingly, in this zero-sum framework of conventional assimilation, ethnicity as a static and primordial status of premodernity has to be relinquished. To pursue full participation in the mainstream society, the later generation of immigrants are left with no option but to dissociate themselves from ethnic structures over time. As long as immigrant groups are embedded in ethnic structures, exclusive identification with parental ancestry is intensified and subjective incorporation will never be accomplished. Binational identification is seen only as a problematic and conflicting transitional phase on the way to the complete assimilation (Child 1943).

However, successive literature on immigrant incorporation has identified that ethnicity is far from being a fixed and transplanted cultural entity. Rather, it is a more flexible and adaptable phenomenon under constant recreation (Gans 1979; Nagel 1994). Accordingly, a unilinear and irreversible process toward cultural, structural, and subjective assimilation into mainstream society and its affirmative outcomes has been under scrutiny for some time (Glazer and Moynihan 1970; Portes and Bach 1985).

The latest attempt to retheorize contemporary immigrant incorporation can be found in studies of the new second generation (Portes and Rumbaut 2001; Portes and Zhou 1993; Zhou 1997). The segmented assimilation theory, in particular, takes the perspective that there could be multiple and segmented processes involved in becoming a member of the host society, instead of a uniform assimilative path for the new second generation (Fernandez-Kelly and Schauffler 1994; Rumbaut

1994; Suárez-Orozco and Suárez-Orozco 2001; Waldinger and Perlmann, 1998; Waters 1994, 1996; Zhou and Bankston 1998).[2] In this framework, the existence of a vibrant co-ethnic community and an ethnic economy in proximity is considered to provide an alternative path to attaining social mobility, rather than being a liability. Furthermore, participating in ethnic structures developed by the first generation is positively acknowledged to provide fertile ground for the long-term maintenance of binational identity. Unwanted pressure to assimilate is resisted and selective acculturation is facilitated through such participation, though it does not necessarily hinder participation in the mainstream society (Gibson 1988; Rumbaut 1994; Portes and MacLeod 1996). The economically and culturally resourceful immigrant community may be able to provide role models toward which the second generation can develop a sense of pride and respect. By extension, the attractiveness of being a member of such a community is enhanced.

The transnational approach pushes this perspective further. Transnationalists draw attention to the persisting cultural and economic networks through which new immigrants and later generations interact across the borders of multiple nation-states (Faist 2000; Louie 2000; Mitchell 1997; Ong and Nonini 1997; Portes *et al.* 1999). Aided by transnational networks of social relations, they are able to maintain socially meaningful attachments with multiple locations. This leads to more cultural autonomy and the proliferation of multi-layered, hybrid identities among immigrants (Wolf 1997).

In such a framework, ethnic structures such as ethnic malls are conceptualized not as the enclosed and transplanted cultural territory of emigration, but as the focal node connecting the host society, home country, and other cities of the global diaspora (W. Li 1998; Lin 1998). Visiting transnational ethnic malls may thus enhance youths' sense of "being Chinese" in a global diaspora, and may be associated with a strong attachment toward Chinese origins. However, it may not necessarily heighten a fixed and bounded identification with parental ancestry. Rather, it may be associated with the manifestation of multi-layered hybrid-hyphenated identity.

In short, we have discussed two possible ways in which the frequency of visiting ethnic malls might be associated with the ethnic identity of the second generation. According to the conventional assimilation perspective, participation in ethnic structures hinders the subjective incorporation of the second generation in a zero-sum way. Thus, those who more frequently visit ethnic malls are more likely to adhere to an exclusive identification with parental ethnic background (e.g. Chinese, Taiwanese). Visiting ethnic malls significantly enhances a strong attachment to ethnicity, which in turn will delay the subjective incorporation into the mainstream society.

The segmented assimilation theory, along with the transnational perspective, challenges such dichotomous and fixed theorization. It considers ethnic malls to be transnational social spaces which are highly salient in processing and distributing ethnic products, and in connecting with the global diaspora. However, it does not necessarily suggest that participants are resistant to the pressure of assimilation, or marginalized. Participation in transnational ethnic structures will help sustain ongoing association with the homelands among second-generation youths, although it does not necessarily hinder their subjective incorporation into the host society. Thus, following these perspectives, we can expect that those who more frequently visit ethnic malls may not be limited to choosing exclusive identification with parental ethnicity. Regardless of a high frequency of visiting ethnic malls, the second generation may develop a multi-layered hyphenated identity (e.g. Chinese-Canadian, Taiwanese-Canadian). The attachment toward their Chinese background may be strongly associated with their frequent visits to ethnic malls, but it does not necessarily mean that they choose an exclusive identification.

## Controlled factors

To fully explore ethnic self-identification and ethnic attachment of second-generation Chinese youths in relation to their involvement in ethnic malls, demographic background must also be considered. Since the recent literature on the ethnic identity of the new second generation suggests that the identity incorporation process could be gendered, we take into consideration the gender effect (Phinney 1990; Rumbaut 1994; Waters 1996). Nativity has also been found to be a driving force for developing an attachment to the receiving society among most second-generation youths (Rumbaut 1994; Portes and MacLeod 1996). Therefore, we also control for the effect of this factor. Literature on the new second generation has also suggested that economic and cultural resources provided by first-generation parents significantly condition the process of identity incorporation of the second generation. Those with a better socioeconomic background are advantaged in resisting undesirable external forces and their attachment to parental ethnicity is enhanced (Portes and MacLeod 1996). The effect of this factor is also considered.

In addition to demographic factors, we also control for network characteristics of second-generation youths, the composition of co-ethnics in their friendship networks. Friends tend to expose youths to different values, lifestyles, and cultural knowledge and influence their social identity. Previous studies found that those who are exclusively embedded in co-ethnic networks are more likely to show attachment to their own ethnic background and culture (Zhou and Bankston 1998; Ooka 2002). Thus we can expect that those who are embedded in co-ethnic friendship networks are more likely to visit ethnic malls and have exclusive ethnic identification and stronger ethnic attachment. In order to control for this spurious effect, the network factor is controlled in the analysis.

The last factor we include in the model is the life satisfaction of the second-generation youths. It has been argued that ethnic minority youths tend to mobilize their ethnicity when they are dissatisfied with life in the new society. In less con-flicting and more satisfying situations, the saliency of ethnicity declines (Rumbaut 1994; Waters 1996). We hypothesize that those who are satisfied with life in the host society are less likely to cling to the exclusive ancestral ethnic identity and less likely to have a salient ethnic attachment to their own ethnic backgrounds (Glick Schiller and Fouron 1999).

In the following section, we will look at a set of models to explore the association between frequent visits to ethnic malls and ethnic identity among second-generation youths in Toronto. Nonetheless, we have to note that the cross-sectional nature of the data prevents any unequivocal attribution of causality. Therefore, this chapter only aims to explore the patterns of association.

## DATA AND METHODS

### Toronto's Chinese ethnic economy

Data for this study was obtained from a survey of foreign-born and Canadian-born Chinese adolescents in Toronto. Toronto has emerged as one of the major destinations for Chinese immigrants in their global diaspora. Although immigrants of Chinese descent have a long history in Canada, the recent growth of Chinese population is mainly due to the influx of post-1967 immigrants, particularly those from Hong Kong, but also from Taiwan and mainland China (Lary and Luk 1994; Lo and Wang 1997). According to the 2001 Census, 1,094,700 people of Chinese origin live in Canada and 435,690, or about 40 percent of them, live in Toronto, a number which is almost double the 1991 figure of 231,820 (Statistics Canada 2003). More than 70 percent of the Chinese in Canada or in Toronto are immigrants and approximately 77 percent of those immigrated to Canada after 1981.

These new immigrants include a significant proportion from the professional, managerial, and entrepreneurial classes, who are well educated, prosperous, and mobile (P.S. Li 1998). They have created a strong demand for Chinese goods and services and have promoted the proliferation of the Chinese ethnic economy in Toronto.

Toronto now enjoys thriving downtown Chinatowns as well as the development of suburban shopping malls. According to Wang (1999), 34.2 percent of Chinese commercial activities are still in the downtown area. About 45 percent are already located in inner suburbs such as Scarborough (30%) and North York (11%). Outer suburbs such as Markham also have a significant proportion. Immigrants from Hong Kong and Taiwan with a better socioeconomic background tend to settle in the Toronto suburbs, such as North York, Scarborough, Richmond Hill, and Markham, and have contributed to the new suburban development. Those from mainland China and Vietnam with a disadvantaged socioeconomic background tend to concentrate in downtown Toronto (Lo and Wang 1997).

Commercial development in the suburbs is largely due to the increase in Chinese shopping malls. There are more than 50 shopping malls and plazas that specialize in Chinese goods and services in North York, Scarborough, and Markham. Market Village and Pacific Mall in Markham make up the largest indoor Chinese mall in North America, with over 300 stores.[3] There are only two Chinese malls (the Dragon Centre and the Chinese Cultural Centre) in downtown Toronto (see Wang 1999 and Preston and Lo 2000 for details).

# Data

In what way is the frequency of visits to these Chinese malls associated with the patterns of ethnic self-identification and ethnic attachment among contemporary second-generation youths growing up in this globalized Chinese economy? To explore this question, this study draws on a sample population of both foreign-born and Canadian-born Chinese second-generation youths in Toronto.

A small-scale survey entitled "Chinese Adolescent Survey" (hereafter called the CAS survey) was conducted between December 1999 and February 2000 with the co-operation of the Toronto Board of Education. Taking into consideration the geographical patterns of their settlement, students from two schools in downtown Toronto and three schools in North York were selected to participate in the survey.[4] According to data released by the Toronto Board of Education, the proportion of Chinese students in the student populations of these five schools ranges from 18.7 percent to 47.6 percent. (This information was obtained through personal contact.) The inclusion of schools in both downtown Toronto and suburban North York with varying degrees of Chinese student population allowed us to represent the heterogeneous characteristics existing within the Chinese population in Toronto.

The original sample included 208 students with Chinese origin, mainly from Hong Kong, Taiwan, and mainland China. Their ages ranged between 14 and 20. Of these 208 cases, those who had been in Canada less than two years were excluded, to avoid the most recent arrivals. In addition, three cases whose parents had intermarried, and 14 cases whose mother tongue had already shifted to English, were also eliminated from the analysis, considering the different degrees of social-ization these youths had received. This left 173 cases of new second-generation Chinese youths to be analyzed.

This data set has two significant advantages. First, it is the most recent survey to specifically look at incorporation experiences of Chinese second-generation youth growing up in an era of globalization. As mentioned, Toronto's Chinese economy has developed dramatically over the last three decades due to the increase of post-1967 middle-class immigrants from Hong Kong and Taiwan and the increase in transnational capital investment (P.S. Li 1998). The recent data allow us to explore to what extent the transnationalization of ethnic economy, manifested in the form of ethnic malls, influences the process of identity incorporation among the new second-generation youth. Second, the data set covers several important aspects of incorporation among second-generation Chinese youths, such as ethnic self-identification and ethnic attachment, friendship networks, and the perception of Canadian society. The detailed sets of questions will enable us to explore the association in a more systematic way.

Despite these advantages, this survey is not free from problems. First, the response rate was low, about 15 percent, which may limit the representativeness of the sample.[5] Second, the survey only covers those who attend public high schools. The sample does not cover anyone who dropped out of school or students in Catholic schools. Given these limitations, results should be understood as exploratory and we should be careful in trying to generalize them to the overall Chinese second-generation population in Toronto.[6]

## Method

This study explores how the frequency of visiting ethnic malls may be associated with youths' ethnic identity. Table 12.1 briefly describes the definition and measurement of the dependent and independent variables included in this analysis.

Since previous studies have identified that ethnic identity is a multidimensional phenomenon, this study aims to look at both ethnic self-identification and ethnic attachment. The first dependent variable is ethnic identification among the Chinese youths. In order to generate their ethnic identity, the open-ended question was asked: "How do you describe yourself (e.g., Chinese, Canadian, Chinese-Canadian, Canadian-born Chinese, Hong Kong Chinese, Taiwanese or something else)?" Answers were then divided into three types: (a) ancestral ethnic identity (e.g. Chinese, Hong Kong Chinese, Taiwanese), (b) hyphenated (e.g. Chinese-Canadian, Canadian-born Chinese), and (c) Canadian. With this information, we explore whether or not the varying degree of involvement in ethnic malls is related to different types of self-identity.

The second dependent variable is the degree of ethnic attachment of these Chinese youths. The survey asked three related questions on ethnic attachment: "How important is being of Chinese origin to you?", "How important is it for you that your future children understand Chinese language(s)?" and "Would you prefer to marry a Chinese person?" Factor analysis identified that these three elements share a common factor. Therefore, we combined the scores of these three questions to create a scale of ethnic attachment. Cronbach's alpha of 0.675 suggests that the scale has a suitable reliability.[7] Cases in the lowest score of 6 were combined with the next category because of their small number.

The first independent variable is the frequency of visiting Chinese malls. The respondents were asked, "How often did you go to a Chinese mall(s) this year?" They were given five response categories: "never," "a few times a year," "once a month," "2 or 3 times a month," and "at least once a week." Since the number of respondents who never visited Chinese malls was very small, it was combined with those who chose "a few times a year." The variable with four categories is used as the interval variable. Ethnic malls expose the youth to products, information, and new trends from their parental country of origin and other parts of the Chinese diaspora. Visiting such places may enable the second-generation youths to sustain connections to the vibrant and continuously changing culture of the country of emigration and the diaspora.

On the other hand, youths can also visit the shopping malls of the wider society (e.g. Eaton Centre, Yorkdale Mall) as an alternative or additional place for their leisure activities. Mainstream malls which do not specialize in Chinese products and services expose the youths to various mainstream cultures and play a different role in their identity construction process. In order to differentiate the unique

*Table 12.1* Definition and measurement of variables

| Variables | Measurement |
|---|---|
| **Dependent variable** | |
| Ethnic self-identification | "How do you describe yourself?" (open-ended question) Hyphenated Chinese = 1; Ethnic Chinese = 0[a] |
| Degree of ethnic attachment (Unstandardized scale: 3–15) | "How important is being of Chinese origin to you?" 1 = not at all important; 2 = not very important; 3 = somewhat important; 4 = pretty important; 5 = very important "How important is it for you that your future children understand Chinese language(s)?" 1 = not at all important; 2 = not very important; 3 = somewhat important; 4 = pretty important; 5 = very important "Would you prefer to marry a person of Chinese origin?" 1 = I would only marry a Chinese person; 2 = I would prefer to marry a Chinese person; 3 = I would marry either a Chinese or a non-Chinese person; 4 = I would prefer to marry a non-Chinese person; 5 = I would only marry a non-Chinese person (reverse coded) |
| **Independent variables** | |
| Shopping in malls | |
| Chinese malls | "How often did you go to a Chinese mall(s) during this year?" 1 = never or a few times a year; 2 = once a month; 3 = 2 or 3 times a month; 4 = at least once a week |
| Canadian malls | "How often did you go to a Canadian mall(s) during this year?" 1 = never or a few times a year; 2 = once a month; 3 = 2 or 3 times a month; 4 = at least once a week |
| **Control variables** | |
| Sociodemographic characteristics | |
| Female | Female = 1; Male = 0 |
| Nativity | Born in Canada = 1; Other = 0 |
| Parental socioeconomic background | Father completed university or above = 1; Other = 0 |
| Composition of Chinese friends | "Now think of ALL of your friends, both in school and out of school (best friends, boyfriend or girlfriend, other good friends, and anyone else who is a friend of yours). How many are Chinese?" 1 = few or less than half; 2 = about half; 3 = more than half; 4 = almost all; 5 = all |
| Life satisfaction | "I am satisfied with my life in Canada." 1 = agree and strongly agree; 0 = strongly disagree and disagree |

[a] The number of cases who chose "Canadian" identity was small (N = 5). Therefore, only the comparison between the two patterns of ethnic identification will be carried out.

association that Chinese malls have with the ethnic identity of the youths, we control for the effect of the frequency of visiting Canadian malls on the ethnic identity of Chinese youth.

Respondents were asked, "How often did you go to a Canadian mall this year?" They were given the same five response categories. Due to the small number of respondents who chose "never," it was combined with those who chose "a few times a year." The variable of the frequency of visiting Canadian malls is used as the interval variable with four categories.

As we have discussed in the literature review section, this study includes another three sets of control variables in examining the ethnic identity of the youths: demographic characteristics, the composition of co-ethnics in the friendship networks, and life satisfaction in the host society. The first set of control variables, demographic characteristics, consists of three variables: the respondent's gender, nativity, and parental socioeconomic background. Gender is a dummy variable, female coded as 1 and male coded as 0. Nativity is a dummy variable that contrasts those who were born in Canada with those who are foreign-born. Parental socioeconomic background is also a dummy variable. Those with a father who completed university are coded as 1, and those with a father who did not complete university are coded as 0. From previous studies on ethnic identity, we expect that those who were born in Canada are less likely to choose an ethnic identity which is exclusively attached to ancestral or ethnic origin. This is because parental socioeconomic resources facilitate rapid assimilation. However, those with a father with a higher-level education may be more likely to develop a strong ethnic attachment since they are more advantaged in resisting unwanted assimilation and sustaining ethnic pride (Rumbaut 1994). On the other hand, Canadian-born respondents may also choose assimilative self-identity and have a lower degree of ethnic attachment, if they follow the assimilative path of incorporation.

The second set of control variables refer to the ethnic composition of respondents' friends. The respondents were asked: "Now think of ALL of your friends, both in school and out of school (best friends, boyfriend or girlfriend, other good friends and anyone else who is a friend of yours). How many are Chinese?" This introduction was used in order to capture the proportion of Chinese in overall friendship networks, including both strong and weak ties. While the original answer category included seven choices—none, few, less than half, about half, more than half, almost all, and all—there are no Chinese youths in the CAS study who have no Chinese friends at all. The numbers with few or "less than half" Chinese friends in their friendship networks were also small. Therefore, these two categories were collapsed. This variable is used as the interval scale variable.

The third control variable looks at the effect of life satisfaction in the host society on ethnic identity. The respondents were asked to indicate their views on the statement, "I am satisfied with my life in Canada." If they strongly agreed or agreed with this statement, they were coded 1. If they disagreed or strongly disagreed with the statement, they were coded 0. We hypothesize that those who are satisfied with life in Canada are less likely to have an ancestral ethnic identity or a salient ethnic attachment.

**RESULTS**

Table 12.2 looks at the bivariate association between the patterns of ethnic self-identification and the varying frequencies of visiting ethnic malls. First, the table shows that the majority (97%) of the second-generation Chinese youths chose their self-identification under the influence of parental ethnicity, with or without hyphen. Only 3 percent of them chose unhyphenated Canadian identity. Given that Toronto is one of the major centers of the contemporary Chinese diaspora, with a large and resourceful ethnic economy, this result is not surprising. It suggests that those who are growing up in proximity to a strong ethnic economy take a unilinear and non-assimilative path for incorporation. Second, the result shows that the patterns of ethnic self-identification are not significantly associated with the frequency of visiting ethnic malls. Frequent visits to ethnic malls do not restrict the youths to choosing an exclusive ethnic identity. Chinese youths are not prevented from developing a hyphenated identity. Ethnic malls provide a space for entertainment, socializing, and shopping for the second-generation youths, regardless of their self-identification.

On the other hand, Table 12.3 demonstrates that the degree of ethnic attachment varies with the different frequency of visiting ethnic malls. For the purpose of a simpler presentation, the degree of ethnic attachment is dichotomized into two categories, split by the mean score: lower and higher degrees.[8] The majority of those who visit ethnic malls at least once a week have a higher degree of ethnic attachment (78% versus 23%). Although the cases are few, all respondents who have never been to Chinese ethnic malls have a lower degree of ethnic attachment. These findings clearly suggest that Chinese youths who frequently visit Chinese malls are more likely to have stronger ethnic attachments. There may exist a reciprocal association such that those who have strong ethnic attachment are more likely to visit ethnic malls. In the following section, we will explore to what extent the frequency of visiting ethnic malls is associated with the patterns of ethnic self-identification and ethnic attachment, controlling for other possible factors.

*Table 12.2* Patterns of ethnic self-identification with varying frequencies of visiting ethnic malls

| Frequency of visiting Chinese malls | Patterns of ethnic self-identification | | | |
| --- | --- | --- | --- | --- |
| | Ancestral ethnicity (%) | Hyphenated identity (%) | Unhyphenated Canadian (%) | N |
| Never | 66.7 | 33.3 | | 3 |
| A few times a year | 31.3 | 62.5 | 6.3 | 32 |
| Once a month | 38.9 | 58.3 | 2.8 | 36 |
| 2 or 3 times a month | 42.0 | 54.0 | 4.0 | 50 |
| At least once a week | 46.8 | 53.2 | | 47 |
| Total (%) | 41.1 | 56.0 | 3.0 | 100 |
| (N) | (69) | (94) | (5) | (168) |

Note: Pearson chi-square = 5.134.

*Table 12.3* Degree of attachment to Chinese background among Chinese youths with varying frequencies of visiting ethnic malls

|  | Ethnic attachment | | |
| --- | --- | --- | --- |
| *Frequency of visiting Chinese malls* | *Lower (%)* | *Higher (%)* | *N* |
| Never | 100.0 | 0.0 | 3 |
| A few times a year | 54.5 | 45.5 | 33 |
| Once a month | 48.6 | 51.4 | 35 |
| 2 or 3 times a month | 45.1 | 54.9 | 51 |
| At least once a week | 22.9 | 77.1 | 48 |
| Total (%) | 42.4 | 57.6 | 100 |
| (N) | (72) | (98) | (170) |

Note: Pearson chi-square = 14.231; $p < 0.01$.

Table 12.4 provides a summary of the descriptive statistics of the sample population. As we have already seen, the majority (56%) of this sample choose a hyphenated identity, while another 41 percent choose an ancestral identity. This sample also shows a relatively higher degree of ethnic attachment (a score of 11.78 out of 15). They tend to visit Chinese malls at least once a month on average, whereas they also visit Canadian malls more often.

*Table 12.4* Descriptive statistics

| *Variables* | *Total sample* |
| --- | --- |
| Dependent variable | |
| Self-identification | 1.619 |
| Degree of ethnic attachment | 11.78 |
| Independent variables | |
| Shopping in malls | |
| Chinese malls | 2.65 |
| Canadian malls | 3.09 |
| Control variables | |
| Sociodemographic characteristics | |
| Female | 0.62 |
| Nativity | 0.22 |
| Parental socioeconomic background | 0.45 |
| Composition of Chinese friends | 3.26 |
| Life satisfaction | 0.81 |
| Total number of cases | 173 |

## Multivariate analysis

Table 12.5 shows the results of the four logistic regression models of ethnic self-identification among the second-generation Chinese youths in our sample. Since the number who chose to identify themselves as "Canadian" was small ($N = 5$), we only look at the differences between those who identify with an ancestral ethnic identity and those with a hyphenated identity. The initial model includes only two variables: frequency of visiting Chinese malls and frequency of visiting Canadian malls. The second model takes into account the effects of sociodemographic characteristics. The third model adds the characteristics of friendship networks to control the effect of structural incorporation on ethnic identity. The fourth model takes into account the effect of psychological factors such as life satisfaction on ethnic identification. The standard error is given in parentheses.

The results largely confirm that there is no statistically significant association between the patterns of ethnic identification and the frequency of visiting Chinese malls. In fact, no included factors except nativity is significantly related to ethnic self-identification. The ethnic identity of Chinese youths in Toronto uniformly shifts toward a binational hyphenated identity such as Chinese-Canadian or Canadian-born Chinese as the generation changes. The relationship is positive and very strong.

The segmented assimilation theory has suggested that the presence of a vibrant ethnic economy in proximity increases the attractiveness of membership in the

*Table 12.5* Logistic regression models predicting the patterns of ethnic self-identification

|  | Model 1 | Model 2 | Model 3 | Model 4 |
|---|---|---|---|---|
| **Shopping in malls** |  |  |  |  |
| Chinese malls | −0.155 | −0.094 | −0.057 | −0.082 |
|  | (0.149) | (0.186) | (0.199) | (0.200) |
| Canadian malls | 0.104 | 0.050 | 0.031 | 0.004 |
|  | (0.188) | (0.229) | (0.232) | (0.244) |
| **Sociodemographic characteristics** |  |  |  |  |
| Female |  | 0.001 | 0.011 | −0.054 |
|  |  | (0.408) | (0.409) | (0.414) |
| Nativity |  | 2.845*** | 2.835*** | 2.853*** |
|  |  | (0.762) | (0.763) | (0.763) |
| Parental socioeconomic background |  | 0.313 | 0.266 | 0.191 |
|  |  | (0.404) | (0.415) | (0.421) |
| Composition of non-Chinese friends |  |  | −0.100 | −0.092 |
|  |  |  | (0.195) | (0.199) |
| Life satisfaction |  |  |  | 0.259 |
|  |  |  |  | (0.539) |
| Intercept | 0.421 | −0.281 | 0.028 | −0.012 |
|  | (0.658) | (0.871) | (1.058) | (1.110) |
| N | 162 | 133 | 131 | 130 |
| Degrees of freedom | 2 | 5 | 6 | 7 |
| −2 Log likelihood | 219.417 | 152.050 | 151.785 | 149.853 |

Note: ***$p < 0.001$, **$p < 0.01$, *$p < 0.05$, ª $p < 0.1$.

ethnic group and could provide fertile ground for the long-term maintenance of a binational identity (Rumbaut 1994; Portes and MacLeod 1996). Given Toronto's Chinese economy's prosperity, our result that shows the lack of development of unhyphenated assimilative Canadian identity and the uniform shift toward a hyphenated identity partially supports this hypothesis. Furthermore, we also learned that those who develop a hyphenated identity do not necessarily have a lower frequency of visits to ethnic malls. The association is negative, but it is not statistically significant.

In Table 12.6, we provide the results of the four multiple regression models of ethnic attachment. The procedure of model construction for ethnic attachment is the same as for the one for ethnic self-identification. The standard error is again reported in parentheses.

The first model looks at the association between the degree of ethnic attachment and the frequency of visiting ethnic malls. The result is consistent with the bivariate analysis. Paying more visits to Chinese malls is positively and significantly associated with stronger ethnic attachment. Interestingly, the frequency of visiting Canadian malls shows a statistically significant and negative association with the degree of ethnic attachment. The more that Chinese youths go to Canadian malls, the less they become attached to their ethnicity. Preference as regards place of leisure and entertainment might be significantly associated with their degree of ethnic attachment, though it is not necessarily associated with their self-identity.

*Table 12.6* Multiple regression models predicting the degree of ethnic attachment

|  | Model 1 | Model 2 | Model 3 | Model 4 |
|---|---|---|---|---|
| **Shopping in malls** | | | | |
| Chinese malls | 0.570*** | 0.478** | 0.327* | 0.316* |
|  | (0.132) | (0.155) | (0.160) | (0.157) |
| Canadian malls | −0.363* | −0.204 | −0.109 | 0.030 |
|  | (0.170) | (0.204) | (0.202) | (0.203) |
| **Sociodemographic characteristics** | | | | |
| Female |  | −0.534 | −0.547 | −0.517 |
|  |  | (0.345) | (0.336) | (0.330) |
| Nativity |  | −0.360 | −0.274 | −0.271 |
|  |  | (0.388) | (0.380) | (0.371) |
| Parental socioeconomic background |  | 0.203 | 0.433 | 0.429 |
|  |  | (0.343) | (0.345) | (0.339) |
| Composition of non-Chinese friends |  |  | 0.446** | 0.360* |
|  |  |  | (0.162) | (0.161) |
| Life satisfaction |  |  |  | −1.272** |
|  |  |  |  | (0.433) |
| Intercept | 11.412*** | 11.515*** | 10.041*** | 10.940*** |
|  | (0.605) | (0.751) | (0.908) | (0.938) |
| N | 169 | 138 | 138 | 137 |
| Degrees of freedom | 2 | 5 | 6 | 7 |
| R-square | 0.112 | 0.102 | 0.151 | 0.203 |

Note: ***p < 0.001, **p < 0.01, *p < 0.05, p < 0.1.

In Model 2, we added the sociodemographic variables to the model. Surprisingly, none of the sociodemographic variables (gender, nativity, and parental sociodemographic variables) is significantly associated with the degree of ethnic attachment. Particularly interesting is the finding that the degree of ethnic attachment does not decline among the Canadian-born youths. Though conventional assimilation theory has suggested that the degree of ethnic saliency declines over generations, recent literature has challenged this proposition (Rumbaut 1994; Portes and Rumbaut 2001). Our finding also supports the notion that strong ethnic attachment remains over generations, regardless of gender and parental background, when the second-generation youths grow up in proximity to a resourceful ethnic economy. However, after these sociodemographic variables were included, the strength of association between frequency of visiting Chinese malls and ethnic attachment was slightly weakened.

The association between the frequency of visiting Canadian malls and the degree of ethnic attachment becomes statistically insignificant when demographic factors are controlled for. Perhaps nativity controlled the spurious effect between the frequency of visiting Canadian malls and the degree of ethnic attachment.

In Model 3, the composition of co-ethnics among friends is added to the model. The results demonstrate that youths with a limited degree of structural incorporation tend to have a stronger ethnic attachment. Of course, this association can be interpreted as meaning that those with stronger ethnic attachment might limit their social relationships beyond their ethnic boundary, thus resisting structural assimilation. The significance or direction of the ethnic mall variable does not change on adding this variable, though the effect is slightly weakened. Those who are embedded in co-ethnic friendship networks tend to have a higher frequency of visiting ethnic malls (Ooka 2002). Therefore, controlling this effect might have slightly decreased its coefficient.

In Model 4, we finally add the life satisfaction variable. The results indicate that those who are satisfied with their life in Canada show a significantly lower degree of ethnic attachment. As we have seen, ethnic background loses its salience when minority youths have less difficulty in the host society (Rumbaut 1994). Our results supported this association.

Even after controlling for all these factors, the results show that frequent visits to ethnic malls are significantly and positively associated with strong ethnic attachment. Overall, these results suggest that in the contemporary globalized ethnic economy, new forms of business development, such as ethnic malls, not only provide business opportunities for the first generation, but also play a role of enforcing and sustaining ethnic attachment among second-generation youth. In particular, we found that Chinese youths embedded in co-ethnic friendship networks tend to visit Chinese malls more often, carrying stronger ethnic attachment. Thus, regardless of the nativity of such youths, those surrounded by co-ethnic friends tend to have stronger ethnic attachment and choose Chinese malls as their place of leisure.

However, we also have to note that frequent visits to ethnic malls do not necessarily hinder their process of subjectively becoming Canadian. Transnational social space manifested as ethnic malls has become a fertile ground to develop a hyphenated hybrid identification grounded in multiple locations. But individuals who participate in such space are not necessarily marginalized from the mainstream society (Itzigsohn and Giorguli Saucedo 2002). Regardless of the frequency of their visits to Chinese malls, Canadian-born youths develop a hyphenated identity and find their way of being Canadian, along with varying degrees of ethnic attachment.

Accordingly, we should not simply assume that the perceived "distinctiveness" of Chinese malls is related to social isolation or exclusive ghettoization, hindering social incorporation. Even those who frequently visit ethnic malls visit Canadian malls as well. For second-generation youths, ethnic malls might be a transnational space where they can substantiate the meaning of being Chinese in their receiving society. However, visiting these malls would not conflict with their way of being Canadian.

## CONCLUSION AND IMPLICATIONS

The purpose of this chapter is to explore the extent to which the frequency of visits to Chinese malls, a focal point of the contemporary global ethnopolis, is associated with the ethnic identity of contemporary second-generation youths. We seek to understand whether or not ethnic malls provide a sociocultural space to enhance a multi-layered and hybrid identity among Chinese youths.

First, we found that the patterns of ethnic identification are not significantly associated with the frequency of visiting ethnic malls. This result does not follow the pattern suggested by conventional assimilation theory. As the generation shifts from the foreign-born to native-born, Chinese youths shift their ethnic identification from those only attached with parental ethnic background to hyphenated and binational identity. However, this shift is not necessarily associated with a lower degree of involvement in ethnic structures. Contrary to the casual public perception of the social isolation and exclusiveness of the Chinese population, Chinese youths tend to enjoy visiting both ethnic and Canadian malls and develop binational and hyphenated identification.[9] Therefore, involvement in the ethnic structures does not hinder the subjective incorporation into the host society, as conventional assimilation has suggested. Ethnic malls should not be regarded as essential and bounded cultural space marginalized from the mainstream society. Rather, they can be understood as a transnational space connected to the homeland and other diaspora communities, and even to the host society, enhancing the persistence of binational and hyphenated identification.[10]

On the other hand, the frequency of visits to ethnic malls is significantly associated with a stronger attachment to Chinese background. The frequency of visiting Canadian malls does not play a significant role in the identity incorporation process once demographic characteristics are controlled. Ethnic malls, the focal point for transnational flows of capital, information, products, and immigrants in the contemporary Chinese economy, may play a unique role in enhancing the sense of being Chinese in the diaspora. Of course, these results have to be treated with caution. Since the analysis is based on cross-sectional data, causal relationships between the frequency of visiting ethnic malls and the emerging patterns of self-identity and the degree of ethnic attachment should not be identified.

Nonetheless, the conclusion, which must follow these complex results, is that one cannot create any simple theory of zero-sum relationship between ethnic identity and ethnic malls, as conventional assimilation theory has suggested. Not only those who exclusively identify with their ancestral background, but also those with binational identification visited ethnic malls for their own purposes. At least we may be allowed to suggest that a new form of business development manifested in ethnic malls contributes to the manifestation of the unbounded and hyphenated form of being "Chinese" and "Canadian" beyond conventional assimilative identities.

What needs to be explored in future research is how the second-generation youth may differentially use particular social space and particular goods in the construction of a contested meaning of being Chinese in the diaspora. More qualitative work, such as in-depth interviews with various subgroups of Chinese youths, should be conducted in order to understand the symbolic role of Chinese malls in their crystallization of ethnic identity.

Some studies on the diasporatic identity of contemporary Chinese immigrants suggest that popular culture coming from Hong Kong and Taiwan circulates globally and provides important elements for the cultural identity of new generations of overseas Chinese (Parker 1995). As centers of the flow of such cultural products, ethnic malls may offer more symbolic and casual ways of being Chinese in the global era. However, as previous studies on ethnicity have identified, cultural packages used to substantiate the group boundary will change over time. Although the pace is slow, some mainstream malls in Toronto have already integrated Asian specialty shops as tenants.

Thus, we need to look at the changing importance of ethnic malls in crystallizing the identity of youths, by taking into consideration the increasing convergence of ethnic malls and mainstream malls.

Overall, in the future analysis of the ethnic economy, we need to go beyond its exclusive focus on the first generation. Especially, we should not examine ethnic economy only as the working place for the first generation. The second generation also take advantage of opportunities provided by the first generation and use this space to serve their own ethnic identity. Expanding our focus to the second generation will be a necessary step in future studies of the ethnic economy under globalization. Do the foreign-born 1.5 generation and the native-born youths give different roles to ethnic malls in their process of identity construction? What is the meaning of ethnic malls for them? Asking these questions will significantly enrich our understanding of whether or not transnational ethnic economy thrives over generations.

Far from solving any puzzles about a new form of immigrant incorporation, one thing becomes clear from this research: ethnic malls can provide a strategic research site to rethink our understanding of emergent forms of multiple identities and hybrid cultures in the era of globalization.

# Notes

1 There are three types of Chinese shopping centres: (1) one- and two-storey enclosed shopping malls; (2) single-storey strip plazas opening into inner parking courts; (3) mixed commercial and office complexes (Qadeer, 1998). This chapter will pay special attention to the enclosed shopping malls, given their large scale and landmark status in the local communities.

2 At least three ideal types of second-generation incorporation are proposed. One path may follow the conventional path of assimilation into the culture and identity of the white middle-class majority. The second path is downward mobility and assimilation into the culture and identity of the inner-city underclass. The third path may combine upward mobility with a kind of selective acculturation in which second-generation youths continue to draw on the moral and material resources of the immigrant community in their attachment to immigrant culture and identity (Portes and Zhou 1993; Zhou 1997; Rumbaut 1997a, 1997b).

3 These suburban Chinese malls are linked to worldwide diaspora networks of entrepreneurs and capital. Some of the shops and companies included are now branch operations linked with overseas corporations such as Bank of East Asia, Bank of China, Ten Ren Tea Company, and Fairchild TV.

4 For details regarding data collection, see Ooka (2002).

5 Regarding the problems in the survey procedures, please consult Ooka (2002).

6 The 1997 Every Secondary Student Survey covers all public secondary school students in the former City of Toronto. Compared with the profile of Chinese students in the survey of every secondary student, we learned that the sample in the CAS survey might overrepresent foreign-born second-generation youths, those with better-educated fathers, as well as those who are more academic-oriented (Cheng and Yau 1999: iii: Ooka 2002). This might be due to the data collection procedure itself, in that more academic-oriented students co-operated with this study. In addition, the inclusion of North York suburban schools might have overrepresented the middle-class or upper-middle-class population among the Chinese in Toronto.

7 Cronbach's alpha is the most commonly used test of the reliability of a scale, which is based on the "internal consistency" of the items. It ranges in value from 0 to 1. Higher value indicates a greater reliability (Green *et al.* 2000).

8 The lower degree of ethnic attachment covers the youths whose scores range between 6 and 11 and those with a higher degree of ethnic attachment refers to the youths whose score is above 12.

9 Though the results are not shown, the preliminary analysis found that the frequency of visiting ethnic malls and that of visiting Canadian malls are significantly and positively correlated (the correlation coefficient is 0.151).

10 For example, cultural events such as Easter, Halloween, Christmas are organized in Chinese malls. Other ethnic groups in the community are also invited to show their musical and dance performance in the malls.

# References

Alba, Richard and Victor Nee. 1997. "Rethinking Assimilation Theory for a New Era of Immigration." *International Migration Review* 31: 826–74.

Anthony, K.H. 1985. "The Shopping Mall: A Teenage Hangout." *Adolescence* 20: 307–12.

Breton, Raymond. 1964. "Institutional Completeness of Ethnic Communities and Personal Relations of Immigrants." *American Journal of Sociology* 70: 193–205.

Cheng, Maisy and Maria Yau. 1999. "The 1997 Every Secondary Student Survey: Detailed Findings." Toronto: Toronto District School Board.

Child, Irvin Long. 1943. *Italian or American? The Second Generation in Conflict*. New Haven, CT: Yale University Press.

Faist, Thomas. 2000. "Transnationalization in International Migration: Implications for the Study of Citizenship and Culture." *Ethnic and Racial Studies* 23: 189–222.

Fernandez-Kelly, M. Patricia and Richard Schauffler. 1994. "Divided Fates: Immigrant Children in a Restructured U.S. Economy." *International Migration Review* 28: 662–89.

Fong, Eric. 2001a. "Introduction: The Chinese Ethnic Economy." *Asian and Pacific Migration Journal* 10: 1–7.

—— 2001b. "Participating in the Ethnic Economy and Psychological Well-Being." *Asian and Pacific Migration Journal* 10(1): 35–52.

Fong, Eric and Emi Ooka. 2002. "The Social Consequences of Participating in Ethnic Economy." *International Migration Review* 36(1): 125–46.

Fong, Timothy P. 1994. *The First Suburban Chinatown: The Remaking of Monterey Park, California*. Philadelphia, PA: Temple University Press.

Gans, Herbert J. 1979. "Symbolic Ethnicity: The Future of Ethnic Groups and Cultures in America." *Ethnic and Racial Studies* 2: 1–20.

Gibson, Margaret A. 1988. *Accommodation without Assimilation: Sikh Immigrants in an American High School*. Ithaca, NY: Cornell University Press.

Glazer, Nathan and Daniel P. Moynihan. 1970. *Beyond the Melting Pot: The Negroes, Puerto Ricans, Jews, Italians, and Irish of New York City*. Cambridge, MA: MIT Press.

Glick Schiller, Nina and Georges E. Fouron. 1999. "Terrains of Blood and Nation: Haitian Transnational Social Fields." *Ethnic and Racial Studies* 22: 340–66.

Gordon, Milton Myron. 1964. *Assimilation in American Life: The Role of Race, Religion, and National Origins*. New York: Oxford University Press.

Green, Samuel B., Neil J. Salkind, and Theresa M. Akey. 2000. *Using SPSS for Windows: Analyzing and Understanding Data*. Upper Saddle River, NJ: Prentice-Hall.

Itzigsohn, José and Silvia Giorguli Saucedo. 2002. "Immigrant Incorporation and Sociocultural Transnationalism." *International Migration Review* 36: 766–98.

Laguerre, Michel S. 2000. *The Global Ethnopolis: Chinatown, Japantown, and Manilatown in American Society*. New York: St. Martin's Press.

Lary, Diana and Bernard Luk. 1994. "Hong Kong Immigrants in Toronto." Pp. 139–62 in *Reluctant Exiles? Migration from Hong Kong and the New Overseas Chinese*, edited by R. Skeldon. Armonk, NY: M.E. Sharpe.

Li, Peter S. 1998. *The Chinese in Canada*. Toronto: Oxford University Press.

Li, Wei. 1998. "Los Angeles's Chinese Ethnoburb: From Ethnic Service Center to Global Economy Outpost." *Urban Geography* 19: 502–17.

Light, Ivan Hubert. 1972. *Ethnic Enterprise in America: Business and Welfare among Chinese, Japanese, and Blacks*. Berkeley, CA: University of California Press.

Light, Ivan Hubert and Edna Bonacich. 1988. *Immigrant Entrepreneurs: Koreans in Los Angeles, 1965–1982*. Berkeley, CA: University of California Press.

Lin, Jan. 1998. "Globalization and the Revalorizing of Ethnic Places in Immigration Gateway Cities." *Urban Affairs Review* 34: 313–39.

Lo, Lucia and Shuguang Wang. 1997. "Settlement Patterns of Toronto's Chinese Immigrants: Convergence or Divergence?" *Canadian Journal of Regional Science* 20: 49–72.

Louie, Andrea. 2000. "Re-territorializing Transnationalism: Chinese Americans and the Chinese Motherland." *American Ethnologist* 27: 645–69.

Mitchell, Katharyne. 1997. "Transnational Subjects: Constituting the Cultural Citizen in the Era of Pacific Rim Capital." Pp. 228–56 in *Ungrounded Empires: The Cultural*

*Politics of Modern Chinese Transnationalism*, edited by A. Ong and D.M. Nonini. New York: Routledge.

Nagel, Joane. 1994. "Constructing Ethnicity: Creating and Recreating Ethnic Identity and Culture." *Social Problems* 41: 152–76.

Ong, Aihwa and Donald Macon Nonini. 1997. *Ungrounded Empires: The Cultural Politics of Modern Chinese Transnationalism*. New York, Routledge.

Ooka, Emi. 2002. "Growing Up Canadian: Language, Culture and Identity among Second-Generation Chinese Youths in Canada." Ph.D. Thesis, Department of Sociology, University of Toronto, Toronto.

Parker, David. 1995. *Through Different Eyes: The Cultural Identities of Young Chinese People in Britain*. Aldershot, England: Avebury.

Phinney, Jean S. 1990. "Ethnic Identity in Adolescents and Adults: Review of Research." *Psychological Bulletin* 108: 499–514.

Portes, Alejandro and Robert L. Bach. 1985. *Latin Journey: Cuban and Mexican Immigrants in the United States*. Berkeley, CA: University of California Press.

Portes, Alejandro and Dag MacLeod. 1996. "What Shall I Call Myself? Hispanic Identity Formation in the Second Generation." *Ethnic and Racial Studies* 19: 523–47.

Portes, Alejandro and Rubén G. Rumbaut. 1996. *Immigrant America: A Portrait*. Berkeley, CA: University of California Press.

———. 2001. *Legacies: The Story of the Immigrant Second Generation*. Berkeley, CA: University of California Press.

Portes, Alejandro and Min Zhou. 1993. "The New 2nd-Generation—Segmented Assimilation and Its Variants." *Annual American Academy of Political and Sociological Science* 530: 74–96.

———. 1996. "Self-Employment and the Earnings of Immigrants." *American Sociological Review* 61: 219–30.

Portes, Alejandro, Luis E. Guarnizo, and Patricia Landolt. 1999. "The Study of Transnationalism: Pitfalls and Promise of an Emergent Research Field." *Ethnic and Racial Studies* 22: 217–37.

Portes, Alejandro, William J. Haller, and Luis Eduardo Guarnizo. 2002. "Transnational Entrepreneurs: An Alternative Form of Immigrant Economic Adaptation." *American Sociological Review* 67: 278–98.

Preston, Valerie and Lucia Lo. 2000. "Asian Theme Malls in Suburban Toronto: Land Use Conflict in Richmond Hill." *The Canadian Geographer* 44: 86–93.

Qadeer, Mohammad. 1998. "Ethnic Malls and Plazas: Chinese Commercial Developments in Scarborough, Ontario." Toronto: Joint Centre of Excellence for Research on Immigration and Settlement.

Rumbaut, Ruben G. 1994. "The Crucible Within: Ethnic Identity, Self-Esteem, and Segmented Assimilation among Children of Immigrants." *International Migration Review* 28: 748–94.

———. 1997a. "Paradoxes (and Orthodoxies) of Assimilation." *Sociological Perspectives* 40: 483–511.

———. 1997b. "Assimilation and Its Discontents: Between Rhetoric and Reality." *International Migration Review* 31: 923–60.

Sanders, Jimy M. and Victor Nee. 1996. "Immigrant Self-employment: The Family as Social Capital and the Value of Human Capital." *American Sociological Review* 61: 231–49.

Statistics Canada. 1996. *Public Use Microdata Files for Individuals, 1996 Census*. Ottawa: Statistics Canada.

——. 2003. *Ethnocultural Portrait of Canada, 2001 Census*. Ottawa: Statistics Canada. 97F0010XCB01003.

Suárez-Orozco, Carola and Marcelo M. Suárez-Orozco. 2001. *Children of Immigration*. Cambridge, MA: Harvard University Press.

Tseng, Yen-Fen. 1994. "Chinese Ethnic Economy: San Gabriel Valley, Los Angeles County." *Journal of Urban Affairs* 16: 169–89.

Vanderbeck, Robert M. and James H. Johnson Jr. 2000. "'That's the Only Place Where You Can Hang Out': Urban Young People and the Space of the Mall." *Urban Geography* 21: 5–25.

Waldinger, Roger and Joel Perlmann. 1998. "Second Generations: Past, Present, Future." *Journal of Ethnic and Migration Studies* 24: 5–24.

Wang, Shuguang. 1999. "Chinese Commercial Activity in the Toronto CMA: New Development Patterns and Impacts." *Canadian Geographer* 43: 19–35.

Waters, Mary C. 1994. "Ethnic and Racial Identities of Second-Generation Black Immigrants in New York City." *International Migration Review* 28: 795–820.

——. 1996. "The Intersection of Gender, Race and Ethnicity in Identity Development of Caribbean American Teens." Pp. 65–81 in *Urban Girls: Resisting Stereotypes, Creating Identities*, edited by B.J.R. Leadbeater and N. Way. New York: New York University Press.

Wolf, Diane L. 1997. "Family Secrets: Transnational Struggles among Children of Filipino Immigrants." *Sociological Perspectives* 40: 457–82.

Wong, Lloyd L. 1997. "Globalization and Transnational Migration: A Study of Recent Chinese Capitalist Migration from the Asian Pacific to Canada." *International Sociology* 12: 329–51.

Wong, Lloyd L. and Michele Ng. 2002. "The Emergence of Small Transnational Enterprise in Vancouver: The Case of Chinese Immigrant Entrepreneurs." *International Journal of Urban and Regional Research* 26: 508–30.

Zhou, Min. 1992. *Chinatown: The Socioeconomic Potential of an Urban Enclave*. Philadelphia, PA: Temple University Press.

——. 1997. "Segmented Assimilation: Issues, Controversies, and Recent Research on the New Second Generation." *International Migration Review* 31: 975–1008.

Zhou, Min and Carl L. Bankston. 1998. Growing Up American: How Vietnamese Children Adapt to Life in the United States. New York: Russell Sage Foundation.

Zhou, Min and John R. Logan. 1989. "Returns on Human Capital in Ethnic Enclaves: New York City's Chinatown." *American Sociological Review* 54: 809–20.

# 13  Conclusion

*Chiu Luk and Eric Fong*

Ethnic businesses have drawn considerable attention in recent decades (Kloosterman and Rath 2000). As Light and Rosenstein (1995) suggested, the resurgent interest is partly a reflection of the growing self-employment rate and partly due to the increase in immigrant populations in various countries. In this concluding chapter, our aim is to discuss all the chapters in this volume about Chinese business in different countries and cities by situating the findings in the literature on ethnic business. We will highlight the contributions of the chapters to the topic. At the same time, drawing from the findings of these chapters, we would like to outline a few central theoretical issues related to ethnic businesses. Given that the chapters focus on the Chinese population, we realize that generalization of the findings to other groups should be done with caution. Nevertheless, we believe that these chapters shed light on important issues in the field, and that they have extended the boundaries of understanding ethnic business. We also discuss the implications of the findings for the study of Chinese businesses.

The study of ethnic business over the years has concentrated on understanding structural arrangements and processes. Subsequently, most studies have explored the internal dynamics of ethnic businesses. While the study of Chinese businesses has a long history, it was not until recent decades that the marriage of the study of Chinese ethnic businesses and the study of ethnic businesses in general placed the discussion of Chinese businesses in a wider theoretical context. Situating the discussion of Chinese businesses within the literature on ethnic businesses provides a larger framework for exploring the operational structures and processes of Chinese businesses. At the same time, it leads the discussion to focus on the structures and processes of Chinese businesses, topics that are largely relevant to ethnic business literature.

In this volume, we have extended the discussion from focusing on the internal dynamics of ethnic businesses to the global influence on ethnic business operations. The discussion situates ethnic businesses in a newly emerged economic context. We argue that the development and operation of ethnic businesses should take into consideration their global economic linkages. In this volume, we have concentrated on three areas in which economic globalization shapes the development of ethnic businesses: (1) ethnic businesses, economic globalization, and ethnic community development; (2) the transnational linkages of ethnic businesses; (3)

ethnic businesses, the local urban structures, and homogenization. Given the heavy focus on the structural and economic dimensions of ethnic businesses in our discussion, the cultural element of ethnic businesses has rarely been mentioned (except briefly in Light's chapter) in this volume.

These chapters collectively demonstrate that ethnic businesses can no longer be studied in isolation from global economic events. Various developments and recently emerged structures and processes of ethnic business are the direct or indirect consequences of economic globalization. Chapters by Zhou and Cai, Li and Dymski, and Lo and Wang show that the emerged structures, such as ethnic media, ethnic banks, and diversified ethnic business size, all reflect the economic globalization linkage. In addition, the chapters by Fong and Lee, Light, Salaff *et al.*, and Ip suggest that processes such as participation in ethnic businesses, and earnings for those participating in ethnic businesses, are influenced by factors in the home country and by city contexts. These determinants are beyond earlier findings that focus on individual and family factors. Therefore, the study of ethnic businesses, even their internal dynamics, should take into consideration the wider context of economic globalization. Finally, chapters by Szonyi, Luk, and Ooka also suggest that local ethnic business developments are not only affected by economic globalized forces, but also have impact and give rise to new expressions of ethnic businesses.

## DIMENSIONS FOR STUDYING ETHNIC BUSINESSES AND GLOBALIZATION

These studies highlight two important dimensions of exploring the relationship between economic globalization and ethnic business. The first dimension is the effects of economic globalization on ethnic business. The areas affected can vary from organizational structures to operational processes.

The most notable effect of economic globalization on the structures of ethnic business is a growing diversity in the size of Chinese businesses, as suggested in Lo and Wang's chapter. Ethnic businesses no longer only include small neighborhood corner stores where all family members help out and work long hours. They also include corporations that hire a considerable number of people and have a substantial volume of sales. Economic globalization not only affects the development of certain industries in cities, but also influences the ethnic businesses involved, such as ethnic media and ethnic malls (as discussed by Zhou and Cai, and Li and Dymski).

Economic globalization also comprises a unique process in ethnic business. An obvious effect is the transnational linkage of business owners. However, Light in his chapter forcefully argued that the relationship between transnational networks and ethnic entrepreneurship has to be considered with caution. Chapters by Ip and Salaff, Greve, and Wong further elaborate this caution. They argued that although ethnic business owners, especially immigrants, rely heavily on their networks back home to provide information and financial support, their occupations prior to immigration can affect the types of resources available to them for setting up businesses. Therefore, not all transnational networks are helpful in immigrant entrepreneurship.

Another process discussed in these chapters is that the knowledge about the home country is updated constantly in the new country through products sold in ethnic malls and shops. As described by Ooka in her chapter, these linkages in turn shape the ethnic identity of the second generation who visit these malls or watch ethnic TV, while Luk pointed out in his chapter that a sense of ethnic belonging is constantly reinforced by business names borrowed from landmarks or famous stores back home. Szonyi's chapter further showed that the impact is not one-directional. He demonstrated that information and products obtained in the destination country can shape social developments back home as businesspeople introduce new ideas and products when they return.

This book also demonstrates the level of "globalness" and "localness" as another dimension of understanding the relationship between economic globalization and ethnic business. Ethnic banking reflects a high level of global linkage of funding between home country and destination. However, some structures and processes related to economic globalization are relatively local in orientation, as discussed by Salaff *et al.* and Ip. Networks back home are not always transferable and useful in the new country. They depend on the local context.

Table 13.1 summarizes the above discussion on the two dimensions: structure vs. process, and global vs. local. Taken together, they represent four possible effects of economic globalization on ethnic businesses that our chapters have explored.

## APPROACHES TO STUDYING ETHNIC BUSINESSES AND GLOBALIZATION

These studies not only highlight the dimensions for studying ethnic businesses and globalization, but also challenge our approaches to understanding ethnic businesses. Although some studies control for the particular industries of the businesses, most of them do not take the type of industry into serious consideration. However, research has shown that each industry has its own unique operations and markets. This uniqueness has been demonstrated in the chapters by Zhou and Cai, and Li and Dymski. Ethnic media and ethnic banking have been confronted by different

*Table 13.1* Globalization impacts on ethnic businesses: a multiple-dimension schema

|        | *Structure* | *Processes* |
|--------|-------------|-------------|
| Local  | Business size, industrial concentration, organizations (e.g. media, malls) | Network resources, ethnic identity |
| Global | Transnational networks, organizations (e.g. banking) | Flow of financial capital, products and knowledge introduced back home |

sets of issues. As the industries in which ethnic businesses are located become much more diversified than before, careful consideration is necessary. There needs to be further elaboration on proposed factors related to ethnic businesses in different industries.

In addition, these studies suggest that the analysis of participation in ethnic business and the operation of ethnic business, especially among immigrants, should go beyond individual socioeconomic and demographic characteristics in the destination country. Findings by Fong and Lee and discussion in various chapters (such as those by Light, Salaff, Greve, and Wong, Ip, and Szonyi) have argued that city context, transnational networks back home, and socioeconomic background before immigration should all be taken into consideration. All these factors highlight the complexity of the decision to participate in ethnic businesses, especially among immigrants, and their operations. It also suggests that analysis of ethnic businesses should further develop the understanding of how contextual factors shape ethnic business participation and operation.

As theoretical understanding of ethnic entrepreneurship becomes even more important due to rapid changes in urban structures in response to economic globalization, a wider perspective that encompasses various factors will become necessary. Theoretical advancement in understanding ethnic businesses is likely to come sooner if social scientists are able to sort out the effects of contextual factors, individual socioeconomic characteristics, and the interaction effect of these two sets of factors on ethnic entrepreneurship.

## UNDERSTANDING CHINESE BUSINESSES AND ECONOMIC GLOBALIZATION

Finally, we specifically highlight the implications of these studies for the study of Chinese businesses. The focus on economic globalization in analyzing issues related to Chinese businesses can be seen as a direction for theoretical development and empirical analyses. Economic globalization can be seen as a thread that links the understanding of Chinese businesses in diverse countries.

The studies reported in this volume suggest that the closer linkages of Chinese businesses due to economic globalization have revealed some major patterns in Chinese businesses in major immigrant receiving countries. They have gone from involvement in a few industries to representing diversified industries, from primary concentration in Chinatown to dispersal to all parts of cities, from mainly local business contacts to growing transnational ties, and the homogeneous outlook of businesses between home and host countries.

Although the studies included in this volume do not directly compare Chinese businesses in different countries, they demonstrate that Chinese businesses, like other ethnic businesses, are affected by contextual factors as well as individual socioeconomic characteristics. Nevertheless, the writers of these chapters have also warned that the implications of the findings from Chinese businesses should be interpreted with caution.

## FUTURE DIRECTIONS

Our goal with this book is to demonstrate the importance of including economic globalization in the understanding of recent developments in ethnic businesses. We have focused our discussion on only the economic aspect of globalization, because we fully understand that discussion of the many dimensions of globalization requires efforts beyond the scope of a single volume of work. Nevertheless, it is worthwhile to explore further various dimensions of globalization, including the cultural dimension. The cultural effects on ethnic businesses have scarcely been mentioned, except in Light's chapter. The topic has been one of the central discussions in the literature (Basru 2002; Redding 1993; Berger 1991; Aldrich and Waldinger 1990). Some writers have argued the importance of culture to explain the operation of ethnic businesses and the rate of participation in ethnic businesses. This argument has been especially prominent in explaining Chinese ethnic businesses. However, the task of situating the discussion of culture within the context of economic globalization requires further elaboration and comparisons of different ethnic groups. Light raised the question of how much the transnational linkages of ethnic businesses are shaped by globalization or by culture. The issue of culture can be related to economic globalization and ethnic business in various ways. How does culture mediate the effects of globalization on the development of ethnic businesses? Can ethnic culture inhibit or facilitate the effects of globalization on ethnic business development? What are the relative impacts of ethnic culture in contrast to economic globalization on the development of ethnic businesses?

Second, the dynamics of how ethnic businesses adopt or resist the impact of economic globalization require further study. This issue is related to a larger issue of the determinants of local and global elements in ethnic business development in a global context. Although all ethnic businesses directly or indirectly are under the forces of globalization, the extent to which and the mechanisms by which they are influenced are unclear. Such research will help us to further situate the discussion of the internal dynamics of ethnic business in a global context, and requires a broader framework. It is highly plausible that "hybrid" structures and processes may be developed in response to both global and local demands. In addition, how the operations of ethnic businesses under the economic globalization shape local interaction not only among co-ethnic businesses but also among co-ethnic businesses and their co-ethnic members requires further understanding.

The insights generated from the studies in this volume hold many lessons for us. The most basic and obvious one is that the study of ethnic businesses should be put in the context of globalization (see Luk 2005). The research, as demonstrated in this volume, needs to be more interdisciplinary and should occur in a variety of geographic locations. This approach would require more comparative work and collaboration among researchers with different backgrounds. We might then be able to update our understanding of ethnic business, which has been a cornerstone of immigrant economic integration for generations.

# References

Aldrich, Howard E. and Roger Waldinger. 1990. "Ethnicity and Entrepreneurship." *Annual Review of Sociology* 16: 111–35.

Basru, A. 2002. "The Interaction between Culture and Entrepreneurship in London's Immigrant Businesses." *International Small Business Journal* 20: 371–94.

Berger, Brigitte. 1991. "The Culture of Modern Entrepreneurship." Pp.13–22 in *The Culture of Entrepreneurship*, edited by Brigitte Berger. San Francisco, CA: ICS Press.

Kloosterman, Robert and Jan Rath. 2003. *Immigrant Entrepreneurs: Venturing Abroad in the Age of Globalization*. New York: Berg.

Light, Ivan and Carolyn Rosenstein. 1995. *Race, Ethnicity, and Entrepreneurship in Urban America*. Hawthorne, NY: Aldine de Gruyter.

Luk, Chiu (ed.). 2005. Special issue, "Contextualizing the Emergence of New Chinatown." *GeoJournal* 64(1).

Rath, Jan. 2000. "A Critical Review of Research on Immigrant Entrepreneurs." *International Migration Review* 34: 657–81.

Redding, S. Gordon. 1993. *The Spirit of Chinese Capitalism*. New York: Walter de Gruyter.

# Index